Praise for *The Tycoons*

"Thorough and highly readable, Morris' exemplary volume does a superb job. . . . Gracefully and eloquently clarifies these men's frequently misunderstood roles in the shaping of modern U.S. commerce."

—*The Providence Journal*

"Engaging and credible."   —*The Washington Post Book World*

"Too often presented either as demigods or mythical beasts, [these men] are returned to their proper stature as mere people by Charles Morris. . . . He also paints rich, intriguing and at times, harrowing descriptions of the extraordinary age of innovation in which they starred—the late 19th century, when the U.S. came into its own."   —*Barron's*

"Morris writes with an uncommonly light touch, even on complex financial matters, and his brisk summary of the achievements and chicaneries of his tycoons makes for . . . a very rewarding evening."   —*Commonweal*

"Morris may change your impression of these men—some for the better (Gould), some for the worse (Morgan)—as he tells their stories against the backdrop of America's rise to power. . . . A forceful storyteller."

—Harvard Business School, *Working Knowledge*

"Morris has a striking command of his material and his analysis is highlighted time and again by vivid sketches and thought-provoking comparisons with contemporary circumstances. Altogether, *The Tycoons* is a valuable contribution to the presentation and interpretation of one of the most vital, yet all too often romanticized periods of American economic growth."

—Kenneth Warren, fellow emeritus, Jesus College,
Oxford University, and author of *Big Steel*

"A fascinating revisionist interpretation."   —*Publishers Weekly*

"An excellent picture of the growth of American business that made the United States an economic powerhouse."   —*Library Journal*

THE TYCOONS

THE TYCOONS

How Andrew Carnegie,
John D. Rockefeller, Jay Gould,
and J. P. Morgan Invented
the American Supereconomy

. . .

CHARLES R. MORRIS

A HOLT PAPERBACK

TIMES BOOKS/HENRY HOLT AND COMPANY • NEW YORK

Holt Paperbacks
Henry Holt and Company, LLC
Publishers since 1866
175 Fifth Avenue
New York, New York 10010
www.henryholt.com

A Holt Paperback® and ® are registered trademarks of
Henry Holt and Company, LLC.

Library of Congress Cataloging-in-Publication Data
Morris, Charles R.
    The tycoons : how Andrew Carnegie, John D. Rockefeller, Jay Gould, and
J. P. Morgan invented the American supereconomy.
        p.   cm.
    Includes bibliographical references and index.
    ISBN-13: 978-0-8050-8134-3
    ISBN-10: 0-8050-8134-8
        1. Industrial management—United States—History.   2. Industrialists—
United States—Biography.   3. Rockefeller, John D. (John Davison), 1839–1937.
4. Carnegie, Andrew, 1835–1919.   5. Gould, Jay, 1836–1892.
6. Morgan, J. Pierpont (John Pierpont), 1837–1913.   I. Title.
HD70.U5M67 2005
338.092′273—dc22   2005041637

Henry Holt books are available for special promotions
and premiums. For details contact: Director, Special Markets.

Originally published in hardcover in 2005 by Times Books

First Holt Paperbacks Edition 2006

Designed by Victoria Hartman

Printed in the United States of America
5   7   9   10   8   6

*To Leo, for freely sharing his extensive
knowledge of railroad technology*

Contents

Preface   xi

Acknowledgments   xv

1 · Prelude   1

2 · ". . . glorious Yankee Doodle"   30

3 · Bandit Capitalism   60

4 · Wrenchings   97

5 · Mega-Machine   119

6 · The First Mass Consumer Society   161

7 · Paper Tigers   187

8 · The Age of Morgan   230

9 · America Rules   271

10 · The Wrong Lessons   292

Appendix I: The Carnegie Company's 1900 Earnings   319

Appendix II: Standard Oil Earnings   331

Notes   335

Index   369

Preface

There are no official league tables for "most powerful country," but by about 1895 America had clearly outdistanced the pack. Few people recognized it at the time. British officials were merely annoyed in 1899 when they realized that they would have to finance their Boer War in America. Just a dozen or so years later, however, the British were in a near panic at the possibility that America might put its financial weight behind Germany.

America was not only the most populous of industrial countries but the richest by any standard—per capita income, natural resource endowment, industrial production, the value of its farmlands and factories. It dominated world markets—not just in steel and oil but in wheat and cotton. It ran huge trade surpluses in goods, and was gaining preeminence in financial services. Its people were the most mobile, the most productive, the most inventive, and, on average, the best educated. It did not have much to say for itself in literature and the arts, but that time would come. Nor did it have the biggest army nor nearly the biggest navy, but no thinking person doubted those deficiencies could be remedied with but a few years' attention.

Attentive European elites were shocked as they came to understand the scale and speed of America's ascendancy. Hardly three decades before, America was still torn and bleeding from a savage civil war, making its living exporting raw cotton, grain, and timber in exchange for Europe's surplus manufactures. The sustained American growth spurt was the fastest in history, at least until the Pacific Rim countries made their run for daylight a century later.

The Tycoons is the story of that leap, told primarily through the lens of a handful of extraordinary men who stood in the vanguard of the surge. But while "Great Men" can dominate historical epochs, they are never the whole story. The America of the tycoons really was different from all other countries. Their stories are therefore interleaved with an account of the characteristics of America, and its people, that made it such fertile ground for the transition.

Andrew Carnegie, John D. Rockefeller, Jay Gould, and John Pierpont Morgan were all in their late twenties or early thirties, all on the first rungs of their careers, in the waning days of the Civil War. In an age of outsized business leaders, no others played so great a role in shaping and channeling the American boom. They forced the pace, drove the transition to ever-larger scales, and, for good and for ill, imposed personal stamps on the national economy that persisted well into the twentieth century.

They were quite different people. Carnegie, Rockefeller, and Gould tapped into the national predilection for speed, the obsession with "moving ahead," the tolerance for experimentalism, to create one of history's purest laboratories of creative destruction. Most businessmen of the time believed in orderly markets and gentlemanly fair profits, but these three came with flaming swords. Morgan was the regulator, always on the side of reining in "ruinous competition," most especially of the kind regularly unleashed by the other three.

The American steel industry was settling into a comfortable cartel when Carnegie commenced his career of disruption. He was no technologist, but rather a masterful consumer of invention. His plants were always the biggest, the most automated, the most focused on pushing prices down. He had the simplest of business mantras: cut costs, take share, gain scale. Profits would take care of themselves.

Gould was a *provocateur,* a master of public securities markets as no one before him, and few since, always attacking, always pushing the possible to precarious new heights. Gould's arena was railroads and the telegraph, the critical infrastructure of the period. Pre–Civil War railroads had expanded cautiously and almost always profitably, staying carefully within their natural territories, and resolving conflicts with gentlemanly "pools." To Gould rail-road pools were as steel cartels to Carnegie—sitting targets for attack.

Rockefeller may have been the greatest visionary and the supreme manager: he took over world oil markets so quickly and effortlessly that it was over before most people noticed, even as he taught the world its first lessons in the power of large-scale distribution. A host of other enterprises followed his lead; within a decade after Rockefeller first sold his kerosene in the Far East, American meatpackers had distribution centers in China and Japan.

Morgan, the most traditional figure of the four, was the one American whom overseas financiers trusted. After mediating the crucial capital flows that supported the extraordinary pace of American investment, he transmuted into a one-man proto–Securities Exchange Commission, and occasionally even a proto–Federal Reserve, laying down the rules for corporate finance, demanding honest accounting, an end to the looting, and fair treatment for securities holders.

Carnegie, Rockefeller, Gould, and Morgan would have been dominant figures anywhere, but few places have ever been as open to people of talent as post–Civil War America; and in America, no field offered opportunities as unlimited as business. America's radically different manufacturing culture, its cult of the innovative entrepreneur, its obsession with "getting ahead" even on the part of ordinary people, its enthusiasm for the new—the new tool, the new consumer product—were all unique.

The final ascension of big companies around the turn of the century can properly be called the Age of Morgan, who asserted control just as the long American boom was visibly running out of energy. Indeed, he helped slow it down. With Gould dead, and Carnegie gone after Morgan's U. S. Steel buyout, he reimposed a gentlemen's version of orderly markets and "administered" prices. U. S. Steel was the paradigm for a broad wave of consolidations, many of them stage-managed by Morgan.

Morgan's consolidations represent both the capstone and the end to the story. It took another seventy-five years, and the root-and-branch assaults by Japan and other countries, before American companies understood the degree to which they had been living off the capital bequeathed by the nineteenth-century tycoons, the founding fathers of the American industrial superpower.

Acknowledgments

One of the pleasures of this book was the discovery of how easily, via Web searches and e-mail, I could drop in unannounced on senior scholars with questions or proposed formulations of events. I often got multipage responses, which led to further exchanges. A special word of thanks to Ken Warren, perhaps the leading historian of the nineteenth-century steel industry, who engaged in an extended correspondence and then read the entire manuscript, saving me from many errors. My gratitude also to Nancy Bryk, David Hounshell, Douglas Irwin, Thomas Johnson, Maury Klein, Thomas Misa, Clayne Pope, and Merritt Roe Smith. My appreciation also to the librarians and archivists at the Library of Congress, the Pierpont Morgan Library, the Rockefeller Archive Center, and the Historical Society of Western Pennsylvania, and a special word of thanks to John Alexander of the American Precision Museum. Charles Kaczynski was a competent and careful research assistant. Responsibility for errors and omissions is, of course, my own.

Charles Ferguson suggested the original idea for the book and read portions of the manuscript. Kim Malone, Dan Woods, Steve Ross, Andrew Kerr, and Sam Solie read most, or all, of the manuscript and made many useful suggestions. Mike Bessie was, as usual, a benevolent presence and sharp critic throughout. I enjoyed being reunited with Paul Golob at Times

Books, and my appreciation to Robin Dennis for her very intelligent and professional editing. And this book marks twenty pleasurable years of working with my agent, Tim Seldes.

Finally, my thanks and love to my wife, Beverly, who endured the production of yet another book with her usual affection and good humor.

PRELUDE

Abraham Lincoln was pronounced dead shortly after seven o'clock on a rain-soaked Holy Saturday morning, April 15, 1865. It was less than a week after Gen. Robert E. Lee's surrender at Appomattox. The little group of officials and family gathered around the blood-soaked bed in Will Peterson's boardinghouse across from Ford's Theater stood silently for several minutes. Then Mary Lincoln's pastor, Phineas Gurley, said a short prayer, and a detachment of soldiers was summoned into the room. They placed the body in a military coffin and whisked it through the sodden crowd keeping vigil outside to the hearse that would carry it to the White House.

The autopsy and embalming were performed in the east wing's second-floor guest room. Edwin Stanton, the volcanic secretary of war, chose the president's funeral garb and insisted that the undertaker leave the black residue of intracranial bleeding that had formed under Lincoln's right eye. Construction started almost immediately on a catafalque, modeled after a Masonic "Lodge of Sorrow," in the first-floor East Room for the public viewing. As the hammering went on through Easter Sunday and the following Monday, a distraught Mary Lincoln pleaded that the blows sounded like pistol shots. The men who carried Lincoln's body to the first floor on Monday night removed their shoes so as not to disturb Mrs. Lincoln.

There was a public viewing in the East Room on Tuesday. With special trains ferrying tens of thousands of people into the capital, the lines—for the opportunity to file through the darkened room and gaze down for barely a second at the dead president—stretched out for hours. A series of private viewings on Tuesday evening included a delegation of Illinois citizens who had come to demand that Lincoln be buried in his home state; Stanton was planning an interment in Washington. The following morning, six hundred guests packed into the East Room for the funeral service. Even men like Gen. Ulysses S. Grant and Stanton openly wept. Some twenty-five million people attended similar services held more or less simultaneously throughout the United States and Canada.

The massive funeral procession on Wednesday afternoon, before some seventy-five thousand spectators, included detachments of black fighting units and crippled veterans, and, most dramatically, the traditional commander-in-chief's horse following the hearse, with empty saddle and boots facing backward in the stirrups. It was the same image that so stirred television audiences at John F. Kennedy's funeral procession a century later.

The procession terminated at the Capitol, where another ornately rendered catafalque awaited the president's coffin. After lying in state for two days, the body was transferred to a special Baltimore & Ohio railroad car for the first leg of the trip back to Springfield, for Stanton had finally acceded to the Illinoisans' demands. Adding a final grace note of sadness, Lincoln's coffin was accompanied by that of his young son, Willie, whom he had adored, and who had died, probably of pneumonia, in 1862. Willie's little metal coffin was removed from its crypt in Washington and encased in a finer walnut container to rest with his father's in Springfield.

On the Brink

A stop-action frame of the United States at Lincoln's death would have caught the mourning nation frozen for the moment in mid-leap, aimed headlong into modernity. The route chosen for Lincoln's last trip home— up the East Coast to New York, then westward along the Great Lakes to the Midwest and Springfield—itself traced a kind of fault line through the stresses of a society moving rapidly away from its preindustrial roots, roughly tracking the shape of a new American commercial geography.

Most notably, because it was by railroad, the trip took just days, instead of the weeks or months it would have consumed not many years before. The locomotives appear small and quaint today, with their big inverted-bell smokestacks and wood-burning fireboxes. But when they jumped across the Alleghenies in the 1850s, the nation shrank radically; for the first time, the urban East Coast was joined in a single national system with the farmlands and resources of the "Northwest"—the name still used for the states and territories between the original northern colonies and the eastern banks of the Mississippi.

A dozen cities along the route hosted formal funeral ceremonies, all of them vying in the rococo excesses of the catafalques, the funeral orations, and the strutting ranks of portly men in costumes and plumes. The first stop after Washington was Baltimore. Both essentially were the same cities as before the war—the capital, disgracefully enough, a malarial mudhole, although now with an array of almost-finished Greek revival buildings, while Baltimore, a thriving mercantile port, was bloated and bilious from its fat-rich diet of wartime trading.

When the trip first turned inland, however, from Baltimore to Harrisburg, it was traversing a brand-new kind of battle salient. Railroads were coming to understand the profits to be made from the country's quickening internal trade, and there was an oil boom in the woods of western Pennsylvania. Bucolic little towns like Titusville had turned into hellholes where

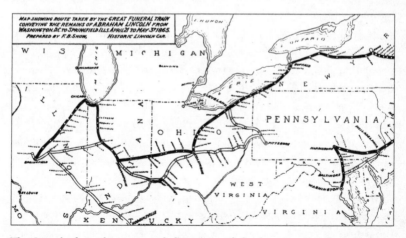

The Lincoln funeral train traced the center of the emerging American business superpower.

streams ran black and the air was misted with oil. The wells' garish night flares flickered over swirling mobs of wildcatters, draymen, prostitutes, and small-time con men, all desperately clawing after their one main chance to get very rich very fast. The Pennsylvania fields were the largest yet discovered, by a huge margin, and within just a few years would supply the illuminating oil for almost the entire civilized world. With stakes like those, the nascent railroad wars would be fierce, often violent, and in a world with no system of law for controlling large corporations, deeply corrupting.

The next stops on the journey, Philadelphia and New York, were both struggling with over-rapid transitions into diversified manufacturing and financial centers. Philadelphia's machine-made textile industry got a huge boost from wartime blanket contracts. Its famed Franklin Institute, the oldest technical institute in the country, was organized in the 1820s with more than a thousand membership subscriptions to promote scientific manufacturing. The boom in New York—printing, light manufacturing, securities and banking—was bursting the boundaries of Manhattan island, and plans were afoot for a colossal bridge to expand the city's footprint across the East River into Brooklyn.

Funeral incidents in both cities pointed up the travails of rapid growth. On Sunday in Philadelphia, three hundred thousand people assembled in miles-long lines to view Lincoln's body, their exhaustion and exasperation sharpened by the city's Sabbath-day refusal to operate public transportation. When a band of pickpockets swept through the lines and cut the crowd-control ropes, there was a wild melee in which a number of people were injured. In New York, the tensions were ethnic. The city, with a larger Irish population than Dublin, was a hotbed of "Copperhead" antiwar Democracy. Irish suspicions that Republican businessmen used the military draft to break labor organizations and to import cheaper black workers—which was almost certainly true—had exploded into the savage 1863 Draft Riots, the most lethal public disturbance in American history. The local Tammany Democratic machine touched off a minor crisis a few days before the funeral procession by decreeing that it would be closed to blacks. After a forceful intervention by Stanton, a small contingent of blacks marched at the tail of the massive parade up Broadway, and were actually cheered by the crowd.

From New York City the funeral train proceeded up the Hudson River to Albany before turning west to cross New York State. Poignantly, unbroken lines of mourners stood vigil over much of the route even during the night, when they marked their presence with bonfires. The only complaint was the speed of the train—in the nineteenth century, twenty miles an hour felt disrespectfully fast.

Western New York State was farm country, populated in great part by German, Swiss, and Scots-Irish immigrants. These were not the yeoman farmers romanticized by Thomas Jefferson: by war's end, some three-quarters of New York's farmers within wagon distance of a railroad depot were efficiency-minded middle-class businessmen running commercial establishments producing wheat, timber, and dairy products for sale. The transformation of New York's farms dated from the opening of the Erie Canal in 1825, and accelerated with the spread of regional railroads in the 1850s. Within a generation, they had decimated New England agriculture, forcing a decisive shift to a manufacturing economy in that part of the country.

New York farmers spent remarkable amounts of money on consumer items—"a lot of trumpery," one farmer humphed in his diary. They stood vigil for the funeral train in factory-made shoes, and their best clothes were purchased ready-made, for superior styling and fit. Middle-class farm wives still worked very hard, but there was visible convergence between their lives and their urban sisters'. They bought cloth instead of spinning and weaving it, and ran off new curtains on sewing machines. Household necessities such as soap and candles came from stores, and many farm homes had new oil lamps, so children could study in the evening. Back-breaking kitchen fireplaces had long since been replaced with "civilized" cast-iron stoves, and travelers agreed that the quantity and variety of New York farmers' food was extraordinary—eons away from the whiskey, salt-pork, and gruel that passed for a reasonable diet earlier in the century.

The first stops after the New York countryside were Buffalo and Cleveland, both bustling Lake Erie port cities that were natural collection points for the oil, coal, and iron industries of western Pennsylvania. From there, the cortege turned back inland to Columbus, Indianapolis, and Indiana's Michigan City—flat, black-earth country, the world's first laboratory for large-scale mechanized farming. The farmers of the "Northwest" were about to give New Yorkers a dose of their own medicine, seizing control of the grain trade and forcing their eastern brethren to specialize ever more intensively in dairies and fruit orchards.

Chicago, the last stop before Lincoln's final resting place in Springfield, self-consciously tried to put on a show as big as New York's, for it viewed itself as the city of the American future. Until the war, midwestern grain and meat products flowed eastward on the Great Lakes and the Erie Canal, or, from south of Chicago, by flatboat down the Mississippi to New Orleans for the coastal sail to New York. By war's end, railroad links east from Chicago had taken over most of the old New Orleans-based trade and were making inroads into the Great Lakes traffic. A grain boom was driving entrepreneurial activity to a fever pitch, while Cyrus McCormick's reaper factory anchored a promising manufacturing base. George Pullman, struggling to get his sleeping car company off the ground, scored a publicity coup by donating the car that carried Lincoln from Chicago home to Springfield. (Or so legend has it. Recent scholarship suggests that he donated all the cars *except* the Lincoln car.)

Springfield was close to the limits of westward rail penetration. There were no train links to the western banks of the Mississippi, and only three tiny, widely separated railroad lines in the whole vast western territories. Western commerce, such as it was, was based on mining—still mostly men with shovels and mules—but entrepreneurs had already spotted the opportunity for ranches to feed the growing demand for meat from the urban east. The splendid western romance of the cowboy and the cattle drive was rooted in just the couple of decades before the railroads completely penetrated the ranch lands after the Civil War. In the South, railroads were not as intensely developed as in the North, but it hardly mattered. For a long time, the area's only important export would be low-technology cotton grown mostly by sharecroppers. The white farmers in the hill country, having depleted their once-rich land, gradually sank back into the old subsistence farming tradition.

Sharp-eyed contemporaries were already rhapsodizing over America's coming economic behemoth, but it was very much in an embryonic state. Railroad routes were still cobbled together piecemeal by local entrepreneurs or enterprising towns. It took no less than ten different carriers to connect the Lincoln funeral route—lines with long-forgotten names like the Northern Central, the Camden and Amboy, the Columbus and Indianapolis, the Lafayette and Michigan City. Since few railroads had the resources to build bridges, engines and cars were still routinely ferried across rivers; the hodgepodge of track sizes interfered with long-distance shipping; and any carrier looking for quality rails and rolling stock did its shopping in England. This was a slouching and stumbling boom, which made the feverish grasping for wealth all the more comical to satirists as various as Mark Twain and Anthony Trollope.

The Artisanal Eden of Abraham Lincoln

Abraham Lincoln would have heartily approved of all of it, even the grasping. As he put it during his first presidential run, "[It is] best for all to leave each man free to acquire property as fast as he can. Some will get wealthy. I don't believe in a law to prevent a man from getting rich [but] . . . we do wish to allow the humblest man an equal chance to get rich with everyone else."

The Republican party that nominated Lincoln for president in 1860 was an awkward amalgam of old-line Whigs, nativist Know-Nothings, radical abolitionists, and antislavery "Barnburner" Democrats, upset at their party's control by southerners. The Whigs probably accounted for the majority of members, and dominated the leadership. The core Whig commitment was to the prodevelopment project of Daniel Webster, Henry Clay, and, further back, of Alexander Hamilton. The conservative wing of the Whig party was somewhat more tolerant of slavery than their moderate brethren, in the name of preserving the Union, and also had a snobbish, antiimmigrant streak, largely in reaction to the impoverished Irish crowding into eastern cities.

The prodevelopment tradition came easily to Lincoln. His political idol was Henry Clay, the great apostle of canals and American self-sufficiency. Lincoln had been a businessman himself, although not a very successful one. He was a tinkerer, had worked as a surveyor, and held a patent on a device for lifting flatboats over river shoals. Lincoln especially enjoyed patent cases, and once said that the most important discoveries advancing civilization were "writing, . . . printing, the discovery of America, and the introduction of Patent Laws." It was typical of him that in a case involving reaper patents, he came armed with models of the machines, and gathered the jurors around on their knees to point out the critical details.

Lincoln's fascination with invention permeated his political statements. After his narrow loss to Stephen Douglas in the 1858 Illinois senatorial election, Lincoln went on the lecture circuit to test his presidential prospects. Instead of focusing on slavery, his signature speech was on "Discoveries and Inventions," which he saw as a uniquely American talent: "[W]e, here in America, *think* we discover, and invent, and improve, faster than any [European nation]. *They* may think this arrogance; but they cannot deny that Russia has called on us to show her how to build steam-boats and railroads."

For generations, historians argued whether the Civil War was primarily about slavery or was rather a showdown between competing economic systems. More recent historiography has shown how deeply Republican antislavery was intertwined with the Whig prodevelopment project. Republicans took economic independence as a prerequisite for political freedom— essentially updating the Jeffersonian vision of independent yeomen for a commercial society. For a brief golden age, Republicans could point to the middle-class polity emerging in the North as their showpiece. With the exception of a handful of large textile mills, northern manufacture was still primarily artisanal, and in the pre–Civil War era, no one anticipated the phenomenon of global mega-businesses. The Republican claim that probusiness legislation, like higher tariffs on manufactured goods, was in the interest of working people was almost certainly true, and was defended in detail by the best economist of the day, Henry Carey. As Daniel Webster once put it, "Why, who are the laboring people of the North? They are the whole North."

But for decades, every development initiative was beaten back by the slave interest, since speeding the settlement of the West, or even investing in rail and canal systems, would inevitably increase the power and population of the free states. To Republicans, and to Abraham Lincoln, southern obstructionism was a piece of a conspiracy to crush freedom everywhere, not just for slaves. If southerners were allowed to extend slavery into the territories, the blights of hierarchy and aristocratic indolence would surely follow, driving out free labor. The word *aristocrat* itself was becoming almost a curse throughout the North, and travelers' reports of the South's pestilence-ridden, barefooted backwardness were staples of the northern press. It was implicitly understood, as one historian put it, that "two profoundly different and antagonistic civilizations . . . were competing for control of the political system."

Lincoln devoted much of his 1859 speaking tour to laying out the Republican social vision: If the government supported individual independence and education, and jump-started a commercial infrastructure, a free, self-improving population would make the most of the opportunity. In a speech at a Wisconsin agricultural fair—after an opening excursus on improving yields through technology (including a bizarre design for a steam plow)—Lincoln attacked the aristocratic "mudsill theory," which he held up in opposition to the Republican ideal of a highly fluid society:

> The prudent, penniless beginner in the world, labors for wages a while, saves a surplus with which to buy tools or land, for himself; then labors on his own account another while, and at length hires another new beginner to help him. . . . There is demonstration for saying this. Many independent men, in this assembly, doubtless a few years ago were hired laborers. And their case is almost, if not quite, the general rule. . . .
>
> By the "mud-sill" theory it is assumed that labor and education are incompatible; and any practical combination of them impossible. . . . [It is] deemed a misfortune that laborers should have heads at all. These same heads are regarded as explosive materials only to be kept safely in damp places.

Nineteenth-century political audiences were extremely well-informed—it was the age's mass entertainment—and Lincoln's listeners perfectly understood whom he was talking about. Slavery's apologists often spoke of the need for a social "mudsill"—"a class to do the mean duties, to perform the drudgeries of life," as a South Carolinian put it. Slavery was only the most visible feature of the deeply antiegalitarian ruling system of the South. Aristocratic power was disgracefully reinforced by the U.S. Constitution's three-fifths rule for weighting slaves in apportionments, and in a series of state political conventions throughout the slave states in the 1850s, the lowland elites steadily disenfranchised small-holder whites.

There was a real edge to Lincoln's attacks on Douglas during their 1858 debates; it derived from his conviction that Douglas, wittingly or not, was a tool of aristocratic interests against the rights of working people:

> [T]he [proslavery] arguments . . . are the arguments that kings have made for enslaving the people in all ages of the world. . . . they always bestrode the necks of the people, not that they wanted to do it, but because the people were better off for being ridden. That is their argument, and this argument of the Judge [Douglas] is the same old serpent that says you work and I eat, you toil and I will enjoy the fruits of it. Turn

in whatever way you will. . . . it does not stop with the negro. I should like to know if taking this old Declaration of Independence, which declares that all men are equal upon principle and making exceptions to it where will it stop. If one man says it does not mean a negro, why not another say it does not mean some other man? If that declaration is not the truth, let us get that Statute book, in which we find it and tear it out!

Once in office, and freed from Southern obstructionism after the attack on Fort Sumter, Lincoln and his Republican majority unleashed a blitz of prodevelopment legislation almost without parallel in American history—a "second American Revolution," in the words of historians Charles and Mary Beard. The Republican achievement has been obscured by the cataclysmic events of the war, although the distractions of war make the farsightedness of the program all the more remarkable.

The Homestead Act of 1862 allowed any citizen, including single women and freed slaves, to take possession of virtually any unoccupied 160-acre tract of public land, for a $12 registration and filing fee. Live on it for five years, build a house and farm the land, and it was yours for just an additional $6 "proving" fee. Over time, the Homestead Act helped settle some 10 percent of the entire land area of the continental United States. Senator Justin Morrill's (R-Vt.) 1862 land-grant college act awarded each state a bequest of public lands which they could sell to finance state colleges focused on the agricultural and industrial arts. No other country had conceived the notion of educating farmers and mechanics, and the Morrill Act schools are still the foundation of the state university systems.

The 1862 Pacific Railway Act made yet another lavish grant of public lands to finance a railway line from the Missouri River to the Pacific Ocean, a dream of the prodevelopment party for more than twenty years. The undertaking was still at the very limits of current technology; the act needed several revisions to get the financing right; and the whole project was plagued by scandal. But the railroad was actually completed more or less as its promoters promised and surprisingly close to the original schedule; over time, its development impact justified the airiest dreams of its supporters. The Republican/Whig agenda was rounded out with major tariff increases and a federal banking act that, for all its flaws, got the country through the war and its financial aftermath.

While Lincoln would never have chosen war as the instrument for extirpating slavery, he did not shrink from it when it was forced upon him, seizing the opportunity to root out the whole twisted aristocratic enterprise. In his own terrible words, from the second inaugural address:

> And the war came. . . . and if . . . it continue, until all the wealth piled by the bondman's two hundred and fifty years of unrequited toil shall be sunk, and until every drop of blood drawn with the lash, shall be paid by another drawn with the sword, as was said three thousand years ago, so still it must be said "the judgments of the Lord, are true and righteous altogether."

That same speech has the famous peroration, "With malice toward none; with charity for all . . ." But Lincoln's intention to rehabilitate the South within the American system could not obscure how radical the change would be. For more than two-thirds of the period from the republic's founding to the Civil War, America had a slaveholding president. The Congress and the Supreme Court had virtually always been dominated by southern majorities. The historian James McPherson points out that in the 1860s, it was the *North*'s social system that was unusual; most other societies, whether or not they legitimized slavery, were organized on the same hierarchical principles as the American South.

Lincoln was fully aware of the North's uniqueness. His speeches emphasize again and again the exceptionalism of America, where the broad populace enjoyed the social and economic underpinnings of political freedom. In no other country was political freedom an intrinsic part of the national project. What country of Europe, presented with a vast wealth of unexploited resources, would have conceived of giving it to its people? Or consciously set out to make its citizens economically independent?

The prolonged American boom that persisted for some forty years after the Civil War—accepting all the reverses and jagged ups and downs—was the greatest in history, at least until the spectacular late twentieth-century growth spurts in the "Tiger" economies of East Asia. Lincoln would have been gratified at the thought, though not surprised. But if he had possessed some magic peephole into the future, even the future of only twenty or so years thence, one can imagine that poor Lincoln, with his moderate-Whig aversion to concentrated power, his mistrust of economic giantism, his hatred of speculators and manipulators of paper, would have blanched.

Young Tycoons

When Lincoln died, Andrew Carnegie was turning thirty, and already wealthy, although he had been a factory bobbin boy hardly a decade and a half before, and had yet even to settle on a career. John D. Rockefeller was only twenty-six, but his Cleveland oil refinery was one of the largest and most profitable in the country, and he may have already formed his design of taking over the entire industry. Jay Gould was twenty-nine, and after a brief, stormy career as a tanner, was trying his hand as a railroad turnaround specialist. Pierpont Morgan was twenty-eight, quietly learning his trade within his father's banking network.

The vast forces afoot in post–Civil War America far transcended any small group of men; but these four would become the greatest of a generation of outsized business leaders, the most prominent of the cadre the press dubbed "The Robber Barons," and by their sheer intelligence, their ambition, and their forcefulness, they laid down the channels that other people followed. They were never friends, and as often opponents as allies; the wary respect they held for each other readily shaded into active dislike. While it would be too much to say that they created the American industrial superstate, it still conspicuously bears their fingerprints.

Carnegie, Rockefeller, and Gould personified the unlimited entrepreneurial opportunities suddenly opened by America's vast resources and its freedom from constraints of class and caste. For the man of fierce business ambition and massive talent, it was the one place, and perhaps the one time, where he could push as far as he could possibly go.

Morgan stood apart from the others. He was not only born wealthy, of the bluest of blue-blood Yankee stock, but he defined his career in reaction to the great entrepreneurs. He worked with them all, especially with Carnegie and Gould, but became a dominant figure only as their careers were peaking. Then he emerged as the boundary-setter, the bringer of order, the creator of the first, porous, institutional webs designed to cushion the disruptions of outsized men.

· CARNEGIE ·

Andrew Carnegie was the most irritating of tycoons. A petite five-foot-three, towheaded, with small hands and feet and a boyish face, he was a tireless bundle of bouncing, gabbling energy, opinionated and obsequious, fawning and provocative, preternaturally quick in apprehension of anything that would advance his interests.

His rise is the canonical American rags-to-riches tale. Carnegie's father was a displaced Scottish hand-loom weaver, and the family emigrated to Pittsburgh when Andrew was thirteen. Andrew zipped through jobs as a bobbin boy, a bookkeeper's clerk, and a telegraph delivery boy, where he picked up telegraphy by watching the operators. He quickly became the business community's favorite telegrapher, and then a one-man wire service, compiling each day's telegraphic news reports for Pittsburgh's newspapers. He was as relentless in self-improvement as in everything else, reading voraciously, and working hard on his accent and grammar. His life was dominated by his mother, Margaret, who imparted the fierce class consciousness of the respectable poor—a wrenching shame of poverty and withering scorn for the unambitious laboring people they were forced to associate with. She and Andrew were inseparable until she died, just before his fifty-first birthday. The Carnegies were nonbelievers, but Andrew still inherited a strong Calvinist aversion to fleshly pleasures. He was immensely charming, and had many friendly associations with women, but probably no intimacy until he finally married a few months after his mother's death, to a young lady who had waited years for that blessed event.

Andrew's big break came when he was seventeen, in the person of Tom Scott, who became his business hero. Scott was one of the era's great railroad executives. Born poor, and working since age ten, he immediately took to Andrew. The need to track far-flung rolling stock made railroads heavy telegraph users, and Scott, who had just been appointed superintendent of the Western division of the Pennsylvania Railroad, was a frequent visitor to Andrew's telegraph office. When he decided that the workload justified a telegraph station of his own, his first choice for an operator was that bright, bustling little "Andy."

Since Scott did so much work by telegraph, he and Carnegie shared an office, and the flow of messages allowed Carnegie almost to inhale the essence of the railroad business. Early one morning before Scott had arrived at the office, Carnegie received a message that a train accident had left traffic in a dreadful snarl. Unable to locate Scott—one wonders how hard he tried—Carnegie took control and issued a flood of orders under Scott's "TAS" signature. By the time Scott was tracked down and came rushing into the office, everything was moving smoothly. This was one time, Carnegie later recalled, that he feared he had gone too far; but after he had nervously explained what he had done, Scott just looked at him strangely, checked that the lines were indeed in order, and let it pass. Shortly thereafter, however, Carnegie was delighted to learn that Scott had been bragging of the exploits of the "little white-haired Scotch devil" in his office, and that he was already known within the railroad as "Mr. Scott's Andy." Even the great J. Edgar Thomson, president of the Pennsylvania, popped his head into the office one day, stared hard at Carnegie for a moment, and said, "so you are Scott's Andy."

Had Carnegie spent his career at the Pennsylvania, there is no question he would have been one of the great railroad executives of the age. His niche as "Mr. Scott's Andy" ended in 1859, when Scott was promoted to vice president of the railroad, and secured Carnegie's appointment as superintendent of the Western division, an extraordinary promotion for his age and experience, more especially since the Pennsylvania's western roads had been hastily built over difficult terrain and were plagued by line breaks and service interruptions. Carnegie plunged into the job. He kept a telegraph station in his home and was on the railroad lines day and night, supervising repairs, rerouting traffic, shoring up system weak points, instinctively grasping, as few railroad men had, that the core challenge was to keep traffic flowing. Shortly after his appointment, he shocked fellow executives by burning stalled cars to clear lines. It was the classic Carnegie technique: focus on an objective, then cut brutally through any conventions, competitors, or ordinary people who stood in your way. Car burning was soon a standard method for clearing stalled trains. The next year, when Scott was appointed U.S. assistant secretary of war for railroad and telegraph services, he naturally brought Carnegie with him, and in a matter of weeks, Carnegie had again performed prodigies of construction to assemble Union troops for the disastrous first battle at Bull Run in 1860.

By the early 1860s, Carnegie was already a rich man. In an age when conflicts of interest were routine, Scott had carefully steered him to investments in companies doing business with the Pennsylvania, like a sleeping car company and a railroad bridge builder, often advancing him the purchase money. The sleeping car investment alone paid Carnegie dividends of $5,000 a year, more than double his salary at the Pennsylvania, on a cash outlay of less than $450. An early investment in the Pennsylvania oil boom, in a property known as the Storey Farm, one of the most fabled of the early Pennsylvania drilling sites, earned Carnegie a staggering $125 for each $1 invested. When he made out his return for the new wartime income tax in 1863, Carnegie showed total income of more than $42,000, suggesting a portfolio in the half million-dollar range, or perhaps $6–7 million in today's money.

Carnegie was so spectacularly talented—with his extraordinary intelligence and dead-accurate Scots practicality, his energy, his immense charm, his feline instinct for a deal—that he simply overmatched everyone else. He was also far better read than most of his peers, with an acquired, but genuine, taste for art and culture, and an attractive writing style. Indeed, he constantly questioned whether he was squandering his talents in business. When his investment income passed the $50,000 mark in 1868, he promised himself that he would work for just two more years to secure that level of income for life, and then devote himself to finer pursuits.

He was kidding himself. The core fact about Carnegie was the drive to dominate—at all costs. But for some reason, although Carnegie was among the hardest of men, he always insisted on parading as a humanitarian idealist, as if his businesses were some kind of social welfare project. So when he was the world's greatest steel magnate, he loved to issue prolabor manifestos and to bask in the attendant adulation, even as he steadily ratcheted up the demands on his workers and as steadily cut their pay. In his telling, every encounter with workers becomes a parable of a republic of good deeds, and each tall tale winds up with a lecture on the virtues of kindness, for "the reward is sweet in proportion to the humbleness of the individual whom you have obliged." At the height of the 1892 Homestead Strike, one of America's deadliest labor-management conflicts, he tells us that the workers "alas, too late" telegraphed him, "Kind master, tell us what you wish us to do and we shall do it for you." (There is, of course, no trace of such a telegram in the extensive files of the strike.)

Carnegie was often pointlessly cruel, even to his most loyal associates. He manipulated his underlings shamelessly, harping obsessively on their smallest failures and taking the credit for their every success. When Henry

Frick retired—Frick, who had contributed as much as anyone to building his empire—Carnegie applied all of his trademark energy and obsessiveness to cheat him of his stake. A proclaimed pacifist, Carnegie chased after war contracts, after promising his wife he never would, and then cheated to get them. He resolved the conflict between his behavior and his stated ideals by lying—egregiously, consistently, and continually. He became, in fact, that most corrupted of liars, one who lies to himself. Even his contemporaneous letters and memoranda of events are likely to be false, to show himself in a better light. It is no surprise that the faults, and occasionally the crimes, of the great tycoons are on the scale of their achievements, but none but Carnegie was so repellantly smarmy.

A few years after Carnegie retired from the Pennsylvania, he became one of the Morgan bank's favorite clients, although his relationship was with Junius Morgan, Pierpont's father, for he did not get on with Pierpont. In the long run, he bested Pierpont, as he did almost everyone else. The crowning deal of Morgan's long career was his buyout of the Carnegie Company in 1901 to create the United States Steel Corporation; in constant dollars, it was the biggest corporate transaction in history until the buyout boom of the 1980s. But that was less a Morgan triumph than a measure of his fear that Carnegie was about to destroy a painstakingly constructed steel cartel. Buying Carnegie out was the only way to get him off the field, and Morgan could thank his angels that Carnegie's wife was pushing him toward his long-stated goal of finally doing some good in the world. Carnegie rubbed it in by lying about his profits when he and Morgan set the price.

Indeed, over a long career the only fellow tycoon who fully matched up with Carnegie in a business setting was the man he liked to called "Reckafellows."

· ROCKEFELLER ·

John D. Rockefeller descended from solid farmer stock on both sides of his family, and while the Rockefellers were often in straitened financial circumstances, he was never truly poor. Indeed, were it not for the bizarrely unstable behavior of his father, John's early years would have been almost the cliché of a midcentury boyhood in rural western New York. "Big Bill" Rockefeller was a trickster character. A large, handsome, overpowering man, he was at various times a farmer and businessman, a traveling medicine man, a magician, and an ersatz doctor, who was once indicted for rape. (Weirdly, he also liked to feign being a mute.) Rockefeller's first biographers noted that his father often disappeared on "long, mysterious, trips"; in fact, as "William Levingston" he was married to another woman and more or less supporting two families for much of John's life. As John's fame grew, he simply rebuffed inquiries about his father—he could hardly admit that his father was "Doc" Levingston, a practicing backwoods medicine man, still bilking the rubes.

Perhaps in reaction to his father's behavior, John was the most sober and industrious of young men—diligent at school, serious about his Baptist religion, scrupulously honest, utterly reliable. His adult life was similarly conventional, at least outside of business. He married young, was close to his wife and children, and in later years worked hard to prevent their lives from being completely distorted by his great wealth. John was better educated than most young men of his time, completing high school and some commercial courses before starting work at sixteen as an assistant bookkeeper for a produce merchant in 1855. Two years later, with a loan of $1,000 from his father, John purchased a partnership in the firm of another merchant, Maurice Clark, a gregarious Englishman about ten years older than himself, and by the time John was twenty, he was already recognized as one of Cleveland's outstanding young merchants—honest, reliable, and with a shrewd sense of commodity markets. The truly portentous event of John's twentieth year, however, was Col. Edwin Drake's success in producing a substantial amount of "rock oil" from a well near Titusville, in Pennsylvania's "Oil Creek" region, so named for its visible seepages of surface oil.

Drake was backed by professional investors who had done the scientific homework to know that Pennsylvania oil, if only it could be produced in commercial quantities, could be the superior illuminant and lubricant the world so desperately needed. Drake's fitful progress was closely watched, and when his well finally bubbled with a large volume of oil, the region went berserk. A local lumberman became a millionaire almost overnight by galloping through the valley and buying out any farmer who would sell. Wildcatters poured into the region, and immediately began to strike wells over an area of hundreds of square miles. Oil Creek shipped an estimated 200,000 to 500,000 barrels of crude in 1860, the year after Drake's discovery, and 2,000,000 barrels in 1861, including some 275,000 barrels sold internationally. (A Pennsylvania barrel, still the standard today, contains forty-two gallons.) About 70 percent of the production was for lighting.

As merchants and commodity traders, Clark and Rockefeller would have traded oil for their customers and must have had some idea of the profits to be made. But the idea of going into oil was brought to them, two years after Drake's strike, by a friend of Clark's, an Englishman and self-taught chemist named Sam Andrews. Andrews, who had some refinery experience, proposed that Clark and Rockefeller back him in opening a refinery, and they finally agreed to put up $4,000, which John regarded as "*very large.*" The new undertaking was organized as Andrews, Clark and Co., although Rockefeller apparently put up the same amount of capital as Clark. At twenty-two, John was still regarded as a junior partner, the guy who took care of the numbers.

The Andrews, Clark refinery, which they dubbed the Excelsior Oil Works, flourished from the start. Rockefeller picked the location—situated for maximum access to rail and water transport. And as he gradually became obsessed with the opportunities in oil, he took over the day-to-day operations of the business while Andrews ran the refinery. Andrews was an excellent refiner, and his products quickly gained a high reputation; most important, he had the sense to recognize that John, young as he was, should make the business calls. For the first time, Rockefeller could demonstrate his extraordinary ability to combine headlong expansion with fanatical attention to efficiency and cost. Within two years, Excelsior was turning out some five hundred barrels a day of refined product. That was paltry production by the standards of just a few years later, but in 1865 it made Excelsior one of the largest refineries in the country and twice as large as any other in Cleveland. Under Rockefeller's management, it was also the most consistently profitable.

The problem was the Clarks. Maurice had brought his two brothers into the business, as buyers and salesmen. One of them, James, who was an ex-prizefighter and a bully, clashed with Rockefeller almost from the start. Worse, Rockefeller didn't trust him. James liked to make risky side deals, padded his expense claims, and bragged about cheating customers. At the same time, Maurice was worried by Rockefeller's appetite for debt and began to take a hard line against continued expansion. As frictions grew, the Clarks made frequent threats to dissolve the partnership. On one such occasion, Rockefeller disingenuously asked them if they really meant it, which they confirmed. The next day, to their shock, they read a notice of dissolution in the local newspaper. They were doubly shocked to find that Andrews had thrown in his lot with Rockefeller; and then, after they had agreed to an auction to settle the ownership of the refinery, were shocked again to find themselves coolly outbid by the twenty-five-year-old Rockefeller. The deal was done on March 2, 1865, just a few weeks before Appomattox.

The Clarks conceded the auction when the bidding hit $72,500. Maurice clearly felt that was an extraordinary price for a one-half interest. In addition, Rockefeller was giving back his half interest in the produce business, which pushed the total price up near the $100,000 mark. In truth it was a steal. The next year, in 1866, Excelsior Oil had total sales of $1.2 million, easily returning the purchase price before the year was out. Within just a few months after buying out the Clarks, Rockefeller and Andrews had started construction on a second refinery, and had set up yet a third business in New York to focus on overseas oil brokerage and sales; it was headed by John's younger brother William, who was becoming an excellent businessman in his own right.

The muckraker Ida Tarbell once dismissed Rockefeller as a man with the "soul of a bookkeeper," an image that has stuck to him ever since. It was true that he loved the completeness and concreteness of good ledgers, and insisted that every entry, every tally, every invoice had to be right; but the "bookkeeper" label does not begin to capture the reality of John D. Rockefeller. If he lacked Morgan's rhinocerous presence or Carnegie's noisy panache, he made up for it with an extraordinary, quiet charisma. As a young man, we see him joining new settings, a church, perhaps, or an association of oilmen, and somehow, without apparent effort or almost without saying anything, he always emerges as the leader. Rockefeller was well built, though not as tall as his father, and a good athlete who enjoyed vigorous work—he loved to pitch in with the men at the Excelsior works. Acquaintances frequently commented on his sense of humor, and family pictures often catch him looking distinctly jolly. His direct, understated, factual style made him an exceptional salesman, and he must have exuded immense self-assurance. From the very start of his business career, he took enormous risks, but so calmly and matter-of-factly as to make them seem perfectly ordinary.

Even during his first years in refining, the characteristic Rockefeller methods were on full display: Move with shocking speed and minimum fanfare. Act with total confidence, but turn on a dime if new facts warrant. March in service of a sweeping vision, but pay obsessive attention to the details. Rockefeller's grand plan may have been in place as early as his buyout of the Clarks, for he moved in a seemingly straight line to world oil dominance under the Standard Oil banner in hardly fifteen years. Although he often played very rough, he was surprisingly free of vindictiveness. When he took over another man's business, he generally paid a fair price, indeed, often overpaid. A typical ploy was to open his books to the target: any sensible man would understand that competition was hopeless and make a deal. If a target was especially obdurate, rejecting all reasonable offers, a switch would finally turn and Rockefeller would suddenly unleash total, blazing warfare on every front—price, supplies, access to transportation, land-use permits, whatever created pain. When the target capitulated— they always did—the fair-price offer would still be available, often with an offer to join the Rockefeller team. It was industrial conquest on the efficiency principle. As Rockefeller kept determinedly in the background, even as the Standard spread across the globe, he began to acquire in the public mind an aura of an almost mystical power.

Rockefeller was by no means free of hypocrisy. Although he was a deeply devout Baptist, his biographer Ron Chernow has documented at least one instance where he clearly committed perjury. But the image of Standard Oil as a kind of criminal enterprise, due mostly to Tarbell, was never accurate. Rockefeller companies unquestionably paid bribes to local officials, but the business environment in nineteenth-century America was a bit like that in today's Middle East: as the English observer Lord Bryce wrote, "It is only by the use of money that [corporations] can ward off the attacks constantly made on them by demagogues or blackmailers." Rockefeller didn't need to cheat to win world oil dominance; he was simply better at the business than anyone else.

• GOULD •

For all the vituperation that descended on the heads of the Robber Barons, especially on Rockefeller, none had so dark a reputation as Jay Gould. To Henry Adams, Gould was "a spider . . . [who] spun huge webs, in corners and in the dark." The Wall Street denizen Daniel Drew said of Gould, "his touch is of death." Drew himself was one of the most unattractive figures in the history of Wall Street—a semiliterate former cattle drover, a coward and a sniveler, constant only in his disloyalties. He was the first master of the "bear raid," attacking the stock of his own companies and reaping profit from the destruction of fellow shareholders, along the way making a mockery of even the flimsy fiduciary standards of the day. Drew's hatred of Gould drew extra venom from the crushing losses he had once suffered when Gould out-traded him. Morgan, who in his early career was also outmaneuvered by Gould, was always torn between keeping him at a wary distance and chasing after his business.

If the Mephistophelian caricature of Gould was overdrawn, there was enough basis in fact to make it stick. Gould had one of the supplest business minds of his, or of any, age. His career coincided with the great epoch of American railroads, the first large, investor-financed, publicly traded corporations. The roads' thirst for capital was insatiable, and in the absence of standards for creating securities or keeping accounts, their books were typically cobwebbed with a murky chaos of conflicting claims. This was the playing field Gould was born for. His subtle intelligence could flicker through every crevice and corner of the most convoluted financial constructions and divine exactly the points of leverage, the strategic positions that could make him, by a few adroit purchases, master of the entire enterprise. Time and again, unsuspecting investors struggling to rescue their business or recover their funds would suddenly be confronted by the specter of Gould, as if risen from the gloom, snatching away both their company and their money. Railroads became the center of Gould's interests early in his career, and more than anyone else, he created the national railroad map that prevails to this day.

Gould's mastery of financial arcana was paired with a strange streak of self-destructiveness. More than once, after a string of victories had left him in possession of the field, he would launch some new, seemingly pointless depredation that laid waste to everything he had worked for—as if launching stock wars was simply what he *did*. His reputation as a looter of his lines, however, is less fair. While he typically underinvested in his roads, he was always financially stretched, and over the years he probably put far more money into his roads than he took out. During his one extended term as president of the Union Pacific, he proved to be a better than average railroad manager—he was a superb financial engineer, took a close interest in operational details, and usually outstrategized his competitors.

He cut the most unprepossessing of figures. Gould's father was so disappointed in the scrawny, undersized son his wife presented after five straight daughters that he eventually gave up farming for a store in town, for Jay clearly wasn't the son to scratch a living from the hardscrabble soil of rural New York State. As an adult, Gould was barely five feet tall, even smaller than Carnegie, but with none of Carnegie's voluble energy. Instead, he made a wan, silent, somewhat hunched figure. During times of crisis, he would usually sit calmly and quietly, betraying tension by tearing small bits of paper. His dark, usually haggard, eyes, the wiry black beard, the subtlety of his methods, his name, all fed rumors that he was a Jew, although there is no evident Jewish ancestry in the family tree.

Burning ambition more than made up for Jay's lack of physical strength. He was essentially on his own from age thirteen, when his father registered him in a high school in a neighboring town and left him with a pile of clothes and fifty cents. Jay quickly found a job as a part-time, self-taught bookkeeper, and also proved an excellent student, with a genuine taste for literature, and a surprisingly mature writing style. He taught himself surveying, and at seventeen he seems to have been the leading surveyor in the county, lobbying for the profession in the state legislature. He raised the financing for a comprehensive county map, which was a major undertaking, and along the way published a competent county history. He stayed in close touch with his sisters, returning home from time to time when prolonged periods of overwork led to bouts of debilitating illness, sometimes severe enough to be life-threatening.

Gould's breakthrough opportunity came in 1856 when he was twenty, in the person of Zadock Pratt. Pratt, in his sixties when Gould met him, was a tanner and backwoods entrepreneur, the leading citizen of his county, an overbearing, hard-handed, booted and Stetsoned pioneer figure, whose taste for young wives lasted well into old age. Nineteenth-century tanners cured animal skins by soaking them in tannic acid derived from a mash of tree bark. It was dirty, dangerous work, requiring vast amounts of timber and water, and was usually conducted deep in the woods. Pratt hired Gould to survey a tanning site, but was sufficiently impressed that he made him a partner and manager of the projected new tannery. So the pint-sized Gould, barely out of his teens, led fifty workmen into the woods and built virtually a full-scale town, including living and food service quarters, a mule-powered bark crushing plant and curing vat facilities, plus a post office, a wagon house, a water race, and eventually a general store. Work proceeded so fast that the settlement was named "Gouldsborough" by acclamation.

Gould was never known as a charismatic figure—adjectives like "furtive" and "elusive" are the kind most often applied. But he clearly won the loyalty of the men of Gouldsborough, for when his control of the tannery was challenged a few years later, the town men fought for him, carrying the day in what amounted to a mini-frontier war. The details of the story are lost, but the broad facts are that after Gould bought out Pratt with the help of a leading leather house, he came to loggerheads with his new backers. (They had assumed the youthful Gould would do as he was told; but the partnership agreement gave Gould total control over the tannery, and he was expanding on every front—more woodland, another tannery, a leather brokerage.) When financial discussions broke down, one of his backers, Charles Lee, hired a crew of toughs and took over the tannery by force. Gould hastened to the town and addressed a spontaneous gathering of about two hundred townspeople and employees, who rallied to his banner. That night he led a group of fifty men, divided into two assault teams, and stormed the tannery from the front and rear. There was a brief, but wild, shooting melee before Lee's ruffians fled. Three men were wounded, including Lee, who took some buckshot in his hand. The local newspaper, doubtless tongue in cheek, blazoned:

Civil War And The Leather Trade
Italian War Eclipsed
Great Fight At Gouldsborough
Gen. Gould Victorious
And Marshall Lee A Prisoner Of War

For Gould it was a hollow victory. The battling had made a shambles of the tannery business and destroyed his reputation in the leather trade. When Gould decided to try his luck in New York in late 1860 or early 1861, his prospects were unpromising in the extreme. At the time he bought out Pratt, he was already a wealthy young man, with a net worth of about $80,000, or close to $1 million in today's money. But the tannery fiasco had almost wiped him out, leaving him little but illiquid woodland holdings. An

1861 credit report states that he "has not settled his affairs & and has no particular location. Is not known to do any business, nor is it ascertained whether or not he is worth anything."

Failure though it was, the tannery episode highlighted the characteristics Gould would display his entire career: the ability to tackle any endeavor, master any field, and, despite his frail constitution, to work prodigiously; the constant pushing against boundaries and restraints; the impulse to expand in every direction at once, sometimes beyond all reason; the unfortunate habit of leaving a trail of dazed and battered partners in his wake; and the sharp reading of legal documents—one scholar has called him "probably the most successful litigant in American history." (While Gould could generally be trusted to keep his word, one had to parse very carefully what that word actually *was,* for agreements would be interpreted in the closest possible way, and always to Gould's advantage.) Most extraordinary, perhaps, was Gould's ability to sustain reverses that would crush another man, then to pull himself off the floor and to carry on, learning more, working harder, never complaining, just looking for the next chance.

The move to New York quickly turned to his advantage, for in 1863 he married Helen Miller, the daughter of a prominent New York merchant. Helen's family was part of the tightly knit New York upper-class commercial society, one that usually married within its own ranks. Helen's father liked Jay, however, and the couple moved in with her parents after the marriage. Six children followed in rapid succession, and Helen and the children were the rock of stability in Jay's life for the rest of his days.

And just as fortuitously, the windup of his leather business in 1861 introduced Gould to railroading. One of his other leather partners held $50,000 in first mortgage bonds on a small railroad in New York's Lake Champlain region. The line was in trouble, and with the market crash following the onset of the war, the bonds had fallen to ten cents on the dollar. It must have taken Gould's entire remaining cash trove, but he bought them and gained effective control of the line. We have only his own brief account to confirm that he spent most of his first years in New York nursing the line back to health. When it merged with a larger line a few years later, his bonds were trading at par, and the stock he had acquired along the way had become quite valuable. He was a player once more, although at the time of Lincoln's death, his name was almost unknown on Wall Street.

The tycoons as young men. *Upper left:* Andrew Carnegie; *upper right:* John D. Rock-efeller; *lower left:* Jay Gould; *lower right:* J. P. Morgan.

· MORGAN ·

Pierpont Morgan was already an experienced banker at the time of Lincoln's death, having started and built his own firm during the war. Certainly, few young men had been as carefully brought up for their trade. Both branches of his family had settled in America by 1640, and he could count Aaron Burr and the evangelist Jonathan Edwards among his relatives. The males of the Pierpont line, his mother's side, were mostly a genteel, otherworldly lot, who made their living as ministers or school administrators. The Morgans were sterner stuff. Pierpont's grandfather, Joseph Morgan, was one of Hartford's leading citizens and a founder of the Aetna Insurance Co. Joseph's first son, Junius, Pierpont's father, was a dry goods importer when he was recruited as a partner by an aging George Peabody, then the leading American merchant banker in London. Peabody brought Junius and his family to London in 1854, and Junius succeeded to sole control of the business a decade later, when Peabody & Co. was formally wound up and succeeded by J. S. Morgan & Co. Pierpont, like his father, was tall, strong, and outgoing. He had Junius's flair for numbers and loved to spend his school vacations working in the countinghouse, as bank back-offices were called. But he also had a raffish streak—with an eye for the ladies and an appetite for risk that occasionally alarmed the very buttoned-down Junius.

J. S. Morgan's core business was short-term trade finance, "discounting bills," as it was called. Its primary customers were American cotton or iron merchants. They typically sold their goods on credit, taking back a piece of paper, or "bill of exchange," which could be cashed at a specific bank such as Barings at some set future date. If a merchant needed cash before the maturity date, he sold his bills at a discount to a firm like Junius's. It was a game of gritty details; Junius needed a close understanding of his principals' businesses and their credit to avoid getting stuck with bad paper. Junius rounded out his banking practice by providing local credit to his clients when they were abroad and by helping to sell American government and railroad bonds, although at this time usually as a secondary underwriter behind one of the bigger European banks.

It was taken for granted that Pierpont would succeed to the firm. After the move to London, Pierpont attended a Swiss boarding school and then the University of Göttingen to work on his French and German. Then in early 1857, Junius placed him in with one of his New York correspondents, Duncan, Sherman & Co., where Pierpont's assignment was to learn the banking business, keep an eye on Junius's New York affairs, and maintain the correspondence with the London office, which included great floods of long, somewhat preachy letters from his father. One incident, which Pierpont relished telling in later years, demonstrated his independent streak. Sent to visit merchant customers in New Orleans, Pierpont saw a chance to make a killing in coffee beans and used Duncan, Sherman credit to take a large position. When the anticipated outraged telegram from New York arrived,

Pierpont laconically replied that the position had been sold out and he was remitting a substantial profit. He later asserted that there was no risk in the deal because he thoroughly understood what he was doing.

After two years, Pierpont, just twenty-four, opened his own firm, and with the help of referrals from Junius rapidly built his business. A quasi-scandal from this period, the celebrated case of the "Hall carbines," shadowed his name many years later. Pierpont collected a large fee for financing a sale of rifles to the hard-pressed general John C. Frémont, the Union commander in the West. What made the deal sleazy was that the government already owned the rifles. A government armory had agreed to sell the rifles before the war at a very attractive price, but the armory wanted cash, which the buyer could not raise. But once war broke out, field commanders were desperate for rifles, and a friend of the Morgans from London, a wheeler-dealer named Simon Stevens, took over the contract and made a deal with Frémont at a very high price. Morgan put up the cash to close the purchase with the armory and ship the rifles west. Morgan's war-profiteering is especially unattractive, since like all the fledgling tycoons he had paid for a replacement soldier instead of submitting to the draft.

With the founding of J. S. Morgan & Co. in 1864, Junius summoned Pierpont back to the family business. Pierpont's firm was dissolved, and Junius paired him with Charles Dabney, an experienced senior partner from Duncan, Sherman, in Dabney, Morgan & Co., widely understood as the New York branch of J. S. Morgan & Co. Later, when Dabney retired, Junius once again paired Pierpont with an older hand, Anthony Drexel, of the long-established Philadelphia banking family, changing the firm to Drexel, Morgan & Co., with the older man again named first.

Junius might have been less cautious, for Pierpont was clearly well prepared. Endowed with a powerful intellect, great financial insight, and enormous personal forcefulness, he enjoyed a growing following on Wall Street, and was praised by Dun's credit service for conducting a "first rate" business. Over the years, Pierpont came to be known for a certain stiff rectitude—a Colonel Blimplike ethos that reduced to a harumphed "Gentlemen pay their debts." His conventionality did not extend to his personal life. He displayed a surprisingly pre-Raphaelite sensibility by marrying a young beauty already dying of tuberculosis when he was twenty-four, suffering the inevitable bereavement four months later. His second marriage, in 1864, was a replica of his father's—a powerful man in a cold marriage with a neurasthenic wife. Unlike his father, however, Pierpont had a succession of mistresses whom he never bothered to conceal from colleagues or family.

Morgan's genius was that of the disciplinarian, not that of the creator. He was the last of the great eighteenth- and nineteenth-century merchant bankers, rather than the pioneer of a new dispensation. He did what his father and other bankers had always done, but in broader strokes, on a bigger canvas, applying his formidable intelligence to ever more complex financial constructions. His fundamental drive was toward order and control, and he was appalled by the storm of "creative destruction" at the heart of the long American boom. He detested "bitter, destructive, competition" that always led to "demoralization and ruin," in the words of Elbert Gary, the Morgan man at U. S. Steel. Often strangely inarticulate, as if rendered speechless by the titanic fulminations in his breast, he railed against the madness for progress and change that wiped out perfectly respectable businesses of perfectly decent gentlemen, against the gale winds of technology that turned economic assumptions upside down and made it impossible for his clients to *pay their debts*! Over the course of forty years, he eventually succeeded as no one else in imposing his own iron will on the American economy, reining in the competitive free-for-all, and setting rules and boundaries that held sway for a half century after he died.

Carnegie, Rockefeller, Gould, and Morgan would have risen to the top in any age, as military leaders, perhaps, or as chancellors to kings. But in post–Civil War America, business had acquired the sense of excitement and purpose that men had once associated with great feats of statecraft or conquest.

It was no accident. The sheer size of America, and its already-impressive industrial base, made it ripe for hyperdevelopment. America was the only country where "worker" was a job description rather than a badge of class. Most Americans seem to have truly believed, just as Lincoln said they should, that their lives would get better, that there was no limit to the vistas to be opened by hard work and imagination. They chose the new almost as a matter of course—new things to buy, new inventions, new ways of making or growing things. It was to cast off the shackles of status, of artisanal guilds, of long-established trade practices, that they or their near ancestors had come to America in the first place. As a radically uprooted people, Americans shed ties of position and place as easily as old shoes. Contemporary observers were astonished that the pioneers pushing into western farm-lands were not landless peasants but mostly successful farmers from Penn-sylvania or New York, looking to move up to larger scale operations.

The freewheeling American style bequeathed a unique business her-itage to an ambitious entrepreneur. Even well before the Civil War, some sharp-eyed Englishmen were becoming alarmed at the radicalism of Amer-ican innovation.

· 2 ·

" . . . GLORIOUS YANKEE DOODLE "

The steamer carrying Queen Victoria and Prince Albert pulled along-side the yacht *America* in tacit salute as it entered the last leg of an all-class regatta around the Isle of Wight on August 22, 1851. The royal couple then peeled off for home, for the only other sail in sight, seven and a half miles back, was the *Aurora,* a light, fast British cutter that should have easily out-sailed a schooner the size and weight of *America.* As the royal steamer passed near the shore, the question from the waiting public was: "Is the *America* first?" "Yes," said the passengers at the rail of the steamer. "What's second?" "Nothing."

The sailing race—ever since known as the *America's* Cup—was organized for maximum world attention as part of the "Great Crystal Palace Exhibition," an unabashed self-celebration of a British nation at the top of its imperial game in the first full flowering of the Victorian Age. More than six million visitors gaped their awestruck way through the massive glass Exhibition Hall in Hyde Park. The hall, more than a third of a mile long and set among 12,000 fountain jets spurting as high as 250 feet, housed 13,000 exhibitions from all the civilized nations of the world. A great feat of engineering in its own right, the hall was constructed of more than a million machine-fabricated iron-framed glass sheets and erected in only twenty-two weeks.

Xenophobic English elites harbored doubts about the wisdom of such a display, worrying that London would be "overrun with foreign rogues and revolutionaries" and British "trade secrets stolen." In fact, for knowledgeable industrialists and civil servants the implications of the Exhibition were far more unsettling than that. It was shameful enough that British yachtsmen had strenuously tried to avoid a direct contest with *America*—the London *Times* reporter said they acted like "wood pigeons or skylarks" who spot "a sparrowhawk on the horizon," once they saw its training runs. But the news from the Crystal Palace suggested that "Brother Jonathan," their bumptious American relative, was also developing an alarming superiority in advanced precision manufacturing, an arena in which Englishmen had thought themselves without peer.

On the very same day as the loss to *America,* an American succeeded in opening the famous, exquisitely crafted, and "unpickable" British Bramah lock—meeting a challenge that had stood for forty years. The lock-breaker was Alfred C. Hobbs, a talented huckster with an excellent understanding of machine manufacturing. He adroitly downplayed that his lock-breaking feat took more than two weeks, then offered $1,000 to any British locksmith who could open his own machine-made locks. When no one could meet his challenge, he collected the Exhibition's lock medal and almost immediately made plans to open a factory in England.

Hobbs's demonstration came just a few weeks after Cyrus McCormick's reaper had decisively bested a feeble array of local competitors in a series of field tests. The usually anti-American *Times,* which had earlier derided McCormick's machine as "a cross between a flying machine, a wheelbarrow, and an Astley chariot," abruptly changed its tune: "the reaping machine from the United States is the most valuable contribution from abroad, to the stock of previous knowledge that we have yet discovered," predicting that it would "amply remunerate England for her outlay connected with the Great Exhibition."

But the praise heaped on reapers and locks was far eclipsed by the adulatory attention showered on Samuel Colt's repeating firearm exhibit—even the Duke of Wellington, a regular visitor to Colt's booth, was heard proclaiming the virtues of repeating firearms. Colt himself was invited to address the British Institute of Civil Engineers, the first American to do so; in a talk attended by leaders of the military and political establishment, he proclaimed the advantages of machine production over skilled craftsmen.

The yacht *America* crushed its British competition at the Great Crystal Palace Exhibition of 1851. It was just one of several alarming (to the British) demonstrations of American technical prowess.

In the meantime, the Vermont gun maker, Robbins and Lawrence, conducted a well-attended demonstration that proved that its machine-made rifles could be disassembled, their parts mixed up, and then randomly reassembled by an unskilled workman using only a screwdriver—a feat of "interchangeability" that British gunsmiths had long declared impossible. Robbins and Lawrence won the Exhibition's firearms medal, while Colt, like Hobbs, let it be known that he too would open a plant to bring American technology to Great Britain.

It was sweet turnaround for the Americans, whose exhibit had been widely derided for its emphasis on the boringly utilitarian—dubbed a desolate "prairie ground" amid "magnificent displays of Russian, Austrian, and French art." *Punch* had first greeted the American exhibit with disdain— "their contribution to the world's industry consists as yet of a few wine glasses, a square or two of soap, and a pair of salt cellars"—but gleefully switched to mocking punctured British pride:

Yankee Doodle sent to town
   His goods for exhibition;
Everybody ran him down,
   And laughed at his position;
They thought him all the world behind;
   A goney muff or noodle,
Laugh on, good people,—never mind—
   Says quiet Yankee Doodle.
CHORUS Yankee Doodle, etc.

. . . .

Their whole yacht squadron she outsped,
   And that on their own water,
Of all the lot she went ahead,
   And they came nowhere arter.

. . . .

Your gunsmiths of their skill may crack,
   But that again don't mention;
I guess that Colt's revolvers whack
   Their very first invention.

. . . .

But Chubb's [another British lockmaker] and Bramah's Hobbs has pick'd,
   And you must now be viewed all
As having been completely licked
   By glorious Yankee Doodle.
CHORUS Yankee Doodle, etc.

The very disconcerting triumph of American technology was no accident, for it was the culmination of developments stretching back many years.

Rise of the Nerds

Thomas Blanchard was the classic nerd, a technology geek, but since he came of age in the Connecticut River Valley in the early 1800s, he was a machine geek. An indifferent student with limited social graces—he was afflicted with a bad stammer—his father early despaired of turning him into a farmer. Told to clear a field of stones, he was apt to mumble that it was a proper job for a machine, then spend his time designing one instead of digging up stones. As a teenager he was shipped off to work for his eldest brother who ran a tack factory—and Blanchard had found his milieu. His first job was hand-fixing heads on tacks, which he hated, so he invented a tack-making machine that turned out five hundred tacks a minute. After winning a patent for the tack machine, Blanchard sold the licensing rights for $5,000—a stupendous sum for a young man—and opened his own manufactory in Millbury, with "water privileges," or the right to build a water mill to power his plant. Like a proto-Bill Gates, Blanchard not only had a genius for machines but was to prove an astute businessman besides.

Blanchard's lasting fame is based on the "Blanchard gun-stocking lathe," a truly original manufacturing breakthrough that dates from 1818, when he was thirty years old. Lathes, or "turning machines," are among the oldest of machine tools, and were well known in both the ancient and medieval worlds. A piece of wood or other material is clamped in place lengthwise next to a fixed cutting blade. As the wood is turned by a handcrank or other power source, the blade inscribes a circular cut. Moving the wood back and forth on its long axis as it rotates against the blade will result in cylindrical shapes for table legs, pike staffs, and the like. Ornamental effects are achieved by adjusting the blade and the wood's position to create bulges, cut deeper grooves, and so forth. Renaissance craftsmen achieved striking results using slides for smooth lengthwise motions and screw-based adjusters for precise placement of the blade. By the eighteenth century, rosette-cutting lathes were a popular entertainment for upper-class gentlemen and "royal hobbyists who enjoyed spending leisure hours creating intricate and pretty bibelots of wood, brass, ivory, or horn." The great limitation of the lathe, of course, was that it was limited to objects with circular cross-sections or, at best, to elliptical shapes that didn't depart too far from the strictly circular.

Blanchard's gun-stock lathe arose from a consultation requested by Asa Waters, one of the Valley's established armorers. Waters had patented a lathe that could cut a tapered gun barrel, but he could not solve the challenge of machining the breech-end of the barrel, where it flattened out and connected to the stock. The fact that Waters turned to Blanchard suggests that he was already a young man of considerable reputation. According to Waters's son, who later was an important manufacturer in his own right, Blanchard listened to the problem, then "glanced his eye over the machine, began a low monotonous whistle, as was his wont through life when in deep study, and ere long suggested an additional, very simple, but wholly original cam motion . . . which upon being applied, relieved the difficulty at once, and proved a perfect success." (A cam is an accessory that adjusts the path of the material or the cutting tool to create an ellipse or other noncircular curve.)

When Blanchard returned with the improved lathe, a delighted Waters said, "Well, Thomas, I don't know what you won't do next. I should not be surprised if you turned a gun-stock!" When Thomas stammered out that he would like to try, workmen who had gathered around the new lathe broke into guffaws. A gun-stock, in truth, is an intricate product that had long been a serious bottleneck at government armories. The wood stock has a variety of subtle curves along multiple axes, with dozens of recesses and connection points for the lock, barrel, and other metal parts, which in the early nineteenth century were all carved out by hand. A skilled team could turn out only eight to ten finished stocks a week. Intrigued, Blanchard mulled the problem, until one day on a trip home "the whole principle of turning irregular forms from a pattern burst upon his mind." A neighbor reported that Blanchard stood in the road shouting, "I've got it! I've got it! I've got it!" while a passing farmer muttered, "I guess that man is crazy."

The concept was as simple as it was brilliant. Blanchard constructed a lathe with two distinct parts, each separately powered. The first comprised the cutting tool, geared to revolve at a high speed, connected on a rigid frame to the "tracer," which was just a freely moving wheel. The second part comprised the target block of wood, which was connected by a similar frame to a finished gun stock, or the "pattern." The target block and the pattern had identical motions, rotating slowly while moving back and forth on their long axes. The tracer wheel rested against the pattern, while the cutting wheel rested against the wood block. As the pattern rotated and moved longitudinally, the undulations of the pattern pushed the tracer wheel back and forth, imparting the same action to the cutting wheel—and voilà, within just a few passes, the wood block assumed the shape of the pattern.*

Blanchard perfectly understood that he had solved a general problem: how to machine any irregular shape at all. He produced prototypes for a host of items that previously could be produced only by hand labor—shoe lasts (forms in the shape of a foot, an essential tool for shoe and boot factories),

---

*A second-generation Blanchard machine, dating from the early 1840s, can be seen at the American Precision Museum in Windsor, Vermont, which is housed in the former main factory of the same Robbins and Lawrence company that won the firearms medal at the Crystal Palace exhibit. It has one of the world's best collections of nineteenth-century machine tools, many of them still in working order, demonstrating as well how multiple machines, running at different speeds, were all driven off the same waterwheel. Strikingly, modern rifle factories still cut stocks with machines practically identical to Blanchard's—except that they cut multiple stocks at a time and have a variety of guards to protect workers from cutting edges and flying chips.

axe handles, plow handles, and wheel spokes. In a tour de force at the Paris Exposition of 1857, he executed a bust of the Empress Eugénie entirely by machine. He also proved to be a pioneer in patent management, doggedly fighting off imitations and carefully specifying the applications and the permissible territory covered by each license. Over a long life, he was credited with dozens of inventions, in almost every field that caught his restless fancy, including steam engine and steamboat technology. He died in 1865, at age seventy-seven, a sophisticated and well-traveled gentleman of considerable wealth. A eulogy said, "One can hardly go into a tool shop, a machine shop, or workshop of any kind, wood or iron, where motive power is used, in which he will not find more or less of Blanchard's mechanical notions."

The striking feature of Blanchard's story, however, is not so much his invention but the reception it was accorded by the military establishment. Even before he finished his gun-stock lathe, he received a letter from the Springfield Armory—along with Harpers Ferry, one of the two government armories—asking what he was up to. Blanchard was to find himself the

Thomas Blanchard's gun-stock machine was a radical manufacturing breakthrough. Both the pattern stock and the target wood block turned slowly and moved back and forth on their long axes. A tracer wheel followed the path of the pattern and imparted the same motion to a rapidly spinning cutting wheel. For the first time, highly non-regular shapes could be manufactured by machine.

beneficiary of perhaps the American government's first attempt at an "industrial policy." The most direct analog may be the period of the 1950s and early 1960s, when the U.S. military was the primary support, indeed, occasionally the only customer, of the American semiconductor industry. During the cold war, the military sponsored high technology to counter the Soviet Union's great manpower advantage; in the wake of the War of 1812, machine manufacturing was seen as a way to offset Great Britain's much greater pool of skilled craftsmen.

When Blanchard's lathe was ready, the armory arranged a series of demonstrations and tests at both Springfield and Harpers Ferry that consumed much of 1819. (Just transporting the machinery between Springfield and Harpers Ferry—from Massachusetts to rural Virginia—would have taken a month or more.) Discussions were put on hold through much of 1820 while Blanchard dealt with a patent challenge, although he also designed a companion machine to cut out the gunlock seating. Finally, in 1822, he and the government negotiated what we would now call a research and development contract. Blanchard would move to Springfield as an "inside contractor" and have the facilities and workers of the armory at his disposal. The government would pick up all the development costs of his machinery and pay Blanchard nine cents for each gun stock he produced. By the time he left the armory in 1827, besides having received $18,500 in Springfield patent fees alone, Blanchard had perfected a system of sixteen machines that carried out all of the multiple stocking operations with a minimum of manual intervention, including cutting and boring the fussiest of the pin and plate seatings. Blanchard's production system was modernized and retooled twenty years later by Cyrus Buckland, one of the great Springfield supervisors, but the fundamental principles were unchanged.

The Crystal Palace Exhibition was the first occasion in which a wide swathe of British opinion makers encountered Blanchard-style production systems, which came to be known as the "American System of Manufacturing." Reactions ran from utter disbelief, especially among British craftsmen, whose gun production methods had hardly changed for a century, to something like fear among industrialists and civil servants. The nastiest shock, perhaps, was how utterly different and radically complete the American approach to manufacturing appeared to be.

Revolutions don't boil up from a vacuum. Blanchard's invention was just one flowering of a unique concentration of machine-geek talent taking shape in the Connecticut River Valley, much as Silicon Valley emerged as a center of innovation a century and a half later. The fact that it happened along the Connecticut River, or happened at all, was, just as in Silicon Valley, the semirandom consequence of basic predispositions and happy chance.

Valley Guys

The Connecticut River rises in the mountains of New Hampshire, then zigzags between New Hampshire and Vermont, and cuts a north-south divide through Massachusetts, passing between Mount Holyoke and Mount Tom, before traversing Connecticut and emptying into Long Island Sound near Old Saybrook. The site of savage Indian-settler wars in the seventeenth and eighteenth centuries, the river valley was beginning to emerge as an important secondary manufacturing center in the 1800s, built around an artisanal culture of small workshops, especially in the metal trades.

The attractions of the river valley started with its splendid endowment of physical resources. First, there was the prospect of almost unlimited power. The river's fall across its entire length was greater than Niagara's.* Even today, upriver dams provide a substantial fraction of the electrical power for the region. Then there was direct water transport to New York harbor; the state of rural roads was such that overland transport longer than thirty to forty miles almost always cost more than shipping goods to New York from any point on the river. And finally, there were the convenient iron mines of Salisbury, Connecticut, just south of the Massachusetts border.

In the first quarter of the nineteenth century, New England manufacturing was "hot." Samuel Slater smuggled British spinning technology into the country in 1791, and the pace of industrialization accelerated after Francis Cabot Lowell stole Samuel Cartwright's power loom designs during an English tour in 1813. The mills drew from a swelling stream of farm girls and boys as New England agriculture withered under the onslaught of high-productivity New York farmers. Mill profits created an ample supply of ven-

---

*The investors who created the town of Holyoke, for example, calculated that even in the dry season, the river provided some 550 "mill powers." A mill power is thirty cubic feet of water per second over a twenty-five-foot fall. The very largest mills consumed only four to five mill powers. The calculation also suggests the professionalism of early American capitalists.

ture capital, with activist investors prospecting for opportunities. The most talented young men perceived that a flair for machinery could be a fast track to financial independence. An English observer commented in 1854:

> [T]here is not a working boy of average ability in the New England states, at least, who has not an idea of some mechanical invention or improvement in manufactures, by which, in good time, he hopes to better his position, or rise to fortune and social distinction.

And finally, there was the nearby Springfield Armory, the nerve center of the American military's drive toward high-technology weapon-making. Ironically, the blueprint for the armory came from the industrially laggard French, with the help of that most committed of pastoralists, Thomas Jefferson. After the American Revolution, Frenchmen helped organize West Point and wrote the first American weapons manuals. The French took a highly rational approach to weapons design—it was called *le système Gribeauval* after the eighteenth-century artillery reformer Jean-Baptiste de Gribeauval, who had made simplicity and uniformity of weapons a career project. One of his disciples, Honoré Blanc, an arsenal expert, was a friend of Jefferson when he was the ambassador in Paris. Blanc insisted that true uniformity meant that parts should be freely exchangeable from one weapon to another. (It is not clear whether Blanc ever achieved such uniformity himself. If so, it would have been on a limited basis in small production lots. He did not use machinery, but rather promoted hand-shaping and filing parts with the aid of precise dies and jigs, or molds, which he may have learned from Swedish clock makers.) Jefferson pressed Blanc's methods on Washington's cabinet, and even attempted to create an armory for Blanc in the United States.

The first American chief of ordnance, Decius Wadsworth, adopted the very Gribeauvalian motto, "Uniformity, Simplicity, and Solidarity." Mechanized production was emphasized from the start. Springfield Armory reported in 1799 that the man-days to produce a musket had been reduced from twenty-one to just nine through "labor-saving machines." Wadsworth's chief assistant and long-serving successor, George Bomford, was a Gribeauval devotée, as was Roswell Lee, who was Springfield superintendent from 1815 to 1833. It was Lee who reached out to Blanchard and invited him to demonstrate his gun-stock machine at the armory. Their mantra was "interchangeability of parts," in the spirit of Blanc. The military impetus behind interchangeability was the difficulty in finding skilled craftsmen to repair weapons in the field*; but in the longer run, the precision methodologies developed under military contracts became a critical technology behind American manufacturing dominance later in the century.

The Valley's venture investors were typically Boston merchant princes, men such as Israel Thorndike, S. A. Eliot, Samuel Cabot, Francis Stanton, and Harrison Gray Otis. Edmund Dwight, a Morgan cousin on his mother's side, wasn't in the same financial stratum as a Cabot, but gained access through his work at the law firm of Fisher Ames, the old Massachusetts Federalist leader. Political connections were taken for granted; these were men who kept Daniel Webster on their payroll while he was in the Senate, and Otis had been a U.S. senator himself. They committed money for the long term, for returns that look modest today—there was considerable excitement over a water-power investment in Waltham, for example, that was returning 15–20 percent a year to shareholders after five years. But money wasn't the only motivator. James K. Mill, a substantial Boston merchant who participated in several investment groups, was absent from his primary business for months at a time getting new companies on their feet. He was clearly extremely capable and worked very hard. One imagines he enjoyed it.

Since these were cotton men, primarily interested in new cotton mills, they did not target precision manufacturing as such. But they envisioned a manufacturing metropolis extending the entire length of the river, and their infrastructure investments benefited manufacturers of all kinds. A common strategy was to buy up stretches of the riverbank as mill sites, build a dam, some worker housing and amenities, then organize a textile mill and a machine company to supply the mill, often with a second round of investors, perhaps a successful mill manager putting up his life savings for the chance to own his own mill. The hope was that with anchor businesses in place, other entrepreneurs would lease the remaining mill sites, or "water privileges," as the youthful Thomas Blanchard did. Investors put large sums at risk. The group that financed the town of Holyoke, for example, started with an initial paid-in capital of $2.45 million in 1847—a huge sum for the

---

*For many classes of products, strict interchangeability was not such an obvious requirement. A prairie farmer was satisfied with a replacement reaper blade even if it took some effort to make it fit. So long as the job was within the typical farmer's skill set, it was "interchangeable" enough. The military definition tended to be a strict one, however—soldiers should be able to unscrew a defective gunlock piece and screw in another that fit just as well. During the Crystal Palace Exhibition and subsequent British investigations, the strict definition was the one generally intended, and is the one I use in this chapter.

time, mostly for a thousand-foot-wide dam (which collapsed on the day of its opening and had to be rebuilt from scratch). After ten years of struggle, they lost it all, although Holyoke eventually prospered as a papermaking center.

The whirl of entrepreneurial activity in the Valley, the presence of the machine-geek culture, and the technical leadership of the Springfield Armory made it the natural center for the military's development of inter-changeability-level precision machining. It took a long time, but in the first half of the century, striving for interchangeability was as important as actually achieving it. Machining is one of a small number of enabling tech-nologies—like electricity in the early twentieth century and information technology now—that accelerate development across a very wide front; and the advances in "American system" precision machining had profound implications for the entire course of the country's economic development.

The Quest for the Holy Grail

Until relatively recently, legend had it that military-precision interchange-ability was first achieved around the turn of the century by Eli Whitney of cotton gin fame, a tale that was assiduously watered by Whitney and his heirs. Whitney eventually became one of the Valley's great manufacturers, but he never achieved interchangeability-standard machining. The source of the story was that he once *promised* interchangeability to win an impor-tant military contract, at a time when he was in serious financial trouble from mismanaging his cotton gin patents. Whitney had very limited manu-facturing experience at the time, and none in rifles; besides not achieving the promised interchangeability, his deliveries were years late and dogged by disputes over their quality. Much later, Samuel Colt also claimed that his pistols were made with interchangeable parts, as did Cyrus McCormick for his reapers and Isaac Singer for his sewing machines, although none of them had actually achieved that standard of precision.* (When pressed

---

*Historians used to take such claims at face value. But modern scholars like David Hounshell and Merritt Roe Smith developed the annoying habit of going back to the artifacts, gathering samples of, say, same-model Colt pistols, and taking them apart to see if the parts are interchangeable. They're not. A dead giveaway is that each part is marked with the number of the specific pistol it fits. Colt's production accounts specify the existence of "fitting departments" where specialized workmen used elaborate arrays of files to assemble the final product. The same was true in Singer's and McCormick's factories.

hard by a British panel on one occasion, Colt retreated to the claim that he had achieved "approximate" interchangeability.)

Achieving consistent interchangeability in volume production turned out to be a much tougher challenge than French military reformers or American ordnance officials had ever imagined. The practical methodologies evolved over many years, and were largely the work of John Hall, a gunsmith from Portland, Maine, and inventor of the "Hall carbine" that became notorious when muckrakers dug into the youthful Pierpont Morgan's dealings with Civil War procurement authorities.

John Hall was born into an upper-middle-class family during the waning days of the Revolution, and judging by his letters, was much better educated than Blanchard. He became fascinated with firearms after a stint in his state militia, and in 1811, at age thirty, he applied for a patent on a new type of breech-loading rifle, which eliminated the clumsy process of pushing ammunition down the muzzle at each reload. As Hall described his invention in an 1816 pamphlet:

> The Patent Rifles may be loaded and fired . . . more than twice as quick as muskets . . . ; in addition to this, they may be loaded with great ease, in almost every situation. . . . [Since] the American Militia . . . will always excel as light troop . . . quickly assembling and moving with rapidity . . . these guns are most excellently adapted for them.

In contrast to Blanchard, who moved easily from one product or technology to another, Hall was grimly focused, with perhaps a touch of the fanatic. He devoted thirty years to his rifle, suffering one cruel turn of fate after the other. Although his work influenced almost every aspect of the post–Civil War manufacturing revolution, when he died he could fairly be considered a failure. He had never made much money, and had to scrape and scratch to educate his children. Despite the accolades accorded his rifle, it never achieved wide distribution and was already obsolete at his death; the credit for his great manufacturing innovations was accorded to Whitney and others.

The first harbinger of the stony path ahead came when Hall applied for his patent. The commissioner of patents, William Thornton, notified Hall that there was a prior claim. From whom? inquired an incredulous Hall. From me! came the reply, although Thornton hastened to reassure him that he was prepared to share the rights.

Thornton, a friend of Jefferson, was the scion of a wealthy American family, educated in Europe, a medical doctor, prominent in Philadelphia artistic and cultural circles, and a bit of a scientific dabbler. After investing in John Fitch's pioneering steamboat in 1788, he insisted that the much-harassed Fitch incorporate "improvements" of his own design, none of which worked. Thornton was admitted to Jefferson's circle when he won the design competition for the projected president's mansion and Capitol building for the new federal city. He was forced to share the award with a professional architect when it turned out that his design was unbuildable. But both Jefferson and Washington loved his facades, and the current White House and Capitol apparently incorporate substantial elements of his original design. Standard biographies treat Thornton as an accomplished inventor, for he "held patents for improvements on steamboats, distilling equipment, and firearms." One can imagine how he got them. The story of Hall's patent has the ring of modern machine-politics graft.

Upon receiving Thornton's letter, Hall arranged to see him in Washington:

> Upon my arrival there a gun was shewn me, the barrel of which was made broad at the butt as large as to receive a piece of metal . . . sufficient to contain a charge of powder & ball. Such a contrivance it appeared to me would never have been of any utility, at any rate was very different from mine. [It has been identified as a British Ferguson, dating from about 1776.] In conversation upon it he remarked . . . that he had thought of a plan which would have resembled mine & had given orders for its construction but nothing (except the drawings) had been done toward it (& they were not to be found).

When Thornton made it clear that a patent would not issue unless it was in both their names, an outraged Hall appealed to James Monroe, the secretary of state, requesting a conflict of claims hearing under the patent law. Monroe blandly advised him not to rock the boat, because "[I]t would be more to my interest to be connected with Doct. Thornton even at the expence of half my right than to have it wholly to myself, because his influence in that case would be exerted in my favor but otherwise would be exerted against me."

To his lifelong regret, Hall caved. He later exacted a measure of revenge, but it cost him dearly. When he and Thornton settled their respective rights under the patent, Hall retained the manufacturing rights, while allocating the licensing income to Thornton. Hall then refused to sign off on licenses, thereby denying Thornton the profits of his blackmail, but crippling the marketing of the weapon.*

Hall's time in purgatory was only beginning. He desperately needed a military contract, but Thornton had become his nemesis, using his connections to block any assistance. Developing his rifle and equipping a factory had strained Hall's resources to the limit, and private sales were disappointing, despite pamphlets claiming his rifle's success against a "bulletproof sea monster" on the Maine coast. Hall finally managed to squeeze a small contract out of Bomford at Ordnance, who liked the weapons, and a trial in 1816 gave them high marks. That led to an offer for a somewhat larger contract, which Hall, to his chagrin, was forced to decline because he was losing his factory. With the War of 1812 over, military requirements had fallen as well.

Hall then upped the ante with the same promise that Whitney had made almost twenty years before, that he would manufacture his weapons by machine in such a way that all parts would be interchangeable, which was sure to get Ordnance's attention. In the meantime, Hall's family, which had some political connections of its own, had gotten the ear of John Calhoun, the new secretary of war. In a series of interventions, Calhoun arranged for two separate trials, and finally a rigorous three-month military review to rate the Hall rifles against standard ordnance, which was conducted in 1818–19. Although Hall thought the report "very guarded," it is actually a ringing confirmation of his claims. His rifles proved more durable, and as accurate and powerful, as the standard rifle—both scoring much higher than any musket—but with an ease of loading that the review board rated as 2:1 over the standard rifle and 3:2 over the musket. The board rated the ease of loading *"of infinite consequence in the rifle,* the diffi-

---

*Thornton and Hall feuded in public in 1819, after an antiquarian asserted that a German Marshal Saxe had anticipated Hall by a century. When Hall defended his priority, he was challenged by Thornton and, not for the first time, asked for an open arbitration, which Thornton airily dismissed with a quatrain:

What I have written, I have written, Pilate said
In answ'ring Jewish infidels, and those ill-bred.
And what I've written, I have written, once for all,
   Whether the attack's
   From Marshal Saxe
     Or from John Hall.

culty of loading this arm being the great objection to its more general introduction." (Muzzle-loading was a special problem for rifles because of foul-
ing of the rifling grooves.)

The consequence was an R&D contract, somewhat like Blanchard's.
Finalized in 1819, it would have answered Hall's fondest prayers, but for a
near fatal Catch-22 that plagued the rest of his days. He was awarded a
salaried armory position, an appropriation for equipment and a work force,
and, to boot, a $1 royalty for each delivered rifle. But the contract had to be
performed at Harpers Ferry rather than Springfield—Harpers Ferry was the
"southern" armory, heavily politicized, in part because of the proximity to
Washington, and technically backward compared to Springfield. Hall put
up an argument, but finally had little choice but to accede, and was to work
at Harpers Ferry the rest of his life. As he had feared, the Harpers Ferry
superintendents, who were all politicians, had no interest in his project and
undermined him at every turn—skimming his appropriations, shortchanging
him on equipment and space, filing endless complaints about the wastefulness and ineffectiveness of his methods—while Hall slowly and steadily
created the manufacturing processes that underpinned mass production
technology for the next century. He later conceded that his own naïve
underestimate of the challenge lent credibility to his critics:

> I was not aware of the great length of time that would be consumed . . .
> to effect the construction of the arms with the perfect similarity of all
> their component parts. . . . I had been told it had been pronounced im-
> possible by the French Commissioners . . . and I know that all attempts
> to effect it in Great Britain and this Country had failed; but from an
> unswerving reliance on my own abilities I expected to accomplish it in
> a *short* period . . ."

Hall had divined, as no one else, that achieving true precision manufacturing entailed reconceiving the entire process in all its details. Better
machines by themselves would not answer. It was essential, for example,
always to begin with an ideal model of the target product, and take subsequent measurements only from that model.* Hall insisted on special-

---

*Hall almost despaired when Ordnance sent samples of his rifles to Simeon North as manufac-
turing templates. Even a man as sympathetic as Bomford had missed the point that a sample
wasn't a pattern, and would inevitably incorporate imperceptible, but possibly fatal, deviations
that would be passed along to all its progeny.

purpose machines for each part, and also special-purpose machines to make the production machines. Placing and fixing a part in a machine required the same attention as the precision of the machine itself. Precision gauges were constructed for every measurement—there were some sixty-three separate gauges for the rifle, leaving nothing to a workman's judgment. The gauges were always made in three sets, one for workmen, one for inspectors, and a master set in the plant manager's office to monitor wear on the other two. Inspections of inspections helped ferret out any nonconforming part, and a final batch of finished rifles was always disassembled, their parts mixed up, and reassembled before shipping. Along the way, Hall made substantial contributions to a wide range of processes, especially in milling and forging, created new systems for controlling cutting tools, and solved the problem of forging shrinkage during cooling, which had stumped all of his predecessors. He also lavished attention on dampening vibration and chatter in his machines, redesigning drives and spindles so they stayed true, and creating gauges to measure a machine's drift from trueness.

It took almost five years, but in 1824 Hall could finally invite Calhoun and Bomford, who had recently moved up to Ordnance chief, to examine a production run of rifles manufactured on his principles. They could see for themselves "the manner in which the several parts, promiscuously taken, came together, fitted and adapted to each other." Just as important, the guns had been manufactured almost entirely with unskilled machine operatives. Both men were much impressed, but before Bomford could move forward with a further contract, Congress intervened, demanding Hall's dismissal. The Virginia delegation, after years of complaints from Harpers Ferry,

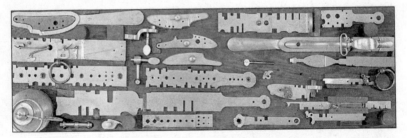

One of the many critical steps toward precision manufacturing was to establish precise gauges for each part. This is a partial gauging set for an 1841 Springfield Armory rifle. John Hall's carbines had sixty-three separate gauges like these.

insisted on a full investigation into the alleged "waste & extravagance of the Publick money on the Patent Rifle." Bomford had no choice but to suspend all production activities pending a full field trial of the rifles and an external review of Hall's manufacturing methods.

Two more years were consumed convening the review boards and completing the investigations, but the final reports were stunning vindications of Hall. After a five-month field trial, the military board expressed "its perfect conviction of the superiority of this Arm over every other kind of Small Arm now in use," and supplied a statistical analysis of its great advantages in speed of firing, accuracy, and durability.

The manufacturing review was even more glowing. Hall's system was adjudged to be "entirely novel" with "the most benefitial results to the country." The inspectors, who were all experienced men, had never before seen arms "made so exactly similar to each other . . . [that] parts, on being changed, would suit equally well when applied to every other arm." They conducted an experiment of freely intermixing parts from 200 rifles drawn from different annual production runs and found that "We were unable to discover any inaccuracy in any of their parts." Overall, they pronounced Hall's work "greatly superior to anything we have ever seen or expected to see in the manufacture of small arms"—especially since it was mostly executed by "boys from twelve to fifteen years of age, at small wages." The board concluded by noting Hall's poor working conditions and hoped that he might "receive that patronage from the Government that his talents, science, and mechanical ingenuity deserve."

The board's hopes were in vain. Spectacular as they were, the reviews still did not quell the sniping from Congress and Harpers Ferry. Bomford at least was able to protect Hall's contract, although it was renegotiated on less favorable terms. When state militias in 1828 demanded to be supplied with Hall rifles, the manufacturing contract, larger than any Hall had been awarded, went to Simeon North, of Middletown, Connecticut. In part to ease Hall's disappointment, Bomford made him inspector of North's output. The relationship got off to a rocky start when Hall arrived at Middletown with his full panoply of gauges and pronounced North's output unacceptable. But North was one of America's great gunsmiths—he had invented the milling machine and had tried to fabricate pistols with interchangeable parts as early as 1807—and as he came to understand Hall's achievement, he replicated the system in his own factory. It took another several years, but in 1834, Hall and North proudly demonstrated to the War Department that parts from both Middletown and Harpers Ferry could be "promiscuously" intermixed and readily reassembled into perfectly functional rifles.

By then Hall was in his midfifties, and seems to have wearied of the struggle. None of his manufacturing innovations was patentable, since they had all been developed while he was in government employ. His rifle, good as it was, was slowly becoming obsolete, and was soon eclipsed by more modern weapons, from gunsmiths like Christian Sharps—the Sharps rifle may have been the favorite of Union troops—and B. Tyler Henry, whose Henry rifle was a prototype for the long-running Winchester. Hall quietly continued on salary at Harpers Ferry, tinkering with his system until his death in 1841. His place in the story gradually faded into a mere footnote—as one popular history written in the 1950s put it, ". . . by 1820, Hall, using Whitney's techniques of interchangeable manufacture, was turning out his rifles at Harpers Ferry."

The American Machine Tradition

The American fascination with machine production is a distinguishing feature of its leap to the front ranks of manufacturing powers. The collection of manufacturing technologies developed by Hall, Blanchard, and, later, men like Thomas Warner and Cyrus Buckland at the Springfield Armory has been dubbed "Armory practice" by the historian David Hounshell, and was a key element in the American technologic gene pool. Merritt Roe Smith has traced the numerous skilled machinists who passed through Harpers Ferry in Hall's day, did their stint at Springfield, and later became key managers throughout the pantheon of great Valley plants—Simeon North's, Nathan Ames & Co., Robbins and Lawrence, Browne and Sharpe. The ties between North, who had replicated Hall's system, and Robbins and Lawrence were very close; and the perfect interchangeability of the rifles that Robbins and Lawrence demonstrated at the Crystal Palace Exhibition were a textbook case of the Hall tradition. Browne and Sharpe, whose connections to Hall ran through Robbins and Lawrence, demonstrated their mastery of the technology in the 1850s by producing the Willcox and Gibbs sewing machines to Armory standards of exactness.

More important than actually achieving parts interchangeability was the commitment to a total Hall-style precision-machining environment. Samuel Colt's great factory at "Coltsville" in Hartford, Connecticut, which became the Mecca of the "American system" in the 1850s, is a case in point. Colt was a promoter, not an engineer, who once made his living staging laughing gas exhibitions. He devised his repeating firearms in the mid-1830s, but his breakthrough did not happen until the Mexican War (1846–48), when his pistol design caught the fancy of Samuel Walker, the legendary commander of the Texas Rangers. With Walker's support, Colt won a patent renewal in 1849 and set up his own factory. To run it, he recruited Elisha K. Root, the manager of an axe and edge-tool factory. Colt made the announcement with his typical George Steinbrenner-like flair: Elisha Root would be "the highest-paid mechanic in New England, if not in the entire country."

Root was a great manufacturer, who made signal contributions to forging and milling technology, and he created one of the outstanding early American factory environments. As one historian has put it, "[C]redit for the revolver belongs to Colt; for the way they were made, mainly to Root." Although he never drove down to that n^{th} degree of precision that Hall had achieved, all of the basic Armory production hallmarks were in place in Root's factories—precise designs, special-purpose machinery, detailed gauging, multitier inspections. As a visiting British engineer noted of the Root factory, "[I]t is impossible to go through that work without coming away a better engineer."

The Valley's influence reached far beyond metal fabrication. Alexander Holley, America's greatest steel engineer in the 1870s and early 1880s, who was responsible for almost all American steel plant designs, was a true son of the Valley, and almost certainly knew Root. They were from the same area of Connecticut, and Holley's father, who served a term as state governor, was a cutlery manufacturer like Root. Holley's plants were a radical departure from those abroad, exhibiting all the features of the broader American machine tradition—continuous processing, the mechanization of unreliable hand processes, and John Hall's style of reconceiving a process down through the finest-grained of production details. British visitors to American steel plants were astonished—not just at their scale and speed but by the "very conspicuous absence of labourers."

Strict Armory practice came into full flower with the rise of America's mass consumer society in the 1880s; indeed, it made it possible. Isaac Singer was a marketing genius who achieved world dominance for his sewing machine. Although he did not manufacture to Armory standards of precision, he ran a well-organized factory system that served until about 1880, when sales soared past the 500,000 mark and Singer suddenly found himself in replacement-parts hell. At his company's rate of growth, the world couldn't supply the craftsmen to keep up with his service and repair requirements. Other companies, like McCormick and the Ball Glass Co., faced up to their problems at about the same time as Singer, while Colt did so a full decade before. In case after case, the men they called on to retool their factories and clean up their processes were in a direct lineage from the old Robbins and Lawrence, Nathan Ames, and other Connecticut Valley tool companies, the true creators of the "American system" more than a half century before.

The list of spinoff benefits could be extended almost indefinitely. Machining steam engine parts to the hundredths, rather than the six-teenths, of an inch greatly improved fuel efficiency and power output. The push toward precision spotlighted improvement opportunities in cutting steels, metal alloys, lubricants, machine power trains, and an ever-expanding host of other satellite industries. Perhaps most important was a style of problem solving. The fact that Americans typically thought of machine solu-tions as a *first* recourse, an integral part of almost any production process, was a major factor in the seemingly effortless move up to manufacturing scales previously undreamed of.

The British Reaction

The Crystal Palace demonstrations by Colt and Robbins and Lawrence came at a time when British civil servants and military officials were struggling with the dark side of imperial glory. Conquest required vast armies and massive supplies of ordnance, and British gunsmiths were not keeping pace. Production had greatly expanded, but at the cost of a distressing falloff in quality. The notion of interchangeable parts was especially attractive, since far-flung armies could not be reliably supplied with the skilled craftsmen to keep hand-crafted weapons in good repair.

But even civil servants who believed the American claims were stymied by the radicalism of the innovations. The workings of the British gun industry were reasonably typical of mid-nineteenth-century manufacturing. It was craft-based and included at least forty trades, each with its own apprenticeship system and organization. The gunsmiths were concentrated in Birmingham; there were about 7,500 in all, about half of them parts makers, with the rest employed as "setters-up," or finishers, generally the most skilled men. Under the typical contract, each of the trades produced its own type of parts, which were shipped to the government for inspection before being assigned to the finishers for assembly. The most labor-intensive finishing task was stock-making, which consumed about a fourth of all the finishers, while the most skilled men were the lock-filers. The gunlock, the key firing mechanism, was the most complicated part, and lock-filers spent years as apprentices learning to painstakingly hand-file the forty or so separate lock pieces to create a unified assembly with a smooth and consistent action. When the Americans breezily described machine-made stocks, and locks that required no hand fitting, they sounded as if they were smoking opium.

Parliamentary and military advocates for reform were greatly bolstered by the opening of Colt's British factory in 1853. It was the first Colt plant designed entirely by Root, and drew a continuing stream of industrial pilgrims. The awestruck comments of British engineers are strikingly reminiscent of the comments of American automobile executives upon first visiting Japanese plants in the 1970s and 1980s. One visitor reported to an official inquiry that Colt's factory

> produced a very impressive effect, such as I shall never forget. The first impression was to humble me very considerably. I was in a manner introduced to such a masterly extension of what I knew to be correct principles, but extended in so masterly and wholesale a manner, as made me feel we were very far behind. . . . In those American tools there is a common-sense way of going to the point at once, that I was quite struck with: there is great simplicity . . . no ornamentation, no rubbing away of corners, or polishing; but the precise, accurate, and correct results.

The second important event of 1853 was a major industrial exhibit in New York, planned as a riposte to the great exhibition at the Crystal Palace. Parliament authorized a delegation for a firsthand look, and the two men chosen as delegation leaders attest to the seriousness of the trip: they were George Wallis, England's leading industrial arts educator, and Joseph Whitworth, arguably Britain's greatest machinist.

To history's lasting benefit, the American exhibition was an organizational fiasco, and was still months from opening when the Whitworth-Wallis delegation arrived in New York. Rather than waste the voyage, the two men divided up their research priorities and undertook separate tours, attempting to gain a comprehensive view of American industrial prowess. They covered thousands of miles, with each man making several return trips, visiting factories throughout the country in virtually every major industry, carefully noting production statistics and methods, the organization of work, the use of advanced machinery, the attitudes of tradesmen, and the social conditions of factories. Both made written reports and supplied extensive supporting testimony to a parliamentary inquiry. The total body of the reports are uniquely informative surveys compiled by unusually well-qualified and disinterested experts.

Their primary conclusion, as summarized by a parliamentary body, was that:

> [I]n the adaptation of special apparatus to a single operation in almost all branches of industry, the Americans display an amount of ingenuity, combined with undaunted energy, which as a nation we would do well to imitate, if we mean to hold our present position in the great market of the world.

Whitworth was especially impressed with American prowess in woodworking machinery—Blanchard's gun-stocking machine being merely a leading case:

> In no branch of manufacture does the application of labour-saving machinery produce by simple means more important results than in the working of wood. Wood being obtained in America in any quantity, it is there applied to every possible purpose, and its manufacture has received that attention which its importance deserves. . . . Many works in various towns are occupied exclusively in making doors, window frames, or staircases by means of self-acting machinery, such as planing, tenoning, morticing, and jointing machines. . . . In one of these manufactories twenty men were making panelled doors at the rate of 100 per day.

For Parliament's purposes, however, the most important findings came from Whitworth's visits to Connecticut Valley gun makers and the federal armories, where he fully documented the reality of strict interchangeability. At Springfield, he insisted on repeated demonstrations of disassembling rifles from different annual production runs, mixing up the parts and then reassembling them without special tools. He also minutely documented the armory's production schedules and manning. Jaws dropped when he reported the elapsed time to produce a finished rifle stock at about twenty-two minutes, including about two minutes of manual interventions, compared to a half day or more of work by a skilled team of craftsmen in England. Final assembly—the job that in England was spread among more than a dozen different "finisher" craft types, each requiring years of training—took only three to three and a half minutes, with no special tools and no files. One could scoff at Yankees who made such claims, but Whitworth could not be so easily dismissed, even though he was effectively consigning entire proud branches of the British metal trades to the scrapheap.

To their credit, Parliament and the military establishment, in the face of outraged political outcries from Birmingham, grasped the nettle and created a new government armory, located at Enfield. It was built entirely on American Armory principles, and outfitted with a full panoply of American machinery purchased primarily from Nathan Ames and Robbins and Lawrence. A measure of the commitment to correct principles was the hiring of James H. Burton, an American who learned his trade under John Hall, to set up the Enfield plant and initial operations. It was Enfield, of course, that produced the famed Enfield rifle that was the mainstay of the empire throughout the Victorian era.

The man who adroitly managed the entire process—from organizing the initial visits to America, through the successive parliamentary inquiries, the commitment to Enfield, and its construction and launch—was a splendid civil servant named John Anderson. With Enfield safely underway, he proudly stated his view of what was at stake:

> The American machinery is so different to our own, and so rich in suggestions that when fully organized it should be thrown open to the study of the machine makers of the kingdom. . . . A few hours at Enfield will show that we shall soon have to contend with no mean competitors in the Americans, who display an originality and common sense in most of

their arrangements which are not to be despised, but on the contrary are either to be copied or improved upon.

Anderson lived a long life; he made many other contributions to British armory practice, and was eventually knighted. But he must have been disappointed by the impact of the Enfield experiment. Outside of the military, British manufacturers were far less eager, and moved much more slowly, to adopt Armory practice, or the "American system." The divergent experiences were a source of much comment by contemporary British and American observers, and remain of continuing interest to historians.

What Made America Different?

A British analyst surveying the relative technical positions of America and Great Britain in midcentury could rightfully argue that there was no cause for panic: the mother country still enjoyed great advantages over its rustic former colony. American woodworking was indeed ingenious—tubs, reapers, even machine tools, were built mostly of wood and leather; but if one believed that the future lay with steel, Americans were not yet even in the field. Almost all quality American edge-tool makers relied on Sheffield steel, with British factories supplying either finished parts or rough blanks to be trimmed and finished locally. American gun-makers switched to American steel suppliers at the start of the Civil War, but switched back as soon as the war ended. (And for all its vaunted superiority in gun-making, the North imported 80 percent of its guns in the first year of the war.) Much the same could be said of engines. American factories were mostly water-powered, but the wave of the future was clearly steam, and American railroad and steamboat lines bought British engines. On the eve of the Civil War, America's biggest manufacturing industry was still cotton textiles, and the British could take sour comfort in the fact that American mills ran mostly on stolen British technology.

But the unexpectedness of the American showing at the Crystal Palace set off alarms. Advanced skills in precision manufacturing was so jarringly inconsistent with the common perception of America that it suggested a sudden economic acceleration. In fact, had national macroeconomic data been available, concerned Englishmen would have seen exactly the acceleration they feared. American income per head jumped from about two-thirds the British level in 1830, when it lagged countries like Portugal, France, and Canada, to virtual equivalence with Great Britain by 1860, far ahead of the next country on the list. Whitworth's emphasis on the prodigious output of American machine-aided factories, in industries as diverse as stonecutting and window-making, implied that England might have already lost the productivity race. Modern research suggests that the crossing point came as early as the 1820s.

In an insightful analysis of the causes for the American surge, Whitworth proposed a list that included the relative scarcity of labor; the country's great natural resources (although he points out that large tracts of the nation were quite barren); the lack of resistance to innovation on the part of workers; fewer barriers to organizing businesses; and most important in his view, the high national rate of literacy supported by a "cheap press."

Modern scholars have considerably tweaked and refined Whitworth's list. Scarcity of labor, for example, may have been a much more important factor in mechanizing midwestern farms than in, say, firearms production. When large farms could be had almost for the asking, especially in the prairie states, no skilled farm worker would choose to become a laborer. Since big farms had the same unforgiving weather-dictated time windows for planting and reaping as small ones, an ambitious, labor-short farmer had no choice but to mechanize. In 1857, *Scientific American* specified the minimum machinery for a one-hundred-acre farm as "a combined reaper and mower, a horse rake, a seed planter and a mower, a thresher and grain cleaner; portable grist mill, a corn sheller, a horse power, three harrows, roller, [and] two cultivators . . ." But it's much harder to relate Armory mechanization to labor scarcities, for both Springfield and Harpers Ferry seemed to have an ample supply of craftsmen. Fear of displacement among Harpers Ferry craftsmen was a prime source of John Hall's political problems.

The abundance of natural resources undoubtedly channeled American technology toward wood, water power, and large farms, but the historian Nathan Rosenberg suggests it may also have affected the pace of mechanization. In deforested England, workmen had to be much more respectful of their wood supplies than Americans, who were prodigiously wasteful. Hand-carving conserved wood better than machines, and British power saws were smaller, thinner, and ran more slowly than American saws to save wood. Whitworth also may have been right about America's probusiness legislative stance. He suggests, for example, that American telegraph companies could get organized much faster than in England, and that telegraph penetration was much deeper as a consequence.

And almost all observers agreed on the extraordinary quality of American workers, the social fluidity of the industrial system, and very high average educational levels. (American school spending doubled between 1840 and 1850, and doubled again by 1860; per pupil spending rose by about half.) A British manufacturer who had spent many years in America told a committee of inquiry:

> . . . the Englishman has not got the ductility of mind and the readiness of apprehension for a new thing which is required. . . . An American readily produces a new article; he understands everything you say to him as well as a man from a college in England would; he helps the employer by his own acuteness and intelligence.

Alfred Hobbs, the American lock maker, who had experience manufacturing in England, was also convinced that British workmen were a major productivity obstacle: "In America they might set to work to invent a machine, and all the workmen in the establishment would, if possible, lend a helping hand. . . . But in England it was quite the reverse. If the workmen could do anything to make the machine go wrong, they would do it."

Whitworth similarly admired "the readiness with which [American workmen] cause new improvements to be received, and the impulse which they thus unavoidably give to that inventive spirit."

The British cataloger of the American exhibit at the Crystal Palace caught that spirit very acutely:

> The absence in the United States of those vast accumulations of wealth which favour the expenditure of large sums on articles of mere luxury, and the general distribution of the means of procuring the more substantial conveniences of life, impart to the productions of American industry a character distinct from that of many other countries. . . . [B]oth manual and mechanical labour are applied with direct reference to increasing the number or the quantity of articles suited to the wants of a whole people, and adapted to promote the enjoyment of that moderate competency which prevails among them.

There really does seem to have been a culture of invention in America. There were hundreds of water-powered sawmills in Massachusetts by the end of the eighteenth century, when they were still relatively rare in England, in part because of opposition from the sawyers, the British woodcutting trade. (Sawyers actually burnt down a new sawmill in Manchester in 1825.) Flour-grinding in stone water mills was hardly changed in England for hundreds of years, but in America, Oliver Evans patented a radical new design for a semi-automated flour mill in 1790 that was widely licensed. The patent drawing shows an extraordinary five-story apparatus with multiple conveyors and belts that could direct grain along several process paths depending on the operation to be performed. As the licensing brochure puts it:

> ... the grain and meal are carried from one story to another, or from one part of the same story to another; the meal is cooled; and the boulting hoppers are attended by machinery, which is moved entirely by the power of the mill, and lessens the expense of attendance at least one half.

While the British invented spinning machines and power looms, the Americans greatly improved the stolen British designs, making them faster and easier to operate, opening up the industry to young women. Within a decade after Lowell built the first American loom, American textile-making productivity exceeded Great Britain's by 10 percent or more. The 1840s even saw the phenomenon of the patent broker, men who traveled by wagon throughout rural areas of the country, displaying recent inventions, and soliciting new ideas, which, for a fee, they would write up and submit as patent applications. It was Lincoln, after all, who said, "We, here in America, *think* we discover, and invent, and improve, faster than any [European nation]." Indeed, there may have been something of a patenting craze. After Asa Waters patented a trip-hammer forge, one competitor grumbled, "I should not think of gitting a patent for . . . applying a trip to welding a gun barel any moure than plating a scythe or a hoe it seems to me that a strange fanatism has operated on sum peope for gitting patents for some simple things." One is reminded of some of the very strange software patents that were issued during the 1990s technology bubble.

The fundamental novelty of the "American system" suggests that it sprang from a unique technology environment. Consider the trajectory of Blanchard's gun-stock machine: the tight network of machine geeks who spread the word of what he was up to even before he had finished; the instant receptivity to his ideas, and rapid creation of an R&D setting to

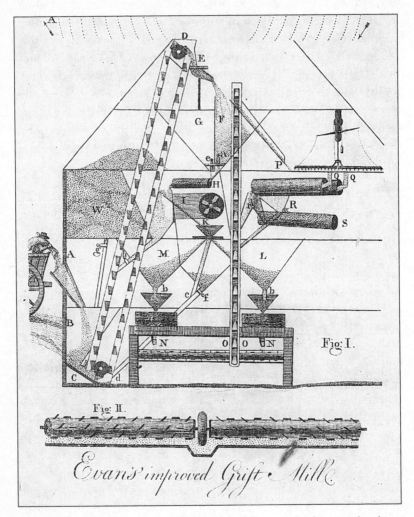

A schematic of Oliver Evans's patented grist mill from a 1797 licensing brochure. The tall conveyor belt on the left raises the grain for storage. Sluice gate settings release it for multiple processing paths, including grinding, cleaning, heating, cooling, and chopping, each of which could be set for multiple repetitions. The mill was water-driven, and Evans maintained that it reduced "the expense of attendance at least one half."

work out a complete production solution; the culture of innovation, supported by quick patenting and wide licensing; the way good ideas radiated and refracted off each other, as from Waters's barrel lathe to Blanchard's gun-stock machine, and then to fully mechanized production environments through the combined work of Hall, men like Buckland at Springfield, and great private machinists like North, Ames, and Robbins and Lawrence. And key to the entire process was a consensus within the government and military that advanced technology was very much a national priority. Driving it all was the sense of opportunity—Lincoln's "prudent, penniless beginner" could strive to become an independent businessman.

What Lincoln had not foreseen was that exploiting American innovation would require larger-scale enterprises than he could have imagined. The path to creating them would be very twisting indeed.

· 3 ·

BANDIT CAPITALISM

Icy nights on the Hudson River shroud the black waters in swirls of white fog. Shorelines were dark in 1868, and the small boat with two sailors and two passengers circled aimlessly, having lost direction in the choppy river. A ferry suddenly loomed out of the fog like a ghost ship, swamping the boat with freezing water and nearly capsizing it. When the sailors finally deposited their charges on the dock at Jersey City, Jay Gould was drenched and shivering in his greatcoat like a rat terrier. His partner, Jim Fisk, Jr., corpulent, expansive, bediamonded, was his usual cheerful, booming self. And why not? They had eluded sheriff's officers in New York, they had booked a whole floor of rooms in a good hotel, they had $7 million in cash, and Josie Mansfield, Fisk's favorite actress of the moment, who was said to strike men dumb with her (rather zaftig) beauty, would join them in due course. The cash had been extricated from the safes of the Erie Railway, although most of it arguably belonged to Gould's and Fisk's nemesis of the moment, "Commodore" Cornelius Vanderbilt. But if one took the title chain just a step further back, it was really the property of European investors.

The late 1860s were raw, explosive times. The massive injection of federal spending during the war years had triggered a wild scramble for wealth and a pandemic of corruption. Every system—physical, commercial, financial—was strained and struggling. Even as federal spending dipped after the war, foreign money came pouring in. Between 1855 and 1865, net foreign investment in America had doubled; in the decade to 1875, it tripled. Most of it came from England. Victorian prosperity was underpinned by Prime Minister William Ewart Gladstone's granitic commitment to Victorian morality in economic affairs—fiscal discipline, free trade, steadfast devotion to gold, and low interest rates. The return on British bonds fell steadily from more than 6 percent during the Napoleonic wars toward 2 percent in the 1880s. But stable prosperity could be boring, especially for adventurous sons and daughters of the upper classes who felt constrained by the modest returns from their "competencies." The greedy monied classes were irresistibly drawn to Wall Street in the 1870s, and to a clever young trader like Gould they looked like so many sheep lined up to the horizon, asking to be sheared.

Gould and Fisk had been forced to repair to the rigors of a Jersey City hotel because they were in the process of extracting one of the country's largest railroads, and biggest companies, from Vanderbilt and the other shareholders of the Erie. The episode was all the more shocking since it was masterminded by Gould, still in his early thirties and a virtual unknown on Wall Street, while Vanderbilt was the richest and arguably the most powerful man in the country, with long experience of financial markets. Still, it was Gould who emerged with the prize, although Vanderbilt wreaked enough havoc in the process that the railroad was damaged goods by the time Gould took control.

Of our four fledgling tycoons, Gould and Rockefeller were the first to make their presence felt in the years immediately after the war. Morgan, back in his father's firm, made the occasional cameo appearance, while Carnegie had cut loose from the Pennsylvania and was casting about for a career, albeit making buckets of money in the process. By 1870, however, Rockefeller had already become the most powerful figure in oil, while Gould's late-1860s "Erie Wars" were a dry run for the strategies that made him the nation's dominant railroad manager of the 1880s. In a pattern he would repeat again and again, Gould took control of the Erie by exploiting immature financial markets, and then violently disrupting the comfortable business patterns of his competitors. The resulting price wars and frantic defensive investments helped force the all-out, lurching style of railroad development that characterized the last quarter of the nineteenth century. Conservatives like Morgan deplored his methods, even as they sought his business, but the national system would never have developed so fast without Gould's provocations.

Opéra Bouffe

The Erie Railway was a lopsided saga of vast disappointments leavened by extraordinary accomplishment. Organized under a special act of the legislature in 1832 to link "the ocean and the lakes," its founders badly underestimated the engineering challenges of building a railroad through the stony, river-streaked hills of western New York. It took almost twenty years for the line to reach Lake Erie—at a point about fifty miles west of Buffalo—and it cost at least six times the original estimates. The railroad was freighted with a sodden history of bad luck and execrable judgments. Its finances were perennially a disgrace and its securities widely mistrusted. An inopportune burst of penny-pinching in 1841 prevented it from owning a direct route into New York City; instead it terminated on the western side of the Hudson, so city-bound freight had to "break bulk" and was ferried across from Jersey City. Traversing its difficult terrain with 1840s technology left a legacy of steep grades, rickety bridges, limited double-tracking (for safe two-way travel), and the wrong rail gauge—an unusually wide one, unfortunately, that substantially increased the cost of roads and rolling stock.

Gould was drawn into the "Erie wars," as they came to be known, in 1867 when some of the railroad's shares that his brokerage held on behalf of English investors were solicited during a struggle for control of the company. There were three warring factions: Daniel Drew, Cornelius Vanderbilt, and a consortium of Boston investors, which included the then-president of the Erie.

Vanderbilt and Drew went way back. Both were in their seventies—rough, unlettered men, who had made their first fortunes in the Hudson River steamboat trade. Neither was a paragon of personal behavior. Vanderbilt was a crude bully—forcing the maids was part of his normal routine, and he once clapped his wife into an insane asylum when she protested a house move. Drew was a whiner and groveler, a vicious enemy and treacherous ally. While Vanderbilt was a gifted businessman and railroad manager, Drew preferred to make money by cheating his own shareholders. A few years before, Drew had tried to trap Vanderbilt in one of his patented Erie bear raids,* but the wily Commodore had caught him out. Perhaps out of deference to their years of steamboat rivalry, Vanderbilt let Drew keep his Erie board seat on the understanding that he would help out in Vanderbilt's drive to take over the Erie—he wanted its Great Lake connections for the collection of railroads he was consolidating under the banner of the New York Central. The Boston group were looking for a similar connection for their New England road, and, besides, were desperate for the Erie's financial assistance. Drew's reasons for quietly opposing Vanderbilt after accepting his favor are obscure; keeping his word, perhaps, was too much of a break with the habits of a lifetime, especially when he could make money by trading against Vanderbilt's strategy.

The first approach to Gould came from Drew through the agency of Jim Fisk. Fisk was a New England farmboy, a year younger than Gould, who had worked as a peddler and circus roustabout before striking it rich as a cotton smuggler during the war. Drew was impressed with Fisk's boldness when he barged into his office one day with a business opportunity, and after executing the deal, helped set him up as a stockbroker. Fisk was an entertainer and a clown—generous, funny, and loyal. A womanizer, a trencherman, a fop, he spent prodigiously in good times and bad. Utterly unscrupulous, he was an artist of good-natured rascality; any law or social convention became a chance for uproarious transgression. There have been few less congruent pairs than Fisk and Gould, but they bonded almost immediately—Gould must have spotted the shrewd intelligence and appetite for hard work behind the buffoonish presentation. Fisk brought the touch of humor to their joint enterprises. Once during an Erie–New York Central price war on cattle shipping, Vanderbilt slashed rates to an absurd penny a head, chortling victoriously as his trains filled up with steers, until he discovered that Fisk and Gould had cornered the cattle market and were making a fortune from his shipping losses—Fisk's idea of course.

Drew had reached out to Gould merely for the shares he controlled. He knew that sooner or later Vanderbilt would discover his treachery and

---

*Drew was the Erie treasurer for many years. A favorite tactic was to lend money to the Erie to bail it out of a tight spot, usually triggering a rise in the stock. He would take back both a note for the loan and a secret trove of stock. As the stock rose, he would sell short (using borrowed stock). When it was time to cover (return the borrowed stock), he would dump his secret trove on the market, driving down the price, so he could buy back the borrowed stock on the cheap and lock in the profit he had made on the rise. Even by the loose ethical standards of the day, this was regarded as reprehensible.

launch a stock market battle for control of the Erie. It is striking, however, that as soon as Gould signed on, he seems to have become the field general in the Drew camp. When Vanderbilt, as expected, declared war on Drew in early 1868 and started buying up Erie in the open market, Gould quietly created $10 million in convertible bonds (bonds that could be traded in for stock), which he deposited in his and Fisk's brokerages. As Vanderbilt bought Erie shares, they would convert their bonds and leak the new shares into the market. So the more stock Vanderbilt bought, the more stock seemed to be available, and the more the price dropped. Vanderbilt was the richest man in America, with a fortune estimated at $100 million, but his wealth was tied up in his enterprises, and as his margin calls mounted,* the Commodore's knees visibly buckled. Just the thought of Vanderbilt failing sent quiet shudders through Wall Street.

Belatedly, Vanderbilt realized Gould's ruse and solicited a friendly judge, the Tammany stalwart George Barnard, for an injunction against the convertible bond issuances. (The legislation creating the Erie meticulously specified its allowable capital structure, but Gould could make a good case that the bonds were legal.) Drew, Gould, and Fisk were in the meantime scrambling to other judges for injunctions of their own. But Vanderbilt was the quicker to court, and finally got a contempt order for the arrest of the entire Erie board, prompting the late-night flight to Jersey City. The boating adventure on the Hudson was quite unnecessary—Drew left by public ferry earlier in the day—but Fisk insisted that he and Gould first have a lavish dinner at Delmonico's so he could entertain his friends with stories of Vanderbilt's discomfiture. Sheriff's officers were hot on their heels when they finally ran for the harbor and commandeered the first boat they found.

For a while, the Jersey City strategy looked almost successful. Vanderbilt was groaning under the weight of his margin calls as the Erie stock price went into free fall. The legal process was frozen in place—the two sides' competing judges had each appointed receivers—but Gould, Fisk, and Drew had the money and all the corporate instruments. Fisk, of course, with his

---

*Vanderbilt, like most big players, borrowed the money for stock purchases from his brokers, who held the stock as collateral for their loans. As the stock price fell, Vanderbilt had to make cash deposits to maintain the value of the loan collateral. These were huge sums of money. Currency comparisons over a gap of almost 140 years are just approximations, but the usual rule of thumb for the late nineteenth century is to multiply by 12–13x, so $10 million becomes $120–130 million. For another sense of the scale, in 1869 $10 million was about 0.15 percent of national product, equivalent to about $17 billion today.

"Gentleman Jim" Fisk was an uproarious scoundrel, a fop, a trencherman, and a womanizer, but he was also very intelligent and loyal to Jay Gould.

Josie installed at the hotel, was hugely enjoying life on an unlimited expense account; but Drew pined for Wall Street and Gould missed his family. After a month had passed, Gould packed up a suitcase of money and entrained for Albany. He was briefly arrested, but with the help of sweeteners from the suitcase, stayed out of jail and set up shop in a hotel room to receive legislators. (Vanderbilt's agents opened their offices on another floor of the hotel.)

Gould and his suitcase were wonderfully persuasive. Within barely a week, the legislature passed a law retroactively authorizing the Erie's financial maneuvers, and he had bought off the Vanderbilt judge who had issued the contempt citation, allowing him to return to the city both triumphant and a free man. A journal maintained by the Erie auditor, a long-time retainer of Gould, shows that Gould and Fisk dispensed almost $600,000 during the spring and summer of 1868, or some $7–8 million in today's money, on "legal expenses" and related items. Important beneficiaries included William M. "Boss" Tweed, who was also a state senator, and Peter Sweeney, Tweed's number two. Forced to sue for peace, Vanderbilt finally exacted a package of cash and stock buybacks worth about $9 million, denuding the Erie treasury. An impecunious Erie was of no interest to Drew, so he resigned his directorship along with Vanderbilt and the Boston group. Elections in the fall returned a Gould board, including both Tweed and Sweeney. Gould was appointed president, and promptly named Fisk comptroller. Fisk, Gould, and a compliant lawyer, Franklin Lane, constituted a majority of the executive committee, leaving Gould, in effect, in total control of the Erie. In the seven years since Jay Gould had arrived in New York, nearly broke, and a failed tanner, he had done very well indeed. He was thirty-two years old.

Gould and Fisk quickly ratcheted up the scale of their embezzlements. Erie's headquarters were moved from a convenient location on the lower Manhattan waterfront to uptown rented offices in a marble Opera House, owned by Fisk and Gould, who had bought it with Erie cash. For Fisk, it was an adolescent's dream of heaven. He lavished some $2 million on redecorations, disported with the downstairs chorus girls, and tapped Erie money to support his new part-time role as an impresario. A house for Josie Mansfield, located conveniently down the street, was part of the package.

Unlike Fisk, however, Gould was actually interested in running the Erie. More important, he had a strategy. Even in its gravely wounded state, the Erie was all the platform he needed to set about teaching the rest of the northeastern roads, including Vanderbilt's New York Central and the vaunted Pennsylvania, what their business was really about.

Railroad Privateer

"Airplane-seat pricing" is the reason a modern business traveler may find herself squeezed into a middle seat next to a grandparent who paid a fifth as much for the same ticket. Almost all the costs of a commercial flight are incurred when the plane takes off, regardless of how many passengers are aboard. Since any additional revenue is almost pure margin, it makes sense to fill empty seats for almost any price at all, and airlines use elaborate pricing models that continually adjust fares to ensure maximum loading. After fare regulation ended in the 1970s, prices plummeted, passenger miles soared, and most lines constantly skitter on the edge of bankruptcy.

The economics of railroads are the same as for airlines, and Jay Gould may have grasped them more quickly and clearly than anyone else. The favored contemporary response to price wars was to form pools, or industry rate agreements, which inevitably collapsed because of cheating. Instead, Gould hoped to control pricing by establishing monopolies over natural regions of commerce. Almost as soon as he won control of the Erie he began an aggressive series of probes aimed at establishing Erie control over a huge swathe of territory stretching from New York City westward, sweeping in the coal, oil, and iron districts of northern and western Pennsylvania and the agriculture and food processing regions west and south of Chicago.

There were three eastern trunk line contenders for his targeted Midwest-to-East Coast traffic corridor: the Erie, the Pennsylvania, and Vanderbilt's New York Central, each of which controlled routes covering roughly half the journey from the coast to Chicago. The second leg could be cobbled together from any one of four lines, one of which already had a close working relationship with the Erie. Of the remaining three, all of them pastiches of smaller routes, one was under the loose sway of the New York Central, while the other two were Pennsylvania allies. If all four routes were arrayed on a map, they laddered in four parallel lines, with the most northern running along the Great Lakes and the most southern through central Pennsylvania; but by one means or another, they all offered serviceable connections to Chicago and the western grain fields for whichever one of the three eastern lines controlled them.

Strikingly, although their western connections were crucial for both the Pennsylvania and the New York Central, neither had taken any special steps to defend them; the Pennsylvania had actually been *divesting* its ownership interests in its western connections. Its executives prided themselves on keeping debt low, extending lines cautiously, and conserving cash. In the pre–Gould days, this was the epitome of good management; the railroad bosses were like peacetime generals who keep the troops fed and equipment working, but haven't a clue about strategic maneuver or positional advantage.

Gould decided to go after all four western legs at the same time. Since he did not trust contracts or working agreements, he needed executive control through leases or outright purchases. His problem was that he had no money. He had agreed to the Erie's settlement with Vanderbilt only weeks before, and injunctions and lawsuits were still whizzing around like spitballs. But mere lack of money never fazed Gould. He could, for example, just buy proxies, which was possible in the nineteenth century. For a small price, Gould would then be entitled to vote the stock for a limited period. A second trick was to use his brokerage firm to borrow quantities of stock in time for a board election, and vote the stock through the brokerage account. There would be many others, ploy upon ploy, as Gould effortlessly churned out new market wrinkles as occasion demanded. His consistent pattern was to move very quietly, assemble stock through a host of dummy accounts, then suddenly emerge in a control position, usually just before a crucial board election.

He almost pulled it off. His first step was to lock up the already-established Erie western route, the Atlantic & Great Western, with a long-term lease. Then, in just a few months, a series of lightning, but well-disguised, stock raids on nearly a dozen different roads put him within an eyelash of erecting a solid wall across all Vanderbilt and Pennsylvania access to the west. He had won outright control over both of the Pennsylvania's western routes; he also controlled about half of the lines in the New York Central's western connections, and was poised to take over almost all the others. A little more time, and all mainline rail service to and from the heart of the American grain, iron, steel, and oil sectors would have been in Gould's hands. Vanderbilt and the Pennsylvania could build more roads, of course, but that would be the work of years; until then they would owe Gould tribute.

Almost as an afterthought amid his blitzkrieg against Vanderbilt and the Pennsylvania, Gould also made a stock play for a small anthracite line, the Albany & Susquehanna. It marked one of Pierpont Morgan's first appearances as a railroad banker. Pierpoint managed to fight off the Gould forces in a picaresque battle involving dubious share issuances, the usual war of injunctions, Jim Fisk and a troupe of thugs getting tossed out of a shareholders' meeting, and a dramatic crash of locomotives in the middle of contested territory. (It is remarkable that Junius had high praise for his son's efforts, for J. S. Morgan & Co. was the *Erie's* investment banker, while Pierpont's firm, of course, was an integral part of Junius's network.)

One wonders if Gould might have succeeded against Vanderbilt and the Pennsylvania if he had moved somewhat *less* deftly, or without quite the blinding speed and dazzling strokes. As it was, incumbent managements felt assaulted; even the Pennsylvania was shocked out of its torpor. Tom Scott led the Pennsylvania's charge in its home-state legislature, which, in the words of one historian, always practiced "state mercantilism" when it came to its favorite company. Pennsylvania money flowed thick and fast to secure anti-Gould shareholder votes and to induce the legislature, in effect, to outlaw Gould's takeovers. It was the same story in Ohio, where courts and the legislature linked arms to block his westernmost takeovers. As Gould had amply demonstrated in New York, in the absence of a national framework of security law, home-state legislatures could skew outcomes however they pleased.

Then, in the summer of 1869, with his railroad wars raging on every side, and the outcome still hanging in the balance, Gould launched, or was swept up in, the infamous Fisk–Gould "Gold Corner." It is one of the most notorious episodes in American financial history, one that demonstrates not only Gould's own self-destructive streak but also the fragility of America's postwar financial markets and the openness of the corruption. The Gold Corner forever fixed the image of Gould as the evil genius of Wall Street; even worse from Gould's perspective, it destroyed an important ally in his railroad wars, fatally tipping the balance against him.

The Gold Corner

Gould's mind ran in labyrinthine channels, and he turned to the gold markets as part of a strategy to improve Erie's freights. Grain was America's largest export in 1869. Merchants purchased grain from farmers on credit, shipped it overseas, and paid off the farmers when they received their remittances from abroad. Their debt to the farmers was in greenbacks, but their receipts from abroad came in gold, for the greenback was not legal tender overseas. It could take weeks, or even months, to complete a transaction, so the merchant was exposed to changes in the gold/greenback exchange rate during that time. If gold fell (or the greenback rose), the merchant's gold proceeds might not cover his greenback debts. The New York Gold Exchange was created to help merchants protect against that risk. Using the Exchange, a merchant could borrow gold when he made his contract, convert it to greenbacks, and pay off his suppliers right away. Then he would pay off the gold loan when his gold payment came in some weeks later; since it was gold for gold, exchange rates didn't matter. To protect against default, the Exchange required full cash collateral to borrow gold. But that was an opening for speculations by clever traders like Gould. If a trader bought gold and then immediately lent it, he could finance his purchase with the cash collateral and thereby acquire large positions while using very little of his own cash.

Gould reasoned that if he could force up the price of gold, he might improve the Erie's freight revenues. If gold bought more greenbacks, greenback-priced wheat would look cheaper to overseas buyers, so exports, and freights, would rise. And because of the fledgling status of the new Gold Exchange, gold prices looked eminently manipulable, since only about $20 million in gold was usually available in New York. He discussed the idea with Fisk, who was skeptical. The Grant administration, which had just taken office in March, was sitting on $100 million in gold reserves. If gold started suddenly rising, it would hurt merchant importers, who could be expected to clamor for government gold sales.

So Gould decided to probe the government's intentions. He made friends with Abel Corbin, a somewhat tremulous retired gentleman who had recently become the president's brother-in-law, and who claimed to exercise substantial family influence. In June, when Grant traveled through New York on his way to Boston, Corbin helped arrange a meeting with Gould and Fisk. The president was Fisk's guest at the private Erie box at the Opera House, and the following evening, the two, along with Gould's friend Cyrus Field, the entrepreneur of the transatlantic cable, entertained Grant and other leading men at a late supper on an Erie river steamer. (How far and fast these two farm boys had traveled!) In Gould's account, he delicately steered the conversation to monetary policy, evoking only grumbles from Grant on the "fictitiousness about the prosperity of the country and that the bubble might be tapped in one way as well as another." That was discouraging: popping a bubble meant tighter money and lower gold.*

Corbin, nostrils quivering with the scent of money, beat nervous attendance on Gould throughout the summer and made several more introduc-

---

*You "pop bubbles," i.e., slow down a boom, by raising interest rates. In 1869, with no central bank, the government would sell gold to mop up excess greenbacks, counting on scarcer greenbacks to push up the interest rate on loans. The combination of an increase in circulating gold and scarcer greenbacks would cause the greenback to rise and gold to fall.

tions. On September 2, Gould, in a transaction Henry Adams calls "worthy of the French stage," purchased $1.5 million in gold for Corbin, which was delicately accepted "only for the sake of a lady, my wife," in Corbin's words, gallantly positioning her to make more than $11,000 on each one dollar rise in gold. That payment is often taken as illustrating Gould's naïve acceptance of Corbin's blather, but it was well earned. Corbin actually seems to have talked Grant into calling off a planned gold sale in early September, and also arranged at least two separate tête-à-têtes between Gould and Grant. As political payoffs go, that was solid value for the money. As a further hedge, Gould made comparable purchases for a senior New York treasury official, Daniel Butterfield, who had been introduced to him by Corbin. When a congressional panel later quizzed him on the purpose of these transactions, Gould was characteristically forthright:

Q. Tell the committee why it was that you bought and carried that gold for these two men without their putting up any margin. Is that exactly business . . . ?
A. No; that is not on business principles.
Q. On what principle did you do it?
A. I did it as a friendly thing.
Q. Was it to interest them in establishing the policy of the country?
A. I supposed that what interest they had would be thrown in that way.
Q. And you considered that an anchor thrown to the windward, did you?
A. Yes, sir.

Gould began buying large quantities of gold in September, but with no visible impact on its price. As Gould, of all people, should have anticipated, speculation begets speculation. Disguise his trading as he might, everyone knew he was the one pushing up gold. The more he bought, the more exposed he looked to bear traders (who profit on a fall), so they sold short on every rise. As Gould told the congressional investigators:

I did not want to buy so much gold. . . . but all these fellows went in and sold short, so that in order to keep it up I had to buy or else back down and show the white feather. They would sell it to you all the time. I never intended to buy more than four or five millions of gold. . . . I had no idea of cornering it.

Reluctantly, Gould turned to Fisk. Fisk's claim that he came in only because Gould was his friend is entirely credible. He was still skeptical, and still concerned that the government would sell gold if its price started climbing. Gould argued that he had fixed that. Fisk checked with Corbin, who told him that Grant's wife had taken a position in gold; that was not true, but Corbin was hopeful. To confirm Grant's steadfastness, Corbin wrote yet another letter urging the president not to intervene in the gold markets, which Fisk arranged to be hand delivered. Fisk's messenger tracked down Grant, who was traveling through Pennsylvania, and handed him the letter (these were informal times). Grant read it through and said there was no return message. The messenger's telegraph, "Delivered all right." was mistakenly transmitted as "Delivered. All right." Fisk assumed that Grant was on board.

Fisk's brokers started buying heavily on Monday, September 20. Through Tuesday, the bears nervously held their ground, with gold stuck stubbornly in the high 130s ($100 in gold bought $130-plus in greenbacks). Then on Wednesday, Fisk took over the floor. A resplendent and intimidating figure, he strode confidently through the Exchange, trumpeting the unlimited resources of the gold clique, bragging that the president, his wife, and White House officials were in on the play, darkly warning that settlement day was drawing nigh for the bears.

A true corner is the slaughter of the bears. A bear who shorts by borrowing and selling a security needs to buy it, or borrow it again, when the borrowing term is up. As the week went on, the short position grew to some $200 million in gold, probably most of it owed to Gould and Fisk, who were lending out all the gold they bought. The $20 million in available gold, that is, was being borrowed and sold over and over, and as the price kept rising, the bears got into a deeper and deeper hole. As Gould disgustedly put it: "[W]hat put gold up so high is that these bears got frightened, and they commenced jumping over each other's shoulders for it. The worst panics ever produced are bear panics." The bears feared that Gould and Fisk would stop the merry-go-round and demand their gold back. Since the amount they were owed was far higher than the amount in circulation, the price could theoretically go to infinity.

Gold closed Wednesday at 141½. Having spent $50–60 million in a single day, the bulls showed no signs of flagging. Fisk was offering $50,000 bets that gold would hit 145 on Thursday. Panic thickened over the Exchange like an acrid cloud. Gould's insistence that he never intended a corner was probably truthful; but for a flamboyant subversive like Jim Fisk, its theatricality would have been irresistible. But by now, Gould's antennae were crackling with warnings. Financial markets were in full flight, with telegraph wires to Washington pulsating with pleas for intervention. Corbin was pleading with Gould for his profits.

Gould made a temperature check on Corbin early on Thursday and found the old man in a state of near-terminal terror. The rumors of official involvement in a gold corner had reached the White House, and Grant's wife had sent her sister, Mrs. Corbin, a stinging letter demanding to know if it was true. Corbin wanted out, plus $100,000 in profits. Gould promised both, but on condition that Corbin keep quiet, for as he told Corbin, he was "undone" if that letter were known. In fact, Gould never paid, leaving an unrecompensed Corbin to marinate in the disdain of his relatives.

Gould could tell Fisk nothing. Fisk's performance had mesmerized the market, and if he showed a flicker of doubt, the entire enterprise would collapse. Gould seems to have felt no qualms on deserting Fisk; if nothing else, one must admire the clarity of his mind. Early on Thursday, he and his brokerage partner, Henry Smith, worked out a strategy that mixed highly visible purchases with much larger disguised sales to let Gould run off his holdings.

Thursday's market closed at 143¼ amid word that Fisk would demand delivery from the bears on Friday, forcing the final corner. Crowds started gathering early, as if for a spectacle in the Roman Coliseum. When pre-opening prices jumped to 145, Fisk ordered one of his brokers, Albert Speyers, to push it to 150. It was accomplished in an instant. After the opening, the price stuck for some minutes at 150, then raced past 155. Fisk told Speyers to "Go and bid gold up to 160. Take all you can get at 160." In the meantime, Gould was telling Smith and another trusted broker, Edward Willard, to speed up their sales, for the collapse was in sight. He had visited Butterfield, who had reassured him that Washington was holding firm. But Gould was a man who maneuvered in a world of lies, and Butterfield's soothings only screamed that he should sell faster. In truth, Butterfield was quietly dumping his own gold and peppering the Treasury with reports on the crisis.

The telegraph informing the New York Treasury that Washington would sell gold was dispatched at 11:45; a second telegraph was sent a few minutes later by a different service just to be sure. By mistake the first was not sent in cipher. Sudden large sales by a select few brokers may have broken the corner a few minutes before the Treasury news was released to the Exchange; Fisk insisted that the early sellers had been tipped by Butterfield, leaving an intriguing loose end for future researchers. The collapse was almost instantaneous; within minutes gold was at 132. Poor Albert Speyers was still shouting out buy orders at 160—he had gone "crazy as a loon," Fisk snorted.

When the market first broke, Gould and Fisk made a dash for the Opera House and barricaded themselves behind armed guards. The Exchange supervisors made some estimated settlements to save illiquid brokerages, but one of Gould's pet judges slapped them with an injunction on the grounds that they had exceeded their authority, which was arguably true. As fortune had it, freezing settlements was exactly the right remedy. When the Exchange washed its hands of the mess, brokers quickly sorted it out among themselves. Most houses just ignored the bubble prices and settled in the mid-130s. Fisk blithely repudiated his losses, producing a forged letter, allegedly from his brokerage partner, Henry Belden, representing that all of Fisk's trading was on Belden's account. Belden took the fall and went into bankruptcy; he later recovered his career with a position in Gould's brokerage.

Fascinatingly, there was never a hint from Fisk that he felt abused by Gould's Thursday and Friday trading tactics. Both men were to-the-bone pragmatists, and Fisk would have understood immediately that Gould had no choice. Their financial positions, in any case, had hardly been affected. Fisk didn't pay on any losses, and Gould certainly didn't collect on his bubble-period trading windfall. Fisk delivered a hilarious version of the entire episode to a congressional investigating committee, enthusiastically spraying mud on all actual and alleged participants, from Mrs. Grant to Gould, winding up with a long description of the Corbins' panic on Black Friday: "His wife and he both looked like death. He was tottling just like that. (Illustrated by a trembling movement of the body.)" Henry Adams was the more impressed because so much of the performance was pure invention.

The impact of the Gold Corner on the national economy was fleeting at worst, but it was devastating for Gould. Besides destroying his reputation, it delivered a knockout blow to his railroad strategy.

Ouster

When the smoke cleared from Black Friday, only one major brokerage was listed among the casualties. Unfortunately for Gould, it turned out to be Lockwood & Co., a strong Gould ally, who just happened to be a major owner of railroad properties at the heart of Vanderbilt's western connections. When Lockwood went into receivership, all of its railroad shares were thrown on the market and were snapped up by the Commodore, who easily outbid the cash-strapped Gould. Vanderbilt was not a man to twice trust luck to save his railroads; before he died in 1877, he had moved decisively to ensure that his entire web of western links was tightly within the New York Central's control.

With Gould's western strategy fatally breached, and financial headlines blaring his market-wrecking Gold Corner tactics, the legislatures in Pennsylvania and Ohio quickly finished off his hopes of encircling the Pennsylvania. The Pennsylvania's escape from Gould's nighttime assault marked the last step in the ascendancy of Tom Scott, who succeeded J. Edgar Thomson as president in 1874. Scott, in contrast to the conservative Thomson, was an exemplar of the railroad-president-as-buccaneer, violently wrenching his board away from its narrow inward concentrations into a near-reckless program of expansion and encirclement aimed at making the Pennsylvania America's dominant national carrier.

From that point, the national railroad wars came to resemble the Chinese game of Go, in which players win points by outflanking and encircling an opponent's positions. In the scramble for territorial advantage, new lines were spun out with abandon, far ahead of business demand. As freight rates were steadily cut, often to absurdly low levels, expansions were financed by watering balance sheets and defaulting on security holders. Reining in Gould's go-for-the-throat style of competition became Pierpont Morgan's great cause for the rest of the century. By the time he finally succeeded, the roads had already fueled the continentwide boom that marked the rest of the century.

Gould hung on at the Erie for two more years, more or less practicing at the job of railroad president—planning some modest line extensions, investigating the advantages of steel rails, engaging in some stock market

brigandage against an uncooperative affiliate. But the years of blazing notoriety, extravagant embezzlements, and ignominious reverses had exhausted
the patience of even the ever-quiescent European shareholders.

The opening wedge was planted by William Duncan, Junius Morgan's
long-time banking colleague at Duncan, Sherman, who approached Gould
with the idea of replacing the Erie's current board with one that could reassure the overseas investors. Gould turned for advice to Junius, who strongly
urged him to open up the 1870 board elections. (One suspects Junius was
playing a double game, giving Gould advice that he knew would sink
him.) At the same time, an erstwhile Gould ally on the Erie's western lines,
James McHenry, decided to stage a coup of his own. He linked up with
Bischoffheimer & Goldschmidt, an important German banking house with
substantial blocks of Erie, and began scouring London and Berlin for shares
to fuel an opposition drive. The Erie counsel, Franklin Lane, the third man
with Fisk and Gould on the Erie Executive Committee, quietly allied with
McHenry while maintaining a pretense of loyalty to Gould.

Another blow to Gould came in the summer of 1871, when leaked
memoranda exposed the enormity of the Tweed Ring's theft from New York
City. To everyone's surprise a reform whirlwind swept the machine out of
office in the fall elections. Tweed fled the country, and Gould's puppet judges
were forced off the bench.

Then Gould lost Jim Fisk. A messy love triangle among Fisk, Josie
Mansfield, and Ned Stokes, another lover of Mansfield, erupted into the
courts and the press. Fisk was clearly the wronged party—Mansfield was
diverting his money to Stokes and both were trying to blackmail Fisk. Stokes
had initiated legal action against Fisk, but when the case turned against
him, he waylaid Fisk in his hotel in January 1872 and fatally shot him.
Onlookers were amazed to see Gould sobbing uncontrollably by the death-
bed. No one has claimed to understand the relationship between the two,
but after Fisk's death Gould seemed oddly passive against the attacks from
the overseas shareholders.

The details of Gould's overthrow suggest that the Erie was cursed by some
demon of sordidness. Bischoffheimer organized a bribery operation to buy out
the Gould loyalists on the board. Two different agents competed as bribery
go-betweens, and a menagerie of slippery characters scrambled for the crumbs
from the anticipated food fight. Simon Stevens, the patriot who, along with
the youthful Pierpont Morgan, sold the government its own Hall rifles dur-

ing the Civil War, somehow bobbed up as an important intermediary. When pressed by a state legislative committee on the reasons for the shareholder revolt, Stevens answered simply: "They had heard most fabulous accounts, that the controlling officers of the road had made enormous fortunes out of it, and they wanted to get their friends into it." For its part, Bischoffheimer ended up with an extraordinary investment banking contract with the post–Gould Erie—a fifty-year agency with the assurance of very high fees with no obligation actually to do anything. The firm made no secret that the contract was in recognition of its heavy bribery expenses.

Gould resigned from the Erie in March 1872, later negotiating a full release from possible shareholder claims in exchange for repaying $9 million to the Erie. The actual payment was a fraction of that amount: it included $50,000 in cash; $5.2 million in wildly overvalued stock in Erie subsidiaries; the Opera House and surrounding properties (like Josie Mansfield's former house), allegedly worth $3 million, probably twice their actual value; plus a grab bag of various releases and rent forbearances from Gould. There was little comment on why such properties were in Gould's name in the first place.

Contemporaries may be forgiven for believing that they had finally drawn Gould's fangs. He was now once more just a lone stockbroker, with no corporate base and no access to a security-printing machine like the Erie. His reputation was thoroughly blasted. A representative of the English shareholders said that whenever McHenry or Bischoffheimer ran into opposition they would just "raise the cry of 'Jay Gould'" and English investors would rush to their banner. But discounting Gould was to vastly underestimate the little man's resilience. Time and again through a long career he absorbed fearsome blows, stoically regathered himself, and plunged back into the fray. Scandalous though his reign at the Erie was, he had forever changed the nature of American railroad competition, and he would return again and again to teach new lessons in how the game was played.

The Erie experience generated other tendrils. McHenry, as it turned out, did not quite win control after Gould's departure, and Peter Watson was elected as the new president. Watson was a lawyer and a competent railroad man; a detailed state legislative inquiry into events at the Erie proved him to be one of the few people on either side of the table with a consistent grasp of railroad accounting. His lasting claim to fame, however, was as one of the original promoters of the South Improvement Company,

Jay Gould was finally ousted from the Erie Railroad in 1872. The three plunging figures, from the top, are George Barnard, a pet Gould judge; David Dudley Field, the Erie and Tweed ring's lawyer (and, incongruously, a famous legal reformer); and Gould.

a nefarious construction supposedly at the root of John D. Rockefeller's takeover of the American oil industry. There was also a history between Gould and Rockefeller; one Rockefeller muckraker, indeed, declared that the whole Standard Oil Trust "must be regarded as the gigantic offspring of the Erie ring."

The First Oil Baron

The notion that John Rockefeller might somehow be a creature of Jay Gould is fanciful to say the least, but there was a grain of truth in the claim—for the rise of Cleveland as an oil refining center was a direct fallout of the new Gould-written rules of railroad competition.

On a map, Pittsburgh seemed ideally positioned to dominate the refining business. Easy river connections from the oil fields jump-started the industry during the first days of the boom, and barge shipping was gradually supplanted by a thickening network of rail lines. From Pittsburgh, refiners enjoyed high-quality, straight-shot Pennsylvania Railroad transport to the port of Philadelphia. (Even in the early days, about 70 percent of refined product was exported.) The trip from the oil region to the Atlantic ports via Pittsburgh was 355 miles, while the comparable route through Cleveland was 629 miles. As one would expect, by the end of the war, Pittsburgh was home to more than a third of the nation's oil refining capacity, while Cleveland, with a 7 percent share, was a distinctly minor player. Yet just a few years later, it was Cleveland that was in the catbird seat. What happened?

Cleveland's opportunity arose by courtesy of the Pennsylvania's short-sighted policy of milking its Pittsburgh-to-Philadelphia traffic monopoly. (Andrew Carnegie railed against this practice for years. Despite his close relations with the Pennsylvania, he always took care to locate his steel plants so they couldn't gouge him, and eventually built his own railroad.) Cleveland was a natural gateway for both Gould's and Vanderbilt's westward routes, and both of them decided to build up Cleveland refining to sop up excess freight capacity outside of the grain season. Since Cleveland refiners could also ship by Great Lake steamers during the seven ice-free months of the year, they found themselves with the bonus of *three* competing carriers. The Pennsylvania's rates from Pittsburgh were high enough that Gould and Vanderbilt could easily match them at Cleveland; and as the two of them inevitably engaged in price-cutting duels, they steadily increased Cleveland's advantage. With Rockefeller and his new partner, the charismatic and aggressive Henry Flagler,* leading the charge, Cleveland rapidly built refining capacity. By the time the Pennsylvania finally began to react about 1870, Cleveland had already zoomed past Pittsburgh as a refining center.

The growth spurt in refining left the industry with a huge capacity over-hang. In the early days, "oil-boiling," as refining was called, was not much different from distilling whiskey, and early refiners used color, smell, and taste to decide which distillates were most suitable for kerosene, heating oil, or other products. Refining economics were even more spectacular than those in drilling. The cost of building a moderately sized refinery was about $13 per barrel for the first production run, which was close to the sale price for refined product; in other words, an investor could recover most of his cash investment with a single run. Hundreds of refineries, some of them handling no more than five barrels a day, sprang up throughout the oil region and at its transportation termini in Pittsburgh and Cleveland.

By the late 1860s, however, the better refiners were starting to ratchet up the competitive barriers as they developed sound empirical understandings of heating cycles, process sequences and timing, still design, and the use of acids and other chemicals to improve product performance and physical characteristics. There was considerable innovation in continuous processing, the use of vacuum and superheated steam technology, and the mechanization of time-consuming tasks like removing sludge buildup from still bottoms. Still sizes increased by a factor of ten, and full-line refiners learned to tune operations to the full range of petroleum products, from heavy paraffins to very light solvents like benzene and naphtha. Standard Oil (as the Rockefeller refineries were rechristened in 1870) was not an innovator in any of these areas, but Rockefeller was an early adopter of proven technologies and constantly on the prowl for talent—buying up Charles Pratt's cutting-edge refinery in 1874, for instance, and picking up the brilliant distillation specialist Henry Rogers with the deal.

There is evidence that Rockefeller was running very scared in this period, for he doubtless divined that the industry was on the edge of a cataclysmic

---

*Flagler, a few years older than Rockefeller, was originally a produce wholesaler, and had made and lost a fortune in salt mining. He returned to produce to recover his finances, and leased an office from Rockefeller. The two had become almost inseparable by the time Rockefeller invited him into the Standard.

shakeout. He pressed on every front to reduce costs, cut waste, and sell more by-products. No opportunity to pick up a nickel of margin was overlooked—creating his own hauling operation, building his own barrel plant, purchasing his own piping supplies. Aside from his management talent, Flagler brought in wealthy in-laws, whose equity investments may have been critical in permitting major operational improvements in the company. Even the most anti-Rockefeller muckrakers conceded the high quality of operations at the Standard.

Rockefeller also may have been unique among oil executives for his understanding of distribution. Kerosene—illuminating oil—was arguably the first global consumer product. (Grain markets were global, of course, but grain was usually processed locally into flour or bread before being sold to consumers.) Rockefeller pursued tightly integrated marketing and distribution operations from the earliest days, rapidly moving from contractual relationships to outright purchase and merger. His network acquisitions from the late 1860s through the first half of the 1870s included pipeline-based crude gathering facilities, tank storage farms, tank-car-loading facilities, domestic and overseas wholesale shipping and distribution operations, and coastal assemblage and ship-loading facilities (Rockefeller built his own and also took over both the Erie and the New York Central oil dock operations). The Standard was therefore the only company positioned to balance refinery output, transportation, and distribution, and squeeze margin increments at every stage. Since the Standard's distribution services, like the New York oil dock operations, were used by other shippers, competing refineries also contributed to the burgeoning Standard cash coffers. The accumulation of minor efficiencies at so many points gradually amassed into a crushing profitability advantage.

The last piece in the mosaic was superior discounts from railroads and other shippers, almost always via month-end rebates from posted freight tariffs. Rebates were typically volume-based, but often involved other considerations, like the free use of Standard storage tank or loading facilities, freight smoothing agreements, and the Standard's absorption of fire risk (very important to the roads in the early days of oil). At one point Rockefeller purchased a fleet of wide-gauge tank cars for the cash-strapped Erie and its allies; naturally, the Standard got first dibs on the cars, paid a lower freight rate for their use, and collected rent when the railroads used them for other refiners.

Two early contracts are illustrative. Both were negotiated primarily by Flagler, who had lead responsibility for shipping and freight management. The first, executed in 1868 and subsequently renewed, comprised a sequence of agreements between a consortium of Cleveland refiners led by the Standard, Jay Gould's Erie and one of its allied railroads, and a crude-oil-gathering pipeline (it piped oil field production to tank-car-loading points) also under the control of the Erie. The companies made exclusive traffic commitments and major rate concessions, while the refineries got some stock in the pipeline. The clear intent of the agreements was to tie the companies into an integrated network and to ensure a steady product flow. While the arrangement made excellent economic sense, it was treated almost as evidence of criminality when it came to light many years later.

The second contract was executed in 1870 between the Standard and the Lake Shore, a Vanderbilt road. Flagler extracted a discount of about 30 percent from posted rates by guaranteeing no fewer than sixty tank car loads a day. According to a Lake Shore executive, J. H. Devereaux, the arrangement effected tremendous savings for the railroad, since it could schedule daily nonstop oil train runs to the coast. The time required for tank car round-trips was reduced to a third of what it was when tank cars were intermixed with other freight, with commensurate savings in rolling stock and capital costs. Tongue tucked firmly in cheek, Devereaux made the offer to any other refiner, provided that it guaranteed the same volumes.

Crisis and Consolidation

By 1871, the crisis Rockefeller had feared was at hand. Refining capacity had ballooned to some twelve million barrels a year, much of it spread around hundreds of mom-and-pop oil-boilers, while crude production was just over five million barrels. For a brief period the producers basked in high prices as refineries bid for their product—wellhead crude went to $5 per barrel in 1871—but big new discoveries soon created a glut of crude as well. The railroads also were under strain. The Erie Wars had triggered vicious price wars, but desperate refiners continued to clamor for ever-deeper discounts and rebates. At the same time, Tom Scott was rapidly expanding the Pennsylvania into New York and New Jersey, and bruiting plans for a powerful east coast refining sector to take on Cleveland and Pittsburgh. Clearly, a cataclysmic restructuring was overdue.

Besides shoring up his own operations, Rockefeller had positioned himself for a shakeout by reorganizing his businesses as the Standard Oil Co., a joint-stock corporation, in 1870. Joint-stock corporations were still uncommon outside of railroads, but their ability to use stock as takeover currency made them an ideal acquisition vehicle. The Standard was capitalized at $1 million (10,000 $100 par shares), including $200,000 of new equity investment, $100,000 of which was paid in at the time of incorporation by O. B. Jennings, brother-in-law to John's younger brother and partner, William, with the rest taken in over the next two years from officers of important Cleveland banks. The remaining shares were distributed among the partners in the same ratio as their old partnership equity.

The crisis came to a head in a remarkable five-month period from December 1871 through April 1872. On November 30, 1871, while he was in New York, Rockefeller first heard of a plan being floated by Tom Scott and Peter Watson, then an executive in the Vanderbilt system, to organize a refiner-railroad petroleum cartel. A new corporation, the South Improvement Company (SIC), jointly owned by the railroads and the refiners, would establish uniform freight rates and freight allocations among the three major trunk lines and allocate production and shipping quotas among the participating refineries. In contrast to most contemporary pooling arrangements, this one had teeth. Oil shipping freight rates would be set very high, at least double the current averages, with almost all of the increases rebated back to the participating refiners. To top it off, the extra charges levied on nonparticipating shippers would *also* be rebated back to the participants. Not to join, in short, was to die. Although Rockefeller and Flagler always claimed that they were extremely skeptical of the SIC idea, Rockefeller took the lead role in selling it to his industry.

Rockefeller returned to Cleveland on December 15 and promptly proposed a Standard buyout to Oliver H. Payne, the primary partner in Clark, Payne, Cleveland's second biggest refiner. Payne was one of Cleveland's wealthiest and best-connected businessmen; the Clarks were Rockefeller's former partners in his first refinery venture. Rockefeller stipulated that he wished to retain Payne as an executive, but there would be no role for the Clarks. The deal was closed in just a few days. Payne, who had been souring on the refinery business, was first invited to examine the Standard's books and was "thunderstruck" at its profitability. He agreed to an all-stock deal valued at $400,000, representing a goodwill premium of $150,000 over the appraised value of the Clark, Payne assets.

In two successive filings on January 1 and 2, 1872, Standard Oil increased its capitalization, first to $2,500,000, then to $3,500,000, by issuing an additional 25,000 $100 par shares. Of the new shares, 4,000 were issued pro rata to existing shareholders, presumably as a stock dividend; 4,400 were purchased by Rockefeller and Flagler; 4,000 were issued to cover the Clark, Payne acquisition; and 900 went for two further acquisitions—a small Cleveland refinery and an internationally focused refining and distribution business owned on the New York waterfront by Jabez Bostwick. Finally, 500 shares were issued, significantly enough, to Watson, while the remaining 11,200 shares were retained against further acquisitions. (See the chapter Notes for the Standard stock tables.) Rockefeller was moving very fast.

On January 2, the SIC was incorporated, with Watson as president. Of the 2,000 authorized shares, Watson held 100 and was the only railroad representative. The Standard held 900 shares, including 360 in the names of Payne and Bostwick. Two refineries with interlocking ownership in Philadelphia and Pittsburgh received almost all the remainder, totaling 80 more than the Standard group. With some haggling, the Erie and Vanderbilt roads agreed to come in, and quickly settled their respective traffic allocations with the Pennsylvania.

Rockefeller was a whirlwind. He and Watson were the key drivers of the SIC, holding meetings up and down the east coast and throughout the oil regions. At the same time, his Cleveland acquisition program went into hyperdrive. By the end of January, he had made buyout propositions to all twenty-six Cleveland refineries. By the end of March, he had closed on twenty-one.

The SIC crashed and burned just as the last Cleveland acquisitions were closing. Despite Scott's protestations, the refiner-incorporators of the SIC did not want to include the producers, and only reluctantly invited in the oil region's bigger refiners, who refused to join. Then in February, through a clerical error, the proposed freight rates under the SIC plan were posted as if they were already in effect. The oil region exploded in shock and anger. There were torchlit parades, fiery speeches, and attacks against the facilities of SIC participants. When Rockefeller and Watson attempted conciliation, they were shouted out of meeting rooms. Most dramatically, for the only time in the region's history, the producers actually enforced an embargo against the SIC's member refineries. Night-riding embargo vigilantes kept waverers in line. By early March, the Standard was effectively out of business, and up to 5,000 Cleveland refinery workers were laid off.

With Scott leading the way, the railroads capitulated in mid-March. Cornelius Vanderbilt said it was all a mistake, bravely blaming his son. George McClellan, the bumbling Civil War general who was now president of the Atlantic & Great Western, denied he had signed on in the first place. Jay Gould at the Erie, ever the pretense-puncturer, promptly sent producers a telegram with the details of McClellan's signup. The railroad's peace offering was a new uniform rate schedule—no rebates or discounts allowed— announced on March 25, basically tracking the rebated schedules in the SIC plan. (The railroads stuck with their no-discount promise for about two weeks.) Jumping on the bandwagon, the Pennsylvania legislature righteously revoked the SIC's charter on April 2. A week later, the triumphant producers announced the end of their embargo.

And a week after that, the trade press first revealed that the Standard, for all practical purposes, had consolidated the entire Cleveland refinery industry. Until the SIC fiasco, most people in the industry had never heard John Rockefeller's name; now he controlled more than a fourth of the country's refining capacity. As the shock waves reverberated through the oil regions—one paper spoke of the South Improvement Company "*alias* the Standard Oil Company"—Rockefeller and Flagler made a conciliatory visit, floating a so-called "Pittsburgh Plan" whereby refiners would sign on to a minimum wellhead crude price—provided the oil fields would limit production to agreed levels. They may not have been entirely serious; galvanizing angry producers into a one-month embargo was one thing, but sustained production agreements were quite beyond the region's organizational capacity. The excursion was still useful to Rockefeller, for he established friendly relations with the two biggest region refiners, John Archbold and J. J. Vandergrift, who had been among his fiercest critics during the SIC fiasco.

Rockefeller and his partners were otherwise not much in the news for the next eighteen months, as they concentrated on a root-and-branch reworking of their Cleveland refining base. Most of their newly acquired businesses were sold for scrap, as a total of twenty-four refineries were consolidated into six large, state-of-the-art installations, designed from the outset for efficient production of the full range of oil by-products. From that point, the Standard was a money-spinning machine. Between 1870 and 1873, the price of kerosene in New York dropped by about 25 percent. Most of the hit was absorbed by the producers, as wellhead crude fell from more than $4 a barrel to less than $2. Per-barrel railroad freight recoveries were squeezed by an additional 15 percent, but refinery per-barrel revenues actually increased by 25 percent. For most of the industry, the revenue kick would have barely stemmed the flow of red ink; for the Standard, it locked in an already powerful profit advantage. Most executives might have considered the "Conquest of Cleveland" the work of a lifetime. But Rockefeller was only thirty-three, and was just getting started.

The Muckrakers' Case against Rockefeller

Ida Tarbell's *History of Standard Oil,* based on her famous nineteen-part series in *McClure's Magazine* from 1901 to 1903, may be considered the *ur*-text, the canonical statement, of the case against Rockefeller. It is a splendid polemic, and has dominated the perception of the man and his rise ever since. Tarbell was a child of the oil region. Her father built the first tank system to contain the runaway flows of some of the earliest oil strikes, and as a teenager during the region's war against the SIC, she proudly saw him gallop to battle as a vigilante enforcing the oil embargo. Her story is a morality play: the stalwart independent producers and refiners of the region fighting a hopeless struggle against a distant corporation personified by a soulless John D. Rockefeller. Its central argument is that the region's producers and refiners had an inherent advantage over any other petroleum center, especially Cleveland. It was the only place with integrated production and refining, and was closer to major eastern markets and ports to boot. She concedes Rockefeller's excellence as a businessman, but insists that he could not have overcome such advantages except by cheating. And she uncovers the cheating in the system of "unjust and illegal" railroad rebates that discriminated in favor of the large shipper.

The great power of Tarbell's prose, unfortunately, conceals the holes in her argument. To begin with, the region's refiners did not enjoy an inherent advantage over the more distant centers; the reverse, in fact, was more likely the case. Wellhead to refinery to market distances were indeed the shortest, as Tarbell says, but the locational advantage came with built-in problems, like unreliable access to supplies and very high land prices—lessors preferred the windfalls from drilling. Much more important, transportation *within* the region was poor. This was rough, mountainous country; the railroad network was rather like many newer urban rapid transit systems—designed to move people between suburbs and city center, but of little help in getting around the city itself. The struggle was to keep up with the shifting locations of high-production fields as older wells ran down and new discoveries expanded the region's boundaries. Region refineries, inevitably, tended to be tied to particular well centers and were typically small and underutilized. It was the smaller operators that Tarbell especially romanticized—men whose lives ran "swift and ruddy and joyous . . . until a big hand reached out from nobody knew where, to steal their conquest and throttle their future." But the hard fact was that with two or three exceptions, the region's refiners were among the least efficient of all. As production technology shifted to favor large-scale, full-line, continuous processing, the consolidated refining centers situated at major transportation hubs acquired an unassailable advantage.

More important, Tarbell did not understand that the great Gould–Vanderbilt–Scott trunk line battles were never primarily about oil; they were about dominating the grain traffic routes to Chicago and the Midwest. In the early days especially, oil freight was hardly more than ballast for the much bigger business of grain shipping. In 1882, the first year petroleum was broken out in the trade data, raw agricultural exports, excluding flour, were more than six times petroleum exports; if flour is included, they were almost ten times as great. Back in the time of the SIC, the ratios would have been even more lopsided in agriculture's favor. Comparing export volumes actually overstates the importance of petroleum, since exports were a much larger share of oil production than in grain.

The railroads loudly lamented their losses on oil shipping, and given the still-primitive state of cost accounting, were probably not intentionally deceitful. But since they originally chased oil freight to use excess capacity, oil revenues needed only to exceed variable costs to be attractive. A careful review by the industry historian Harold Williamson suggests that the oil traffic was almost always profitable, which canny businessmen like Gould and Vanderbilt would have understood intuitively. The fact that both the Erie and the New York Central chose to build up Cleveland, therefore, was not a consequence of Rockefeller scheming. Gould and Vanderbilt were struggling for control of the western grain trade, and Cleveland was the natural hub for both of their systems. There was never the slightest chance of their investing to build up the oil regions as a competing transportation center.

The second part of Tarbell's argument—that rebates were somehow "illegal"—is simply false. There was no law against rebates, on either the federal or state level, and they were standard practice among all carriers.* Nor were they especially "secret." Railroads struggled to prevent disclosure of *particular* rebates, for obvious reasons, but freely conceded, and as frequently complained about, the generality of the practice. Nor is it true, as frequently claimed, that rebates violated "the common law" against contracts in restraint of trade. In the first place, under the common law, contracts in restraint of trade were not criminal, they were *unenforceable*, which is rather different.† And second, the rigid predisposition of Elizabethan courts against covenants restricting trade had given way to a much more relaxed attitude "as the exigencies of an advancing civilization demanded," in the words of a British authority. British courts generally recognized such agreements so long as they were "reasonable"; and in particular, neither courts nor Parliament saw anything wrong with price cartels that were not aimed at "raising prices or annihilating competition to the detriment of the public." British railroad law prohibited only the granting of "undue or unreasonable

---

*Railroads doubtless settled on rebates as the preferred method of discounting to window-dress performance for bondholders. By booking the base rate as revenue and showing the subsequent rebate as a cost, rather than as a revenue reduction, railroads could bulk up their top-line revenue growth. Some midwestern "Granger" states later passed antirebate laws, but most were quickly repealed when railroads responded by raising rates. In any case, they applied only to intrastate shipping.

†When he was on the federal Court of Appeals, William H. Taft (the future president and chief justice) wrote that contracts in "restraint of trade at common law were not unlawful in the sense of being criminal . . . but were simply void and were not enforced by courts." After he became a steel magnate, for example, Andrew Carnegie could routinely enter, and then violate, steel price-fixing pools without worrying that his pool partners would sue him. But the agreements themselves were not illegal until the 1890 Sherman Act. Courts are similarly reluctant to enforce contractual restraints on alienation of land, but they are not "illegal," and parties are free to abide by them. The supposed common-law criminality of contracts in restraint of trade is repeated even by usually careful historians, but as far as I have seen, only in connection with Rockefeller. By contrast, historians and contemporaries tend to praise people like Albert Fink, who oversaw the most important railroad pools of the era, which were clearly contracts in restraint of trade. Fink's pools, moreover, were designed to *raise* prices, while Rockefeller's pressure on the roads tended to force prices down.

preference or advantage," a rule that would seem to admit most of the discounts awarded the Standard, since they generally reflected economic substance, like volume guarantees.

In any case, it is especially misleading to suggest that common law provided clear guidelines for settling novel issues in the United States. When the Sherman antitrust legislation was passed in 1890, everyone agreed that it incorporated the common law, but it took twenty years of split U.S. Supreme Court decisions, usually registered in strikingly testy opinions and dissents, to reach a consensus on what the common law was. The law was finally resolved in favor of the "reasonableness" position by the Supreme Court in the 1910 Standard Oil breakup case: "[A]t a very remote period," the Court wrote, ". . . all such contracts [in restraint of trade] were considered to be illegal. . . . [but in] the interest of the freedom of individuals to contract, this doctrine was modified so that it was only when a restraint by contract was so general as to be conterminous with the kingdom that it was treated as void"—in other words, "reasonable" restraints on trade would pass muster until they approached actual monopoly. Progressive justices, like Oliver Wendell Holmes, Jr., and Louis D. Brandeis, aimed at entirely jettisoning "common law principles" because they were so often a mask for untethered judicial prejudice.

Finally, the claim that rebates, even if legal, were "unethical" is meaningless; these were legal discounts negotiated with powerful vendors for the benefit of shareholders. Many people thought that rebates were wrong, but they had not managed to translate their views into legislation. The pressure for common carrier rate regulation finally gained ground in 1887, with the passage of the Interstate Commerce Act, and federal rate setting became a reality in 1906. The experiment was finally abandoned in the 1970s, as economists reached a near-consensus that regulation had resulted only in higher rates and unresponsive service. No one argued that regulated rates were the more ethical alternative.

There are additional ethical questions, however, related to Rockefeller's rollup of the Cleveland refineries. Did he pay fair prices? And how important, and how improper, was the SIC pressure?

The loudest complaints about Rockefeller's prices came from men who received less than they had invested. Today we would take that for granted, even for businesses that weren't designated for the scrap heap. We assume that a new breakthrough, as in telecommunications or the Internet, will cause a burst of business formation, followed by a harsh consolidation as the victors emerge. Businessmen in Rockefeller's era, however, placed a much higher value on stability. A "fair return" from an established business was akin to a right in property, or as an influential congressman argued, "[E]very man in business . . . has a right, a legal and a moral right, to obtain a fair profit upon his business and his work."

Rockefeller took the modern view. The game in Cleveland was over, especially after the merger with Payne. Rockefeller regarded almost all of his acquisitions as highly inefficient, and made no secret that he was going to shut them down. In his view, it was magnanimous to pay anything at all. He did so, it seems, primarily to save time, for he was marching to an insistent drummer—the quicker and cleaner the restructuring, the faster he could move on to the next arena. All the evidence is that his prices were based on fair, apparently scrupulously fair, appraisals of the purchased assets. Many sellers conceded the reasonableness of the prices, and those who followed Rockefeller's advice and accepted Standard stock often became quite wealthy. Although Tarbell deplores a similar Rockefeller takeover of the oil region refiners a few years later, even she does not allege price-gouging. Her complaint is that, although refiners may have received large sums of cash, they had lost a valued way of life. Whether newly wealthy refiners would have agreed is not known.

Did Rockefeller use the threat of the SIC to exert pressure on sellers? Unquestionably. Was the threat unethical? In this instance, it does seem so. Recall that the coercive feature of the SIC was that if a refiner refused to join, he would not receive the SIC rebates, *and* his foregone rebates would be paid to the other SIC members. One cannot imagine that the second provision could pass even a common law test of reasonableness. The railroads insisted, however, that since all refiners would be welcomed in the SIC, there would in fact be no discrimination. But that was disingenuous. The whole point of the SIC was to reduce and rationalize capacity, so it would make no sense to admit small refiners unless they agreed to merge with their powerful bigger brothers. The SIC was all along intended as a pressure tactic, as Tarbell alleges.

Nor is there any way to defend the secret Standard stock grant to Peter Watson, the president of the SIC. It was a sizeable grant, with a book value of $50,000, or about what Rockefeller was paying for two modestly sized refineries. As Rockefeller and Watson surely expected, refiners looking for an independent opinion on a buyout offer often turned to Watson. A good test of unethical behavior is that you are ashamed to have it known. When Rockefeller was asked under oath whether Watson owned Standard stock, he lied. It is highly doubtful that the corrupt deal with Watson affected the ultimate outcome in Cleveland; but Rockefeller still had good reason to be embarrassed by it.

On balance, while there were skeletons aplenty in John Rockefeller's closet, he was not a brigand, or embezzler, or stock manipulator in the manner of the early Jay Gould. Most of the accusations against him are for violating standards as reformers wished them to be, not as they actually were. The best current analog may be Microsoft's Bill Gates. He and his crew have played very rough over the years, often skirting the edges of the law. But they were also the first to understand the global opportunity in desktop software and executed their strategy brilliantly. As a committed Baptist, Rockefeller must have had long conversations with his God about the Watson perjury and his other bad deeds. But his misdeeds were not the reason he conquered his industry: he won because he was faster in apprehension and more deadly in execution than any of his contemporaries.

Carnegie Chooses a Career

During the years that Gould was making headlines with his Erie Wars and Gold Corner, and Rockefeller was executing the first phase of his takeover of the oil industry, Andrew Carnegie was bouncing from flower to flower— as if he were taking soundings on the limits of his talent.

A bare listing of his activities gives some flavor. By 1865, the year he left the Pennsylvania, he had recapitalized his original sleeping car investment, reorganized two iron companies into the Union Iron Mills, and organized the Keystone Bridge Co. During a nine-month world tour in 1865—part of his continuing quest for social polish—he encountered processes for putting steel caps on iron rails, and when he came home, started a company to experiment with the new Bessemer steel (unsuccessfully at this point). As competition between his sleeping car company and the interloper George Pullman heated up, he negotiated a tricky joint venture for a major Union Pacific contract, settled a contentious patent dispute, and merged the two companies in 1870. He went into the telegraph business in 1867, merged with the much larger Pacific & Atlantic Telegraph Co., executed major contracts with the Pennsylvania, went into the telegraph line construction business, and eventually sold his telegraph holdings to the Western Union, a deal in which he and a few favored insiders like Scott and Thomson did much better than the average shareholder. In all of these deals, Carnegie entered with a small stake, then came in with both feet as he saw an opportunity to scale up—reorganizing, reenergizing, and recapitalizing—almost always emerging as the lead shareholder. He was also becoming an accomplished bond salesman: by 1870, as if with his left hand, he had become an important investment banker for the Pennsylvania, structuring several imaginative transactions, and moving easily among major European investment houses such as J. S. Morgan, the Barings, and Frankfurt's Sulzbachs.

Carnegie's most famous project, perhaps, was the St. Louis Bridge, vaulting across the Mississippi in a single five-hundred-foot leap of iron and steel—"sensational and architectonic," in the words of the great architect Louis Sullivan, who first saw the bridge as a boy. The bridge was especially noted for the first American use of pneumatic caissons for sinking the piers, a precedent even more famously followed by the Roeblings, *père et fils,* in the construction of the Brooklyn Bridge a decade later. The caissons were massive, hollow stone pylons footed by iron blades. They were floated to the pier site, overturned into the water, and sited on the bottom. An airtight roofed work area at the foot of the caisson was filled with compressed air to prevent water seeping in at the bottom. Workmen descended by a stairway, entered through an airlock, and as they excavated, the mud and silt was shuttled to the top through another air lock. Reporters were entranced by the caissons' strange working conditions far under the water. The compressed air environment was fetid, working torches glowed strangely and flared unpredictably, and every moment was shadowed by the risk of sudden flooding from a compression failure. At depths of about sixty-five feet, the workmen began to suffer a mysterious, extremely painful, illness—what we now call the "bends." None of the doctors had seen it before, so they decided it was the fault of the men's drinking habits. Altogether, decompression sickness killed sixteen workers.

The organization of the St. Louis Bridge project offers a fine example of Carnegie's methods. Railroad bridges were entrepreneurial ventures, usually financed by bond sales, which were repaid from railroad leases. The St. Louis Bridge Co.—primary owner Andrew Carnegie, silent partners Tom

Scott and J. Edgar Thomson—clinched the St. Louis contract in 1867 mostly for its ability to deliver a long-term lease with the Pennsylvania. The company both financed the project and supervised construction on a total cost-plus-10-percent basis. The actual construction was carried out by the Keystone Bridge Co. (which had an excellent reputation as a bridge builder)— primary partner Andrew Carnegie, silent partners Scott and Thomson. The Keystone contract was also at cost-plus-10-percent. Moving farther down the chain, Keystone purchased its structural iron and almost all other iron supplies from the Union Iron Mills, primary owner Andrew Carnegie. The St. Louis Bridge Co.'s investment banker, finally, was one Andrew Carnegie, and he earned a handsome commission by placing the bridge bonds with Junius Morgan (who was much taken with Carnegie's acuity and crispness), and then going on tour to sell them to investors. The St. Louis deal was by no means one of his most complex. On another Mississippi bridge deal at about the same time, his younger brother Tom, who was becoming a valued partner, protested because there were so many entities involved that he had never heard of. Another partner said not to worry: they were all Andy.

In the case of the St. Louis Bridge, Carnegie actually may have earned his multiple layers of compensation. The local genius of the bridge was Capt. James Eads, a brilliant amateur engineer, who was usually either splendidly right or disastrously wrong. Carnegie's operating partner in Keystone, Andrew Kloman, was a supremely talented bridge builder, who preferred a much lighter, simpler design. After a series of rows with Eads, Kloman simply walked away—Keystone had a lot of other bridge contracts— and left him to Carnegie to manage, which took all of Carnegie's finely honed personal skills. Eads turned out to be right about the caissons; and he was right about the advantages of using steel in certain high-stress elements of the superstructure; but the bridge was grossly overbuilt, and was delivered years late and far over budget. In the spring of 1873, an exasperated Junius Morgan responded to a typically "unreasonably positive" Carnegie update with:

> We are glad to hear there is some prospect of the St. Louis Bridge being ready for traffic during the present year. . . . We have been told the same story for the past <u>three</u> years; we shall therefore not encourage too strong hopes of the accomplishment of what we have been so long anxiously waiting for.

Carnegie held Junius in awe—he was the gateway to the race of godlings who dispensed world-shaking amounts of money. To be rebuked so stingingly must have twisted the little Scotsman's bowels.

It got worse. The bridge company ran out of cash in the fall, and Carnegie had to arrange yet another financing through Pierpont. The barely concealed dislike between the two may have stemmed from this first transaction. Junius always liked Carnegie, but one can imagine Pierpont curtly dismissing the Scotsman's tale-spinning when he set out his terms. The money came in two tranches, the second of which was contingent on the span being closed by December 18. The crews came within a whisker of missing the date: one span was badly misaligned, and they struggled for weeks to connect it, succeeding only on the day the financing was scheduled to expire. Pierpont had already proved himself a banker who could pull financings without a flicker of sympathy. Failure to receive the second tranche of funds would have bankrupted the St. Louis Bridge and conceivably threatened all the rest of Carnegie's enterprises.

The bridge did indeed open to much fanfare, on July 4, 1874, and accounts were happily settled with all of Carnegie's various enterprises. The bondholders did not fare so well, as the bridge company slipped into insolvency the very next year. (The Morgans managed an exit for their investors in 1881 by leasing the bridge to Jay Gould. The negotiations were characteristically painful, and when Pierpont finally wired his father the terms, Junius replied laconically, "Think Mr. Gould exercised usual sagacity," and advised his bondholders that the terms were "somewhat less favorable than hoped.")

Carnegie may have sensed that he'd been pushing his luck. The St. Louis Bridge had come close to being a financial disaster, and he and Scott had also suffered a major reverse in connection with the Union Pacific, the transcontinental railroad. Scott had been invited in as part-time president, and used Carnegie to arrange a clever financing in London, for which Carnegie earned stock and a board seat. It may have been the proudest moment of Carnegie's life to that point—from telegraph boy to director so quickly! Then when the stock rose he arranged a quick-profit sale of most of his and Scott's holdings. The rest of the board were astounded when they discovered the sale and asked for both Scott's and Carnegie's resignations. Carnegie, one imagines, was equally astounded to discover that there were business rules beyond the rapacious ones he'd learned from Scott.

Andrew Carnegie's companies built the great St. Louis Bridge, a design forerunner of the Brooklyn Bridge. J. P. Morgan gave Carnegie a hard date for closing the span; missing it might have bankrupted the Scotsman. The crews made the deadline only by hours.

At the same time, his string at the Pennsylvania was clearly running out. Except for his oil field investment, his fortune had been built primarily from supplying services or goods to the Pennsylvania. Carnegie's companies were always high-quality, high-performance vendors, but his real edge came from Scott's and Thomson's inside positions. But the same directors' standards that had caught him and Scott short at the Union Pacific were spreading to the Pennsylvania as well. The Pennsylvania's directors, in the aftermath of the strains from the Erie Wars, conducted a full-dress operational review, and were unpleasantly surprised at their executives' extracurricular activities. It wasn't just Thomson and Scott; other senior managers followed the same practice, investing in George Westinghouse's air brake company, for example. They were ordered to stop, in no uncertain terms, in 1874. Executives could comply or resign, as some chose to do. (The report was particularly harsh on Scott, for fiscal mismanagement as well as his conflicts of interest. Quite likely he was on the brink of being fired.)

Outrageous as they sometimes were, the conflicts are more understandable as remnants from the pioneering company-building days of the 1840s and 1850s. Back then, fledgling roads often encouraged their executives to share investment risk in new technologies.* It was not until roads grew much richer and more powerful during the Civil War that risk sharing transmuted into profit skimming. At the Pennsylvania, at least, the truly rapacious era lasted only about ten years or so; other roads, with varying degrees of alacrity, gradually followed the Pennsylvania's lead and adopted codes of conduct for their own executives.

But by then Carnegie had already found his new religion. During a bond-selling trip to England in 1872 he had visited the giant new steel works at Birmingham and Sheffield. Here was industrial scale that made the heart leap—no more maunderings of early retirement. Carnegie's life plan for the next thirty years was suddenly clear.

The confidence of all businessmen, however, was about to be put to a severe test, in the Great Crash of 1873.

---

*The business historian Naomi Lamoreaux has correlated insider dealing in the nineteenth century with the scarcity of business information. The willingness of a Tom Scott to coinvest with his company was a good "market signal"—in effect, a substitute for data.

· 4 ·

WRENCHINGS

To an observer on the Pittsburgh hills on the night of July 21, 1877, the two-mile-long stretch of Pennsylvania Railroad yards running along Liberty Street on the Allegheny River would have looked like the burning of Atlanta. Angry mobs, thousands strong and many of them armed, torched some thirty-nine buildings and more than thirteen hundred cars and engines. The flames from a massive grain elevator leaped high into the sky, like a beacon of rage.

The violence started after Tom Scott demanded that Washington send a contingent of National Guard to break a spreading railroad strike. When the soldiers marched into the city on the afternoon of the twenty-first, they were met with a volley of stones from an angry crowd. The troop responded with gunfire, killing at least twenty people, then beat a disorderly retreat to the railroad roundhouse, a huge locomotive maintenance facility between 26th and 28th streets on Liberty. The torching of the rail yards started at the roundhouse, clearly with murderous intent. A mob pushed burning cars down tracks into the soldiers, who saved themselves with railroad hoses. The next morning was a Sunday, and as the crowds thinned and smoke built dangerously, the soldiers decided to fight their way out. This time the gunfire was apparently initiated by the crowd, and when the soldiers returned fire, they used a Gatling gun. Twenty-two or twenty-three people were killed,

The 1877 strikes were the most lethal in American history and affected most major cities. Violence at Pittsburgh's Pennsylvania Railroad yards was among the worst anywhere. After soldiers fired on crowds, mobs torched 1,300 cars and most of the company's buildings.

including several soldiers. The *Commercial and Financial Chronicle* (the *Wall Street Journal* of the day) deplored the "saturnalia of violence and pillage," but laid equal blame on "bungling mismanagement at Pittsburgh."

Strikes spread throughout the country the next week. Eleven people were killed in a railroad strike at Reading, Pennsylvania, on Monday. By Tuesday and Wednesday, there were general strikes in Chicago and St. Louis, ugly clashes among police, troops, and workers, and a number of deaths. Strikes in San Francisco turned into murderous anti-Chinese riots. Virtually every major city saw some kind of disturbance before the violence finally dissipated from sheer exhaustion and the inexorable buildup of troops. On August 5, the head of the response team in Washington reported to the president and secretary of war that there was "peace everywhere."

The 1877 strikes were by no means the first in America. But along with the bloody "Molly Maguire" Pennsylvania coal field confrontations between miners and Pinkertons a few years before, they were the first to have such a nasty, class-based edge. Superficially, the Pittsburgh crowds looked a lot like midcentury mobs in Europe, and newspapers freely invoked the specter of the "Commune," the 1871 rising in Paris. Tom Scott, despite his hardscrabble roots, played the role of outraged plutocrat to perfection.

It was the strangest of decades. For generations, historians treated the 1877 labor risings as a reaction to the "long and merciless depression" of the 1870s, one that was usually described as the second worst in history after the collapse of the 1930s. More recent research, however, makes it clear that if there was a "depression" at all, it was brief and mild; in fact, the decade saw some of the fastest growth on record, and marked the point where American heavy industry began decisively to narrow the technology and productivity gap with Great Britain. But the times still *felt* awful, for bankers and businessmen and ordinary farmers and factory workers alike. There was a deep current of social unrest: farm protests swept through the midwest, industrial strikes left dead and injured on both sides of picket lines, and the characteristic easy-money, antimonopoly brand of American Populism first took root.

America was careening toward modernity. The momentum of technologic and commercial exploitation had been building since the 1840s and 1850s, even as traditional social structures were disrupted by the Civil War. The Whig vision of a frictionless, monadlike society of independent artisans and farmers was being swallowed up by its own relentless logic of development. The infrastructure of modernity—fast, cheap transportation; ready access to primary materials like coal, iron, and oil; real-time communications; smoothly flowing channels of finance capital—demanded behemoth-scale institutions, sprawling, soulless, autistically focused on pouring out more steel, more coal, more stocks and bonds, more of whatever they happened to do. During the 1870s, the wrenching forces of modernization achieved maximum torque on the old ways of living and governing and doing business. The captains of modernity, the Carnegies, the Rockefellers, the Goulds, and their admirers; all the people yearning to strike out on new salients, buy more things, behave in new ways; immigrants seeking release from the encrusted semifeudal strictures of Old Europe: they all reveled in the change. Probably half the country hated it.

The Crash of 1873

The banking house of Jay Cooke & Co., its portfolio stuffed with unsellable Northern Pacific railroad bonds, closed its doors on September 18, 1873, triggering a banking crisis and, in the traditional telling, initiating the "Great Depression of the 1870s." The shock of Cooke's failure would be hard to overstate, for he was widely perceived as America's leading private banker, and there had been little inkling of the difficulty he was in. The *Commercial and Financial Chronicle* said that the news was "received with almost derisive incredulity on the part of the mercantile public."

Cooke's was the one name on Wall Street that reverberated far beyond the financial community. He was a marketing genius, who had single-handedly stabilized the Union's finances in the darkest days of 1862–63 by mounting a massive town to town, almost house to house, bond sale, the first true retail bond drive in history. Cooke went on to place two massive federal bond issuances, totaling almost $1 billion, while charging razor-thin commissions and bearing all the marketing expenses. His retail customers also proved to be ideal security holders. Ordinary folk bought for long-term savings, not for speculation; their bonds disappeared into sugar bowls and mattresses instead of weighing on securities markets. While Cooke made only modest profits on the bonds, he emerged as one of the world's best known bond bankers, a man that even the Barings and the Rothschilds were happy to partner with.

A string of Wall Street houses toppled in Cooke's wake. The stock exchange suspended trading, and New York clearinghouse banks closed for more than a week. Official opinion at first resisted the bad news. The *Chronicle,* whose commentary was usually quite acute, derided the notion that the "present Jay Cooke panic" signaled that anything was seriously awry, for "Since the close of the war there has never been a time when our mercantile community have been in a better condition than now."

In fact, the country was undergoing a full-fledged banking crisis, one that persisted into mid-1874. Like fiber optic lines in the 1990s, railroads had been built far ahead of actual demand; Cooke's Northern Pacific was just an especially egregious example. The *Chronicle* doggedly insisted that railroad earnings still easily covered their debt service obligations, which was true—if you ignored the havoc from constant-dollar debt service in an era of falling nominal prices. Eighty-nine railroads had defaulted on their bonds by the end of 1873, and the default count grew to 108 over the following year. This was a time when railroads accounted for about 80 percent of total stock market capitalization—even a budding mogul like Rockefeller stayed away from the public securities markets—so a crisis in the roads devastated the entire Street.

The *Chronicle* had been worrying about a cash crunch since late summer. Crop exports were weak in 1872, so the new year opened with an unusually large trade deficit, which was financed by short-term borrowings abroad. The loans were deposited in New York, leaving the banks temporarily brimming with cash. As railroad issues sold poorly throughout the spring, Wall Street supported its bond inventories with call loans, which banks could pull at any time. New York banks, in short, were financing long-term borrowers with foreign hot money, just as Thai and Malaysian banks did in 1997. Then July and August brought the good-bad news that western farmers were harvesting a spectacular crop, and cash started flowing west to start the grain trains rolling. In the best of circumstances, a financial squeeze was inevitable. Pierpont Morgan was one of the few Wall Street figures to call the turn correctly, and demanded payment on most of Drexel, Morgan's outstanding credits well before the crash hit. Not very public-spirited, perhaps, but good banking.

Events in Europe turned a tight patch into a perfect storm. After his lightning victory in the 1870–71 Franco-Prussian war, Prussian chancellor Otto von Bismarck exacted stiff tribute from the French in 1872 and 1873. The total payment, $1 billion in gold, was about the same size in real terms as the World War I reparations exacted at Versailles, with the difference that the French actually paid it, virtually all at once, and from a much smaller economy than the Germans had in 1919. Raising the money was arguably the greatest tour de force of nineteenth-century banking, and the crowning achievement of the Rothschild family, especially its French branch. But the enormous transfer of funds disrupted the continent's bourses throughout 1873, even in Germany, and cash flows from Europe to America fell sharply. Europeans had long been souring on American railroads because of outrages like the Erie Wars. But now, even if they had wanted to help, there wasn't a sou to be had.

Sophisticated observers stumbling through the ruins of the Crash of 1873 could see little but economic desolation ahead. More than a year later, President Grant's message to Congress spoke of the continuing "prostration in business and industries." On the raw numbers, in fact, he was quite wrong: the American economic engine was demonstrating its real power, churning ahead as never before.

A Most Peculiar Decade

The new evidence for the 1870s is a product of the young discipline of "cliometrics" or economic history. Simon Kuznets produced the first comprehensive set of nineteenth-century national growth tables in the 1940s, and his student, Robert Gallman, devoted much of a long career to extending and refining them. The reconstructive work is extraordinary; researchers spend years poring through trade and business reports to pin down arcana like inventory cycles.

The data are consistent and unambiguous: the 1870s was a decade of very strong growth. Depending on your starting point, or whether you use five-year averages, as Kuznets and Gallman prefer, average real (inflation-adjusted) annual growth rates were somewhere between 4.5 percent and 6 percent, among the fastest, if not the fastest, decadal growth rates on record. (A more recent analysis places the real annual growth for the decade at a blazing 6.7 percent and per capita growth at 3.9 percent, both probably the fastest ever.) There *was* a recession in 1874, after a spectacular 1872 and near-flat 1873, but growth recovered sharply thereafter, maintaining a vigorous pace well into the 1880s. Consumption grew even faster than total output. At a time of high immigration and rapid population growth, real consumption per person grew by almost 50 percent over the decade. No country in Europe had nearly so strong a record.

Railroad construction slowed dramatically, of course, especially in the middle of the decade, but virtually every other measure of physical output, including railroad freight loadings, was up strongly. The population grew by 26 percent from 1870 to 1880, but fuel consumption doubled, metals consumption tripled, oil production was up fivefold, and the real value of manufacturing output increased by two-thirds. America had no steel production to speak of in 1870, but was neck and neck with Great Britain by the early 1880s. Henry Frick, the leading Pennsylvania coke vendor (for iron and steel smelting), remembered the 1870s as an "awful" time, even though his coke output tripled in the last half of the decade.

Tonnage measures of food production and consumption grew spectacularly. The volume of grains and cotton consumed at home increased by 50 percent, while exports of wheat were up threefold, corn fourfold, and cotton by 60 percent. Per capita beef consumption increased by 20 percent, while exports shot up ninefold. Employment also grew steadily, at a compound annual rate of 3 percent a year, against an annual population growth of 2.3 percent. By the end of the decade, Americans were better fed, better clothed, and better educated; they had bigger farms with higher output, had access to a much broader range of metal products, like stoves, wash tubs, farm tools, and machinery, and were far more likely to enjoy the benefits of artificial lighting.

So why did it feel like a depression? One reason was that *prices* fell throughout the decade and beyond, in a slide that was steep, relentless, and continuous. The wholesale price index fell by 25 percent from 1870 to 1880, a decline that continued through the 1880s at about half that rate, before flattening out at essentially zero inflation in the 1890s. Falling prices were reflected in falling money incomes. Because prices, in the main, fell faster than incomes did, *real* income grew strongly, but shrinking pay packets, or diminishing cash returns from crop sales, still felt awful. A small number of contemporary analysts speculated that the fall in prices was giving "the wage-earning class a greater command over the necessities and comforts of life."* But the average American was a farmer or an artisan, a housekeeper or a small businessperson in a rural town, and had no way of knowing what was happening to overall price levels. Like people in any age, as their money incomes went down, they forgot about their new curtains, and tools, and kerosene lamps; as far as they knew, they were getting poorer, and they were mad as hell about it.

But it's not just that people were fooled. So dramatic and broad-scale a price restructuring, just like a period of rapid inflation, caught vast numbers of businesses and workers on the wrong side of the adjustment. The financial sector was hit very hard. Railroad stocks dropped 60 percent at their trough, and most other private-sector securities such as coal and iron bonds were closely tied to the fortunes of the roads. In theory, falling prices benefit creditors, but the realignment was radical enough to cause disruptions on all sides. The annual rate of business bankruptcies doubled, and a large

---

*An important, if not precisely answerable question is how well unskilled labor did in this era. Unskilled jobs were certainly growing, but there would have been strong competition from arriving immigrants and newly freed slaves. One 1905 researcher compiled unskilled wage series covering most of the nineteenth century. Her findings suggest that unskilled wages dropped faster than prices in the 1870s (wages were down 31 percent, wholesale prices 25 percent), but workers more than made up for it in the 1880s (wages *up* 17 percent; prices *down* 13 percent). Such data series are impressionistic at best, but are, unfortunately, the best there are.

number of savings banks failed as they were caught in a mismatch between falling deposits and the nominal value of their loans. There are reports that in major cities wages dropped much faster than food prices. Charitable organizations in New York City reported that relief rolls quadrupled, to 20,000, and public construction reportedly came to a dead stop, although that was partly due to the tightfisted city administration that succeeded the disgraced Tweed machine. Construction on the Brooklyn Bridge, on the other hand, the largest project in the city's history to that point, continued through the decade.

Still, when contemporary reports insist on how bad things were, they mostly point to falling prices, as if a "20% fall in retail prices" represented a real loss in value. One much-cited contemporary analysis, for example, tracked railroad revenues, pig iron and coal shipments, merchandise exports and cotton consumption, all in price terms. Pig iron was closely tied to railroad construction, and actually did suffer a terrible decade: prices were halved from 1873 to 1876 and volumes fell by 25 percent. But cotton and coal production both rose steadily in physical units, with minimal year-to-year variations, although output in price terms was flat. Merchandise exports were strong even in price terms. Exports slipped in 1875, but only by comparison to the banner crop export years of 1873 and 1874; otherwise they were stronger than any previous year on record. Overall, from 1870 to 1880, merchandise exports increased by 96 percent in price terms, and, obviously, considerably more than that if deflation is accounted for.

Many reports of hardship are clearly fanciful. Estimates of unemployment in the mid-1870s range from a half million to five million. The numbers at the upper end of that range are quite implausible. The 1870 labor force was only thirteen million, more than half of them working on farms. The *Chronicle*'s 1874 report that "half a million of men at the least are computed to have been partially or wholly thrown out of work by the stoppage of railroad building" could not possibly have been true, even on the most extreme assumptions of job losses among outside contractors. There were only 230,000 railroad workers in 1870, and 78,000 primary iron- and steel-workers. ("Primary" iron and steel manufacturing included rails, but not most other end-products.) A modern estimate of the crash-related job loss in iron and steel manufacturing, which was mostly railroad-driven, is just 21,000. There are no reliable data on year-to-year employment fluctuations for this period, but decadal census-based data show that total employment grew some 40 percent between 1870 and 1880, from thirteen million to eighteen million. It strains credulity that such strong growth was accompanied by mass unemployment in mid-decade.

Although the *Chronicle* would have been acutely aware of layoffs in big steel companies, the vast majority of manufacturing workers were scattered throughout the country in artisanal shops or modestly sized factories. Outside of railroad-related businesses, there are few signs of a downturn. Annual production of Singer sewing machines, for example, quadrupled over the decade, to 500,000 units in 1880, without a single down year. The Studebaker wagon and carriage works doubled its production between 1872 and 1874; when it was interrupted by a fire, the company rebuilt its factory and continued its strong growth. Philadelphia's mostly artisanal textile manufacturers doubled employment in the 1870s,* while Providence's jewelry industry also enjoyed healthy growth. McCormick Reaper had several poor years, but aside from the disruption of the 1871 Chicago fire, its biggest problems were factory foulups and infighting between the McCormick brothers, not slowing demand. This was the era when the Midwest came to dominate grain production: the number of acres devoted to wheat farming went up by 75 percent, mostly on larger farms that were highly dependent on modern machinery.

Times really were tough on railroad workers, for the roads were under considerable duress. The Pennsylvania, generally considered the best managed of the roads, was badly stretched by its defensive acquisition program in response to Gould's attacks earlier in the decade, and found itself in a serious cash squeeze during the post–Cooke money market disruptions. But although Tom Scott loudly lamented falling prices, he cut costs so aggressively that the Pennsylvania's net earnings actually rose, even in the recession year of 1874. Ton-mile rates had fallen by more than half since the war, according to an internal analysis, but year after year, as freight loadings soared, the road consistently earned a bit more than half a cent per ton-mile, give or take a few hundredths of a cent. The Pennsylvania wasn't unique; the annual *Poor's* compendia show that, nationwide, railroad operating margins improved slightly during the 1870s.

---

*When clear evidence of rapid growth contradicts the "Depression" tradition, historians often slip into oxymoron, as "Despite the downturns of the 1870s, Philadelphia textile sectors expanded mightily . . ."

The problem for the roads was that they were overleveraged,* and the burden of fixed interest and dividends became steadily worse as deflation took hold, which explains the large number of defaults. The Pennsylvania's board, moreover, like most railroads, made it very clear that maintaining faith with its investors took priority over all else, and they bore down especially hard on their workers. During the 1877 strikes, the *Baltimore Sun* conceded: "The level of [the railroad workers'] struggle to live is very sad. . . . Many of them declare that they might as well starve without work as starve and work." Even the *Chronicle* editorialized: "[T]hose who speak flippantly of the matter, saying . . . that a dollar a day is enough for bread, and whoever cannot live on bread and water is no man, at all, do not show either a wise head or a feeling heart." Railroad managers might have learned another trick from Jay Gould, who, in 1877, was running the Union Pacific. Unlike his peers, he was unburdened with worker-management ideologies, or indeed with ideologies of any kind. He readily met with his strike leaders, made a few modest concessions, and everyone went cheerfully back to work.

Supply Shock?

But if production was rising, the question remains of *why* prices were falling. The simplest explanation is that it was a consequence of America's return to the gold standard in 1879. After Jay Gould's 1872 Gold Corner, the greenback had settled into a trading range of 125 to 130 greenbacks for $100 in gold. Achieving parity with gold and the British pound would therefore require a 25 percent or so rise in the greenback. As the greenback's value rose, the greenback price of goods should fall, and in fact they did fall, by just about 25 percent over the decade. World gold stocks were also flat,

---

*The prevailing theory of railroad investing was that operating cash flow (revenues less operating expenses) belonged to investors, so roads typically retained quite modest cash reserves after paying dividends and interest. Capital investments, like line extensions, were supposed to be financed by new securities, not from retained earnings. Since dividends were based on the par value of the stock, they were fixed in dollar terms, just like bond interest. It is the fixed dividends and debt service on falling nominal revenues, not falling operating margins, that explains the high rate of defaults. One should not shed tears for the investors: since most railroad shares traded well below par, a par-based dividend at the usual 7–10 percent offered windfall yields that should have fully compensated for the extra risk.

which would similarly tend to push down prices in an era of increasing production.

But the standard monetarist explanation for the fall in prices doesn't quite fit the facts. If the government wanted to bid up the greenback until it reached parity with gold, it would have restricted its supply and raised interest rates. Lincoln proposed just such a strategy for his second administration, but as soon as the tight greenback policy started to bite, Congress forced Andrew Johnson's new administration to back off. From that point there are almost no signs of monetary tightening right up to the restoration of gold/greenback parity on January 1, 1879. For most of the 1870s, in fact, money was easy and interest rates fell. The *Chronicle*, which had documented the extreme tightness of money in 1873, marveled the following spring: "money is so plentiful that banks find it hard to lend"; and a year later reported that the money market "has not for many years shown as much tranquillity as now." When the new Rutherford B. Hayes administration took office in 1877, America's booming trade surpluses were already pushing the greenback toward parity. Export-import houses started substituting greenbacks for gold well before the official resumption date, which turned out to be a nonevent. On resumption day at the Gold Exchange, someone wrote "PAR" in huge block letters on the price-tracking board, and everyone went home. There was not even a party.

The 1870s seem to have been the rare case of a "supply shock." A supply shock is a *good* thing; it is the infelicitous term economists use for a sudden, and permanent, improvement in productive capacity, what Federal Reserve chairman Alan Greenspan recently called a "paradigm shift." With the massive post–Civil War investment in infrastructure, force-fed by the likes of Jay Gould, transaction costs were dropping like a stone. Telegraphic and cable communications were driving down the risks and costs of financial services. John Rockefeller was teaching the world that lower prices meant bigger markets and higher profits. Railroad innovations like the through bill of lading, or "waybill," and the "car accounting office" eliminated countless middlemen and extra handling steps. (With the waybill, a customer paid a single fare, and the bill traveled with the goods, ensuring proper routing and payment. Car accounting, and the gradual standardization of track gauges, allowed lines to haul each other's freight cars instead of unloading and reloading goods.) Economies of scale were taking hold in production of most primary products. The cheaper, better, steel flowing out of Andrew Carnegie's new steel plants made possible mass-produced tools and consumer products that cost less, lasted longer, and worked better than anything that had gone before.

The currency realignment, in other words, came as a natural fallout from larger tidal movements. The British pound sterling was the nineteenth century's proxy for gold, much as the dollar was after World War II. As American productive capacity reached parity with, and then surpassed, Great Britain's, the greenback and sterling realigned by themselves. Falling nominal prices signified strength, not prostration.

The roughly parallel developments in Great Britain suggest the power of the forces that were afoot. There was a British "Great Depression" starting in the 1870s, which lasted much longer than the contraction in America and which exhibited much the same dissonance between perceptions and the underlying data. As one historian put it:

> Prices certainly fell but almost every other index of economic activity— output of coal and pig iron, tonnage of ships built, consumption of raw wool and cotton, import and export figures, shipping entries and clearances, railway freight and passenger traffic, bank deposits and clearances, joint-stock company formation, trading profits, consumption per head of wheat, meat, tea, beer, and tobacco—all these showed an upward trend.

Yet just as in the United States, "an overwhelming mass of opinion . . . [agreed] that conditions were bad"—although "the wails of distress did not come from the mass of the people, who were for the most part better off, but mainly from industrialists, merchants, and financiers." The British, in fact, had more to complain about than Americans, for the quarter century after 1870 was a period of "hollowing-out" of British industry. Real growth continued, and living standards rose, but Great Britain decisively lost competitive advantage to the United States in almost every field, especially manufacturing—much as occurred in 1970s America, when there was decent growth, despite the oil recessions, but pervasive gloom over the loss of competitive leadership to countries such as Japan.

One of the most striking developments in America was the industrialization of farming. As grain and meat production and transport became much more efficient, America dominated international food markets from the mid-1870s on, in a competition that turned primarily on price. The agricultural transformation brought great wealth to the Northwest, and improved diets not just in America but throughout the world, but at the same time, it made the lives of huge numbers of people simply miserable.

The Birth of the Factory Farm

Among the unexpected fallouts from Jay Cooke's failure was a land boom in the far Northwest, especially in Minnesota and the Red River Valley of the Dakotas. The Northern Pacific had received enormous federal land grants, some thirty-nine million acres in all, and many shareholders and creditors chose to settle their claims in land when the company defaulted. For the first time, eastern capitalists found themselves owning vast tracts of unimproved western land—a fertile, flat, stoneless, treeless grassland like few others in the world. A farmer could plow a straight line for months, according to the local tall tale, then turn around and harvest on the way back. This was land ideally suited to the mass production of wheat and corn; being capitalists, the new owners noticed and began to invest.

"Bonanza" farms, so-called because of their huge profits, were farms of several thousand acres with factory-style production management, maximum use of machinery, small resident staffs, substantial reliance on seasonal labor, and usually nonresident investor-owners. Operations came to be organized and standardized to the point where they were run in great part by nonfarmers. The core management staffs looked like a normal company's—bookkeepers, cost accountants, purchasing specialists. The farm work was broken into discrete tasks, like loading bound sheaves, maintaining twine-binding machines, and transporting equipment or grain, so it could be staffed with more or less the same laborers and draymen that an oil refinery or a steel plant used. Bonanza farms were never the majority of farms in the Northwest, or even close to it, but they defined a radically different style and approach to a traditional problem.

The prototypical bonanza farm was the Cass-Cheney farm near Fargo, founded in 1874 and financed by George Cass, the Northern Pacific president, and George Cheney, a railroad board member. (Cass was a capable railroad executive brought into the Northern Pacific by Cooke much too late to prevent the 1873 collapse.) Their primary goal was not so much to make money—although they did very well—but to demonstrate the value of the railroad's holdings. Their most interesting and important decision was to hire Oliver H. Dalrymple to run their properties. This was risky, for Dalrymple had already gone bust from grain speculations, but also brought what modern business gurus call a "transformative" management style. He was a Yale Law graduate who had come to the Northwest to practice law, had switched to farming, and had briefly become the Northwest's "wheat king" by developing a bonanza-style three-thousand-acre wheat farm before losing everything in his bankruptcy. Cass and Cheney had the insight to structure the ideal incentive arrangement: Dalrymple was paid well from the start, but his big payoff was that as his operation succeeded he could gradually win full ownership.

Cass and Cheney had their nervous moments, as Dalrymple, like a mini-Rockefeller, expanded into grain elevators, Great Lakes steam transport, and a host of related enterprises. But within just a few years it was clear that the farm operations were a spectacular success. The "Dalrymple farm" had grown to thirty thousand acres by the early 1880s, employing upwards of two thousand men at various times of the year. Dalrymple's total holdings eventually grew to one hundred thousand acres throughout the area.

From the outset Dalrymple laid out multiyear schedules for bringing the land under cultivation. Sod-busting—breaking up the tough prairie grass roots—was the most expensive investment, usually costing considerably more than raw land. Dalrymple's schedule of breaking sod on five thousand new acres per year probably would not have been feasible without the new steel plow blades. By 1878, the first Cass-Cheney/Dalrymple spread operated with 126 horses, 84 plows, 81 harrows, 67 wagons, 30 seeders, 8 threshing machines, and 45 binders. Plowing was usually done in one mile square (640-acre) sections. Huge gang plows, pulled by up to five horses, would be chained a dozen or more abreast marching in straight-line one-mile runs to minimize turning. Harrowing, seeding, harvesting, and threshing followed in quasimilitary sequence, then the land would be replowed before freezing set in. The automated binders used up to a freight-car load of twine. Steam-powered threshers could process five thousand bushels a day, pouring out their golden streams into freight cars waiting at the farm's siding. In 1881, Dalrymple, with thirty-six threshers, was loading three full trainloads a day, or thirty thousand bushels. By 1883, just a few years after Alexander Graham Bell first demonstrated the telephone, the bigger Northwest farms had already installed telephone connections between far-flung sections. In his second full year of operation, Dalrymple produced wheat at fifty-two cents a bushel for a market that was buying at about a dollar. By 1890, wheat farms west of the Mississippi were producing perhaps a quarter of the world's supply.

Bonanza farms were constantly evolving. The first generation of farms, for instance, were solely devoted to wheat—Dalrymple even imported the oats for the horses—and it took a while to learn the limits of extreme monoculture. The fact that the outsiders tended to be "book farmers" was actually helpful, for they hadn't learned century-old lore at their daddies' knees and were quick to reach out to agronomists for advice on seeds, fertility maintenance, and erosion. (The land-grant colleges financed by the 1862 Morrill Act were just then turning out their first batches of scientifically trained advisers.) A distinct corn belt also developed as the 1880s progressed. Wheat farming tended to drift westward—California was an important center by the 1890s—while corn stayed close to Chicago, since corn-fattening was the last stage in preparing cattle for slaughter. Mass-market grain production fed the burgeoning Minneapolis flour milling industry; Pillsbury is one of the early important names.

Labor productivity steadily increased. The first generation of bonanza farms roughly doubled labor output, and the steady improvement in machinery, especially the advent of the gasoline engine in the early twentieth century, doubled it again. (Steam power never made much of an impact in field work because of the cost of wood or coal fuel.) *Land* productivity actually declined. It was cheaper to break new land than to husband existing plots, so yields tended to drop as more marginal lands came into production.

Part of a seventy-horse plowing team on a North Dakota bonanza farm.

Extravagant waste of natural resources was the common thread through the American development story.

Subtler interactions among railroads, the telegraph companies, and the grain markets—the culmination of twenty-five years of incremental improvements—also paid huge productivity dividends. Not long before, farmers had bagged up their grain and sold it on consignment to merchants. Traditional trade documents tracked the grain to the final sale so the payment could work its way back over the mountains to the farmer. Lots of fingers plucked snippets of the money along the way. Since the farmer usually couldn't wait for his money, he would sell his "bill" to a local bank at a deep discount.

By the mid-1870s, however, there was a fully integrated national system of grain exchanges, with elevator storage, grading and weighing standards, and a telegraph futures market called a "grain call," all underpinned by precise and reliable railroad delivery schedules. Grain was commoditized. The farmer's specific bushels of wheat became certificates for x bushels of "no. 2 hard red winter wheat" that could be readily bought and sold through a near-instantaneous telegraphic pricing system. Farmers and big grain users, like Pillsbury, could make their deals even before the fields were planted, if they chose, and cover their exposures by hedging on the exchanges. Huge "frictional" costs, or pure economic waste, like the deep discounts once charged for the farmer's trade bills, disappeared. Transaction commissions and costs were razor thin, prices fell, but gross volumes and profits rose, while the increased stability fed the growth of national cereal and flour brands.

The Disassembly Line

A rough parallel to the bonanza farm developed at about the same time in the meat industry. The Texas cattle ranch was born out of the devastation of the Civil War. Antebellum beef and pork production was distributed through the mid-Atlantic and border states and along the southern coasts from the Carolinas to Louisiana. The herds were hit hard by the fighting, with losses of up to 20 percent in the North and 50 percent in the South. Meat prices were very high after the war, and varied as much as eightfold from region to region.

Entrepreneurs soon realized that the open ranges of Texas were home to millions of semiwild "mavericks," mostly Texas longhorns. The problem with longhorns was that they carried a devastating tick-borne cattle disease (the longhorn was immune), and many states prohibited driving longhorns through their territories. In 1867, a twenty-nine-year-old Illinois cattle buyer named Joseph McCoy convinced the Union Pacific to run a cattle spur to Abilene, Kansas, and prevailed upon state legislatures to permit the train passage of Texas steers. McCoy's initiative gave birth to the "long drive" from Texas to Abilene, and the romance of the cowboy and the cattle town. In the 1880s, Jay Gould extended a vast, more or less unified, railroad system through the Southwest, consigning the drive to the realm of the dime novel.

Eastern and European capital quickly flowed into large-scale ranching. Barbed wire may have been the essential invention, although careless attitudes by the federal government and railroad companies toward their land grants also helped—many ranchers simply took over vacant land with no pretense to title. The XIT ranch, organized in the mid-1870s, with more than three million acres and six thousand miles of barbed wire, was the largest in American history. The available evidence suggests that big ranches were quite profitable: one of the first British-owned ranches, a half-million-acre spread organized in 1881, earned a 28 percent dividend its first year. Getting cattle to distant markets was never uneventful, however. Longhorns were not known for their docility, and before the era of the Mississippi bridges, they had to be unloaded and ferried across the river. A St. Louis paper reported in 1872:

> Yesterday was a good day for Texas steers on the rampage. They could be met almost anywhere in the city. A Texas steer when he is in good spirits can make things decidedly lively on a crowded thoroughfare. Several portions of our city were enlivened by this means yesterday. One very sprightly fellow with horns nearly a yard long interviewed Mr. Lawrence Ford (of Bridge, Beach & Co.) on the corner of Chestnut and Commercial street, and was very sociable.

Even with bridges, the huge distance from the ranches to customers was a drag on profits. By 1880, when 80 percent of Americans lived east of the Mississippi, almost 60 percent of cattle were being raised in the west. Steers were traveling thousands of miles on trains: they were loaded at ranch-country depots, carried to switching points like Chicago, and from there to the main population centers on the east coast. Slaughtering and dressing was carried out by thousands of local butchers; in urban areas, many of them were substantial businessmen, dressing and brokering meat for retail outlets.

It was obvious that huge savings could be effected by processing the animals closer to the ranches. Live steers occupied three times the car space as their equivalent in dressed product; they lost weight during transshipping, died en route, got banged around so the meat was bruised and spoiled, and had to be regularly debarked, fed, and watered all along the way. The key was refrigeration: fresh beef had only a one-week shelf life, but it took up to three weeks to distribute product from a location like Chicago. Eastern milk producers had begun to use freight cars with ice stuffed in their walls in the 1850s, and an Indiana slaughterer, George Hammond, experimented with refrigerated shipments of dressed beef to Boston merchants as early as 1869, but his cars were too inefficient for summer shipping, and his meat sometimes spoiled even in winter.

It fell to Gustavus Swift, a Massachusetts butcher, to break the refrigeration barrier with a design that added a mechanical forced-air circulation system. He demonstrated the point with a prototype car that delivered good-quality Chicago meat at high profits to his brother, who was also a butcher in Boston. To his disappointment the railroads showed no interest in the new car, and several even refused to carry it. The carriers' stonewalling isn't surprising. All the lines had singled out the boom in cattle transport as a superior earnings opportunity, and most were making large investments in stock cars and stockyards. Swift was not a wealthy man, but he scraped up the money for ten cars and found a Canadian railroad willing to carry them. They were an instant success, allowing large markdowns over local butchers from the very start. Swift and his brother organized the Swift Packing Co., and Gustavus moved to Chicago while his brother handled the marketing of "Western Beef" up and down the East Coast. The railroads capitulated, and in hardly more than a half decade the entire industry was transformed.

Philip Armour, a New York native who had made a modest fortune as a California gold rush butcher, jumped into refrigerated shipping immediately, and quickly challenged Swift for industry leadership. Armour may have been first to appreciate that distribution costs outweighed the costs of slaughtering and packaging. Much as Rockefeller did in oil, Armour cut out local middlemen, setting up regional meat-finishing centers, and even providing train-based retail services to rural towns. Meatpackers found themselves in the same catbird seat as oil refiners—controlling the bottleneck between a diverse and unorganized ranching industry and a widely dispersed consumer market. Very quickly the industry consolidated into four major players—Swift, Armour, Hammond, and Nelson Morris, another Chicago slaughterer—with a few other firms, like Wilson or the Cudahys, holding the fifth position from time to time. Most of the firms expanded their holdings up and down the value chain, from stockyards and ranches to wholesale distribution centers as far away as Tokyo and Shanghai.

The big packing houses were the heart of the business. Most of them were in Chicago, but others were steadily brought on line in Omaha, St. Louis, and points west. The packing house "disassembly" line, an inspiration for Henry Ford's factories, became one of the lurid wonders of the world. The actress Sarah Bernhardt, after a tour, pronounced them "horrendous but fascinating." A steer was forced down a ramp, a worker called a knocker stunned it with a sledgehammer, and it was swept up by an overhead meat hook and moved rapidly through gutters, slicers, splitters, skinners, rump sawyers, hide droppers, and trimmers—there were as many as seventy-eight different jobs on a beef disassembly line. It was fast, hard, dangerous work—the speed of the line and the blur of wickedly sharp instruments exacted a fearful toll of injuries and deaths among the workers. The costs of slaughtering and packaging fell sevenfold, even as the scale of operation opened up profit opportunities in byproducts. One of Armour's very early investments was a glue factory, and all the houses expanded aggressively into hides, oils, and tallow. Hog processing was different in detail, but the pattern of development was roughly the same. Per capita meat consumption grew rapidly, especially in the 1880s, as the full impact of the factory system made itself felt.

The transformation of the food industry illustrates the daily disruptions of an accelerating boom. In production terms, the country was clearly on a roll. Physical output of food and manufactured goods were all up strongly. Employment was growing faster than the population. People were eating better and had more real purchasing power. But old ways of life, long settled expectations, all the fixed stars for measuring stature and progress, were violently wrenched out of place. On Dalrymple's farms, transient workers outnumbered year-round staff by as much as twenty to one. Transients were mostly solid working men, not hobos or bums, and followed a reasonably well-defined route, from early spring farm work in the Southeast to the fall harvests in the Northwest and lumberjack camps in the winter. Living conditions on the bonanza farms and lumber camps were often quite decent. Prodigious quantities of hard physical work required strong men who had to be fed well and boarded in healthful conditions. But with even the best of amenities, how many of them could have aspired to such a life? Where was the opportunity to marry, put down roots, and raise a family? Or to save that "surplus" whereby, as Abraham Lincoln promised, a man "buy[s] tools or land, for himself; then labors on his own account another while, and at length hires another new beginner to help him"?

It's no surprise that the protest movements that bloomed throughout the farm belt in the 1870s—the Grangers* are the best known—had a common theme of victimization by impersonal forces—railroads, eastern capitalists, riggers of commodity markets. The cold data bear out almost none of their complaints. Railroads did sometimes exploit monopoly positions on local connections,† but freight rates fell at least as fast as farm prices in the postwar period, and after the mid-1880s, much faster. Farmers were generally not heavily mortgaged—only about a third of all farmers had mortgages at all, in part because the Homestead Act and railroad land grants made land so cheap. (Roads like the Northern Pacific were desperate to get land into the hands of freight-generating farmers.) Interest rates fell steadily, and lenders were usually looking for customers. There is evidence that lenders rarely foreclosed on defaulted farms; when times were bad, it just wasn't worth it. Overall, late nineteenth-century "terms of trade" turned decisively in farmers' favor: it took fewer and fewer bushels of wheat to buy a reaper or a bolt of good cloth.

But it is the lurking, poorly grasped perils that make you paranoid. Most

---

*The Granger movement won a mass following in the mid-1870s, but steadily lost importance thereafter. Its primary focus was railroad rate regulation. A number of western states passed "Granger laws"; most were of little effect, except perhaps in Illinois. (Railroads often countered "uniformity" requirements by raising all rates sharply, forcing legislatures to back down.) For most purposes, they were superseded by the federal Interstate Commerce Act, passed in 1887.

†But higher short-haul rates did not necessarily mean exploitation, as reformers assumed. Short-haul routes were considerably more expensive to operate because of more frequent stops and greater investment in stations and loading facilities per mile. The Interstate Commerce Commission eventually leveled rates, forcing long-haul shippers to subsidize local haulers—good politics, but poor economics.

farmers would have been terrified as their markets delocalized. Traditional farms were diversified—even in a poor commercial season, a farm family usually had enough food and, in a pinch, could home-produce many of their other needs. The prewar generation of eastern wheat farmers were also close to their markets and could understand, and to a degree anticipate, ups and downs in their customers' behavior. But a mechanized monoculture grower on the Northwest plain lived in a much more volatile world: a shift of weather patterns on the Russian steppes could wipe out his year. Specialization and mechanization increased revenues and profits, but also multiplied the risk of catastrophic failure. Men who prided themselves on crop management burned late-night kerosene lamps puzzling over balance sheets. Times were good, according to the numbers, but the loss of control was frightening.

The packing industry is a case study in how industrialization was creating millions of jobs; by century's end, meat packing was the largest industrial employer in the country. But that was cold comfort to the butchers and middlemen/wholesalers wiped out by Swift and Armour. Headlong modernization must have greatly increased the levels of frictional unemployment even as overall job numbers moved up strongly. The new jobs were in the wrong place, or were jobs that skilled tradesmen would never consider taking—at least at first. Modernization also was very hard on small merchants. Meatpackers were not the only large manufacturers taking control over their own distribution and retail chains. Singer Sewing Machine is another early example. American radicalism typically bubbled up from the petit bourgeois, for they, not the oppressed poor, were often the first victims of modernization.

Finally, some large fraction of the jobs in the new industrial economy were simply dreadful. A nineteenth-century meatpacking line was a medieval vision of hell—gory, filthy, unremitting, unforgiving of even the slightest slip or misstep, and freezing cold besides (all the plants were refrigerated so they could run year-round). There were no set work schedules; even the longest-term workers showed up each day and worked as long, or as briefly, as they were told. Almost all pay was piece rate. Wages did increase strongly over the first twenty years of the industry, especially in real terms, but hours got longer and the lines got faster as well. Rural Irishmen and Polish peasants were delighted to get jobs in meatpacking—both were likely to have known real starvation—but the disassembly line was a world removed from the industrial Eden of artisanal enterprise that Lincoln had envisioned as the future of America.

America's extractive and infrastructure industries—oil, steel, railroads—were careening toward modernity even faster than agriculture, which perfectly suited apostles of progress like Andrew Carnegie, John Rockefeller, and Jay Gould. Most businessmen reacted with fear at the violent disruptions of the 1870s. Top of the food chain feeders saw only a world ripe with opportunity.

· 5 ·

MEGA-MACHINE

Philadelphia's Centennial Exposition was the biggest bash of America's hundredth birthday celebration in 1876. Much like Great Britain's grand Crystal Palace Exhibition, it was an unreserved paean to technology, without the adumbrations of dangerous new competition that had so alarmed knowledgeable Englishmen in the 1850s. Opened by President Grant and Emperor Dom Pedro of Brazil, the exposition was as sprawling and unconstrained as the nation itself—attracting ten million visitors from all over the world with some 30,000 exhibits spread over 236 acres in Fairmount Park. The main exhibition hall, nearly a third of a mile in length, was the largest building in the world. Thomas Edison was there to demonstrate his automatic telegraph; Alexander Graham Bell first showed off his telephone. Composers and poets from Richard Wagner to John Greenleaf Whittier contributed the hymns that burst from massed orchestras and choirs at the opening ceremony. One young lady wrote: "Dear Mother, Oh! Oh! O-o-o-o-o-o-o-o-o!!!!!!"

The center of attraction was Machinery Hall, with a goliath steam engine powering thirteen acres of machinery through a liana-forest of belts and shafting. The engine, designed and built by George Corliss, a Providence manufacturer, was forty-five feet high, with two ten-foot pistons and a massive flywheel, fifty-six tons, thirty feet in diameter, rotating thirty-six times a minute. On opening day, Grant and Dom Pedro climbed up on the apparatus before a packed, hushed hall and pulled the levers that released the steam. There was a hiss, a visible shudder, the pistons slowly began to move, and then the flywheel turned, picking up speed as the shafts and belting stirred, and all the machines moved, hesitantly for a moment before springing into life with a vast clatter, sawing logs, shaving metal, printing wallpaper and newspapers. The pharaonic immensity of the Corliss engine became the symbol of the Exposition. But its silence—the product of beautifully precise engineering—was as awesome. Amid all the busy machine-clamor, the engine dispensed its vast reserves of power serenely, as a god would do. Walt Whitman came and sat before it for a full half hour. William Dean Howells wrote:

> The Corliss engine does not lend itself to description; its personal acquaintance must be sought by those who would understand its vast and almost silent grandeur. It rises loftily in the centre of the huge structure, an athlete of steel and iron with not a superfluous ounce of metal on it; the mighty walking beams plunge their pistons downward, the enormous flywheel revolves with a hoarded power that makes all tremble, the hundred life like details do their office with unerring intelligence. In the midst of this ineffably strong mechanism is a chair where the engineer sits reading his newspaper, as in a peaceful bower. Now and then he lays down his paper and clambers up one of the stairways that cover the framework, and touches some irritated spot on the giant's body with a drop of oil.

The metaphor of the Mega-Machine captured the scale shift that was underway in America. With the upsurge of railroad building at the end of the decade, America doubled the track mileage of Europe. The railroads, in turn, were a primary force in the expansion and centralization of iron, steel, and coal operations and the industrialization of food production. The separation of population centers and food supplies became the norm, which was something new under the sun. Mega-Machine was also the natural metaphor for the megaorganizations arising to mediate the transition. Merely substitute the word *corporation* for *engine* in the snippet from Howell, and *manager* for *engineer*.

Seizing on the openings created by the 1873 crash, Carnegie, Gould, and Rockefeller all played primary roles in driving the scale shift—Carnegie the expansion in steel, Gould in railroads, and Rockefeller, who started with

The great Corliss engine that powered the machinery at the Philadelphia Centennial Exposition became a symbol of America's mechanical prowess. President Ulysses S. Grant stands on the dais in this engraving.

the cleanest slate, actually creating an entity that came closest of any to the perfect global machine of the metaphor. Morgan plied his trade as a banker, and would emerge after yet another market break in the 1880s as the regulator of machines that other people built.

The Edgar Thomson Works

Prior to the Civil War, the array of four-story brick textile mills in Lowell, Massachusetts, were America's most imposing manufacturing plants. Andrew Carnegie's Edgar Thomson Steel Works, opened in the summer of 1875 and covering 106 acres on the banks of the Monongahela River just outside Pittsburgh, was an altogether different proposition. The rail mill alone was bigger than a football field.

More than sheer size, the process flow signaled a new era. Pig iron was melted in giant cupolas, then poured into twelve-ton "tipping cupolas" that fed the stream of iron directly into Bessemer converters. A converter looked like a giant black dinosaur's egg; standing on end, it was as tall as a big tree. When it was full of molten iron, air was pumped into the center of the mass by steam-powered blowers, igniting oxygen with a thunderous shudder and triggering a chain of violent chemical reactions that left an almost pure, silvery pool of liquid steel. The converter, which was suspended on swivels, was tipped to pour the steel into oblong ingot moulds on moving rollers. As described by the plant's designer, Alexander Holley, the ingots were dropped "hot out of their moulds" into railroad cars and were "not again lifted." Moving rollers collected the ingots, still red-hot, at the rail mill where they were cut and trimmed, then:

> . . . pressed with uniformity and precision . . . by hydraulic fingers. . . .
> As a result, they cool almost perfectly straight . . . [in contrast to] rails
> which have been bent and twisted by hand operations, which cannot, of
> course, be precise and uniform. One man and a boy, by means of levers,
> operate all this moving and curving machinery, and also the saws.

The cold saws were marvels in their own right. "Massively fitted" and "rigidly counterweighted" so they would stay true at speeds of 1,800 revolutions per minute, they could cut "a sixteenth-inch slice off the end of a rail."

Holley was the greatest steel plant designer of the era, and the "ET" works were his baby. The ET was the first he had built from scratch—all of his other plants were retrofits—and with Carnegie, when efficiency was at stake, cost was no object. In effect, it was Holley's chance to do everything right; in his own words:

As the cheap transportation of supplies of products in process of manufacture, and of products to market, is a feature of first importance, these
works were laid out, not with a view of making the buildings artistically
parallel with the existing roads or with each other, but of laying down
convenient railroads with easy curves; the buildings were made to fit the
transportation.

The river site offered convenient barge connections for the indispensable
supplies of coke, while the plant buildings were adjacent to both the Pennsylvania's main line and the Pittsburgh branch of the Baltimore & Ohio.
(Carnegie counted on the Pennsylvania as a major customer, but bitter
experience had taught him to protect himself on railroad rates. The name
"Edgar Thomson"—after the Pennsylvania president—was an all too trans-
parent peace offering for setting up the competition with the B&O.) The
ET's internal product flow moved via its own narrow-gauge railroad, with
tracks depressed or elevated as needed so materials were always loaded or
unloaded downward. Time-consuming manual tasks were eliminated as far
as possible. Since 2,000° temperatures quickly destroyed the fire-brick lining in the converters, Holley designed the converter bottoms to be snapped
in and out, so brick relining would not interfere with production uptime.
Almost thirty years later, an English expert detailed the hallmark features of
American steel-making—the absence of manual processing, the continuous
flow of material, the pervasive mechanization; all of them, along with a gim-
let eye to the costs of sourcing and distribution, were in place from the
beginning.

The ET works is one of the clearest highway markers on America's push
to the front ranks of manufacturing nations. Carnegie, of course, wasn't
playing the pioneer as a gift to his adopted country. The plant was profitable
almost from the moment it opened, producing a 20 percent return on
investment by its second full year of operation. "Where is there such a business!" Carnegie crowed.

Steel Is King

If you believed in America, you believed in railroads. And if you believed in
railroads, you believed in steel. It was insatiable demand for steel rails by

American railroads that made steel a mass production business and led to its gradual supplanting of iron for most industrial purposes. The conversion to steel from iron rails was led by the Pennsylvania's Thomson in the mid-1860s. The Pennsylvania, in the heartland of American heavy industry, had the most intensive traffic patterns and heaviest freights of any system, and its managers were alarmed at the ever-shorter service lives of iron rails. Thomson began experimenting with imported steel rails in 1861, and by mid-decade was convinced they would give him eight times the service life at only twice the cost. Since there was only a handful of American suppliers, the Pennsylvania, with characteristic thoroughness, created its own steel company, Pennsylvania Steel, with both Thomson and Tom Scott as major shareholders. The steel company was spun off after the board forbade management cross-holdings in suppliers in 1874.

High-quality steel, especially for bladed weapons, was known almost from the beginning of history. Damascus steel, which originated in India, was the best-known of the ancient steels, while a beautifully executed Toledo sword was de rigueur for the wealthy medieval knight. Sheffield was already an important British steel center by the time of Chaucer, and its craftsmen began to develop comparatively high-volume production methods in the eighteenth century. Even in the 1870s, American toolmakers who needed high-quality cutting steel bought from Sheffield.

Traditional steel-making began with a high-quality iron ore. The ore was mixed with a carbon fuel, usually charcoal or coal, and later, coke, and melted in a furnace (smelting). The hot-blast furnace, invented in 1828, achieved very high temperatures by injecting superheated air, allowing the use of more abundant lower-quality ores. Since iron has a strong preference for oxygen, its impurities tend to be oxides that bind to the carbon in the fuel and are precipitated out as slag; nonoxide impurities were sequestered by additives like limestone. As the heavy iron sank to the bottom of the furnace, the slag was poured off the top, leaving a relatively pure, but carbon-rich, iron. High-carbon iron is fine for castings, but is brittle and hard to work. The softer, malleable "wrought iron," which accounted for the bulk of traditional sales, must be nearly carbon-free. (It was originally made by hammering out the carbon, hence its name.) Steel is wrought iron with small amounts of carbon added back to reach a balance of hardness and malleability. From the mid-eighteenth century, wrought iron was made by "puddling"—reheating the iron in a furnace with a high-oxide lining and slowly working it with a pole until the carbon was precipitated out. The last step in steel-making was to "recarburize" molten wrought iron by slowly working it in a carbon bath, separating out small quantities of steel by color and texture.

Making a modest batch of steel could take a week or more, and traditional techniques were carefully passed down from father to son; one Sheffield recipe started by adding "the juice of four white onions." Superb product, like Sheffield's "crucible" steel, which was made in clay ovens to withstand the high temperatures required to remelt normal steel for further finishing, was both fiercely expensive and much in demand. As the underlying chemistry was better understood in the nineteenth century, steel came to be defined as a purified iron with a carbon content between 0.1 percent and 2 percent. Definitions remained controversial throughout the 1880s, as steel users like the Pennsylvania drove toward consistent quality standards and testing protocols.

The breakthrough to large-scale steel-making came in the 1850s from the prolific British inventor Henry Bessemer. Bessemer guessed that if he simply injected cold air into a chamber of molten iron, the oxygen in the air should, by itself, ignite the carbon in the iron and burn it off without puddling. It worked the first time he tried it: the oxygen almost instantly turned the iron white hot and burned off the carbon and most other contaminants in minutes, leaving the purest iron. Add back a small amount of carbon while the iron was still superheated and you had steel—the chemical violence in the chamber took care of the mixing. A process that had taken days, or even weeks, was reduced to twenty minutes or so. The fuel savings alone were as much as sevenfold.

Bessemer patented his invention in 1855, and his demonstrations were ecstatically received by the industry. Ecstasy turned to consternation when steel-makers trying it on their own got only a brittle, granular mess. Bessemer had unwittingly started with an ore that was unusually low in phosphorus, which turned out to be the one type of ore his process worked with. It was twenty years before the phosphorus problem was solved by a Welsh iron chemist and his cousin, a police court clerk, who came up with a "basic" furnace lining called the Thomas-Gilchrist process that precipitated out the acidic phosphorus. By that time, Bessemer's process had a rival in Charles Siemens's "open hearth" method. Siemens used a furnace similar to an iron puddler's, but achieved the required superheating by recycling waste gas

An 1880s-vintage Bessemer converter. It has just completed its "blow" and is beginning to tilt to pour its newly made steel into ingot molds.

through a clever array of brick chambers. The process was slower than Bessemer's, but many steel-makers thought it gave them better control.

Alexander Holley brought the gospel of steel to America. He is not much known now, but was important enough in his day that his statue, in full mustachioed glory, stands in New York City's Washington Square Park. Holley was a physically impressive polymath, born into a well-to-do Connecticut cutlery manufacturing family, and spent his formative years in the midst of the Connecticut River Valley machining boom. Holley naturally gravitated to machines and machine-assisted processes. He graduated from Brown University as a mechanical engineer, wrote a treatise on ordnance and armor manufacture, worked as a designer of locomotives, wrote reports on European railways, edited the *Railway Review,* wrote hundreds of articles for the *New York Times* on technical subjects, and was the moving spirit behind the formation of the American Society of Mechanical Engineers (ASME). Hearing of Bessemer's experiments, he went to England and convinced Bessemer to assign him the rights to the patents in America. By the time of his death in 1882 at the age of only fifty, Holley had personally designed six of the eleven Bessemer plants in America, and had consulted on three more, while the remaining two were copies of one of the plants he designed.

Holley's first design, in Troy, New York, was a radical departure in almost every feature from the plants he'd seen in England. From the start, Holley's plants were marked by continuous processing, a high degree of mechanization, and careful attention to materials management and process controls. In his designs, his speeches, and his addresses and articles for the ASME, he alternately scolded and goaded the industry to higher standards, better designs, more careful chemistry, less wasteful operations. "Where Bessemer left the process that bears his name, Holley's work began," one contemporary commented. When British steel-makers spoke with mixed admiration and fear about "American practice" in the 1880s, they were talking mostly about Alexander Holley.

There were two problems to be overcome before Holley could seed America with Bessemer mills. The first was the requirement for low-phosphorus ore, which was solved by the discovery that vast, but largely unexploited, ore reserves in the Michigan Upper Peninsula were ideal for Bessemer mills. The second was a dreadful patent snarl. There were two other competing patents in England and America besides Bessemer's. The incentive for a settlement was the dangling plum of a royalty contract from the Pennsylvania Steel Company. After prolonged haggling—and much mediating by Holley—the patents were pooled in 1866 in a new corporation that eventually took the name of the Bessemer Steel Association. The association was owned by the steel companies who were awarded the patents, so it ensured orderly accounting for the patent holders.

The members of the association did not fail to notice that they had also created an ideal forum for running a steel cartel. After 1876, they refused to issue patent rights to new entrants, and apparently subsidized the last patentee, the Vulcan Iron and Steel Works in St. Louis, as it struggled during its start-up phase. The association's attempts to control prices and assign market shares were never especially successful, in part because Carnegie typically broke the sharing agreements when it was in his interest to do so, but more fundamentally because of the spread of the Siemens open-hearth process in the 1880s. The key technical players in the association's meetings were Holley, John and George Fritz, brothers and innovative steelmen who ran the Bethlehem and Cambria works respectively (George died in 1873), and later Capt. William Jones, the formidable ET plant manager, and a fertile innovator in his own right.

King of Steel

Steel was Carnegie's first full-time commitment to a business since his early days at the Pennsylvania, and an ideal platform for displaying his superb talents as a chief executive. He was the controlling partner in the Keystone Bridge Co. and the Union Iron Mills,* which fabricated bridge parts; but except for the St. Louis Bridge, where he got stuck with the unenviable task of managing Captain Eads, he tended to act as the promoter and bond salesman, leaving bridge construction to his partners.

---

*The Union Iron Mills was famous for its "Lucy" blast furnace; at seventy-five feet tall, it was the largest in America when it was built in 1872. "Lucy" was Tom Carnegie's wife—blast furnaces were usually named after executives' wives, perhaps a trace of Victorian misogyny. Another Pittsburgh group soon built a furnace on the same dimensions, the "Isabella." The two were quickly locked in a production competition that set record after record well into the 1880s and was followed closely in the trade press and Pittsburgh papers.

Carnegie circled cautiously around steel for some time before taking the plunge. He had invested in a small plant that tried its hand at Bessemer steel in 1866 without success, in part because of problems with the ore. He had also prevailed upon a reluctant Thomson to try steel-capped iron rails, but they were a dismal failure. He had chafed at Eads's insistence on steel parts on the St. Louis Bridge; he eventually had to concede that Eads was right, but the steel was necessary only because Eads had vetoed the Keystone's original, very sensible, iron design. But Carnegie's lingering doubts were swept away by the huge British Bessemer plants he visited in 1872. Few businessmen understood the economics of scale as well as Carnegie: if steel could escape the realm of the hand craftsman, it would have a very big future indeed.

Carnegie put together a steel plant syndicate as soon as he got back to America, quickly raising $700,000. He put up $250,000 himself, while William Coleman, Tom Carnegie's father-in-law, put in $100,000, and also chose the plant's site on the Monongahela. The rest of the financing came from Pittsburgh businessmen, including William Shinn, a vice president of the Allegheny Valley Railroad, and David McCandless, one of the city's most respected leaders. (Respected enough that Carnegie named the new company Carnegie, McCandless & Company, although McCandless was one of the smaller investors.) The Union Iron Mills partners, Tom Carnegie, Andrew Kloman, and Henry Phipps, each put in $50,000, though they were skeptical of steel. Carnegie also sold a small amount of his own stock to Thomson and Scott, but later bought it back during the 1873 market crisis.

Holley was engaged almost immediately; he had made the first contact himself as soon as he heard of the new plant. His offer—$5,000 for the drawings and $2,500 a year for construction supervision—was one that could not be refused. The drawings took Holley only six weeks; he'd been thinking about the ideal plant for years and needed merely to fit his concepts to the Monongahela site. It was also Holley who introduced Carnegie to Captain Jones, who had fortuitously left the Cambria Works when Holley started his ET engagement. Jones may have been the greatest steel plant superintendent of the nineteenth century. He'd gotten his first job in an iron foundry at age ten, knew iron and steel inside out, was worshiped by his men, and was a creative inventor to boot—the ET rail-straightening apparatus that Holley was so proud of was Jones's invention, as was a later iron-mixing machine, a critical component of the continuous flow process.

When word spread that Jones was joining the ET, two hundred of Cambria's best men chose to follow him.

Shadows fell with the 1873 market crash, just as construction was moving into high gear. The ET was running out of cash—they had underestimated start-up costs—and wise men were telling Carnegie to put on the brakes. This was the precise moment when Carnegie was in most trouble on the St. Louis Bridge. The desperation bridge refinancing through Pierpont Morgan was not concluded until after the crash, and Morgan had set the strict December deadline for the closing of the span, which was met only by a hair's breadth after weeks of frantic work. Tom Carnegie and Kloman probably did not know how strapped Andrew was, but they were acutely aware of the shaky position in St. Louis.

Carnegie's financial stringencies led to a painful break with Tom Scott. Scott, still keeping his day job at the Pennsylvania, became president and chief shareholder of the Texas & Pacific Railroad in 1872. Carnegie didn't like the deal, but put in $250,000 as a friend, although he declined any management role. When the T&P got into serious trouble the next year, Scott, with Thomson adding his voice, pleaded with Carnegie to put in more money, or at least to help with Junius Morgan. Carnegie refused, fully acknowledging that Scott had a claim on him, but as he later put it, he was still a Scots and wasn't going to do anything stupid. That was doubtless part of it—the T&P was unrecoverable—but Carnegie also didn't want to admit that he had no money and that his reputation was at a low point with the Morgans.

Carnegie later boasted of the ET start-up, "A man who has money during a panic is a wise and valuable citizen." But the truth was that his funds were tapped out, and the decision to proceed with the ET was gutsy to the point of foolhardiness. On paper, Carnegie was a wealthy man: his personal balance sheet showed $2.1 million in assets at the end of 1873 and a net worth of $1.7 million. But it was almost all in stock, most of it illiquid securities in his own companies, with railroad-related shares the next largest category. His cash balance was under $5,000, and while he also showed $66,000 in receivables, some of them were probably very doubtful; this was a time that his companies, like the Union Iron Mills, were having trouble with their collections. His financial statements, moreover, recorded securities at par. That was the practice of the time, but it would have grossly overstated their value, since all shares, and especially railroad shares, were in free-fall. Carnegie did sell some of his Pullman shares, probably the stars of his portfolio, but there was no way he could float the ET on his own or come up with any money for Scott. The $250,000 he already had in the ET was all he could afford.

Somehow the ET stayed on schedule, aided by the collapse in construction and materials prices and the contractors' desperation to keep working. Then, as soon as Carnegie could certify that the St. Louis Bridge was finally completed, he boarded a boat with Holley for a pilgrimage to London and Junius Morgan, where they extolled the brilliant future in steel. (It is interesting that he didn't save time and boat fare by dealing through Pierpont. He probably had endured enough of Pierpont's famous brusqueness, while Junius, who clearly liked him, seemed more susceptible to his silver-tongued sales pitches.) Steel rails were fluctuating around $100 a ton in 1874, and he and Holley were confident that, with their huge converters, mechanized rail mill, and automated handling and loading, they could produce them for only $69. Morgan was sold, and agreed to float a bond issue of $400,000, enough to take out some of the weaker partners and see the project through. It is not likely that any other bank could have come up with the money in such an unsettled time. Missing the December deadline on the St. Louis Bridge would have bankrupted the bridge company, almost certainly forced a shutdown of the ET project, and might have ended Carnegie's foray into steel. On such threads the course of history hangs.

Carnegie gave a preview of his steel strategy two months before the ET got its first order. The occasion was a meeting of the Bessemer Association in June 1875, called by the "Fathers," the CEOs of the Bessemer companies, to discuss the continued depression in steel markets. Since the ET was nearing completion, Carnegie, McCandless was invited to send a representative. Carnegie chose to go himself—a clear sign that he attached special importance to the event. He doubtless knew through Holley and Jones, who were very plugged in at the association, that the Fathers were planning to lay down a market-pooling proposal.

The report of the meeting comes from an employee who was present at Carnegie's postmeeting partners' briefing and who recalled it many years later. The Fathers had duly proposed their pricing and market-allocation plan, which had obviously been agreed well in advance; Cambria was awarded the largest share at 19 percent, and so on down the list, with the ET, as the newest company, receiving the smallest allocation, at 9 percent. Carnegie jumped to his feet to claim the same share as Cambria, since the ET was the largest and most efficient plant in the industry. Otherwise, he announced, "I shall withdraw from [the pool] and undersell you all in the market—and make good money doing it." Carnegie had bought shares in all the other companies—all but the ET were publicly traded—so he knew what their costs and salaries were, and proceeded to lay out how much lower they were at the ET. Making all allowances for Carnegie's propensity for exaggeration, and the fallibility of second-hand accounts, something like that surely happened, for the ET, which had yet to produce an ingot, was allotted the same share as Cambria, the largest in the pool. The fact that his first full year's production barely covered the original 9 percent allocation wouldn't have bothered Carnegie: he was staking out a position as an agent of disruption. The story also illustrates Carnegie's lifelong disdain for pools. He was happy to join them, and was vigilant in enforcing them when it was in his temporary interest to do so, and as freely violated them when they were not.

Within twenty years, Carnegie Steel, Inc.—the product of successive reorganizations that consolidated all of Carnegie's steel-related properties, including the ET, the Lucy Furnace Works, the Union Iron Mills, acquisitions like the Homestead Works, and a host of coke, coal, and ore properties— was the largest steel company in the world, with total production about half that of Great Britain's and about a quarter of America's. It was also the most profitable by leagues, and was widely perceived as the market leader. By the 1880s, its structural steel handbooks, which covered beam and section designs, as well as loading and stress tables, were the industry bible. Its great capital resources enabled it to keep on the pressure during good times and bad. As a British scholar put it, "When demand slumped, the firm with the newest equipment—it was often Carnegie's—found that its losses were least (or those of its rivals most) when it reduced its prices so as to run fully occupied." With the purchase of the Frick Coke Co., Carnegie Steel enjoyed a dominant position in coke, and its acquisitions of vast Lake Superior ore reserves gave it a nearly overwhelming advantage in high-quality ore.

The rise of Carnegie Steel was not based on any hidden advantage or technical edge. Carnegie was a relatively late entrant to the industry, and all of his American competitors used essentially the same Holley plants as he did. The St. Louis Vulcan Works, for example, was virtually a duplicate of the ET; Holley himself once described the ET's rolling mill as the best in the United States, "[e]xcepting the mill of the Bethlehem Iron Company, as it will be when completed," which Holley, of course, was just then, in 1878, in the process of completing. The company's competitive advantage, it appears, was mostly Carnegie—his relentless pressure, his hounding to reduce costs, his instinct to steal any deal to keep his plants full, his insistence on always plowing back earnings into ever-bigger plants, the latest equipment, the best technologies. Other companies went through cycles of rise and decline, as founders got comfortable, shareholders demanded payouts, or good times allowed workers and managers to cruise a bit—as almost the entire British steel industry did after the great rail boom of the 1880s. But for twenty-five years Carnegie never let up.

Although Carnegie held no title, he was clearly the boss: the very ambiguity of his role may have increased his power, for there were no channels or protocols that might limit his access. Until Captain Jones's death, from a blast furnace accident in 1889, they maintained an active correspondence in which he goaded Jones with Cambria production figures, although the ET almost always outproduced them: the "ET nag is beginning to show in front as usual," Jones crowed in mid-1881. The correspondence also suggests the degree of involvement Carnegie had in day-to-day affairs. Here is Jones, writing in 1883, for example, as part of an extended exchange on a method for eliminating a step in the rail-making process that had been espoused by Holley:

> I tried this week rolling direct from shears but I confess I do not like it, and am sure it will increase our percentage of seconds besides being too severe on the machinery . . . better and cheapest as well as the best plan is to re-heat on my proposed new arrangement I hope to have plans ready in a few weeks to show you what I am aiming at.

Carnegie also insisted on railroad-style cost accounting, with impressive results. Jones's monthly reports carefully spread labor costs over each product and process, tracked all raw material inputs and percentages of waste and scrap, as well as defective manufactures and returns, uptimes and idling of major plant components, like furnaces and converters. Month-to-month trends and annual comparisons were split out by ton produced, by furnace, by type of ore, by source of the coke, by type of transport. Some reports are clearly the results of special analyses, like an analysis of alternative conversion processes and an 1883 study of metal losses, which was a major bugaboo of Holley's. The report samples surviving in the archives are often heavily annotated in Carnegie's swift, elegant hand. He later said that managers hated the reports and it took years to get them right. Carnegie had a fine eye for talent, but he was a high-tension manager, battering his partners with questions on anomalies, or slippages, and especially on quality problems, which he abhorred, writing, for example, that complaints from a railroad were:

> . . . very sad indeed. No one can hold his head up when he looks at them. Now this will not do and should not be repeated. It is ruin to send out bad rail especially to Eastern lines where inspection is always severe. . . . I would rather today pay out of my own pocket 5000 dollars than have had this disgraceful failure occur.

Carnegie's quasi-official role in the early years was as the company's salesman, a job that he filled superbly. ET production was then almost 100 percent devoted to rails, and Carnegie's connections among railroaders were both deep and broad. He was also an inveterate haggler, and while he hated to lose a deal on price, he never left money on the table. Price negotiations with John Garrett, the head of the B&O, who was as devoted a haggler as Carnegie, were always battles. In one prolonged negotiation, when Cambria was significantly underbidding the ET, Carnegie stuck with his price, but got the sale by demonstrating that the B&O's profits from shipping the order would offset the discount from Cambria, which had to ship via the Pennsylvania. (Typically for Carnegie, he was unmoved when the reverse argument was pressed by Henry Frick, who became chairman of Carnegie Bros., the ET's parent, in 1889: Frick wanted Carnegie to ease up on his constant war against railroad shipping rates, since the roads were his main customers.)

The dual roles as primary owner and chief salesman gave Carnegie the ideal vantage point for tuning production and pricing, and evaluating the profitability of new investment. He understood the subtle absorptions of fixed costs that improve margins as production is pushed further out the curve of the possible. As he put it early in the ET's life:

Two courses are open to a new concern like ours—1st Stand timidly back, afraid to "break the market" [or] . . . 2nd To make up our minds to offer certain large customers lots at figures which will command orders—For my part I would run the works full next year even if we made but $2 per ton.

Carnegie loved Jones's devotion to "hard-driving," or pressing the limits of furnace capacities and constantly striving toward higher temperatures in blast furnaces and converters. The British thought hard-driving was wasteful, since furnace linings had to be replaced more frequently, but Carnegie had the cost figures to back up his strategies. Significantly, hard-driving was most effective with very large blast furnaces, which suited Carnegie's taste exactly. He must have gnashed his teeth when he could not bid on a major Pennsylvania order in 1878 because the ET had no spare capacity; and there were major plant additions in 1879 (including a massive new blast furnace). Finally, since Carnegie traveled more than anyone else in the company, and was constantly on the lookout for new technologies, he was among the best informed people within the company on technical developments.

Over the years, the reinvestment imperative became a major source of contention between Carnegie and his partners. Carnegie insisted on keeping salaries low, since the partners stood to become wealthy through their shareholdings. (The exception was Bill Jones. He didn't want stock—he claimed to be a simple man—but felt he deserved to be the highest-paid superintendent in the industry. He asked for $20,000 a year, but said he would settle for $15,000. Carnegie, in a brilliant stroke, gave him $25,000, binding his loyalty for life.) Dividend payouts were also very low, only about 1 percent, a risible amount by nineteenth-century standards. Carnegie himself had no difficulty financing a regal life style, for he owned such huge blocks of his companies, and had many other investments besides. But his partners, although they were well-to-do, did not have nearly the incomes of their peers in less successful companies. There had also been flare-ups over stock valuations when two partners had departed under contentious circumstances. The rules for stock withdrawals were finally standardized only in 1887, with the so-called Iron-Clad Agreement. It provided that a withdrawing partner would get a book-value payout, with larger withdrawals scheduled over a period of years. A partner could also be forced out upon a three-quarters partners' vote—a provision that obviously did not apply to Carnegie, since he owned more than half the stock.

There was always a double standard for Carnegie and his partners. He was adamant, for example, that they should not have outside business interests, although in the 1880s, he spent half his time in the United Kingdom playing newspaper tycoon. Unlike Rockefeller, Carnegie always displayed an approach-avoidance relation with his enterprises. When he had to, as during his stints with the army railroads or as the Pennsylvania's western superintendent, he could throw himself into the work. But one suspects it was a massive exercise of will, for his instinct was always to recoil from gritty reality, and from ordinary workers. He usually stayed well removed from Pittsburgh, preferring to manage through written reports and correspondence (he insisted he wasn't managing, merely expressing opinions). It may have made him more effective. By staying clear of operating responsibilities, he was free to criticize and harass without worrying about possible shortfalls in his own performance. (He was responsible for sales in the early days, of course, but no salesman fears a quota if he has final say on price.) Had he been more involved, with more to account for, he may not have been so obdurately unreasonable, so unwilling to understand how there could be a defective shipment, or budget overruns, or unplanned furnace downtimes. He might have been easier to live with, that is, but a less successful tycoon.

Gould, Back from the Grave

The wise men of Wall Street had seen Jay Gould safely buried with a bloody stake in his heart in 1872. To their shock, just two years later, he walked the earth yet again, suddenly in control of the Union Pacific, one of America's greatest, if most troubled, roads. Given his lurid record during the Erie Wars and in the Gold Corner, investors worried in public that he would just "*steal* all [the UP's] available money . . . and ultimately leave the long bond holders out in the cold." The *New York Times* was caustic about "the elevation of Mr. Gould . . . following upon the heels of an infamous career."

Of all the railroads beaten down by the crash of 1873, the UP may have been laid the lowest. The UP was the transcontinental link from the Atlantic to the Pacific, a cornerstone of the Whig development program rushed through Congress in the darkest days of the Civil War. It was also one of the heroic engineering feats of the age. Muletrains fought through blizzards to haul rails up Rocky Mountain passes. Tunnels of extraordinary length were blasted through solid rock, and spidery bridges flung over nearly bottomless chasms. Workers were killed by Indians, were taken by grizzlies and cougars, and died from falls or from exposure after becoming separated from their party in the trackless wilderness. And yet when the "Golden Spike" linked the UP with the Central Pacific at a point just north of Utah's Great Salt Lake, in May 1869, the road was within shouting distance of its schedule and budget.

Engineering may have been among the least of its problems. As a creature of Congress, the UP was plagued by politics at every stage of its life. Critical decisions, like choosing the eastern terminus for the line, triggered frenzied lobbying. A core problem was that, in their zeal to protect the public purse, suspicious congressmen riddled the legislation with protective provisions that made the road's securities unsalable. The promoters, who included Massachusetts senator Oakes Ames and his brother, Oliver, therefore fell back on a common railroad financing device, the independent construction company. Since the road was entitled to collect federal construction subsidies as each section was completed, the construction company could sell its own stocks and bonds and repay investors as the subsidies were earned. But since the same men managed both the construction company and the railroad, there was an almost irresistible opportunity for self-dealing. Perversely, the managers called the construction company the Crédit Mobilier of America, after a well-known French development bank (they liked the cachet). Small-town congressmen naturally smelled foreign influence, and suspicions rose higher when the French bank collapsed amid a noisy scandal of its own in 1867.

The American Crédit Mobilier scandal, which broke in 1872, has forever fixed the reputation of the Grant administration as equal parts farce and scandal. Letters showed that Oakes Ames had spread Crédit Mobilier shares among congressmen to win passage of critical legislation five years before. Ames, who insisted he had done nothing wrong, was outraged when one congressman after another denied having anything to do with him or with the Crédit Mobilier. So he laid his notes before the committee, with names, dates, and the amounts of money involved, forcing the panicked investigators into embarrassed retreat. It almost ruined James Garfield's career—he had taken a $370 check from Ames—while Vice President Schuyler Colfax, who had received stock from Ames when he was speaker of the House, was dropped from the 1872 Grant reelection ticket.* Ames was eventually censured for attempting bribery, but amid much editorial guffawing, the congressmen were exonerated on the theory that they hadn't understood Ames's intentions—as if congressmen as a class were entitled to a defense of diminished responsibility.

As Gould later told it, he became involved with the UP almost by accident. He had emerged from his Erie ouster as a wealthy man, and the runup in Erie shares during the market boom of 1872 and early 1873 made him wealthier still. He cooperated in some profitable railroad stock operations with the Vanderbilts, of all people, through the person of Cornelius's son-in-law, Horace Clark. When the Vanderbilts took a position in the UP, Clark became the UP president. According to Gould, Clark told him it was an attractive stock, so he instructed his broker to buy whatever became available below 30. When Clark died after a short illness in the spring of 1873, his brokers liquidated his UP holdings, causing a sharp price drop. Gould's broker snapped it up, and Gould unexpectedly found himself in a control position. It was only at that point, he said, that he learned that the road had serious problems, including $5 million in unsecured call debt and $10 million in bonds due in just a few months. Worse, operations were floundering from a prolonged stretch of rudderless leadership.

The story of the stock purchase might be true, since Gould's tall tales were always grounded in bits of truth, but it is inconceivable that he took over the road by inadvertence or without understanding its problems. Before he bought his UP shares, Gould had become a major shareholder in Pacific Mail, a freight and steamship operation that competed directly with the UP for Asian trade, so he had an excellent understanding of the competitive

---

*By the standards of the Erie, the Crédit Mobilier scandal was decidedly small beer. Robert Fogel's careful reconstruction concludes that, given the risks assumed, the promoters, who put up a lot of their own money, did not earn unreasonable returns. Ames did lie about one critical point, however. When he was testifying on construction reimbursement rates in 1866 he said that the UP still had not found a practical path across the continental divide. In fact, not long before his testimony, a cavalry detachment had rescued a UP engineering crew under attack by a Crow war party. The intrepid chief engineer, Grenville Dodge, noticed how the Crow melted away when the cavalry appeared. Trailing the escaping Crow, he found the long-sought western passage. Ames's correspondence leaves no doubt that he had been informed. Presumably, if Congress had known, they would have set a lower reimbursement rate, and to that extent UP investor returns were excessive. Dodge's exploit gives a flavor of the heroism that was part of the UP routine.

landscape. Gould was no longer just the stock-jobber of contemporary legend. He had been badly bitten by the railroad bug, and the UP was the perfect vehicle for rebuilding his reputation.

The smoothness of Gould's takeover in early 1874 also suggests considerable behind-the-scenes preparation, for it was accomplished with the full cooperation of the key group of Boston investors. Oakes Ames had died within a year of the Crédit Mobilier flap, but Oliver Ames continued on the board, and Oakes's son took his father's seat. Gould did not take a title, but had a seat on the executive committee and had four additional board seats, which he filled with his brokers. Sidney Dillon was named UP president. He was from New York, but had long been involved with the Bostonians. He was an imposing, energetic sixty-one-year-old and one of the country's most experienced railroad construction executives; for the rest of their lives, he and Gould were the closest of allies. Russell Sage, who had been president of the Pacific Mail, also grew very close to Gould. From that point, in the words of historian Maury Klein, "The surest sign that Jay had taken hold of a company was the accession to its board of Gould, Sage, and Dillon."

Gould's performance at the UP quickly turned Wall Street's forebodings into hosannahs. For most people, it was the first time they had seen his talents deployed in a constructive cause. In less than a year, in a sustained market operation that dazzled professionals, the UP's debt problems had been cleared up, while the Pacific Mail had been brought firmly under UP control,* removing an important source of price instability. Management had been streamlined and centralized under Silas Clark, a career railroad man who became another lifelong Gould loyalist. Costs were down, and prices had been strengthened across the board. Gould worked personally with western ranchers to make the UP more cattle-friendly, while land sales, coal earnings, and other nonfare revenues were all on the upswing. Earnings jumped 27 percent in 1874 and another 30 percent in 1875. By early 1875, the UP's bonds were closing in on par, and the stock price had quadrupled. Trading in UP shares frequently accounted for more than half of Stock Exchange activity.

---

*When merger discussions with Pacific Mail broke down, Gould executed one of his classic bear raids, driving down the price of the stock, then stealthily snapping it up at bargain prices. Pacific Mail executives woke up one morning to find themselves working for the UP. The exercise was a warning to all but the most powerful companies that with Gould at the helm, the UP had sharp teeth.

When Gould declared the company's first-ever dividend in the spring of 1875, he metamorphosed into an almost mythic figure. A railway journal commented on Gould's "magical wand" and went on, "The truth is that one man holds almost undisputed sway over the movements of the Stock Exchange. . . . Under these extraordinary circumstances, to write of the New York Market is simply to describe the movements of Jay Gould." Professionals gradually accepted that he was in for the long haul instead of just dressing up the UP for a quick stock sale. Even Collis Huntington, the formidable senior partner in the Central Pacific, who had long been at odds with the UP, was changing his view. He still feared that Gould "will play us false, although I am not sure that I have any good reason for thinking so."

But the UP was by no means out of the woods, for its obligations to the government were in a terrible tangle. The Pacific Road legislation—governing both the UP and Huntington's CP—framed the construction subsidies as loans, paying interest at 5 percent of net earnings as soon as the road was completed. But there was no definition of "completion"—the government argued it was in 1869 when the Golden Spike was driven; the UP, not unreasonably, thought it was in 1874, when the roads qualified for their final land grants. The government also defined "net earnings" as earnings *before* interest was paid, while the roads assumed "net" meant after interest. While the interest was in dispute, the Treasury refused to pay its bills for mail services, an important part of the transcontinental freight.

Grant and his cabinet signed off on a compromise in 1875 that provided for a straightforward schedule of fixed payments, but for some reason never submitted the legislation—possibly because of appeals from stock market bears who had been badly burned by the UP's advance. The next year, the last for the Grant administration, the Pacific Road amendments got lost in a ferocious lobbying campaign by Tom Scott to rescue his bankrupt Texas & Pacific. Saving the T&P became a major plank in the notorious "Compromise of 1877": Rutherford B. Hayes won crucial Southern support in his deadlocked presidential contest with James G. Blaine in return for ending Reconstruction, withdrawing Northern troops, and financing Scott's railroad and some flood control projects. Collis Huntington, who should have been shoulder to shoulder with Gould, dissipated most of his energies opposing the T&P to keep Scott out of California. In the end, Hayes got the critical Southern votes, but never delivered the railroad legislation. Scott was distracted by the 1877 railroad strikes, and was ill and partially paralyzed after

1878. He retired from the Pennsylvania in 1880 and died the following year. Meanwhile, memories of Crédit Mobilier and the Gold Corner scuttled any hopes of congressional action on the Pacific Roads.

The years 1878 and 1879 were difficult for Gould. The only railroad legislation that finally came out of Congress actually worsened the UP's position, dashing his hopes for a reasonable compromise with the government. On top of that, he took heavy losses by shorting the stock market in anticipation of America's return to the gold standard. (Resumption went so smoothly that it triggered a miniboom. Gould's genius was in corporate finance; his record as a market analyst was mediocre at best.) Rumors abounded that Gould was in trouble, as he indeed may have been.

But his enemies were mistaken if they took comfort in his woes. A decade before, he had taken control of the Erie after a devastating struggle that had decimated the Erie's treasury, enriched his primary adversaries, and left him in an apparently hopeless competitive position. His response had been to attack, on every front, against all of his competitors, all at the same time. The year 1879 found him bedraggled and battered, but not nearly so weak as he had been in 1869. And once again he went on the attack, and this time rewrote the nation's railroad map and made himself the most powerful financial player in the country, very close to being the master of all he surveyed.

Gould (Almost) Conquers All

By about 1883, after four years of unrelenting assault on all sides, Gould emerged in control of virtually the whole center of the country's railroad system, even as he was aggressively expanding his operations eastward and into the West, Northwest, and Southwest. He also controlled Manhattan's rapid transportation system; he had buttressed his image by investing in newspapers; and as the primary owner of the Western Union company, he dominated the national system of telegraphy. His powers had become the stuff of legend, and deservedly so, considering the weakness of his initial position. The *New York Times* was reduced to helpless amazement:

> But straightaway we are assured that "JAY GOULD" is at the bottom of the whole affair, as he is said to be at the bottom of everything that goes

on nowadays. We strongly suspect that he will yet be found to . . . have had something to do with the hard Winter, frozen water-pipes, and plumbers' extravagant bills. He doubtless formed a "ring" with the plumbers sometime last Summer, and then produced the recent severe cold, so as to get all his machinery to work.

And later:

The yacht of Mr. JAY GOULD, it appears, ran through a tug yesterday for the purpose of hitting a schooner on the other side. The natural conjecture that Mr. GOULD had "gone short" of both of the injured vessels will, we trust, prove to be baseless . . . but he ought not to prey upon our merchant marine.

Competitors sought safety in paranoia. A railroad executive lamenting Gould's control of Western Union wrote to a colleague: "I am so fully convinced that Gould . . . read[s] all messages that look like R.R. messages that I dare not trust the wires except with a cypher which I change from day to day." A more practical assessment came from an executive of the Texas & Pacific after Gould bought the line from Tom Scott in 1881:

I never had much respect for Tom Scott's ability to *accomplish* any great undertaking. He can give everybody a Pass, and get them to say he is a "big Injun" and good fellow—but he is not the man to lay down a Hundred or Two Hundred Thousand Dollars Cash, to carry a scheme of his own. . . . [Gould is] the reverse of Scott; he is a one man power; consults no one, advises with no one, confides in no one, has no friends, wants none—is bold. Can always lay down Two or Three Hundred Thousand Dollars to accomplish his plans and *will* do it if he thinks it will pay.

Most railroad men in Gould's day understood that railroads were natural monopolies, since few localities generated the traffic to support competitive lines. The conventional solution was to enter into gentlemen's agreements to respect preestablished competitive boundaries, dividing up the traffic in a "friendly" way. Such "pooling" arrangements became standard practice in the decade after the Erie Wars—watching Scott nearly run the Pennsylvania aground in his furious reaction to Gould's 1869 onslaught was sufficient caution on the pitfalls of unrestrained competition. The doyen of pooling was Albert Fink, who had come up the ranks at the Baltimore & Ohio before becoming a senior executive at the Louisville & Nashville, where he organized a comprehensive pool for the southeastern lines in the mid-1870s. Fink then became the first commissioner of the Eastern Trunkline Association, an even larger pool, and by dint of meticulous paperwork and proselytizing zeal, quickly signed up almost all the railroads east of the Mississippi. It was a high point of the will-o'-the-wisp pursuit of rationally ordered industrial relationships that so preoccupied late nineteenth-century businessmen, none more so than Pierpont Morgan. Fink's lasting contribution may be as an evangelist for cost accounting, in part to support revenue and pricing agreements among his pool members.

Gould did not think like most railroad men. Like Carnegie and Rockefeller, he regarded pools as refuges for the weak, although useful for masking predatory intentions. The solution for the fragmented state of the railroads was to consolidate, not to negotiate elaborate paper compacts. Roads that were willing to join his network would find him a fair purchaser; holdouts would find themselves under attack in the securities market. Since railroads' enormous capital requirements could be met only by a wide distribution of securities, even the strongest roads were vulnerable. Gould chose his battles with discretion, and never engaged in pointless warfare with men as capable and as determined as himself, like Huntington. (He once did propose a local pooling arrangement to Huntington, but it was carefully designed to meet both of their interests, was quickly understood and accepted, and lasted for almost fifty years.) But he was quick to spot men like William H. Vanderbilt, whom the gods who look after market traders put on earth to be shorn. As Cornelius's oldest son, "Willie" had assumed leadership of the family properties on his father's death in 1877, and Gould stripped away the great railroad and telegraph holdings one by one, the way a wolf takes bites out of a running deer.

By 1883, Gould had become the dominant owner of, or controlling shareholder in, or chief executive of, literally dozens of railroads, some of them only for brief periods of time. The blur of activity sent shock waves of alarm through competitors even as it delighted stock traders, many of whom grew wealthy divining what Gould was up to and following in his wake. It wasn't easy, for his intentions were always veiled in clouds of misdirection. Even people who understood that he wasn't just stock-jobbing, but wanted to run a big chunk of the rail system, were confused by his identification with the Union Pacific. But once Gould despaired of settling the government's claims against the UP, he quietly reduced his holdings, using the profits to shift into other lines. He moved so quickly and so silently that competitors who thought they had a truce with the UP would be shocked to find themselves under siege by Gould—discovering much too late that Gould was acting for the Kansas Pacific, or the Missouri Pacific, or the Wabash.

When he was at the Erie, Gould had simultaneously attacked the four major systems that stood between him and the Midwest. He forced a major restructuring of rates and system coverage, but came out the loser when he lacked the money to follow through on his initial victories. A decade later, he had plenty of money, but the position was much more complex, involving many more roads. The UP controlled the main transcontinental artery, but was surrounded by formidable combinations intent on nibbling away at its franchise. To the east stood the Iowa Pool, a collection of eight lines, with a common strategy of building westward. Charles E. Perkins, one of the more competent and determined railroad executives of the period, would prove a formidable foe, but in 1878 his fellow Iowa Pool executives were not yet heeding his warnings about Gould. To the far west, Huntington and his three partners, Mark Hopkins, Charles Crocker, and Leland Stanford, had pretty well locked up California, but the important Rocky Mountain ore trade, centered around Denver and stretching from New Mexico to Montana and eastward to the Black Hills, was still wide open, although there were a variety of ambitious contenders. Finally, the Southwest was strewn with the blasted hopes of earlier entrepreneurs, as symbolized by the sun-bleached bones of Tom Scott's Texas & Pacific. But Gould had worked hard at cultivating cattlemen at the UP and surely understood how meat packing was transforming southwestern ranching.

When the smoke cleared, Gould was chief executive and primary owner of one of the major Iowa Pool lines, the Wabash; had control or near-control positions in several others; and was playing havoc with the pool's careful rate and market sharing arrangements. He had taken over the two most important Rocky Mountain lines, the Kansas Pacific and the Denver Pacific, and merged them with the UP, taking a very large payoff in UP stock. He also controlled the main gateway from the Southwest to St. Louis through the Missouri Pacific, and had used that position to win more or less total control of the southwestern roads, including a revived Texas & Pacific. Lines that he controlled by one means or another included the Northwestern; the St. Joseph & Denver City; the Denver & South Park; the Denver & Rio

Grande; the Central Branch Union Pacific (no relation to the UP); the Pueblo & St. Louis; the Bee Line; the Delaware, Lackawanna & Western; the Kansas & Texas; the Quincy; the Iowa; the Peoria; the Hannibal; the New Orleans Pacific; the Iron Mountain; the East St. Louis & Carondelet; the International Great Northern; the Wilmington; the Reading; the Central of New Jersey; plus several major bridges, including the St. Louis Bridge, which he had taken off the Morgans' hands at a price that made Junius and Pierpont blush. And that is not a complete list.

Almost every one of those deals was negotiated personally by Gould, which is astonishing. Rockefeller's rollup of the refining industry was taking place at the same time, but refinery deals usually just required striking a book-value price with one or a few owner-partners. The wide distribution of railroad securities meant that even small deals could involve a large number of parties, many with conflicting interests, and many of them abroad, multiplying the burden of analytic work and legal preparation. Unlike Morgan, who built an impressive staff of senior partners to work on his railroad restructurings in the nineties, Gould did most of the work himself. He had lawyers he relied on, and he regularly took counsel with Dillon and Sage, and often the cable mogul Cyrus Field, but the heavy lifting on strategy and analytics was all his. At the same time, he somehow stayed actively involved in the strategic management of his primary roads, restructuring finances, launching major construction and extension programs, and reassuring investors. (Maury Klein, the leading Gould scholar, makes a convincing case that, contrary to legend, and with the large exception of the Erie, Gould was not a looter of roads; he was, to the contrary, a superb strategist and better than average manager, who often put more money into his roads than he took out.) Amid all this blaze of activity he was the same hunched, frail figure, keeping his counsel, speaking only on the edge of audibility, maintaining his exquisite manners.

Vanderbilt detested him, and Gould crowded him from every side. In 1879, under heavy pressure from Gould on his westward routes, Vanderbilt decided to sell a large block of New York Central stock through Drexel, Morgan. Gould demanded that he be a part of the underwriting syndicate— i.e., get an insider's price and pick up investment banking fees besides. It looks like an intentionally humiliating exercise of power. Gould, of course, could justify taking a position in the New York Central, although he did not keep much of the stock, and there was reputational value from being a co-underwriter with Drexel, Morgan, but he was also training Vanderbilt in the proper degree of fear. That Vanderbilt let it happen must have earned Gould's scorn.

At the same time, Gould was using his railroad empire to attack Western Union, the crown jewel of the Vanderbilt holdings. Railroads and telegraphs were symbiotic businesses. Track rights of way were ideal for stringing lines, and stationmasters could double as the local telegrapher, since the roads all used telegraphy for traffic management. Gould, who always had an eye for collateral revenues, was attracted to telegraphy from his days at the Erie. His acquisition of the Western Union was completed in 1881, and is a classic illustration of the inexorability of a Gould offensive.

When Gould gained control of the Union Pacific, it possessed a telegraph company shell, the Atlantic & Pacific, but leased its lines to the Western Union. Gould and a few other directors purchased the A&P for a song, infused a small amount of cash, and began to compete with Western Union for railroad contracts. A few years before, Carnegie had also bought a small telegraph company and made a quick profit by "flipping" it to Western Union. Gould repeated the process with the A&P, getting a better price by throwing in a railroad that Vanderbilt coveted. But that was just a practice scrimmage. He waited a bit, and then after the Supreme Court had ruled against exclusive railroad contracts with telegraphy vendors, and he had built a bigger war chest and a much bigger portfolio of railroads, Gould created another telegraph company, the American Union.

Very quickly, all of the important Gould lines proceeded to sign up with the American Union, on terms the Western Union found ruinous. Gould then attacked Western Union's eastern stronghold by executing a contract to operate the independent Baltimore & Ohio telegraph company, which was owned by John Garrett, a longtime Vanderbilt opponent. Gould's railroads began to cut down Western Union connections and replace them with the American Union's. (This was pure vandalism, and directly violated the "no exclusivity" court decision Gould had celebrated.) Gould newspapers— by now he owned the *New York World* and had cultivated other friendly editors—publicized his statements about the evils of the telegraph monopoly, just as a mysterious bear attack materialized on Western Union stock. The stock dove further when it was revealed how much the American Union price war had damaged Western Union's profits. Gould, of course, used the price fall to amass a large position. The coup de grâce was Gould's announcement that the Pennsylvania would cancel its contract with Western Union and sign on with the American Union. The terms were outrageously in the Pennsylvania's favor, but who cared?

At that point it was over. Vanderbilt's board was reeling; they were mostly passive investors who just wanted their old dividends. A board contingent called on Gould and found him all sweet reason, as hopeful for peace and concord as they were. (Like Rockefeller, Gould never jeopardized a good deal by trying to squeeze out the last penny of advantage.) All flowed according to script. Western Union bought the American Union in a stock deal that made Gould the largest shareholder, with control of the board. Vanderbilt said he was happy with the outcome—as one scholar put it, happy to "hand over a large part of the value which his father had created, to his father's arch-foe—Gould."

Investors had no reason to be disappointed. Gould quickly disciplined transatlantic cable companies who had been whipsawing Western Union on connection rates by launching his own cable company and forcing a much more favorable arrangement. A few years later, Robert Garrett, John's son, who succeeded to the B&O and its telegraph business on his father's death, launched a price war to leverage Western Union into a buyout. Gould made no statement and engaged in no negotiations; instead, he impassively underpriced Garrett step by step, forced him into insolvency, and picked up the property on the cheap. In Klein's words, Garrett, unfortunately, "was no Gould, and the man on the other side of the table was." From that point, Western Union was secure at the top of its industry, and Gould maintained control of the company for the rest of his life.

Gould never achieved his objectives in railroads, although his influence was enormous. As much as any other individual he determined the final shape of the national system; the many thousands of rail miles built after he left the scene were mostly filling in the basic map as settlement thickened. In the process he also defined the pitfalls and potentials of securities markets, pitilessly exposing careless specifications of rights and priorities, putting a high degree of polish on the oldest methods of market manipulation, and inventing a host of new ones besides. There is hardly any securities wrinkle, even in the most recent market booms and busts, that was not limned in some way by Jay Gould. Pierpont Morgan was among those who learned those lessons well: in his financial restructuring of the railroad industry in the 1890s, his bonds and mortgages were crafted, almost point

After the Western Union takeover, a rather impish-looking *Puck Magazine* version of Jay Gould enjoys his stranglehold over commerce and the press.

for point, to eliminate the hidden traps that were always so obvious to Gould.

Perversely, it was Gould's genius as a market manipulator that undermined his achievements. His core strategy was to align coherent properties by obtaining control through the security markets, but he never wielded his empire into a consolidated entity. At Western Union, he could wage localized struggles with the resources of the whole company; but each unit of his sprawling railroad empire was owned by a separate coterie of investors. If one road was made a loss-leader to secure traffic for a broader array of properties, traders would attack its stock, and investor suits would fly. A market-based strategy, moreover, is always at the mercy of market movements. A fall in one stock might jeopardize share-collateral supporting some other holding. A serious market downturn in 1883, just as he reached the peak of his power, left him scrambling for cash, rushing from one collapsing dike to another. Few observers thought he could survive that episode. That he did so, more or less handily, and even returned to the control of the Union Pacific in 1890, is testimony to his extraordinary intelligence and determination. But by then he was already dying, although he kept it secret, trying to push his son, George, to the head of his enterprises. George, like Willie Vanderbilt, seems to have been a perfectly capable, intelligent, and reasonably hard-working man, but with no spark of his father's genius.

The economist Joseph Schumpeter once wrote that the American railroad boom meant "building ahead of demand in the boldest acceptance of the phrase," a strategy that was widely understood to entail "operating deficits for a period which it was impossible to estimate with any precision." One could quarrel with how wide the understanding was. A British journal commented on one of Gould's bond issuances in 1881:

> The brokers' circulars, which find their way through the post into every country house and rectory, were at one time full of the Wabash. Not one person in a thousand had the least idea where the road was, or whence it drew its traffic, or what sort of men conducted its affairs. . . . People rushed in to buy the shares with their eyes shut.

The perennial gullibility of the small investor aside, Schumpeter's basic point is surely right, at least with respect to western railroads.* Postwar railroad investments were typically of the "If you build it, they will come" variety. It is extraordinary to consider that such a vast assemblage of investment capital—at the time probably the largest and most concentrated in world history—was made for enterprises that mostly had no customers. The large land grants that typically accompanied western railroad charters, after all, were expressly designed to *induce* demand; western settlers sometimes got better deals on railroad land than under the Homestead Act. Market crazes, however, are usually based on fundamental truths, the occasional tulip mania to the contrary. Railroad promoters, just like Internet entrepreneurs in the 1990s, were correct in their perception that a business and consumer revolution was afoot—and were correct as well that the biggest gains would go to the first-movers. It's when the revolution has been absorbed into daily routines that sober second thoughts focus on the wastefulness. For railroads, the transition came sometime in the 1880s. A good milestone is Charles Perkins's 1882 comment that the entrepreneurial phase of railroad

---

*During the first period of intense railroad building in the 1840s and 1850s, most roads were apparently profitable from the outset. But they were built in thickly settled eastern states, or the eastern edges of the "west," and usually lagged demand.

development was essentially over; from that point the main challenge would be the "economical maintenance of the *machine*." Another way to put it was that the age of Gould was ending, and the age of Morgan—and under his protective umbrella also the age of corporate management—was about to begin.

Rockefeller's Machine

Railroads, and especially the Pennsylvania, are often credited with being the forerunners of modern corporate management. But Standard Oil bears comparison with any of them. It was as large and complex as any railroad, its operations were spread throughout the globe, and it may have been the only big business to control its entire value chain from production and processing of raw materials down through distribution to wholesalers and in many areas even to retailers.

Few consumer products have spread as rapidly as kerosene for lighting. Hardly a decade after Colonel Drake's well came home in Titusville it was the world's lighting choice. Hamlin Garland, in his tales of a hardscrabble childhood on a remote Great Plains farm, tells of the evening he came home from the fields in 1869 to the amazing transformation from a kerosene lamp on the dining room table, and how soon daily schedules reorganized themselves to take advantage of the longer day. That was the same year that the Stowe sisters, Harriet Beecher and Catherine, instructed readers of their *America's Woman's Home* that kerosene gives "as good a light as can be desired," suggesting a "student lamp" for late-night studying. Kerosene lamps—plain ones for ordinary people and elaborately decorated ones for the better off—were ubiquitous, as was kerosene, which was sold through pharmacies and grocery stores. The Standard's bright blue five-gallon cans were known throughout the world, with market shares in Europe, Russia, and China similar to those in America.

Rockefeller had completed his Cleveland takeover before the 1873 financial collapse. Financial markets, in any case, had minimal impact on the oil industry, and even less on Rockefeller's continuing drive toward consolidation. Since the Standard was already serving a world market, it was relatively insulated from temporary jags and bumps in America. Personally,

Rockefeller was very wealthy,* and was moving with his usual deftness on a national expansion almost as soon as his Cleveland acquisitions were digested. Within a half dozen years, Rockefeller had acquired more or less the whole of the national refinery capacity, and by the mid-1880s controlled petroleum distribution, and was moving into production as well.

The national acquisitions were accomplished with extraordinary speed and smoothness. The first stage came in 1874 and 1875, when Rockefeller quietly bought out the major players in each refining center—Charles Pratt's refinery in New York; the Warden interests (Atlantic Refining) in Philadelphia; Lockhart, Waring, and Frew in Pittsburgh; and the largest refineries in the oil region, including John Archbold's. Those transactions were remarkably strife-free, as if they happened by consensus. His initial targets were the most powerful and technically advanced in the industry; their executives had each won the top-dog role in an important region of the country and were not used to taking orders. Yet they all seem to have bought into his quiet insistence that consolidation was the path to salvation; that the Standard would be the entity that survived the mergers; and that he was the man to lead them. Warden's son recalled that his father was invited to examine the Standard's books and was astonished at its profitability, just as Oliver Payne had been in Cleveland a few years before. Each of the acquisitions was executed with Standard stock, which, for deal pricing purposes, was valued at almost three times what it had been in the Cleveland takeovers. The entire sequence is testimony to the mesmeric personal power of Tarbell's "bookkeeper."

The rollup was also managed with great stealth. An express condition of the first round of acquisitions is that they were to be kept secret. All of the acquired companies retained their management teams and their names, and, at least nominally, their own stock. Each of them then pursued a regional acquisition strategy in its own name and with its own stock or cash. The process in each region varied little from that in Cleveland; once the

---

*Rockefeller's personal annual statements are in a very similar format to Carnegie's. I could find statements for one or the other for a number of years in this period, but only one, from 1889, for the same year. Compared to Carnegie's $2.1 million in assets in 1873, for instance, Rockefeller's 1875 statement shows $1.1 million. About 45 percent was in Standard stock and 40 percent in local real estate, with only small outside shareholdings. He had clearly surpassed Carnegie by the mid-1880s. By 1889, he listed assets of $37.4 million compared to Carnegie's $13.6 million.

first couple of deals were done, the momentum for joining became irresistible. Almost everyone was in the fold by the end of 1878, with some trailing deals stretching on into 1879. Rockefeller's name was still not widely known, and even industry experts didn't know for sure what had happened until a Rockefeller lieutenant, Henry Rogers, who had himself come to the Standard with the Pratt acquisition, testified in 1879 that the Standard controlled "from 90 to 95 per cent of the refiners of the country."

Did the secrecy give the Standard an unfair advantage? Without question, although Rockefeller never apologized for it. It certainly made business sense, since even in Cleveland worthless companies had popped out of the woodwork as word spread that the Standard was making a clean sweep. An instance where "unfair" clearly tipped into "unethical" was in Baltimore. John Garrett of the Baltimore & Ohio undertook to organize his own local refinery interest in opposition to both the Pennsylvania Railroad and the Standard. He forged an alliance with the Camden refineries, the largest of the local players, and made elaborate anti-Standard plans without knowing that the Camden had long since become a Standard property. There were, of course, no disclosure rules governing corporate acquisitions, so no laws were violated, but Garrett almost certainly had a winnable common-law action against Camden and the Standard for deception.

For the most part, Rockefeller appears to have paid reasonable prices. John Archbold, who had been one of the most pugnacious of Rockefeller's critics before joining the fold, was point man in the oil region. (He eventually rose to president of the Standard and, true to form, was the most belligerent, indeed disrespectful, of all Standard executives in dealing with the government.) During a whirlwind of buyouts in 1877 and 1878, Archbold's letters to Rockefeller clearly suggest that speed was more important than price: over one stretch of several weeks he reported a deal almost every other day. He also obviously had a great deal of authority to close transactions.

For example, Archbold called the Valley Oil Works a "pretty well located small concern." He opened the bidding at $8,000 to $10,000 and closed a deal at $11,000, which he admitted was a "large price for the property + do not doubt" that he could have waited them out. "[W]hether the difference is worth the aggravation is the question," which accorded exactly with Rockefeller's usual approach. Another works estimated their book value at $15,000 and asked $25,000. Archbold reported that they claimed to be making "a fair profit" and would "prefer to take their chances on [going it alone]. . . . I doubt we can trade with them much under the figure named." In two other deals, he seems worried that he had gone too high: "As I telegraphed yesterday, completed the purchase of a Refinery + property at that point, for a consideration of . . . Twelve thousand dollars. I found it a very difficult trade to make + was compelled to make some concessions to the parties that I disliked very much to make." And in yet another: "I am quite sure that in view of all the circumstances attending the case you will agree with me as to the fairness of the transaction." Archbold also complained about continuing refinery start-ups: "The Fools as you see are not all dead," but later decided that they were "pure black-mailing operators."

The takeover of distribution was much noisier, but was over by about 1883; the clashes, such as they were, were the last in the American oil industry for a long time. The most spectacular, in 1877, pitted the Standard against Tom Scott, who had been watching Rockefeller's advance with growing fear and envy. Rockefeller's natural transportation allies were the Erie and the New York Central, who both shipped from Cleveland. In the early 1870s, he took over both railroads' oil loading and shipping operations in New Jersey and Brooklyn and invested heavily in their expansion and modernization. Most oil was exported, and under William Rockefeller's leadership, the Standard's dominance of the international market was even greater than at home. Scott saw a direct threat to his own Philadelphia-based shipping facilities, which he controlled through a subsidiary, the Empire Transportation Co.

The Empire had begun life as a fast-freight forwarder, just one of the many companies that Scott and Thomson had created to pick the meatier bones left on the Pennsylvania's table. Its superb chief executive, Col. Joseph Potts, had built it into a major transportation business in its own right, with a particularly strong position in petroleum. Besides owning fleets of tank cars, it was one of the first creators of gathering pipelines in the oil region, assembling oil from producing wells into centralized tank farms at railroad connections. Potts's ambitions were unbounded: he believed that fast-freight companies, by controlling transshipping points, loading facilities, and specialized carriers like tank cars, could emerge as the freight balancer and rate-setter for all railroad traffic. The cross-ownership with the Pennsylvania ensured that the Empire's facilities were designed to optimize Pennsylvania traffic. Rockefeller, of course, fully appreciated the importance of gathering facilities. By the early 1870s, he had pieced together an even larger network oriented toward Cleveland and New York.

Rockefeller's inexorable momentum was ominous for both Scott's and Potts's businesses, so they joined forces in early 1877 to construct a Pennsylvania-based petroleum refining and shipping cartel to squeeze out the Standard. Their strategy included both rate wars and competitive operations. The Empire reduced pipeage charges to almost nothing to lock up the few remaining independent refiners, while Scott made deep preferential rate cuts on Empire-sourced freight. Potts bought an independent refinery on Long Island, started building a new refinery in Philadelphia, and sent agents into the oil region to pay market-breaking prices to corner the crude supply.

It was delusional. The Pennsylvania was more oil-dependent than other roads, and the Standard, despite its bias toward New York ports, still provided two-thirds of its oil traffic. Standard-controlled gathering pipelines surrounded the Empire's, and the region was flooded with surplus crude supply. Rockefeller paid a visit to the Pennsylvania's headquarters in March, asking them to desist; when Scott refused, Rockefeller immediately launched total war. The Standard's Pittsburgh refineries were shut down until a connecting line was built to the Baltimore & Ohio, so not a gallon of Standard product shipped on the Pennsylvania. A crash tanker construction program rushed six hundred new cars to the Erie and New York Central to pick up the slack. Both those roads matched Scott's price cuts at every step, the Standard pipelines undercut Potts's rates, and Standard agents easily outbid Potts for crude supplies. The dramatic shift of refinery and oil port business away from Philadelphia brought howls of pain from local oilmen, while plummeting Pennsylvania revenues alarmed Scott's shareholders. With a huge war chest and no public security holders, Rockefeller could fight a no-quarter war for as long as Scott and Potts chose to bleed. Characteristically, he kept the war very focused. As A. J. Cassatt, a later Pennsylvania president, told a House committee, "They simply insisted that they could not make any arrangement with us for the transportation of their oil so long as that transportation was carried on by an organization which was their rival in the refining business. . . . That was the only point that they insisted upon." The consequences for the Pennsylvania were dire beyond the sheer loss of money. Drowning in red ink, Scott made the deep slashes in railroad manning schedules and pay that precipitated the lethal 1877

John D. Rockefeller was in his mid-fifties when he sat for this portrait, and at the peak of his powers, although he would shortly retire from the company. It captures the aura of absolute self-assurance that allowed him to dominate a fractious global industry without, it seems, ever raising his voice.

labor confrontations in Pittsburgh. With Pittsburgh in flames and his business a wreck, he had no choice but to capitulate.

Rockefeller could not resist mocking Scott in private: how the great man swept into a room of Standard executives to make his surrender, as if he had carried off the laurels. But he was happy to allow Scott his atmospherics. A deal was quickly struck to fold up the Empire; since the Pennsylvania controlled his company, Potts had no say in the matter. In Cassatt's words, "We made up our minds that it was a mistake." The Pennsylvania took all of Potts's rolling stock, while the Standard took the pipelines and all of the petroleum and harbor facilities. As usual, Rockefeller did not haggle over the price of $3.4 million. He even let Scott demand that $2.5 million of it be paid in cash within twenty-four hours, necessitating flying visits by him and William to their New York and Cleveland bankers to gather up funds. When his other partners balked at including a fleet of antiquated lake barges in the deal, Rockefeller bought them himself. There were no hard feelings against Potts, and he eventually became an active director of the Standard's pipeline subsidiary. After several more smaller acquisitions, all the gathering pipelines were in the Standard's control.*

There was one more high-profile struggle to be won, and it arose because Rockefeller, for once, had missed a beat on new technology. A group of entrepreneurs from the oil regions, led by one Byron Benson, started work on a seaboard pipeline, the Tidewater. These were experienced men who had cut their teeth building a gathering pipeline to circumvent the Empire, before they had been crushed by Scott. A seaboard pipeline was a new order of challenge, involving much longer distances over difficult mountain terrain, using much larger pipes and unprecedented pressures. Even with very heavy-gauge pipe, the line actually writhed as pressure and temperature changes made the metal dance. Benson and his colleagues reached an

---

*The producers charged exploitation by the Standard when production soared following huge new strikes at Bradford, Pennsylvania, in the mid-1870s. The evidence is ambiguous. Because they were so fragmented, and because most drilling leases were structured to ensure rapid exploitation, drillers typically produced as much oil as they could without regard for demand. The gathering pipelines moved oil to railroad connections and stored it until it was loaded into tank cars. The pipeline charge appears to have included the storage; in effect, the producer regarded it as free. When Bradford production kept rising, the Standard, which was the only pipeline/gatherer after 1877, either could not, or chose not to, add tank space fast enough to keep up with the surplus. Its solution was to refuse to store oil that had not been sold, forcing the producers, they claimed, to sell at firesale prices—to the Standard, of course, which was nearly the only buyer. In the Standard's eyes, the excess production was none of its doing. It ultimately built a "prodigious amount of tankage" at Bradford, but, whether out of malice or not, dragged its feet for at least a year or so before committing to a crash program on the required scale. A plausible reading is that the Standard did resist the producers' demands for a while (although still building a lot of new tankage), using its power to refuse to store unsold oil. But it finally decided that the din of bad publicity wasn't worth it, and built the tankage to accommodate the runaway production. In truth, since that new tankage was likely to be surplus once the market caught up, it's extremely unlikely that independent companies without the Standard's resources would have responded as well. (The Empire's Bradford facilities were quite inadequate before the Standard takeover.)

arrangement with an independent railroad, the Philadelphia & Reading, in 1877, and the Reading president, Franklin Gowen, put up half their capital; they also raised additional money from New York investors, including George F. Baker, president of the powerful First National Bank. The first phase was to pipe oil to a Reading terminus at Williamsport, in eastern Pennsylvania, with the road handling the second leg to the coastal refineries. Benson and his group also started building their own refinery near Philadelphia, to forestall a squeeze-out by the Standard.

The railroads had the most to lose, and they were determined not to give up without a fight. The Standard's stake was not nearly so clear, but, apparently after some internal debate, they chose to stand shoulder to shoulder with the roads. In the ensuing battle only the Tidewater covered itself with glory. The Standard and the railroads fought back with rate cuts, preemptive land purchases on the Tidewater's route, obstruction of tanking and tank car orders, and a large dollop of political bribery. The Tidewater overcame all obstacles. At one point, with a critical lease at risk if the land wasn't crossed by a certain date, operations were mired in a five-foot blizzard. The men hauled pipe forty miles through the drifts and made their deadline with only seven hours to spare. The moment of triumph came in late spring of 1879 when the expectant crowd at Williamsport heard the hollow roar of air being pushed ahead of the oncoming oil.

It was a clear victory for the Tidewater. Ever the realist, Rockefeller conceded that the future of oil transport lay with long-distance pipelines and kicked off a massive construction program that quickly dwarfed the Tidewater's. For his part, Benson and his shareholders had signaled almost from the start that they would be happy to be acquired. Interestingly, instead of an acquisition, the Standard and the Tidewater agreed on a market-sharing agreement that preserved the Tidewater's then-current 11.5 percent of the long-distance pipeline business, and implicitly protected their coastal refineries. Rockefeller, as usual, held no grudges, and had nothing but respect for Benson. From that point, Tidewater Oil enjoyed a long success as a kind of pet independent, prospering within the protective shadow of the Standard. Ninety percent of the industry, Rockefeller had decided, was enough.

The Standard's commitment to long-distance pipelines was the beginning of the end of the railroads' dominant role in petroleum transport. Rockefeller began to negotiate what were effectively reverse-rebate arrangements, guaranteeing the roads minimum returns for maintaining their oil-shipping facilities whether or not he used them. The last step in achieving total industry dominance was to integrate backward into crude production, which took place gradually through the 1880s.

In an industry like oil, structural factors of the kind Rockefeller exploited favor larger integrated firms; but in the usual case, one would expect three or four major winners to emerge, as happened in, say, steel, automobiles, electrical equipment, and other industries. But with Rockefeller at the helm of the Standard, it was not only the world's number-one oil company but there was no one in second place.

Running the Machine

A word on Rockefeller as a manager, for he has a claim to be not only the first great corporate executive but one of the greatest ever. He had the rarest of talents for adjusting to each new stage of the Standard's growth. He seized on the initial opportunity in oil in the 1860s with extraordinary entrepreneurial vision and energy; he always seemed to see the future plain, and drove relentlessly to put the Standard at the head of the pack, quickly adjusting tactics to each sudden turn in the road. After consolidating Cleveland, he demonstrated an equal capacity for running what was a very large enterprise for its time. He managed to delegate well, but also to remain in close touch with operations. Even as the Cleveland operations grew to employ several thousand workers, he reputedly knew almost all of them by name. And he did all that at the same time as he was aggressively expanding the range of his strategic conquests.

Then, as the Standard grew to become the largest and most far-flung enterprise in history to that time, he shifted his operations to New York, the company's new center of gravity, and proved to be a superb big-company administrator, building a modern organization that was both highly decentralized and highly unified. A full century before Ralph Cordiner and Jack Welch built GE's famous management tracking systems, Rockefeller was doing something very similar at the Standard. Here is Rockefeller's most severe critic, Ida Tarbell, on the subject:

> In the investigation of 1879, when the producers were trying to find out the real nature of the Standard alliance, they were much puzzled by the

sworn testimony of certain Standard men that the factories they controlled were competing, and competing hard, with the Standard Oil Co. of Cleveland. How could this be? Being bitter of heart and reckless of tongue, the oil men denounced the statements as perjury, but they were the literal truth. Each refinery in the alliance was required to make each month a detailed statement of its operations. These statements were compared and the results made known. If the Acme at Titusville had refined cheaper that month than any other member of the alliance, the fact was made known. If this cheapness continued to show, the others were sent to study the Acme methods. Whenever the improvement showed, that improvement received credit, and the others were sent to find the secret. The keenest rivalry resulted—each factory was on its mettle.

If anyone personified William Dean Howell's image of the engineer at the center of the Corliss engine—now and then laying down his paper to touch "some irritated spot on the giant's body with a drop of oil"—it would have been Rockefeller. Carnegie's drive to the top of the steel industry feels almost hormonal—boundless energy, aggression, and ambition fortunately channeled into something constructive. Rockefeller's seems much more a matter of sheer intelligence in pursuit of an ever-larger scale of elegance and order. Carnegie pushed and badgered, shamelessly playing executives against each other, and too frequently crushed his best men, like Henry Frick. Rockefeller's management style, by contrast, was quiet and reasonable, even though, unlike Carnegie, he never held a majority stake in the Standard. If he had the final word, it was because his very talented executives believed in their hearts that he was smarter than everyone else.* He always reached out for the ablest executives he could find, gave them plenty of running room and support, and kept most of them bound to him for the rest of their careers. For such an aggressive and acquisitive company, the relative lack of vendetta in takeover battles, and the willingness to bring former enemies into the fold, are further evidence of the consistently high order of intelligence at the company's center. Rockefeller's style was not to

---

*This is yet another area of similarity between Rockefeller's Standard and Bill Gates's Microsoft. Even after Microsoft had become quite a large organization, its very talented corps of executives habitually deferred to Gates, not because he was the largest shareholder but because he was still the smartest kid on the block.

destroy good men or good companies but to enlist them in the cause. When Rockefeller withdrew from an active management role, in about 1895, Archbold, from the oil region, succeeded him as president, while Rogers, from the Pratt refineries, became vice president.*

Altogether it was an extraordinary performance. Rockefeller's record, and his later years, were both marred by the eventual violent public revulsion against his company, which he never understood. His failure to comprehend, or even engage with, the broader public may have been the flip side of his uncanny abilities within a business context, where success and failure were relatively unambiguous, and objectives quantifiable and easy to agree. To paraphrase Henry Adams on the nation's founders, Rockefeller's range may have been narrow, but within it he was supreme.

---

*The original team broke up in the 1890s, after a twenty-five- to thirty-year run. Rockefeller himself seems to have retired long before the rest of the world knew it. Flagler fell in love with Florida and, after about 1892, become Florida's first railroad and land development tycoon. By the end of the decade, Rogers and William Rockefeller were running a deals operation that nearly rivaled the Morgan bank's, although they kept their desks at the Standard. Archbold stayed devoted to the company, but there is a near-consensus that the Standard was not well served by his pugnacious instincts during the trust-busting years.

· 6 ·

THE FIRST MASS CONSUMER SOCIETY

The Centennial Exposition wasn't Philadelphia's only grand opening in 1876. Almost as spectacular was the debut of John Wanamaker's "Grand Depot," which he trumpeted as a "New Kind of Store" and the "largest space in the world devoted to retail selling on a single floor." A converted Pennsylvania Railroad station, occupying a full city block at Thirteenth and Market Streets at the center of the city, it dazzled with color and bustle. Lit by the stained glass ceiling in daylight and by hundreds of gas lights at night, the counters were arranged in concentric circles, as much as two-thirds of a mile long, with 1,100 counter stools, so a lady could sit and discuss her purchase. And, indeed, the seventy thousand people who showed up on opening day were mostly women, as Wanamaker intended, just as starched-bloused young women predominated among his sales staff. The most visible males were the lordly floorwalkers stalking between the counters in cutaway coats. By the 1890s women were permeating even the executive ranks. Edward Filene called his Boston store an "Adamless Eden."

Wanamaker was the first to use the term "department store," but his store was in the *grand magasin* style pioneered by Aristide Boucicault's Bon Marché in Paris, and first realized in America by A. T. Stewart's 1862 "Cast Iron Palace" on New York's Broadway. Stewart and Boucicault proceeded to leapfrog each other in grandeur, and set the pattern for the proliferation of metropolitan American shopping palaces. New York City could boast of Macy's, Bloomingdale's, Lord & Taylor, and B. Altman, while Brooklyn had its Abraham & Straus, Boston its Filene's, Detroit its Hudson's, Chicago its Marshall Fields, San Francisco its Emporium; even Indianapolis and Milwaukee each had a Gimbels.

Most department stores had men's departments, but the marketing crosshairs were focused on women. Besides clothing, all the stores featured fabrics, ribbons, sewing materials, ready-made dresses, lingerie, sheets and pillowcases, household items, baby departments, perfumes, soaps, and toiletries, each with its own department and trained staff. The marble, the statuary, the gilded chandeliers were designed to make "shopping" an elegant form of purposeful recreation: a lady could intersperse explorations of the various departments with a stop at the tea room, or the well-appointed lounges, or even listen to an organ recital. Some New York stores expressly targeted higher-income clientele, but mainstream department stores aimed at the "middle-class" homemaker. They amazed and flattered her with the elegance of the environs and with the deference of the salesclerks, but canny retailers understood that their homemaker wasn't wealthy, and had instincts of thrift and austerity stamped in her genes. They could pull her in with spectacle, address her as a "Lady," and encourage her to linger, but they could not persuade her to buy unless they gave good prices, reliable quality, and no-question returns. The customers enjoyed looking at a $300 lace shawl, but the embroidered chemises for seventy-five cents were the fast-moving items.

Department stores were the surface foamings of a tectonic reshaping of American social and economic arrangements that was gaining speed in the 1870s and 1880s. Not many years before, farm wives made their soap and candles from vats of boiled animal fat, one of the nastiest of a woman's duties. By the 1840s and 1850s, better-off farmwomen bought their soap and candles from regional manufacturers, like Cincinnati's Procter & Gamble, which topped eighty employees and $1 million in sales before the Civil War. P&G got a taste of large-scale operations with war supply contracts, but the postwar spread of kerosene lamps hit their candle business hard. Then a lucky accident in 1879—a worker left a soap churn on for too long—produced a soap that floated, which they dubbed Ivory. After risking $11,000 on an advertising campaign, P&G found themselves with one of the first blowout national consumer brands. Within a decade, they were

The grand opening of Wanamaker's in a converted railroad station. The ceiling was stained glass, and counters as much as two-thirds of a mile long circled the floor. Note the signs for "Ladies' Furnishing Goods," "Gloves," "Laces," and "Linen Sheeting."

hawking more than thirty brands of soap, sales had quadrupled, and they were jockeying with Colgate and Palmolive for first place in the hearts and pocketbooks of American women.

None of the Morgans, or Loebs, or Belmonts, or Barings, who shoveled billions of dollars into American railroads, and telegraphs, and steel mills, and iron and coal mines, thought about selling wrapped and scented ladies' soap. But that, it emerged, was what all that infrastructure was for. P&G used tree resin instead of animal tallow for the fatty acids in their soap, so Ivory's booming sales entailed big logging operations, wood processing and transport, steel machinery for soap making, coal-fed steam generators and heating plants, and increasingly mechanized cooling, cutting, wrapping, storing, and shipping operations. Then there were small armies of drummers to fill the order books, and legions of clerks and bookkeepers to track orders, send invoices, register payments, and monitor production. Delivering lower prices, greater variety, and consistent quality, as Wanamaker was promising, with a pleasing shopping environment to boot, became possible only at scale. And big retail operations entailed ever bigger scales all the way back the line—the P&Gs and the Wanamakers were marching in lockstep.

There were casualties. Soap making was an important sideline for most urban pharmacy shops, and the *American Journal of Pharmacy* lamented in 1884:

> . . . it [is] necessary to produce a variety of soaps, at cheap prices. This has been brought about by competition and the inability of the public to discriminate between a well-made and a common soap. . . . The cheaper soaps, being more readily soluble in water, produce a lather more quickly than a pure soap, and as the public does not as a rule make comparative trials as to the lasting powers . . . the sale of the best soaps has of late fallen off considerably, and the cheaper kinds have taken their place.

The pharmacists were probably right on the merits of handmade versus mass-produced soap, whether or not it floated. But the millions of people with modest new margins of disposable income knew only the nasty yellow soaps from the local grocer. In the America of the last quarter of the nineteenth century there was a background roar that astonished and alarmed arbiters of public virtue, as it has in developing societies ever since: it was the roar of a burgeoning new demographic—the middle class—clamoring for *more stuff*.

The New Middle Class

"The most valuable class in any community is the middle class," Walt Whitman proclaimed in 1858, "the men of moderate means, living at the rate of a thousand dollars a year or so." Note that Whitman had to define his term, for the notion of a "middle class" was just gaining currency in mid-century. The historian Stuart Blumin points out that in America "middle class" had quite a different connotation from Great Britain's "middling classes," a rigid stratum of small artisans and shopkeepers squeezed nervously between the ruling elite and the mass of worker-proles. In America, middle class was less a well-defined social layer than a state of mind, a commitment to fluidity, as noted by the always-acute Alexis de Tocqueville in the 1830s:

I do not mean that there is any lack of wealthy individuals in the United States; I know of no country, indeed, where the love of money has taken a stronger hold on the affections of men. . . . But wealth circulates with inconceivable rapidity, and experience shows that it is rare to find two succeeding generations in the full enjoyment of it.

Echoing de Tocqueville, the historian David Potter defined the quintessential nineteenth-century American as "the completely mobile man, moving freely from one locality to the next, from one economic position to another, from one social level to levels above." Mobility, indeed, is central to the American national epic. A key argument in Lincoln's case against slavery was that it supported an aristocracy determined to undermine America's promise that "the humblest man [has] an equal chance to get rich with everyone else."

Historians have performed prodigies of digging to determine the truth of that cherished mythology: Was America really such a place of opportunity? Did ordinary people regularly rise above their station? Was America actually transmuting into a genuine middle-class society? The answer is "Yes"—a "Yes" with many qualifications to be sure—but in the main the conventional picture of American social and economic fluidity is grounded in fact.

Conventional economics assumes that inequality should increase in a developing society, since capital formation tends to concentrate within the wealthier classes. The American results at best weakly confirm that hypothesis. Wealth inequality was very high in the Robber Baron era, of course, but it is even higher today. (See chapter Notes for details.) Nineteenth-century economic mobility was also quite high, however, and in both directions, although de Tocqueville's supposition that rich families tended to lose their standing was not true. Both the richest fifth and the poorest fifth tended to hold their positions, while rapid up and down movement was concentrated within the middle three-fifths.

Occupational mobility was substantial: in two eastern cities, between a third and 40 percent of low-level manual workers moved into higher occupations during their working careers. Samples drawn over shorter time periods in a wide range of cities show 10–20 percent of blue-collar workers moving into white-collar jobs, which was a much bigger step up than it is now. In rural areas, occupational mobility was at least as high. Over ten-year census periods, half or more of farm laborers in Utah were reclassified as farmers, while 15 percent or so became skilled craftsmen. Rural mobility in

Wisconsin was much the same: most farm laborers or tenants became farm owners within a decade or two. Upward mobility was even stronger over generations: an 1890 sample of sons of blue-collar workers showed that 43 percent were in white-collar jobs. Wealth shifts showed a similar pattern. The average Wisconsin farmer tripled his property's value between 1860 and 1870. Even in a relatively stagnant city like Newburyport, Massachusetts, where there was little change in the local occupational structure, 48 percent of laborers owned property in 1870, compared to only 11 percent in 1860.

European travelers marveled at the prosperity of American workers, even though pay scales were so low that wives usually had to hire out as cleaners or seamstresses just to make ends meet. Partly it was because Americans really were better off than their peers in Europe, even at the low prevailing pay scales. English workers ate less than half the meat that American workers did, while the Irish had hardly any meat at all. A substantial portion of American bottom-rung workers, moreover, were recent immigrants who tended to be young and single and spent disproportionately on clothing and entertainment, so the impression of living the high life had considerable truth. Still, large-scale immigration—5.2 million immigrants in the 1880s alone, on an 1880 population base of 50 million—exerted constant downward pressure on entry-level wages. (But upward mobility was quite high among some immigrant groups. German immigrants in Poughkeepsie moved up the occupational ladder more than twice as fast as native-born workers.)

Being middle class was about much more than money. It was a style of speech, dress, and manners, a whole approach to living. In contemporary commentary, middle class became fairly tightly tied to nonmanual job categories. Even though a department store salesclerk earned considerably less than a skilled worker, she was more likely to be considered middle class. The department stores worked hard to project that image, and put considerable training effort into polishing up their clerks' speech and deportment— they wanted ladies to serve ladies. In the early days, female help were "shop girls," which sounded tawdry. Most stores quickly shifted to "saleswomen," and by the 1890s the clerks themselves were insisting on "salesladies." For an immigrant Irish girl, clerking at Wanamaker's was immensely status-conferring, and only the best and the brightest could make the cut. The work was very hard; sixteen-hour days were standard during the Christmas rush. But complaints by labor historians that sales-clerking was a "dead-end" job seem anachronistic. The girls were delighted to have escaped the factory or domestic work, and the store ambience was thrilling.

The low pay for female salesclerks was an exception; pay for most non-manual workers was surprisingly high—crossing the manual/nonmanual divide was a big financial step toward a middle-class life style. *Harpers* ran an article in 1887 about a "typical" American worker and his family, who had a pleasant house and garden in Brooklyn. The father was a carpenter, averaging $900 per year, close to the top of the scale a carpenter could expect. His two daughters and his son lived at home, and all were employed. The girls worked in a straw hat factory, bringing home $712 between them (although they were embarrassed to tell their friends they were factory girls), but the son, who clerked in a wholesale house, made $1,092—in short, he was the only one who qualified as middle class under Walt Whitman's $1,000 per year test.

Although white-collar jobs accounted for only about 7 percent of total employment in 1880, they were clearly the wave of the future. Between 1870 and 1880, the number of clerks and copyists in offices quadrupled, the number of bookkeepers and accountants doubled, insurance office staffs doubled, bank and railroad office staffs nearly doubled, and the number of commercial travelers quadrupled. Clerical workers were overwhelmingly male. While entry pay was often very low, advancement could be rapid. The young John Rockefeller had no intention of spending his life as an assistant bookkeeper, but it was a perfect way to learn what a business was really about. Edward Tailer was a Rockefeller contemporary, and no tycoon, although ambitious enough. He left school to clerk for a New York dry goods importer, but complained about the pay, only $50 a year. By the time he was twenty-one, he was making $450 a year; he jumped to another firm the next year for $1,000, then became a traveling salesman at $1,200, and had his own business when he was twenty-five. "Apprentice merchant" was a better job description than clerk.

The business historian Olivier Zunz has analyzed clerical job applications at a Chicago-based railroad from the 1880s and 1890s. Applicants were almost all under twenty-five, almost all native born, most had been to high school, and their letters were literate and clear, either written in a highly legible hand or neatly typed. They stressed their work habits, their character and reliability, their sobriety and ambition. Many, like Rockefeller, had some business college. The average pay for the railroad's clerical workers in 1880 was $800 a year, substantially above the area's norm of $500 for a skilled craftsman and $300 for an unskilled worker. One claims agent, who was making $1,200 a year at age thirty, had his own house, a wife and four children, and could afford a cook. Salaries for many white-collar jobs were often much higher. Almost all male Treasury clerks had annual salaries higher than $1,200 in 1881. Male and female buyers at Macy's in 1871 got base salaries of $1,200–1,500, probably with commissions on top, and a buyer in the late 1880s was guaranteed $4,000. Accountants and bookkeepers were getting $2,000 even in the earlier years of this period, while $1,500 salaries were apparently common in insurance companies. (The rising pay scales, moreover, coincided with steadily falling prices.) Working wives were rare in white-collar households.

A follow-up of a young male clerical cohort in Boston from 1870 through 1885 found that a fourth had become professionals or independent businessmen, although almost as many, surprisingly, had become manual workers, although mostly in skilled categories. By 1885, however, advancement no longer required opening a business. Exponential growth in the range and reach of white-collar occupations meant that an ambitious young man could often achieve status, power, and a good income over the course of a career with a single firm. As the white-collar population expanded, there was an increasing presence of "ethnics" in the ranks. A sample of clerical workers in 1890 Philadelphia showed that 31 percent were ethnics—in all likelihood German or Irish—while unskilled manual jobs were filled by Italians or the newest immigrants from Eastern Europe.

The rigidity of the "collar line"—blue versus white—was under constant challenge, especially by artisans who had achieved middle-class lifestyles. Incomes reported by artisan-proprietors, in fact, tended to be low, about the same as those of ordinary skilled craftsmen. But that may be a reporting phenomenon: ex-artisan businessmen generating solid, middle-class incomes tended to label themselves managers or merchants. And as their businesses grew, white-collar tasks would have occupied much of their time—selling, ordering supplies, hiring and training workers, keeping the books. Already in midcentury, successful artisan-businessmen could be seen self-consciously seeking a firmly middle-class position without losing contact with their trade. One way was to participate in "scientific" mechanical societies that examined new tools or technologies, recommended quality standards, or lobbied for trade protection. The ASME, during Alexander Holley's presidency in the 1870s, was one of the earliest and most successful of such organizations. A stomach-churning decision for the small manufacturer who valued his relations with his craftsmen was whether to adopt mechanized processes that would de-skill the trade.

One's home was usually the most visible status marker. Earlier in the century, most people lived on family farms that looked and smelled like rural factories. Survival was a matter of brutally hard labor and lots of kids. Houses were painted once when they were built, if at all; yards were full of garbage and foraging animals; soap was for clothes, not for people. Accelerating growth in the 1840s and 1850s, and the steady commercialization of agriculture, was reflected in bigger farmhouses, more hired help, improved hygiene, and the spread of niceties like tableware and carpets. By 1870, most Americans no longer lived on farms, and the growing distance between work and residence, reinforced by public transit, converted the house to the locus of family bonding after daily activities—a "home." With the opening of the Brooklyn Bridge in 1883, Brooklyn quickly evolved into a bedroom suburb of Manhattan. The "lunchroom"—a "piggery at swilltime"—was dotted throughout business districts.

Technology drove the transition. The stud-frame "balloon house," pioneered in the lumber-short Midwest in the 1830s, drastically reduced raw material costs and facilitated larger, more flexible designs.* Wood machining was always an American specialty, and furniture factories, many of them around Michigan's hardwood forests, churned out great quantities of decent, very inexpensive furniture. Even in the 1850s, as British investigators of the "American system" had discovered, a substantial fraction of new doors and windows were mass produced in factory settings. By the 1870s, machine-manufactured complete house kits were available on a mail-order basis: one manufacturer advertised a range from $350 three-room houses to a $5,000 four-hundred-seat spired church. There was a proliferation of design styles—"Romanesque Revival," "Chateau," and "Queen Anne" were all popular—and a ready availability of machined ornamentation, like cornices and scrollwork. Power looms drove the cost of decent wool carpets well below

---

*"Balloon houses" were a conceptual forerunner of the steel-frame skyscraper. Previously, walls were self-supporting, requiring heavy construction. Once the frame provided the support, the wall became a much lighter-weight weather screen.

$1 a yard. When machinery could grind pigments finely enough to suspend in oil, paint production made the jump from a craft to an industry, with multiple color choices stocked in mass-produced, sealed metal cans. The cost of new homes fell to levels affordable by manual workers, if they could finance them. Mortgages were short, usually five to seven years, and required substantial down payments, but building and loan societies proliferated by the tens of thousands to fill the savings gap.

Home spaces became more formalized and standardized. The middle-class home had an entrance hall, a formal parlor, or "sitting room," often a second, or less formal, sitting room, a dining room (which was actually used for eating), a kitchen, and a scullery area on the first floor. The "backstairs" in the kitchen was for children or servants, while the front hall stairs were reserved for stylized descents to greet guests. Bedrooms and the bathroom were on the second floor. Children commonly had their own beds, but still shared rooms. As houses grew in size, it became normal to take in boarders, even in middle-class areas; boarding, indeed, became the standard housing for single people in cities, and they were often treated almost as family members. Farmhouses followed similar designs—the farmer complaining that his house was "bigger than the barn" was a stock joke.

Sanitation lagged population growth by several decades. Water-borne diseases like cholera and typhoid remained dangerous killers well into the twentieth century, accounting for a quarter of all infectious disease deaths in 1900. Wives, or servants, were still lugging water from pumps in the 1870s, but by the end of the decade most larger cities were piping (unfiltered and unchlorinated) water into homes in many, if not most, of their residential areas. Privies were not connected to sewage systems. The backyard latrine—or in many working-class areas, the neighborhood latrine—gradually gave way to indoor privies. Water closets, which flushed into a pit, were suitable for less settled areas, while urban designers experimented with a host of "earth closet" contraptions. Many cities had gas lighting, at least in better neighborhoods, and almost everyone had a kerosene lamp. Pierpont Morgan famously wired his house for electricity in 1882—it required a basement generator—but residential electricity would not become standard until the 1920s.

The role of middle-class women was transformed along with their homes—wives became "homemakers," arbiters of domesticity, society's officially designated civilizing force. Their men had to be taught to eat with forks, to stop pouring their tea into a saucer to cool, and never, ever, to spit in the house. *Harpers* noted that wives "legislate for our dress, etiquette, and manners without fear of a veto. . . . It is indeed, the subtlest, and most pervasive influence in our land." Home economics courses popped up in high schools and land grant colleges. The "educated consumer" was a brand-new role, and there was an outpouring of advice books and instruction manuals on making proper use of the new abundance. Being middle class was suddenly a life strategy, not just an economic category, and one that was mostly managed by women. Tactics included smaller families, greater concentration on child-rearing and child education, careful budgetary management to maintain the required status signals without extravagance, and inculcating children with habits of prudence and respectable deportment.

The nonwealthy upper middle classes lived very well. The Marches, Isabel and Basil, the protagonists of William Dean Howells's *A Hazard of New Fortunes* (1890), are in their midforties and making a move from Boston to New York as the story opens. Basil is leaving a boring job at an insurance company for an editorial position that pays $3,500 a year, while Isabel's inheritance pays $2,000. Their combined income, in today's dollars, would equate to about $66,000.* They are very nervous about the move, especially about money. They own their Boston home; they have a live-in housemaid, Margaret, and a laundress; they are widely traveled, always going first class with many trunks; they have two daughters and a son, Tom, who is graduating high school. Tom had naturally planned to enter Harvard, and is irritated at the prospect of attending Columbia instead. When they commence house-hunting, Isabel sets out her requirements for a New York flat:

> The *sine qua non* are an elevator and steam heat, not above the third floor, to begin with. Then we each must have a room, and you must have your study and I must have my parlor; and the two girls must each have a room. With the kitchen and dining room, how many does that make? . . . And the kitchen must be sunny. . . . And the rooms must *all*

---

*The interpretive issue here is between the use of currency comparisons and purchasing-power parities (PPP), which attempt to correct for price differences. Today, for example, a middle-class Chinese can buy very inexpensive personal services, like housemaids and such, that are not captured in dollar/renminbi currency comparisons. PPP ratios make the Chinese household appear much richer. On a PPP basis, the Marches were clearly better off than the typical insurance company middle manager today, but the purchasing baskets are too different to construct meaningful comparisons.

have outside light. And the rent must not be over eight hundred for the winter. We can only get a thousand for our whole house, and we *must* save something out of that, so as to cover the expenses of moving. [They later agree on a room for Margaret as well. Tom will live at his college.]

Howells amusingly recounts the Marches' shock at New York prices and their eventual decision to settle for only six rooms and a bath, at a far higher price than they expected to pay—Margaret can be squeezed in, the girls will share a bedroom, Basil will forgo his study, and they will send the laundry out. New York, of course, was a special case, as it is today. A house design that was popular in Philadelphia "for people of moderate means," according to the designer, had 3,375 square feet on three floors. It could be built for $3,000 to $3,500, a price that would have been easily within reach of the Marches. Stuart Blumin notes that these were "much larger homes than those of late eighteenth century middling folk." (Quite likely, it is also larger than Professor Blumin's house; it's about 50 percent larger than the median home in America today.) A house that size naturally assumed servants.

Middle-class behavior and values percolated through much of the population. Even in the smaller homes of manual workers, wives self-consciously added little touches to their front rooms to make them look more like "parlors"—family pictures, carpets, some flowers. Workers' real wages rose steadily in the 1870s and even faster in the 1880s, and lower-class women began adjusting their income-producing activity to comport with their domestic duties, although they mostly still had to work. In short, poorer women got the worst of both worlds, as so often in lower-income families today. But there were discernible shifts in employment patterns; for example, Irish women began taking in boarders rather than work outside the home. Working-class children did not remain in school as long as middle-class children, but their attendance rates still rose. Urban schools, both public and parochial, and settlement houses catechized the middle-class virtues of hygiene, prudence, thrift, and hard work.

The 1880s and 1890s saw a sharp ratcheting-up of reformist interest in public education, which was sustained well into the twentieth century. Much of it was prompted by the business demand for capable workers, and had a grimly functional tone—as in "the student should be able to quickly adapt to the rigors of the industrial assembly line"—and there was a conscious funneling of immigrant and working-class children into manual training courses. This same period saw the widespread introduction of the graded school—no more one-room schoolhouses—standardized testing, and minimum standards and certifications for teachers. School enrollment rates rose sharply during the 1870s, then fell back after 1880. The slippage probably reflected rising immigration, for secondary school enrollments shot up 150 percent in the decade of the 1890s alone. Commercial training schools offering night classes at low rates sprang up like mushrooms.

Middle-class values spread so fast in part because the status was attainable for almost any young person with energy and ambition. Horatio Alger's novels flew off the shelves. The rewards of moving ahead were palpable—because there were suddenly so many things to buy.

Things

If you wished to buy a piano in 1895, you could check out the "Windsor" upright in the Montgomery Ward catalog. For $170, they would ship you a new instrument, with ivory keys and an overstrung scale,* done up in "hardwood with highly polished surface and finished in imitation of Rosewood, Ebony or Mahogany." For $40 more, you got a higher quality action, the new three-pedal design, and mahogany wood. The catalog spelled out how easy and safe it was to order:

> We will ship any Windsor Organ or Piano on trial to any railroad shipping point in the United States, subject to the following conditions: Upon receipt of order we will ship the instrument to our own address, send a sight draft with bill of lading attached to your banker's. When the shipment arrives at destination, the purchaser will be required to deposit with the bank the price of the instrument, but with the understanding that the money is to be held fifteen (15) days. During this time the instrument may be given a thorough trial at your home. . . . If you find that it is not in every way satisfactory you can return it to the station agent at any time before the expiration of the time specified, and by obtaining bill of lading . . . and presenting same at bank, the entire amount deposited will be refunded.

---

*"Overstringing," or the diagonal arrangement of the bass strings, was still a fairly recent innovation to enable a deeper, richer bass sound. The catalog provided a fair amount of technical detail aimed at the knowledgeable buyer.

The 1895 catalog filled 623 oversize small-type pages stuffed with wood-cuts illustrating every product. There were saddles, tools, and knives and guns galore; page after page of library tables, bedroom "suits," and book-cases; more than forty styles of ladies' summer cloaks, men's shirts from twenty-five cents to $2 each, and ten different kinds of men's suits from a casual sack style to evening wear; plus a vast array of jewelry, painted per-fume bottles, china, kitchenware, stoves, toys and games, baby clothes and carriages, corsets, "high quality pillow shams," and plumbing gear. The Sears 1897 catalog included arsenic wafers for the complexion ("perfectly harm-less when used according to directions"); "Nerve and Brain Pills," which made Viagra-like claims; laudanum (a mixture of opium and alcohol); and a terrifying "Princess Bust Developer" that looked like an iron toilet plunger, but promised a "round, firm and beautiful" bust with regular usage.

Ward was a young Chicago hardware salesman when he mailed a one-page product list to customers in the Illinois Grange in 1872, listing ready-made clothing items that were hard to buy in rural areas. His idea was that he could purchase and ship items from Chicago, and pass on the savings in inventory and the cost of middlemen. It caught on wonderfully, and he issued new product sheets almost every two months until 1874, when he put out his first catalog—eight 3x5-inch bound pages. He added a woodcut picture with each product in 1880, and by 1884 the catalog had ballooned to 240 pages, listing more than 10,000 items.

Ward's Chicago operation was suddenly a big business, with armies of clerks and shippers, and more than $500,000 in inventory. Many of his prod-ucts, like the Windsor piano and the Montgomery Ward Sewing Machine, were private label manufacture, taking advantage of his buying power to push prices down. All of his customers had a standing invitation to visit his plant, and 285,000 people took him up on it during Chicago's 1893 Columbian Exposition. Richard Sears, whose operations outstripped Ward's by the early 1900s, got his start in 1886 selling watches by mail; Alvah Roebuck joined as the watch repairman. Sears's main innovation was aggressive adver-tising, some of it outrageous. By the 1880s almost all department stores had their own mail-order operations: if a lady in California wanted to buy from Bloomingdale's, she had only to write and request their catalog. When John Wanamaker became postmaster-general in 1889, he ensured that mail-order catalogs had the most favorable rates, since they were "aiding the dissemi-nation of knowledge."

Left: The first Ivory ads were dense with print and full of cleaning advice. But by the 1890s, Procter & Gamble's "Miss Blossom" ads were selling "a style of loveliness."

Below: Bicycle manufacturer and evangelist Albert A. Pope's posters became a minor art form. This poster advertises Pope's Columbia "safety" bicycles.

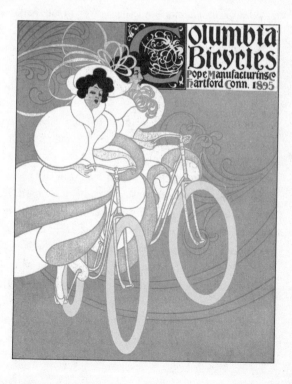

All of these businesses operated below the radar screen of megacapital-ists like the Morgans. Their primary capital expenses were for real estate and inventory, which could be financed by traditional mortgages and bank working capital lines. But that was true only because they could "external-ize" the cost of all the shipping infrastructure that Morgan, the Barings, and others had already paid for. The 1886 Bloomingdale's catalog, for instance, instructed its purchasers to send postage with the order, and advised that they should send a follow-up inquiry if they had not received an order con-firmation within ten days, or fifteen days if they lived on the Pacific coast. (Not twenty years before, much of Bloomingdale's marketing area had been reachable only by wagon train.) By the 1890s train speeds were at least as fast as they are now, and there were a host of "express" companies that handled the shipping from a merchant's loading bay through the rail network to the customer's front door, through networks of local contractors managed by telegraph. In most parts of the country, people could count on thirty-day or better order turnarounds, a cycle time that changed only marginally until the spread of air freight companies almost a century later.

When railroad men and their investment banks adopted their "if you build it, they will come" strategy, they were not thinking of a consumer rev-olution: Gould, Vanderbilt, and Scott went to war over grain, iron, and oil freights, not corsets and ribbons. Pennsylvania managers, who took great pride in the high polish of their shipping and scheduling machinery, were unpleasantly surprised in the 1890s to find themselves ensnarled in a thickening maze of short-term hauling and small freights. Consumers were taking over, and there was considerable management foundering until the road learned to adjust.

Julius Rosenwald, who joined Sears in 1895 and assumed operational responsibility from a very in-over-his-head Richard Sears, was arguably the first retail management genius. Sears executed the first retail public share issuance in 1906, through Goldman, Sachs, one of a new breed of Jewish investment banks (Lehmans was another) that focused on the retail and consumer goods businesses overlooked by the Morgans and Kuhn, Loebs of the world. Rosenwald needed the capital infusion to build continuous-processing, mechanized railroad- and roller-line-based goods assembly and distribution systems, much like those Alexander Holley had pioneered in steel.

Rosenwald's security issuance marked a final stage of business consciousness raising. Ever since the 1870s there had slowly been dawning the stupendous realization that consumer wants are illimitable. The mother in a novel of immigrant life tells how, when she and her two daughters were all working, she replaced old rags with "regular towels," and began to acquire dishes and tableware,

> so we could all sit down at the table at the same time and eat like people. . . . We no sooner got used to regular towels than we began to want toothbrushes. . . . We got the toothbrushes and we began wanting tooth powder to brush our teeth with, instead of ashes. And more and more we wanted more things, and really needed more things, the more we got them.

History had never seen an explosion of new products like that in the America of the 1880s and 1890s. Branded foods followed the lead of the meatpackers, starting in the 1880s. Store shelves offered Cream of Wheat, Aunt Jemima's Pancakes, Postum, Kellogg's Shredded Wheat, Juicy Fruit gum, Pabst Blue Ribbon Beer, Durkee's salad dressings, Uneeda Biscuits, Coca-Cola, and Quaker Oats. Pillsbury and Gold Medal wiped out local flour millers. (Wives started buying cake mixes in the 1890s, but baking one's own bread was still a badge of honor.) Advertising flourished right alongside. (N.W. Ayer, one of the first of the big advertising companies, got its start with John Wanamaker's.) So Jell-O was the "quick and easy" dessert; Schlitz beer was made with "filtered water"; Huckin's soups were "hermetically sealed"; no human hands had touched Stacey's "Workdipt Chocolates." H. J. Heinz created a fifty-foot-tall electric pickle—with 1,200 lightbulbs—in Times Square in 1896. The sign blinked Heinz's "57 Good Things For The Table," listing each one in lights. You'd "Walk a Mile" for a Camel, and hum the jingle for "Sunny Jim" cereal. The Great Atlantic and Pacific Tea Company, A&P, was the first national grocery chain, and Frank Woolworth's "nickel-stores" were sweeping through the country.

The speed of the branded-food triumph could have been due to the naïveté of consumers, or perhaps to the execrable quality of local stores' barrel-food. One suspects it was both; nostalgia buffs too readily assume that consumers were fooled. Packaged brands brought people in large swathes of the country their first access to more varied diets. Many local

At the 1893 Chicago Exposition, spectacular engineering talent was at the service of pure entertainment. The famous Ferris wheel rose 264 feet above the ground, each carriage bigger than a Pullman car, and it could carry two thousand people at a time.

grocers, moreover, were sinks of poor hygiene, bad storage conditions, adulteration, and outright misrepresentation (hog fat for butter, for example). The packaged food industry had its own scandals, especially in meat, but safety and consistency was probably a great improvement over the general store. As a bit of nineteenth-century doggerel had it:

> Things are seldom what they seem;
> Skim milk masquerades as cream;
> Lard and soap we eat for chease;
> Butter is but axle-grease.

A vast range of products made life simpler: Bissell carpet sweepers, Gillette "safety" razors with disposable blades, rubber boots and shoes, zippers, ice boxes (often with an opening on a house's outer wall, so the iceman could fill it), Levi's for workers. Or made life more fun: roller skates were a craze in the 1870s; bicycles in the 1890s. James Bonsack's automatic cigarette-making machine went into production in James Duke's factory in 1886. By 1900, Americans were buying more than four billion cigarettes a year, almost all of them from Duke, including still-current brands like Lucky Strike. A pre-Duke cigarette maker invented the baseball card. Young women were discouraged from smoking, but had a "mania" for cosmetics. Handbag stores prestuffed their bags with branded lipsticks and rouge. Helena Rubinstein and Elizabeth Arden, between them, dominated the business by the early 1900s. Household walls were festooned with chromolithographs, color facsimiles of paintings by American artists such as Audubon, Bierstadt, and Winslow Homer. Currier and Ives were among the first to produce paintings specifically for chromolithography. Mark Twain's Connecticut Yankee knows he is in a strange place because the medieval castle has no "chromos" on the walls.

Residential mail service triggered a postcard craze, and then a greeting card craze. Postcards with photographic scenes were popular collectibles; one company produced 16,000 different views. Thomas Edison invented the phonograph in 1879, but Emile Berliner came up with the popular "gramophone" and the flat "record" in 1889; his system could make thousands of records from a single master. Versions of the modern jukebox proliferated in the 1890s, and it was a natural accompaniment to the drugstore soda fountain—a pharmacist could pull in $500 worth of nickels a week. Both were an index of the increased leisure time of young people. Middle-class parents kept their kids in school instead of sending them off to the factory, and were discovering that the demographic between child and adult was a previously undreamed-of species.

Home entertainment sales boomed—lawn tennis and croquet, board games, and stereoscopes. Two stereoscopic slides viewed in front of a light source produced a three-dimensional scene. Millions of slides were produced—natural wonders, stories, religious matter; Oliver Wendell Holmes, Jr., once boasted that he had seen more than 100,000 stereo views. George Eastman introduced the celluloid film roll for his Kodak in 1888. A Kodak-sponsored photography contest in New York in 1897 drew 26,000 people. By 1900, the country had more than 1.5 million telephones. Improvements in printing technology produced an outpouring of magazines, inexpensive novels, and city newspapers. Plant lighting made morning papers possible, and publishers pulled in readers with sports pages, comics, puzzles, women's pages, and advice columns. Dorothy Dix's column started in 1896. Professional entertainment—baseball, boxing, vaudeville, burlesque, Barnum's circus, and the "Amusement Park"—were fixtures even in smaller cities. The Ferris wheel at the 1893 Chicago Exposition was 264 feet high, each of its cars was larger than a Pullman coach, and the fully loaded wheel handled more than two thousand people at a time.

Armory Practice Redux

The full wealth effects of a mass consumer society are not captured by raw income data. It's not just that the average person has more money, but that technology creates entirely new classes of products while radically reducing the cost of products once available only to the elite. In that respect, the American consumer boom represented the final flowering of the Connecticut Valley machine tradition of Thomas Blanchard, John Hall, and the great superintendents at the Springfield Armory. The woman who breaks the bobbin on her sewing machine while running up curtains at home and the soldier in the field with a broken gunlock present a common problem—neither can get full value from their product if it requires the attendance of a skilled craftsman. Isaac Singer's worldwide distribution of his sewing machine was a new chapter in consumer marketing, but it was not until the 1880s that he finally understood the requirements of consumer support. Singer's business went through painful adjustments for much of that decade to bring its output closer to Armory standards of precision: if a part breaks, just screw a new one in. The bicycle industry that fed the cycling enthusiasm of the 1880s and 1890s was one of the first where manufacturers understood the importance of Armory standards from the outset, and nicely illustrates the direct gene transfer from Valley practice to mass consumer manufacturing.

The "father" of the bicycle in America was Albert A. Pope, a Boston merchant who became infatuated with bicycles when he saw a British high-wheel cycle at the 1876 Philadelphia Exposition. He traveled to Europe, learned how they were manufactured, and returned to create a bicycle industry in America. Pope seems to have understood the opportunity for a mass production industry from the very start, because he was determined that, unlike the European products, his would be produced with "interchangeable parts," an advantage he promoted in his earliest brochures.

Pope contracted production of his first bicycles to the Weed Sewing Machine Co., which, along with Singer and Willcox & Gibbs, was one of the three original sewing machine makers. Both Weed and Willcox & Gibbs used manufacturers directly from the Valley community—Brown and Sharpe for Willcox & Gibbs, and the Robbins & Lawrence/Sharps Rifle Co. for Weed. Robbins & Lawrence had worked closely with Simeon North, the first outside contractor for John Hall's rifles; and it was a Robbins & Lawrence rifle that took the gold medal at the 1851 Crystal Palace Exhibition. But Weed and Willcox were better technologists than marketers, and never won more than a small percentage of the trade—although by the time Pope contacted them, Weed had taken over the Sharps factory and was producing sewing machines as its main line business.

A superb businessman and marketer, Pope bought up every American bicycle patent he could find and evangelized his cycles by financing bicycling magazines and sponsoring bicycle clubs, competitions, and trade shows. He organized local pressure groups, coordinated through his "American Wheelmen's Association," to demand better roads, and his bicycle posters, some by Maxwell Parrish, became popular artwork. Pope achieved impressive volumes even with his high-wheelers, which were an athletic challenge and a bit dangerous—more of a sport than a means of transportation. Business really took off with the introduction of the "safety bicycle," essentially the same design as a 1950s Schwinn. Almost anyone could ride it.

Pope introduced his Columbia safety bicycle in 1890 and bought out the Weed company to bring manufacturing within his own control. While Weed was an excellent manufacturer, it had never strayed far from established Armory practice and always maintained other manufacturing lines. Pope eliminated all nonbicycle production, reorganized the plant, and introduced innovations in forging, assembly, and especially in finishing processes, where consumer markets posed much more demanding challenges than arms makers had faced. By the mid-1890s, American bicycle production was in excess of 1.2 million units a year. Pope wasn't always the largest producer, but he never lost his reputation for the highest quality. Almost all of his competitors were also from the Connecticut sewing machine and small arms tradition. Important manufacturing innovations from other bicycle companies included steel stamping and primitive assembly lines, all critical, if groping, first steps toward the mother of all mass production systems—that for Henry Ford's Model T, now less than twenty years away. Pope himself was an early experimenter with automobile manufacture, and may also have made the first commercial motorcycle (with a regular bicycle chain if the motor failed).

The early 1890s now feels like a long-ago era. That is why pictures and descriptions of the "Model Home" at the 1893 Columbia Exposition's Electricity Building are so surprising. It has electric lighting, electric stove, hot plate, electric washing machine, electric carpet sweeper, electric doorbells and fire alarms. In short, it looks like us. Ordinary people were reaping the benefits of the vast constructions of the Gilded Age titans. Not at all paradoxically, large-scale infrastructure allowed many consumer industries, like paints, furniture, and household tools and utensils, to achieve competitive efficiencies at quite modest scales. Electricity liberated smaller manufacturers from the tyranny of the steam engine or the water run. The city of Cleveland, for example, became a major center of venture-backed electricity-related manufacturing in the last quarter of the century, more or less replicating the development pattern around the Connecticut River fifty years before. Midsize manufacturers achieved access to national markets through the agency of large-scale retailers. As a Sears executive later put it with considerable insight, their success came from concentrating "money, organization, and brains in the distribution field, and, paralleling that, the growth of efficiency of the small manufacturer." A Sears or a Wanamaker was an impresario of brand competition, presiding over a free-for-all in price, quality, and variety that spiraled into the massive outpouring of goods of a modern mass consumption society.

The country that had been trembling on the brink of modernity at Lincoln's death, discovered thirty years later that it had made the leap. And it was scary.

Anxiety

The flip side of American fluidity was status anxiety. The sure connections between one's father's place in society and one's own, the reliable guides to behavior so firmly attached to one's station, were all gone. The psychological costs could be heavy. De Tocqueville, as usual, was one of the first to note it:

> Thus not only does democracy make every man forget his ancestors, but it hides his descendants and separates his contemporaries from him; it throws him back forever upon himself alone and threatens in the end to confine him entirely to the solitude of his own heart.

But it was not just the individuals seeking their own way who were anxious. Here is the longtime quasiofficial moralist, Henry Ward Beecher, in the 1840s, sounding much like a modern-day imam:

> We grade our streets, build our schools, support all our municipal laws, and the young men are *ours;* our sons, our brothers, our wards, clerks, or apprentices. . . . [But there is] a whole race of men, whose camp is the Theatre, the Circus, the Turf, or the Gaming Table . . . a race whose instinct is destruction, who live to corrupt, and live off the corruption which they make. . . . and when they offer to corrupt all these youth . . . and we get the courage to say that we had rather not; that industry and honesty are better than expert knavery—they turn on us in great indignation with, *Why don't you mind your own business—what are you meddling in our affairs for?*

The irony, or poignancy, in Beecher's fulminations is that he was so vulnerable himself. Although his advice manuals roundly condemned seducers, he was famously involved in a seduction scandal with a member of his congregation in the 1870s. He appears also to have been an addicted shopper. His compulsive lecturing, commanding top-market fees for endless rounds of selling prudence and frugality, was in part to keep up with his compulsive spending. One hopes he was a tortured soul—it would at least inspire sympathy.

America had once been an archipelago of small towns in which hierarchy commanded deference and local opinion bounded behavior. But the country's extraordinary social and geographic mobility was creating a horizontal society. When every man or woman is free to constantly recreate himself or herself, one never knows who one should be or, just as frightening, whom one is meeting. In her wonderful study, *Confidence Men and Painted Women,* Karen Halttunen describes the elaborate social rituals that developed during the American Victorian era, the nervously managed systems of social signaling to identify who was real, who was fake, who was dangerous.

Anxiety was compounded by the rapid shift to paper-based wealth. Herman Melville's 1857 novel *The Confidence Man,* set on a steamboat trip, becomes a kind of "Ship of Fools," as passenger vignettes compound into an escalating series of paper swindles. Fear of deception led to a cult of candor and simplicity in midcentury, then, comically, to paroxysms of anxiety as it dawned that the truly deceitful person would appear the most sincere of all—which prompted an absurd outpouring of instruction on spotting the dishonest person by his face or her hands. By the 1870s, the middle classes may have been gaining their sea legs, for they began poking fun at their own canons of correctness and accumulating pomposities.

But there were grounds enough for middle-class anxiety, some of which struck at core features of traditional family life. Maintaining firm domestic control over children, and investing in their educational advancement—key elements in the middle-class life strategy—was feasible for most couples only with small families. Not only were they forgoing economic contributions from their children but they also were stretching out the period of dependence. William Dean Howells's Basil and Isabel March are better off than most of the middle classes, and clearly enjoy their lifestyle—Isabel's ability to pursue literary activities, the flexibility to consider the move to New York. One cannot imagine it is an accident that they have only three children, for having many more would have placed so much of that at risk.

American fertility rates declined steadily throughout the nineteenth century, but the reasons for the decline shifted over time. In the first half of the century, the decline was Malthusian; it can be traced mostly to later marriages and earlier female deaths. But the downtrend after midcentury looks intentional, for it is especially concentrated in middle-class families. Taking into account child mortality rates, the middle classes barely reproduced at replacement levels, or at about the same rate as in America today.

We now know a surprising amount about how they did it, thanks to a documentation project conducted over thirty years by a remarkable woman named Clelia Duel Mosher, which has been only recently exhumed and analyzed by scholars. Mosher was born in 1863, and like any good Victorian girl took her father's advice to live at home after secondary school, tending a small greenhouse business. She did so, that is, until she had socked away enough money to go off to college and medical school. She attended Wellesley, Wisconsin, and Stanford, where she received her bachelor's and master's degrees in biology, before getting a medical degree from Johns Hopkins. She later spent many years on the faculty of Stanford, with a special interest in women's health. Of interest here is her detailed survey on reproductive and contraceptive practices among educated women of her own age (born between 1860 and 1870). Her respondents had all finished secondary school, most had some college, and all were married to well-educated men.

The very frank responses to the Mosher surveys show that virtually all these women consciously managed family size by practicing contraception and limiting coital frequency. Compared to college-educated women of the same age in the 1955 Kinsey survey, they had sex only about half as often—about once a week, compared to nearly twice a week for the Kinsey sample, although very few resorted to abstinence. They used a variety of contraceptive practices. In about a third of the cases, contraception was primarily "male-directed"—condoms and/or withdrawal, which were about equally unreliable, given the uncertain quality of the day's condoms. The rest relied on "female-directed" techniques, primarily douching and fertility timing. (Although doctors did not yet understand ovulation cycles, statistical models suggest that fertility timing combined with the reported coital frequencies should have been about as effective as other available techniques.) A few were experimenting with newer devices, such as cervical caps; the diaphragm was not available until the twentieth century. Mosher did not ask about abortion, but there are suggestions that abortion rates in this group were quite low.

Mosher's data both confirm long-held expectations and hold several surprises. The data clearly support the conventional assumption that falling fertility among middle-class women was a conscious economic strategy. And given the marital discipline these couples exercised, it is reasonable to assume that the Victorian era's public restraint in sexual matters evolved to reinforce a policy of "careful love." But Mosher's women relied much less on abstinence and far more on artificial techniques than many historians had assumed—and this long before Margaret Sanger "pioneered" the acceptance of birth control. The apparent low rate of abortion, if the inference is correct, also runs contrary to historians' expectations. A final interesting data point: once Mosher's women reached menopause, they had sex about as often as Kinsey's sample did, and almost as frequently as in their first years of marriage, suggesting again that low coital frequencies in the early years were an adaptive strategy rather than a consequence of generalized prudery.

In such an officially prudish society, the cartoonishly erotic, pinched-waist and bustled dress standard for middle-class women is especially odd; it may have been an infantilizing strategy, a last-ditch resistance to growing female independence. But the control exercised by women within the confines of family life, as consumers, lifestyle managers, and sexual partners was already transmuting into markedly greater public assertiveness, in causes such as suffrage, birth control, and temperance. By the early twentieth century, that energy would spill over into a much broader, often women-led, social reform agenda.

An analyst recently wrote about modern China, "As . . . more and more Chinese people are able to start affording life's little luxuries, China's domestic economy is starting to become a powerful engine of growth in its own right." Nineteenth-century America was the trailblazer for that virtuous cycle of consumer-driven growth, and it presented industrialists and financiers with an entirely new order of demands—to achieve ever-greater scale, but with much greater product varieties and to higher standards of precision. The technical challenge was one that few entrepreneur-managers were up to. To cope, companies had to assemble entirely new sorts of managerial and technical bureaucracies. The age of the consumer, that is, could not get under way except in parallel with the age of the corporation.

· 7 ·

PAPER TIGERS

Mrs. O'Leary's cow probably didn't do it, but there's no doubt that the city took far too long to react. By the time the first hose company got to the fire in Patrick O'Leary's barn in the Southside slums of Chicago, on a windy October night in 1871, at least five buildings were ablaze and the fire was out of control. It took two days for the *Chicago Tribune* to get the story out, since its own "fireproof" building was lost in the conflagration. It was "a perfect sea of leaping flames. . . . No obstacle seemed to interrupt the progress of the fire. Stone walls crumbled before it. It reached the highest roofs, and swept the earth of everything combustible."

Chicago was one of the fastest growing cities in the country, with a notoriously corrupt local government. No one had paid much attention to zoning or fire regulations, or even to ensuring reasonable water supplies for its fire department. Most of its buildings were wood, and even masonry structures weren't fireproof—in short, the city was a tinderbox. The "Great Fire" burnt out about 2,500 acres of prime land; thousands of buildings were lost, or about a third of all the assessed value in the city. One hundred thousand people lost their homes.

The good news was that the city had to rebuild. Chicago became the locus of the most spectacular sustained burst of architectural development in the country's history. Especially in the 1880s and 1890s, the Chicago

School of urban architecture—Louis Sullivan was its greatest exponent—pioneered clean, elevator high-rise, glass-enclosed steel-frame designs, with minimal ornamentation, well-lighted, open interior spaces, and separate shafts for utilities. As one leading Chicago architect put it:

> Bearing in mind that our building is a business building, we must fully realize what this means. . . . These buildings, standing in the midst of hurrying, busy thousands of men . . . should [carry] out the ideas of modern life—simplicity, stability, breadth, dignity. . . . [S]o imperative are all the commercial and constructive demands, that all architectural detail employed in expressing them must become modified by them. Under these conditions, we are compelled to . . . permeat[e] ourselves with the full spirit of the age, that we may give its architecture true art forms.

The technical challenges that the Chicago school overcame, and the development of an aesthetic of functionality, are fascinating stories in themselves. But the interesting question for us is why were companies suddenly buying huge office buildings? Or more precisely, why did white-collar staffs start growing so fast that paper management—forms and ledgers, file jackets, filing systems, bookkeeping machines, typewriters and carbon paper, business charts and graphs—had become a major industry in its own right by the 1890s?

The Conquest of the Clerks

Economists say that bigger companies need paperwork to substitute for internal markets. It's a nice point. In Lincoln's era, an ax maker bought semifinished wood and steel and sold the finished wares to wholesale merchants. As long as there were several suppliers and several distributors, he was reasonably sure of getting fair prices on both sides. But life was much different for a Carnegie Steel. By the 1880s and 1890s, it supplied its own coke and iron ore, its own pig iron, and much of its own rail and lake shipping facilities, and it maintained its own sales force. How, therefore, to compute profits on steel? First, one had to tot up the costs for the coke, the ore, the shipping, and everything else. But in the absence of normal invoices from outside suppliers, one needed careful internal cost records, which required an ever-growing army of clerks.* Standard Oil's operations were even more far-flung, and even more integrated, while big railroads housed a wide diversity of businesses, like their own coal mines, lumber forests, and extensive real estate operations. It's no surprise that all of these enterprises paid close attention to cost tracking from their earliest days.

But economists' explanations skip past the daily textures of business life. At bigger scales and higher speeds, the little details became ever more crucial. No one understood this better than Alexander Holley, the guru of American steel-making. Before his untimely death in 1882, he was a one-man tsunami of productivity suggestions. In his reports to the Bessemer Association and addresses to professional societies, he scolded his clients for their backwardness. Best-practice steam engine technology could have saved the equivalent of a quarter of labor costs at most plants. Inefficient furnaces were oxidizing away huge amounts of metal. The Germans were pulling ahead in the use of overhead belt conveyors. It was absurdly wasteful to support 119 rail-shape standards. Better management of furnace linings, more intelligent reprocessing of scrap, more aggressive application of continuous processing were all big cost and quality opportunities. You could not argue with Holley: he was widely acknowledged as the most deeply knowledgeable steel engineer in the country, was constantly traveling the world in search of best practices, and could fully document his recommendations. The whole course of his work was to force steel-makers out of their old rule of thumb operations into analysis-based management.

Two related crises in steel toward the end of the 1880s could have been object lessons from the Holley catechism. The first involved a shift to heavier rail standards. The weight of standard freight cars and locomotives, and the intensity of traffic, had all roughly doubled; it was very hard on rails, and rail service lives plummeted. The roads responded by increasing rail specifications from fifty-to-sixty-six pounds per yard to eighty-four-to-one-hundred pounds. But the big new rails had terrible service records, conjuring up memories of the iron rail failures of twenty years before. The second crisis related to structural steel. With their extensive bridge experience, the

---

*Today we call it "transfer pricing." It is one of the fiercest of intracompany battlegrounds, since there is no "right" way to allocate cost and revenue, and minor changes can materially affect executive bonuses.

Carnegie companies dominated structural steel in the 1880s, especially in Chicago. They not only made the largest, deepest beams, but produced the industry design bible, the Carnegie "Handbook," which included industry-standard sections—the details of joints and other critical segments—as well as sophisticated formulas for calculating beam and load relationships. In 1890, however, a large Carnegie beam for an important Chicago building shattered when it fell off the delivery wagon, causing much consternation in the industry.

It took till almost the end of the century to conclude that both problems stemmed from the "hard-driving" production methods of American Bessemer mills. The clue was that there were no performance issues with rails or beams made from open-hearth steel, which was just beginning to make inroads in the 1880s. The difference, it turned out, was that open-hearth steel was worked more slowly. High-durability steel requires not only the right chemistry but also tight, finely grained molecular structures. Rolling (or hammering) forces the molecular restructuring, but it occurs in jumps and is temperature-dependent—the cooler the rail or the beam the better. Since heavier steel components took longer to cool, they needed to be rolled or shaped more slowly: in short, hard-driving methods on scaled-up modern components turned out a deeply flawed product. (Holley had long warned about working steel at excessive temperatures.)

It was an especially bitter pill for Carnegie, who had been one of the primary advocates of hard-driving, and who had resisted the gradual encroachment of open-hearth. Carnegie therefore suddenly found himself playing catchup, as the structural industry made a mass move away from Bessemer steel. Once he realized his mistake, however, he moved with characteristic speed, and by the mid-1890s the Homestead Works had been almost entirely converted to open-hearth, for both the armor plate and structural markets. The rail market took another decade to make the shift.

Holley's initiatives, and the disturbing problems in rails and structural steel, were characteristic of the new challenges that all companies faced as they shifted into modern production modes. Keeping up inevitably involved hosts of new job categories. The Pennsylvania may have been the first mover, with the appointment of Charles Dudley, a Ph.D. chemist, to organize a testing and research laboratory in 1870. Steel companies started to hire chemists shortly thereafter; by the 1890s, they were adding physicists to analyze slices of beam crystal structures. By the mid-1880s, Standard

Oil had built a full-scale petroleum laboratory; its lubricant business, for example, had expanded to dozens of different lines, based on market research on target applications and their likely performance conditions—resistance to heat or cold, whether outdoors or indoors, what speeds, presence of contaminants. Railroad labs developed specification and testing protocols, and conducted rigorous tests of component failure modes to get control over their suppliers. Companies started to keep vendor histories and records of product performance. Industry committees sprang up by the dozen, serving as cross-company forums to hash out technical issues and to develop standard rail shapes, brake and signal conventions, structural loading formulas, safety practices, and much else. Operating manuals grew thicker, as did bid documents and contractual materials. Authority for railroad rates was shifting from senior executives to regional freight agents, whose stock-in-trade was detailed data on local business trends, traffic demands, and inventories of rolling stock.

The conscious wedding of academic research to industrial practice sparked a mini-boom in professional organizations. Between 1870 and 1900, no fewer than 245 professional societies were founded in America—for chemists, engineers, metallurgists, lawyers, doctors, economists, and others—aimed at improving professional standards and qualifications, ensuring the dissemination of the latest academic research, and influencing government and industrial policy. The spreading "institutional matrix" for science-based industry was fed by the impressive American investment in higher education, including the extensive network of the 1862 Morrill Act land grant colleges. The undergraduate population grew from 52,300 in 1870 to 237,000 in 1900, and the number of graduate students jumped from fewer than fifty to about six thousand. Quality, of course, was very uneven, but no European country came close to matching the breadth of opportunity. America was also an aggressive recruiter of science "stars" from German universities, and Germans played a major role in the founding of the industrial research laboratories at General Electric and AT&T in 1900. Overall, the effect was toward greater systematization of product and process development, ever more intensive application of standards, and better operating predictability—in a word, bureaucratization in its best sense.

At the same time, the complexities of company finance were growing apace. For a long time railroads had been virtually the only businesses that raised capital on semipublic markets. A new rail line, especially in the west, had to shell out millions for track and rolling stock before it earned a nickel. When Rockefeller went into oil refining, by contrast, he and a few friends could swing the costs of an oil refinery by themselves, and get it on line and churning out profits within a few months. Almost all his growth from that point was financed internally. (Rockefeller borrowed aggressively from banks, but those were mostly cash flow loans that were quickly repaid, not long-term investment capital.) Bridges and coal mines were usually financed with bonds, but investors treated them, reasonably enough, as railroad financings. Carnegie sold bonds through Junius Morgan to finance the Edgar Thomson Works, but that was exceptional, occasioned by his straitened circumstances in the 1873 crash. For the most part, Carnegie guarded his independence from investment bankers and securities markets as jealously as Rockefeller did.

In the 1880s, however, Wall Street began to build a market in "industrial" securities, essentially shares in businesses other than railroads and

As corporate enterprises increased in scale, paperwork became a major industry in its own right. The rapid expansion of office work opened new career possibilities for women. Pictured above is a mid-1890s insurance office.

banking. While public markets offered greater financing flexibility for big companies, they multiplied record keeping and correspondence requirements. Ironically, it was that most inward-focused of companies, Standard Oil, that indirectly created much of the impetus for industrials in the first place.

Corporate law was the province of American states. Typically, corporations were not allowed to own stock in other corporations, and there were usually burdensome restrictions on out-of-state corporations. Rockefeller's Cleveland takeover was accomplished by merging the acquisitions into Standard Oil, an Ohio corporation. But the legal status of the wide-ranging acquisitions in the 1870s was increasingly anomalous. Matters came to a head after John Archbold joined the Standard and led the buyouts of the oil region's refiners in 1879 and 1880. Rockefeller failed to get a bill through the Pennsylvania legislature that would have allowed him to reorganize and consolidate the separate properties. (Memories of the South Improvement Company still made him persona non grata in the state. That condition didn't last: a decade or so later, wags complained that Rockefeller had "done everything to the Pennsylvania legislature except refine it.")

The solution was the "Standard Oil Trust," the invention of Samuel C. T. Dodd, a leading region attorney, who joined the Standard about the same time as Archbold and was to be the company's long-serving general counsel. Dodd's trust structure became the standard technique for large combinations through the 1880s, until it was made unnecessary by the New Jersey Holding Company Act of 1890, which specifically enabled multilayered, multistate corporate structures. By that time, the term "trust" had become shorthand for almost any large business combination, regardless of its legal form.

Dodd's creation was as simple as it was cunning. The shares of all the constituent Standard companies, which eventually numbered thirty-nine, were put into the hands of a board of trustees in exchange for trust certificates. In theory, the trustees' sole legal function, as a congressional committee noted in 1889, was "the receipt of the dividends declared by the various corporations and the distribution of the aggregate of them to the holders of the trust's certificates, pro rata." The trust did not even own property: the Standard Oil building in New York City where the trustees worked was owned by the Standard of New York. The reason for the elaborate subterfuge, in the committee's words, was to shelter "the trusts and the trustees thereof from the charge of any breach of the conspiracy laws of the various

States, or of being a combination to regulate or control the price or production of any commodity." Maintaining the fiction required some blatant lying, as when Henry Flagler insisted to the committee that the trustees' role was "merely advisory. No power as such is ever used," and claimed never to have heard of a system of multistate market districts that had obviously been laid out at headquarters. The charade was ended in 1892 by incorporating as a New Jersey holding company and replacing the trust certificates with Standard of New Jersey stock.

An unintended consequence of the trust form was that all the constituent holdings had to issue corporate shares as the common denominator for trust certificates. Although the reorganization of the Standard did not involve any new capital—shareholders simply exchanged one form of security for another—its imitators, like the Cotton Oil Trust, the Linseed Oil Trust, the Lead Smelting Trust, the Whiskey Trust, and others, usually needed cash and issued large volumes of new shares, as did a later series of nontrust combinations in the steel industry, like American Steel and Wire, American Tin Plate, and National Tube.

The reputation of industrials was greatly enhanced by their performance during the market crash of 1893—at least they did much better than railroads, which had overexpanded yet again. After the merger boom among industrial companies in the first years of the twentieth century, their shares achieved roughly the same market presence as railroads. The creation of the Dow Jones Industrial Index in 1895 and John Moody's Industrial Manual in 1900 were signposts of their growing importance. Rockefeller's personal stock holdings in 1896, to take one example, were about 30 percent industrials, not including his gas and oil interests, while the remainder of his securities were in railroads and steamship lines. The spread of the corporate form and the ever wider distribution of corporate securities greatly multiplied paper requirements—prospectuses, annual reports, multicompany accounting and financial reports, and all the internal tracking systems to support them. Considering the paucity of mechanical aids, the breadth and sophistication of the financial systems at a company like turn-of-the-century Carnegie Steel are very impressive. The blast furnace cost tracking systems, for example, listed some eight thousand items. Furnace superintendents met monthly to review results and suggest improvements. The company calculated that the system saved $4 million the first year it was in effect.

Finally, one further consequence of the shift to bigger, more bureaucratized companies was a radical restructuring of the relation between workers and bosses.

Labor organizations had a long history in the United States, and work stoppages over wages and hours were common; but before the 1870s, unions tended to be local and craft-based: if the New York City hatters staged a walkout, it wasn't likely to be coordinated with their brothers in Philadelphia or Boston. In the artisanal mode of manufacturing that prevailed before the Civil War, moreover, the owner-managers of factories were usually from the same craft ranks as their workers, and most establishments were small enough to foster a spirit of communal enterprise. British investigators in the 1850s had been particularly struck by that point. Even in large plants, the artisanal mode survived well into the 1880s through the system of internal contracting: various operations were farmed out on a piece-rate basis to local specialists who supplied their own equipment and craftsmen and were allocated their own plant floor space.

The consolidation and scaling up of Holley-style continuous-process manufacturing businesses in the 1870s and 1880s—besides iron and steel, in oil, chemicals, flour, meat—eliminated many traditional craft categories. Labor historians sometimes speak of the "de-skilling" of manufacturing, which is not entirely accurate. It took considerable judgment and experience to be a senior operator in a high-speed rail rolling mill, and, often enough, the tasks eliminated were the most dangerous and exhausting ones, like hand-pouring molten steel into ingot molds. A British team visiting in the 1880s commented that American steelworkers "have to be attentive in guiding operations, and quick in manipulating levers . . . [but they] do not work so hard as the men in England." But even if the work was easier, the new process model entailed an immense loss of power for established craftsmen. The skills required in the modern factory were invented and controlled by the employer, and didn't take years of apprenticeship to acquire. The same visitors were struck by the short training periods required for raw hands in American mills; one Carnegie executive claimed he could make a farmboy into a melter, previously one of the more skilled positions, in just six to eight weeks. Integrated operations also eliminated the last vestiges of internal contracting. Line employees now worked only for other hired hands, increasing their psychological distance from senior managers. One labor historian has summed up the transition as one "from artisans to workers."

The new factory model prompted the first halting moves toward industrial unions; "worker in a steel plant" became a more important category than "iron puddler," so it made no sense to fragment labor along the old craft-based union lines. The Roman-candle growth of the Knights of Labor in the 1870s was one of the first expressions of that impulse, but the Knights collapsed after the 1886 Haymarket Square bombing, a victim of fierce repression and its own disorganization. (Haymarket Square, in Chicago, was the scene of a labor rally following a violent confrontation at McCormick Reaper. The bomber was never found, but he was more likely to be an anarchist, who were active in Chicago, than a Knight, although both were involved in organizing the rally. Seven policemen were killed, just one by the bomb, the rest from gunfire, which may have been mostly their own.)

The Amalgamated Iron and Steel Workers was one of the strongest industrial unions to emerge after the debacle of the Knights, although it still officially represented only skilled tradesmen. The confrontation between the Amalgamated and Carnegie Steel at the Homestead Works in 1892 is not only a permanent blot on the history of American labor relations—there may have been as many as thirty-five deaths—but a disfiguring stain on the character and reputation of Andrew Carnegie. From a longer view, the government's intervention against the Homestead strikers, and two years later during the famous Pullman strike near Chicago, was so unhesitating, and so crushing, that it effectively squelched the industrial union movement. After Homestead and Pullman, an intimidated labor movement retreated to the cautious, craft-based tactics of Samuel Gompers's American Federation of Labor (AFL)—until John L. Lewis rekindled the cause by leading his miners out of the AFL in 1935.

Homestead

Labor issues created terrible conflicts for Carnegie. He panted after public adulation and couldn't resist an applause line, even when it exposed him to charges of flagrant hypocrisy. Since the early 1880s, he had taken to spending approximately half of each year in England and Scotland, where, flaunting his Scots Chartist roots, he purchased a small stable of Radical newspapers and contributed generously to Radical causes ("Radicals" were roughly equivalent to modern "Liberals"). When he began to publish essays broadly defending the rights of labor against his benighted fellow executives, Gladstonian reformers practically canonized him as the paragon of the enlightened modern capitalist. How, indeed, could they have resisted a cherubic, open-pursed little tycoon spouting elegantly phrased reformist maxims? A sample of Carnegie's preachments:

> I am a strong believer in the advantages of Trade Unions, and organizations of work men generally, believing that they are the best educative instruments within reach.

> We expect from the presumably better-informed party representing capital much more than from labor; and it is not asking too much . . . that they should devote some part of their attention to searching out the causes of disaffection among their employees.

> To expect that one dependent upon his daily wage . . . will stand peacably and see a new man employed in his stead is to expect much. . . . [T]he employer of labor [should rather] allow his works to remain idle . . . than to employ a class of men who can be induced to take the place of other men. . . . There is an unwritten law among the best workmen: "Thou shalt not take thy neighbor's job."

The most deplorable features of the Homestead tragedy—the fierce commitment to cutting pay rates despite high profits, the insistence on breaking the union, the use of Pinkerton guards to protect strikebreakers—are usually laid at the feet of the steel company's chief executive, Henry Frick. While publicly supporting Frick, privately Carnegie assiduously shifted the blame to his "young & rather too rash" partner. Every aspect of the Homestead episode, however, was consistent with Carnegie's previous policies. He constantly focused on wage-cutting, with only Captain Jones resisting him: "I do not like a prospective reduction of wages." Jones wrote him in 1878, "Our men are working hard and faithfully . . . Now mark what I tell you. Our labor is the cheapest in the country." And in 1884, "We cannot reduce mechanics <u>more than</u> 10%. We are not paying at present any extravagant wages to our mechanics."

Jones's one major victory was a three-shift, eight-hour day on the grounds that it was "entirely out of the question to expect human flesh and blood to labor incessantly for twelve hours"; he argued as well that the extra productivity would more than cover any additional costs. Under Jones, the

Edgar Thomson Works was the only three-shift steel plant in the country,* and while it was also the most efficient and profitable as he had promised, Carnegie hated the thought that other companies may have had lower labor costs. The 1883 acquisition of Homestead, a two-shift plant, besides bringing an unruly labor force, created conflicting manning profiles within the Carnegie empire. In 1888, roughly the period of his most prominent pro-union declarations, Carnegie ruled that the ET would go to twelve-hour shifts. The ET men struck, and Carnegie closed the plant. He did meet personally with the strike leaders and thought he had reached a settlement. When that fell through, Jones was instructed to hire Pinkertons and reopen the plant with strikebreakers, while Carnegie retreated to Atlantic City. Although it received little outside notice, the confrontation dragged on for almost five months with only "the usual disorders" and "a slight loss of life." There was more violence at the ET in 1891 (Jones's death in a blast furnace accident occurred in 1889), but the company used its own armed men, deputized by the local sheriff, rather than Pinkertons. At least one worker was killed in the disorders, apparently by other workers.

Frick made a temptingly convenient scapegoat for Homestead. Fourteen years younger than Carnegie, he had built his H. C. Frick Co. into the dominant vendor of iron-smelting coke when he was still in his early twenties; by age thirty he was a millionaire. Although he could be charming, no one called him lovable. Widely acknowledged as a superb manager, he was taciturn, grimly intense, and subject to explosive rages—and he made no secret of his antipathy to organized labor. Carnegie had been an admirer of the coke company, and Frick, who was hungry for growth capital, encouraged him to invest to the point where Carnegie and his companies owned a majority position. Carnegie recruited Frick to the steel business after his brother Tom's death, and his own serious illness, in 1886, and Frick became president of the ET company in 1889. At Frick's urging, in 1892 Carnegie

---

*Both the two- and three-shift systems were on seven-day weeks. At Carnegie's plants, Christmas was the only scheduled day off. As a practical matter, men had time off when orders slowed or plants were renovated (which usually took a week or more in January), but those periods operated as minilayoffs, so the men were not paid. There were no benefits in the modern sense, although Jones instituted a system to help men finance company homes at favorable rates. Finally, all plants apparently had some mixture of shift lengths. Men doing very heavy work, of the kind that was most frequently mechanized, were generally allowed to work shorter shifts; and even in the three-shift days at the ET, a man who was truly just pulling levers would likely be put on a two-shift system.

merged all his steel properties into a new company, Carnegie Steel, the largest steel organization in the world, with Frick as chairman and chief executive. Their relations were never easy. With the notable exception of Jones, Carnegie was intolerant of independent executives; although nominally only a shareholder and "advisor," he insisted on being informed on everything, freely overruled the men supposedly in charge, and could be extremely patronizing in doing so.* As John W. Gates, another steel executive, put it: "No one in the Carnegie organization controlled Mr. Carnegie, but he controlled every other man."

There is little dispute about the bare facts of the Homestead strike. At the time of the strike, it was Carnegie's only union plant, in the sense that in 1889 the Amalgamated, much to Carnegie's irritation, had managed to establish itself as exclusive bargaining agent for the roughly eight hundred workers in the skilled categories. The Amalgamated, however, took an enlightened view of technological progress, expressly accepting that tonnage-based pay scales would fall as productivity rose, and that mechanization would gradually eliminate traditional job categories. (British steel executives would have found such flexibility extraordinary.) Carnegie executives, however, detested making job classifications a matter for union discussion, since the agreements tended to accrete into binding precedents and practice rules.

The union had not expected a serious confrontation in 1892; the only scheduled negotiation was a fairly routine updating of the wage scale. Both Carnegie and Frick, on the other hand, were resolved on a break; as one director put it, the "Amalgamated placed a tax on progress, therefore the Amalgamated had to go." At one point, Carnegie even drafted an announcement withdrawing recognition from the union, but Frick preferred to come to a negotiating impasse first, and began active preparations for a long strike, laying in supplies, reinforcing the plant fence, and building a sales inventory of high-margin products.

A key issue in assessing Homestead is Carnegie's attitude toward the use of strikebreakers, which he privately insisted was "foolish . . . repugnant to every feeling of my nature." Before he took off for Scotland,

---

*In a long, querulous cable to Frick listing Frick's shortcomings, Carnegie instructed, "Please read to managers." He also had the habit of mixing his instructions with airy travel notes: "But Good night. Off for Venice tomorrow." Or: "Yours of 19ᵗʰ received upon my return from Yachting," as if to underscore the difference between his position and the workaholic Frick's.

Carnegie met with Frick in New York and handed him a memo that restated his public position against the use of strikebreakers. It is hard to know what to make of that memo, especially since Carnegie himself had used strikebreakers at the ET not long before. Perhaps he had already repressed the memory, as he was fully capable of doing, or he may have regretted his action. But the use of a written memo at a private discussion, instead of a forceful oral presentation, looks like he was speaking for the record. Conceivably, Carnegie thought a written statement would be a salutory curb on Frick's antiworker impulses. More likely, he was creating a paper trail for posterity. Since the two men had already devoted "long and serious talks" to a possible strike, it is hard to believe that the topic of strikebreakers hadn't already come up. It would have been in character for Carnegie to have expressed reservations on strikebreakers, but to have left Frick a free hand while taking care to tidy up the record in case things went badly. Frick could hardly have cared, for he was delighted that Carnegie was leaving. Back when Frick was still managing his coke company, Carnegie, as majority shareholder, had forced a strike settlement favorable to the workers because the loss of coke supplies was costing him steel profits. Frick resigned and had to be cajoled back by Carnegie, but had no confidence in his consistency or judgment.

As it turned out, Frick and the union almost reached a settlement, and negotiations stretched to the point where Carnegie urged him to break them off. But they eventually foundered just as the old contract was ending, and Frick closed the works. As management's intentions had become clear, the Amalgamated had also made careful preparations, particularly taking pains that the entire workforce would act together. On July 1, workers' committees, with many of the men armed, took over the plant to ensure a complete shutdown. When the local sheriff declined to assault the plant, Frick ordered a force of three hundred Pinkertons, which he had assembled in Philadelphia, to take the plant from the river. The Pinkertons, almost all raw recruits with no training, and who were paid even less than the steelworkers, arrived on July 6 on a barge towed up the Monongahela. The workers had assembled on high ground above the disembarkation point and trapped them in a hail of gunfire. In the ensuing gun battle, the tug took off, leaving the barge floating helplessly. After some hours, and with the barge set afire, the Pinkertons surrendered and were allowed off the barge and up the bank. There they met an enraged, mostly female, gauntlet and were severely beaten before being hauled into the town as prisoners. A standard estimate—there are no precise numbers—is that one Pinkerton and seven workers were killed in the initial gunfight and three more Pinkertons were killed by the gauntlet. (Larger fatality numbers include estimates of deaths from disease and other factors during the long work stoppage.)

The fight ended with the workers' committees in full control of the town and the plant, but they sensibly gave way when eight thousand militiamen arrived on July 12. Carnegie, distraught and raging in Scotland, cabled that he would return to take control, but was shouted down by his partners. So he stayed firing off cables back home, while hiding from the press and Republican political leaders who feared that the confrontation could cost them the fall presidential election. (Democrat Grover Cleveland indeed unseated President Benjamin Harrison.) One of his first angry reactions, to his cousin and fellow director, George Lauder, however, is about tactics: "Matters at home *bad*—such a fiasco trying to send guards by Boat and then leaving space between River & fences for the men to get opposite landing and fire. Still we must keep quiet & do all we can to support Frick & those at Seat of War."

Public sympathies shifted radically when Alexander Berkman, an anarchist and longtime consort of Emma Goldman, walked into Frick's office on July 23, shot him twice in the neck, and then stabbed him three times. Amazingly, Frick wrestled Berkman to the ground and prevented his swallowing a lethal poison as he was being subdued by guards. Frick then remained at his desk, refusing anesthetic so he could guide a surgeon in removing the bullets lodged in his back and neck. After his wounds were dressed, he stayed at the office a while longer cleaning up paperwork and preparing a press statement: "I do not think I shall die, but whether I do or not, the Company will pursue the same policy." At home, a son, who was born on the day of the fight with the Pinkertons, lay dying. Frick attended the baby's funeral a week and a half later and a few days after that took his regular trolley car back to the office. His preternaturally cool performance won wide admiration, although as his biographer notes, it also suggests "something of a fanatical quality."

Under militia protection, a thousand men, or more than a quarter of the normal complement, were back at work by the end of July—many of them slept at the plant to avoid retribution at home. The other Carnegie plants were relatively undisturbed, although the Duquesne Works, a new plant recently acquired by Frick, had gone out for a week. Samuel Gompers made a speech calling for boycotts of Carnegie products, but refused to call for sympathy strikes. By October, Carnegie was expressing irritation that the plant was still not running full bore. The union officially threw in the towel in November, precipitating its rapid decline. Carnegie plants were nonunion from then on, and after the 1901 steel mergers, U.S. Steel remained a nonunion shop until the late 1930s. Management took full advantage of its victory. After allowing some months for the passions from Homestead to subside, wage scales were cut very sharply—by as much as 60 percent, according to a local newspaper, which reported that "These are the lowest scales of any in this section, union or nonunion."

The company's resistance to negotiated manning schedules is understandable. In just three years, the Amalgamated's manning agreement at Homestead had accumulated fifty-eight pages of footnotes explicating the rules of job classification. But Carnegie's and Frick's fierce commitment to cutting pay makes almost no sense, particularly when it so regularly provoked debilitating strikes. The 1890s marked the peak of the mechanization drive that had characterized the Carnegie company from its inception, and the labor content of a ton of steel was dramatically and continuously falling. As early as 1883, Captain Jones reported that he had reduced the labor cost of rails by a quarter, from 20 percent to 15 percent. New machinery in 1885 eliminated fifty-seven of sixty-nine men on the heating furnaces and fifty-one of sixty-three hands in the rail mill. In the 1892 Homestead negotiation, the company hoped to eliminate 325 of about 800 skilled positions. By 1897, Homestead had a quarter fewer men than in 1892, although production was far higher. Between 1896 and 1897 alone, labor costs per ton of Bessemer steel were reduced by 20 percent, while in open-hearth the labor cost reduction was about a third.

The extraordinary productivity at Carnegie plants put them in a different class from their competition. During a rail price war in 1897 Carnegie Steel pushed the other companies to the wall by driving rail prices from a previous low of $28 a ton to only $18, and at one point to an almost unimaginable $14. The chief executive of Illinois Steel, its biggest rail competitor, conceded that no one could match Carnegie's costs. In a year when almost no other steel company was operating profitably (Illinois actually prepared bankruptcy papers), Carnegie Steel racked up a stunning, record-high $7 million in profits, a number that *tripled* over the next two years. At the time of the Homestead strike, labor costs at Carnegie Steel were only 15.7 percent of sales, while earnings on sales were 8.6 percent. An offer of a 5 percent wage increase, which workers would have found quite generous, would have cost the partners less than 10 percent of that year's $4 million in earnings. By the end of the decade, profits on sales had soared to a remarkable 20 percent, while the labor costs of sales had dropped to only 10.5 percent. As one historian wrote of the entire industry, its "dismal labor policies represented a social choice to retain profits rather than distribute them as wages"—an observation that applies with even more force to Carnegie than to his competitors.

Screwing down the wage rate wasn't even smart business. Standard Oil offered an instructive example. Rockefeller detested unions as openly as Frick, but a congressional committee investigating the trust reported that "[a labor expert] agreed with practically all other witnesses who gave evidence on this point that the Standard Oil Company pays good wages and gives steady employment to its men." Not surprisingly, while the company was not unionized, it had been virtually free of labor strife.* After Homestead, Carnegie had protested to England's prime minister William Gladstone, "The Works are not worth one drop of human blood. I wish they had sunk." He would readily give up the works, that is, but a dime more on the daily wage was beyond him.

The problem went beyond wages. Living conditions in the Pittsburgh steel towns, all observers agreed, were appalling. Hamlin Garland wrote a famous account of Homestead in 1894:

> The streets of the town were horrible; the buildings were poor; the sidewalks were sunken, swaying, and full of holes, and the crossings were sharp-edged stones set like rocks in a river bed. Everywhere the yellow mud of the street lay kneaded into a sticky mass, through which groups of pale, lean men slouched in faded garments, grimy with the soot and grease of the mills.

---

*The most serious stain on the Rockefeller labor record is the famous "Ludlow Massacre" of 1914 (some years after the quotation above), which cost the lives of twenty coal miners and their relatives. The mining company was not managed by the Rockefellers, but the family was its major shareholder, and John D., Jr., who ran the family interests, was very well informed. He defended the incident at first, but Ludlow eventually converted him to the cause of labor reform. John D., Sr., was seventy-five at the time and more or less completely retired from business.

An 1890s Pennsylvania steel mill town. "Hell with the hatches on," one traveler called them.

The town was as squalid and unlovely as could well be imagined and the people were mainly of the discouraged and sullen type to be found everywhere where labor passes into the brutalizing stage of severity. . . . Such towns are sown thickly over the hill-lands of Pennsylvania. . . . They are American only in the sense in which they represent the American idea of business.*

British observers were similarly depressed. Stephen Jeans, secretary of the British Iron Trade Association, who was a great admirer of Carnegie and

---

*Although Garland does not comment on it, there is a distinct feeling in his interviews that, horrible as the life was, the men *liked* the mills—hot steel men swaggered, they got a masculine kick from the danger, and they bragged about it.

wrote a penetrating report on turn-of-the-century American steel plants, was surprised at the workers' living conditions, which left "a good deal to be desired" compared to those of British workmen. Another British visitor of the same period was more graphic:

> If Pittsburgh is hell with the lid off, Homestead is hell with the hatches on. Never was [a] place more egregiously misnamed. Here there is nothing but unrelieved gloom and grind. . . . I was not surprised at the English workman who told me that if anyone would give him five dollars a week he would go home and live like a gentleman in—the Black Country. . . . Trade unionism has been put down with an iron hand, dipped in blood. . . , but it is a plant which does not die when it has anything to feed on, and here it has much. . . . The management shows obvious signs of nervousness on the subject, and nervousness is weakness.

Carnegie's mendacity on labor matters is breathtaking. He would wink and smile at pre-Homestead rumors that his men were making up to $25 a day. Just a few years after Homestead, he wrote that people "may be surprised to know that we do pay the highest wages in the world. Every man at Homestead last year made two dollars and ninety cents per day average. This embraced common labor as well as skilled." If anyone else paid rates as high, he insisted, "I have never known of it." Actual wage rates were hardly a third of that figure. When Stephen Jeans was mystified at the stories that Carnegie plants paid an average $4 a day in wages, he checked personally with Carnegie, who assured him that the actual average was $2.25, which was still quite good. Jeans then puzzled over information from a plant superintendent that wages were much lower than that. It never occurred to him that Carnegie would simply lie.

Carnegie's one creditable action after Homestead was that he came to the plant the following year and spoke to the men. He came, he said, not "to rake up, but to bury the past," and, while stressing that he had "neither the power nor disposition to interfere . . . in the management of the business," he emphasized his strong support of Frick, a man of "ability, fairness, and pluck." Otherwise, one can watch him testing out Homestead narratives. He wrote to a leading Republican that the company "thought the three thousand old men would keep their promise to work and therefore opened the works *for them*. The [Pinkertons] were intended only to protect them." Other fictions included a last-minute letter ordering Frick to back away that somehow didn't arrive in time, and, finally, the desperate "Kind master, tell us what you wish" plea from his workers that was "alas, too late." And there was, of course, the convenient memo he had left with Frick. At least some contemporaries were beginning to see through the humbug. Here is the *St. Louis Post-Dispatch*:

> Count no man happy until he is dead. Three months ago, Andrew Carnegie was a man to be envied. Today he is an object of mingled pity and contempt. In the estimation of nine-tenths of the thinking people on both sides of the ocean he had not only given the lie to all his antecedents, but confessed himself a moral coward. One would naturally suppose that if he had a grain of consistency, not to say decency, in his composition, he would favor rather than oppose the organization of trades-unions among his own working people at Homestead. One would naturally suppose that if he had a grain of manhood, not to say courage, in his composition, he would at least have been willing to face the consequences of his inconsistency. But what does Carnegie do? Runs off to Scotland out of harm's way to await the issue of the battle he was too pusillanimous to share. A single word from him might have saved the battle—but the word was never spoken. Nor has he, from that bloody day until this, said anything except that he had "implicit confidence in the managers of the mills." The correspondent who finally obtained this valuable information expresses the opinion that "Mr. Carnegie has no intention of returning to America at present." He might have added that America can well spare Mr. Carnegie. Ten thousand "Carnegie Public Libraries" would not compensate the country for the direct and indirect evils resulting from the Homestead lockout. Say what you will of Frick, he is a brave man. Say what you will of Carnegie, he is a coward. And gods and men hate cowards.

The Creation of the Carnegie Company

By 1895, after Frick had been at the helm of Carnegie Steel for only three years, the relationship was clearly breaking down. Carnegie initiated the split, exhibiting immense animosity toward Frick, possibly reflecting lingering resentments from Homestead. For his part, Frick was thoroughly sick of the accumulated irritations of living under Carnegie's thumb—as he explained with characteristic directness:

> Mr. Carnegie, . . . I desire to quietly withdraw, doing as little harm as possible to the interests of others, because I have become tired of your business methods, your absurd newspaper interviews and personal remarks and unwarranted interference in matters you know nothing about.

At least some of the partners were alarmed. An agreement was finally worked out that Frick would give up the presidency but retain the title of Chairman. John Leishman, not yet forty, was appointed president, and Frick ceded him a 5 percent interest in the company from his own 11 percent stake. Henry Phipps, a long-time partner now semiretired, professed himself much relieved, writing to his nephew that "A.C. must have climbed down a very long and steep way." By all accounts, Frick was doing a fine job, especially in integrating the far-flung Carnegie steel businesses into a unified operation. Carnegie had organized each major component as a separate company—probably because it increased his control over the managers. Frick built the "Union Railroad" to tie together all the Carnegie plants, and gradually developed a fully integrated business structure, from ore through initial distribution, much as Rockefeller had done. The last link in the chain, a Great Lake steamship line, opened on his last day at the company in 1899. As the early company historian, James Bridge, wrote, at that point Carnegie Steel controlled "every movement of its material, and all its operations, from mining of the crude ore to the shipment of the finished steel, paying no outsider a price."*

The Frick-Carnegie tensions markedly eased in the first days of the new management structure. Frick stayed very active in the company, but lightened up on his work schedule, began to travel more, and started his famous art collection (he had a surprisingly good eye). But the stars once again shifted against Frick when Leishman, grievously over his head in the presidency,

---

*See the chapter Notes for more detail on Frick's performance record. In Carnegie's defense, he and Frick most commonly differed over Frick's proclivity to enter, and stick to, steel market sharing and price-maintenance agreements. Carnegie didn't mind joining pools, but in economics-speak, whenever the pool price was higher than the market-clearing price, Carnegie would cut prices and take share. The earlier quote from John W. Gates about Carnegie's disruptiveness was specifically with reference to Carnegie's upsetting a price-maintenance agreement. But while Frick had his flaws, the company prospered mightily during his tenure, and it is hard to see Carnegie's behavior as anything but destructive. The core problem may have been Carnegie's inability to share a spotlight.

asked out in early 1897, and was replaced by Charles Schwab, only thirty-four, but a clear up-and-comer, and a special favorite of the old man.

Schwab proved to be one of the greatest of American steel executives. He was a store clerk when he caught the eye of Captain Jones, and, at seventeen, started at the company as a dollar-a-day stake driver. Six months later, Jones had him running a major blast furnace construction program. At age twenty-five Schwab was thrown into, and straightened out, a very troubled postacquisition Homestead Works, which had been seriously mismanaged during its short history, and after Jones's death in 1889, Schwab was his natural successor. A fine picture of Schwab's presidential style can be gleaned from the minutes of the weekly operating committees: he was crisp and decisive, deeply informed, and with an easy, collegial, command. The plant rank-and-file loved him; he was one of their own and a regular back-slapping presence on the factory floor, although he held the line on costs and wages as hard as Carnegie and Frick. He was also formidably self-educated in the technical aspects of steel-making and controlled the roadmap for technology investments. On top of all that he was a charmer and a jester, with just the touch of sycophancy that made him dear to Carnegie. Although Schwab stayed on good terms with Frick, his mere presence fed into Carnegie's lamentable tendency to adopt one favorite at a time and make everyone else miserable. With Leishman gone and fair-haired "Charlie" ensconced in the presidency, Carnegie's bilious energies inevitably refocused on Frick.

Adding to the frictions was Carnegie's uncharacteristic turn to caution in the 1890s. Instead of his usual cheerleading for new investment, he shifted to something nearer obstructiveness. He resisted the trend to open-hearth steel in the structural market, and vetoed the acquisition of the rich Mesabi ore ranges around the Great Lakes, allowing John D. "Reckafellows," as Carnegie called him, to snatch the ore region from under his nose. Rockefeller later professed to have been "astonished that the steel-makers had not seen the necessity of controlling their ore supply." Fortunately for Carnegie, Rockefeller was more interested in his Great Lakes shipping interests than in iron, and leased the fields to Carnegie Steel at very attractive rates. Carnegie's ore subsidiary company almost immediately violated the leasing agreements, drawing a shocked response from Frederick Gates, who managed the Rockefeller portfolio. For the second time, Rockefeller passed up the chance to squeeze Carnegie and agreed to a reasonable settlement.

Sometime in early 1898, Carnegie's partners, with Frick and Henry Phipps in the lead, floated the idea of either selling the company or buying out Carnegie. Mostly they wanted to get rich. The deals market was heating up, and Carnegie's tight-fisted approach to dividends had not allowed them to realize the wealth commensurate with the value of their stakes. But there are also discreet hints of the attractions of running the business without the constant second-guessing from Scotland. Carnegie vacillated maddeningly on the idea—sometimes luxuriating in the notion of a glorious retirement and a career in philanthropy, sometimes insisting that their best days were still ahead and no sale could give them real value. Phipps began to spend much of his time in Scotland, enlisting Carnegie's wife's support for a sale, and sending Frick weatherlike updates on their senior partner's moods.

Valuation discussions were tense. Frick thought his coke company was worth $70 million by itself, which was high even by modern standards. Carnegie was thinking of a $250 million valuation for the steel businesses, which was also high but closer to reality. Steel output was suddenly growing at a breakneck 20–25 percent a year, and profits were up two-thirds, to $11.5 million in 1898, and looked to keep on growing strongly. For Carnegie, even contemplating such valuations was a violent departure from his long habit of pouring scorn on the inflated numbers of his fellow industrialists. Conservative practice focused on book value: a business was worth no more than its actual investment in plant, inventory, and other hard assets plus undistributed profits, less liabilities and depreciation. Carnegie Steel's book value in 1898 was $49 million, while the coke company's was $5 million. Anything more, in the traditional view, was just "water," an unsecured claim on future success. Normal valuation rules, however, were just then being turned upside down by Pierpont Morgan's highly capitalized deals in steel and other industries. To the frustration of his partners, the hot deals market led Carnegie into reveries about how much *more* he could get if he only waited a few more years.

Finally, in the first week of the new year of 1899, at a partners' meeting at his New York home, Carnegie gave the go-ahead to a sale at $250 million, stressing that his consent came "with great reluctance" and only for the sake of "his oldest Partner," Phipps. He immediately began to worry that the price was too low, since he expected very high 1899 earnings (which, in fact, came in even better). But Frick was given the mandate to put together a sale, as Carnegie hovered anxiously in the background.

To Frick's great chagrin, the Rockefeller interests declined to bid, and discussions quickly broke down with the Morgan representatives. They thought Carnegie's price was high—they also may have been tapped out of ready funds—and insisted on an all-stock transaction, while Carnegie wanted half stock and half gold bonds. (Elbert Gary, who was informally looking after Morgan's steel interests, said he "received no encouragement at all" from Morgan, but also noted that Morgan had not yet focused on his steel businesses and knew little about them.) The partners explored a recapitalization on their own—in effect, taking the company public—but that also got tangled in valuation arguments.

Frick was then approached by "Judge" William H. Moore, a prototype of the 1980s leveraged buyout artist. He and his brother John had just organized several big steel deals, as well as the mergers that created the National Biscuit and the Diamond Match companies; in short, he was just the type of operator Carnegie detested. To make it worse, Moore had once mocked Carnegie for knowing only how to make steel, and nothing about "making securities, preferred and common stocks and bonds." Carnegie exacted $1 million for a ninety-day option to Moore for a buyout at the same price offered to Morgan. The option price was subsequently recalculated to $1,170,000, but Frick and Phipps put up the additional cash themselves on the understanding that Carnegie would not keep the money if the deal fell through. (There was no written agreement to that effect, but Carnegie had confirmed that intent in a note to the board.)

Word of the impending deal quickly leaked out. *Iron Age* wrote a highly laudatory piece on "Andrew Carnegie's Retirement," although Carnegie must have bristled at the attention they paid Frick, whom they called "the principal factor in [the company's] phenomenal development," just as he had been "one of the principal factors in the industrial development of the United States." John Gates wrote Carnegie a congratulatory telegram, while Schwab and Frick gleefully projected how easily the expected 1899 profits would support the buyout debt. But then Moore unexpectedly ran into trouble with his financing. While he did manage to pull together another proposal, and the glowing press notices continued to flow, there was no longer a chance of closing within the option period.

Frick and Phipps made the pilgrimage to Carnegie's castle in Scotland to arrange an extension. Carnegie was cold: "not one hour," he told them; it was high time for the partners to refocus their "attention to business." The meeting seems to have ended cordially enough, with some discussion of recapitalizing on their own. But a slow-burning anger was building in Carnegie, which is understandable, especially for one so thin-skinned and protective of his reputation. His personal creation, the greatest steel company in the world, had been trapped in a failed financing by a disreputable operator, and he felt the fool. And he blamed Frick.

When the option expired in early August, Carnegie not only kept Moore's million-dollar option payment but told Frick and Phipps that he was keeping their $170,000 as well. According to Carnegie, he was upset because he had not known Moore was running the deal, and on top of that, had just discovered that Frick and Phipps had arranged to divide a $5 million stock bonus if the deal closed, which they indignantly denied. Both sides were exercising selective memory. It is extremely implausible that Carnegie didn't know about Moore. He would never have allowed an anonymous syndicate to shop his company, and his demand for the large option payment was consistent with his mistrust of Moore. Besides that, the deals world was very small, and Carnegie was very plugged in, so he couldn't easily have avoided knowing who was involved. On the other hand, there is also no question Frick and Phipps had made the offending bonus arrangement. But it wasn't a secret, for they had described it in a cable to Carnegie early in the deal. Presumably, if he had objected then, they would have dropped it. In any case, it was hardly as egregious as the ones he had routinely arranged for himself in his bridge deals.

Relations between Frick and Carnegie never recovered. The final detonation came over coke prices. Carnegie claimed that Frick Coke had committed to delivering its coke at a permanent price of $1.35 a ton, or less than half the market price. There was in fact no such contract, although Frick conceded that he and Carnegie had discussed one. As Frick also pointed out, he was just a minority holder in the coke company, despite its name, and he had no authority to make contracts. Besides that, siphoning profits from Frick Coke for the account of the steel company was a

The Steel Tycoon: Andrew Carnegie, late 1890s.

breach of duty to the coke company's minority holders. Frick was clearly right on the merits, but Carnegie understood his stance as a "Declaration of War," as Frick expected him to.

Carnegie immediately wrote his closest partners and Schwab that Frick had to go, and that he was coming to Pittsburgh to take charge of the ouster. For his part, Frick had no interest in staying on; he quickly submitted his resignation and left on a short vacation. But Carnegie was now in full-blown attack mode and was determined not just to oust Frick but to lock in the coke rate and take control of the coke company. His weapon was to be the "Iron Clad Agreement" that he and his partners had signed after Tom's death in 1886. The Iron-Clad permitted the expulsion of a partner by a three-quarter vote; in such a case, the expelled partner got only the book value of his stock, which would have wiped out about 80 percent of the fair market value of Frick's holdings.

Carnegie pushed through the expulsion vote. It was clearly vindictive, since Frick had already resigned, but only Phipps and another small holder refused to sign it. When Frick returned from his vacation in early January 1900, Carnegie delivered his ultimatum personally: produce the coke deal he wanted or get expelled under the Iron-Clad. Listeners on the other side of the door heard Frick's explosion: "For years I have been convinced that there is not an honest bone in your body. Now I know that you are a god damned thief!" Accounts differ on whether Frick actually chased Carnegie from the room. It was the last time the two men ever met or communicated directly.

As it turned out, for one of the only times in his life, Carnegie was forced into a near-total retreat. Frick beat him to the courtroom and sued for a fair valuation of his holdings. It quickly emerged that the Iron-Clad didn't apply to Frick, that it may have been improperly executed in the first place, and that it had not been consistently enforced. Frick's lawyers also subpoenaed Carnegie Steel's books and records, so enterprising reporters started publishing details of the company's extraordinary profits, at a time when America's very high steel tariffs were under attack by Democrats in Congress. Both Carnegie and Frick were deluged with pleas to stop the idiocy—Mark Hanna, the Republican kingmaker, and George Westinghouse each weighed in personally.

A settlement was finally worked out in March, one that was all that Frick could have hoped for. A new corporation, the Carnegie Co., was created as a New Jersey holding company, with a market capitalization of $320 million, half in 5 percent bonds and half in stock carrying a 5 percent dividend. All the shares in the old companies were converted fifty/fifty into Carnegie Co. bonds and shares. The Carnegie Co. was a pure holding company: it held the shares of the coke and steel companies, and twelve other steel-related businesses, most of them quite small, and collected dividends to service the payments on its own securities. Carnegie was still the real boss, but his long-suffering partners finally got their payday. The yearly interest and dividend payments were nearly $1.8 million for Phipps and just short of $1 million for Frick, while Carnegie's own 60 percent interest brought a whopping $9.6 million.

Just before the deal closed, Carnegie was beset by doubts on the valuations, for he wrote an anxious note to the company treasurer, Lawrence Phipps, asking how he could be sure the securities were really worth so much. The return answer was soothing, but hardly reassuring. The company's shares did not trade on an exchange, and Phipps quite correctly wrote that "The Directors have recorded their opinion that the Stocks of the Operating Companies are of full value . . . so that the Carnegie Company books must be opened on that basis." Absent a public market, that is, the shares were worth whatever the directors said they were worth.

In truth, the valuations were far too high. The write-ups over book value were aggressive enough. The coke company was valued at $70 million, or Frick's high estimate, for a thirteenfold write-up, while the steel company's write-up was a more modest 3.7 times. What really mattered, however, was the interest and dividend burden, which, at $16 million, could have been crippling. The record-breaking $21 million of profits in 1899 left a comfortable margin, but it was the first year ever that earnings would have been sufficient to cover the new level of payouts.* (Dividend payments, of course, unlike interest, are not mandatory. But contemporaries attached great importance to living up to dividend commitments, and Carnegie would have been a laughingstock if it were discovered that he had missed a dividend immediately after the deal.)

Carnegie confidently expected $40 million, or even $50 million in earnings in 1900, which would have been ample cushion. But after getting off to a spectacular start, business slowed sharply in the spring and summer, and total earnings were not much above 1899's.† There was a one-time $12.9 million dividend bonus on closing, which the company clearly hoped to pay out mostly in cash. But except for an initial pro rata cash distribution of $750,000, no further cash payments were made in 1900. Carnegie and

---

*Earnings in 1898 are often shown as $16 million. Steel and coke earnings, in fact, were $11.5 million, but the company also booked several extraordinary items: $2 million for a railroad right-of-way payment and $2.5 million of paper profits from a variety of security write-ups. The write-ups were a deviation from the company's normal practice of carrying its subsidiaries' securities at cost. My guess is that Frick and Phipps were quietly building their case for recapitalization or sale of the company. In Carnegie's notes, he usually crossed out the $16 million and wrote in $11.5 million. The company did not use depreciation accounting, so interest and dividend payments had to be covered from book earnings.
†See Appendix I for details. Carnegie claimed, and other histories repeat, that the company made $40 million in 1900. That is about a third higher than the actual figure.

several other wealthier directors agreed to take their dividend in paper, while payment was simply deferred for everyone else. Although the company had plenty of cash at the outset of the year, it was coming under strain in the fall. The steel company's November earnings were only $362,000, or less than a tenth the average monthly profits in the first quarter, and not nearly enough to cover even the monthly interest burden. In July, Carnegie suggested delaying interest on the bonds to finance continued investment; Schwab and the other directors were politely appalled. In fact, Carnegie's personal income statement for the year suggests that he collected considerably less than the full amount of interest he was entitled to, and no dividends.

It is amazing to see Carnegie, the sworn foe of watered balance sheets, signing on for such a burdensome structure. It can't all be blamed on Frick. The $320 million valuation was among the very highest discussed within the company. And just a month before, Carnegie had rejected out of hand a settlement offer from Phipps and Frick for only $250 million. There was pressure from Carnegie's partners for a high-cap deal—their thirst for a big payday, after all, had been building for almost thirty years. But he was used to that, and could easily have insisted on something lower. Quite possibly, he was sick of the publicity surrounding the string of $200-million-plus steel mergers by the Morgan syndicates, the Moores, and others. Putting together an even bigger deal may have salved an ego still bruised from the failed transaction of the previous summer.

Clearly, whatever fault lay with Carnegie and Frick, it was the stimulus of Pierpont Morgan's megamergers that placed such lofty valuations within the realm of rational discussion. There were other players in the market, such as the Moores, but they would have had limited credibility unless Morgan had confirmed their valuations with deals of his own. During the decade from about 1895 to 1905, Morgan's transactions, and those of lesser figures like the Moores, transformed the contours of American business; they will be the main topic of the next chapter. Another consequence of the sudden spate of giant corporations was a burst of activity under the rubric of antitrust.

Trust-Busting

No other country carried the animus against trusts to the degree that America did. All governments scratched their heads about the best way to deal with the very large companies that were popping up everywhere at the close of the nineteenth century, but nowhere else was trust-busting, as Richard Hofstadter put it, "a way of life and a creed." Most other countries, especially on the continent, freely granted monopolies in railroads and similar businesses, and as often encouraged bigness in the name of national competitiveness.

The antimonopoly fervency in America traces back to Andrew Jackson and earlier. Hofstadter locates it in a culture of "farmers and small-town entrepreneurs—ambitious, mobile, speculative, antiauthoritarian, egalitarian, and competitive." The path to salvation in mainstream American Protestantism was one of deep existential solitude: puny humans marching half-blind across a black plain buffeted by forces cold, cosmic, and violent. That was also a fair job description for a Minnesota wheat farmer, or for a small manufacturer caught in a Wall Street financial panic. The same mind-set assigned quasi-biblical status to a rigorous form of laissez-faire economics. Business competition fit neatly within the metaphor of constant struggle: it forged the character and discipline required for the larger battle.

By the time of the Interstate Commerce Act (1887) and the Sherman Antitrust Act (1890), however, the force of religious millennialism and the agrarian reform impulse were both attenuating, especially with respect to railroads. Since farmers had been the beneficiaries of a prolonged, and very steep, fall in railroad freight rates, the question of maximum rates hardly came up during the hearings. The hot-button issue for Interstate Commerce Act (ICA) advocates was instead the glaring inconsistency between very low long-distance shipping rates and proportionately much higher short-haul rates. But by this time, the aggrieved parties were eastern merchants. Astute western businessmen-farmers had long understood that it was precisely such rate discrimination that kept them in business.

There was no mystery to railroad rate-setting: the roads charged whatever they thought the traffic would bear. When long-haul west–east lines first opened, railroads marked up their rates proportionate to the distances and got very little business. Western wheat came to dominate world markets only after railroads made it very cheap to get to the coast. New York farmers and grain merchants were the big losers, but the chances of Congress requiring the roads to *raise* rates from the west were approximately zero.* What farmers did care about, on the other hand, was rate *volatility*, since the perennial price wars frequently caused a violent seesawing of tariffs. The Eastern Traffic Association, the large eastern rail pool that Albert Fink managed with great competence through most of the 1880s, had brought a measure of stability to eastern rates, at least while times were prosperous. While few congressmen could openly contradict the years of reformist antipooling rhetoric, many had come to believe that regulated pooling might offer the most reasonable path to achieving rate stability.

Much the same ambivalence surrounded the passage of the Sherman Antitrust Act. Grass-roots worries about "monopoly" had temporarily subsided: Free Silver was the only Populist platform plank William Jennings Bryan needed to adopt to gain the Populist party's endorsement in 1896. At the same time, rising academic lights, like John Bates Clark and Richard Ely, the founder of the American Economics Association, were beginning to question the validity of the traditional laissez-faire canons, and at least some congressmen were aware of their thinking. There was also a groping appreciation that in industries like steel and oil, global competitiveness required large-scale production and distribution units. Just as with the ICA, many years of reformist momentum had finally built to the point where the public expected action, but it was suddenly not at all obvious what a legislative program should look like.

In short, it wasn't necessarily corruption or incompetence that produced such toothless compromises in both the original Interstate Commerce and Sherman Antitrust acts. Congressmen may have consciously crafted "wait and see" bills. The new commission that emerged from the ICA had extensive surveillance powers on whether rates were "reasonable and just," but no rate-setting power or powers of enforcement other than bringing an action in federal court. While there was a proscription against long-haul/short-haul rate discrimination, it was vitiated by the qualifier that it applied only

---

*The historian Albro Martin has pointed out that railroad rates disadvantaged *every* business with respect to its peers to the west, and similarly conferred an "unfair" advantage over any business to the east. New York, unfortunately, was where you ran out of east.

under "substantially similar conditions or circumstances," which courts proceeded to read very narrowly—merely the presence of competition was enough to defeat the "substantially similar" test. Only rebates and pooling were quite definitely disallowed. As an indication of the bill's fragmented support, one of its sponsors, New York senator Orville Platt, who had been educated in railroad rate-making by Fink, refused to sign it over the anti-pooling clause.

The language of the Sherman Act was similarly cautious. The first draft's prohibitions against actions that would limit "full and free competition" were replaced with traditional common law formulations: the law forbade only contracts or combinations "in restraint of trade or commerce" or attempts "to monopolize any part of . . . trade or commerce." Sophisticated congressmen were fully aware of the flexibility of the common law precedents. Reformers thought they won a round by imposing horrific penalties for violations—prison terms, huge fines, and forfeit of corporate property. But when it became clear that courts would never impose them, even the reformers lobbied for reductions.

The unintended effect of both laws was to speed the pace of mergers. For the first decade or so after the Sherman Act's passage, the Supreme Court, by narrow majorities, followed a strict interpretive line: if the Act barred "any" combination in restraint of trade, it meant *any*—while the minority insisted that even the strict interpretation implied a reasonableness standard, since every contract theoretically acts as a restraint on trade. In the early 1900s, the Court gradually swung behind an accommodationist position more akin to the British common law approach. By the time of the 1911 Standard Oil breakup, the "reasonableness" banner had carried the field, although the company's assumed "90%" market share was taken as sufficient evidence of unreasonable concentration, while U. S. Steel's roughly 50-percent-plus market share passed muster. (In a triumph of prejudice over logic, for many years the Court not only insisted that labor unions were "combinations in restraint of trade" but also refused to apply the same reasonableness tests they used for business combinations.)

The Court's benign view of mergers, however, was paralleled by a very strict standard for reviewing agreements *between* companies aimed at dividing markets or maintaining prices. In the *Northern Securities Co. v. U.S.* case (1904) the Court did not permit a Morgan-brokered holding company designed to resolve a years'-long war between the E. H. Harriman and James J. Hill lines to the far Northwest. One of the offending features of the structure, according to the Court, was that it was not the "real owner of the stock in the railroads" but merely "the custodian or trustee." *Northern Securities* culminated a long string of decisions that left no doubt of the Court's hostility to "loose" combinations like Albert Fink's railroad pools. You didn't need a genius lawyer to figure out that if you wanted to combine, a genuine "tight" merger had the best survival prospects, as long as you merely stayed under a Standard-scale "unreasonableness" threshold.* The national railroad system eventually consolidated around six or seven large networks, and the Interstate Commerce Commission (ICC) was finally empowered to set all interstate railroad tariffs in 1906. Once the Commission began prescribing tariffs, rates generally rose.

Spotlight on the Standard

The Standard, like no other company, was a magnet for intense, angry antitrust scrutiny, especially after Ida Tarbell's *History of Standard Oil* completed its nearly two-year serialization run in *McClure's Magazine* in 1903. Between 1904 and 1906, at least twenty major antitrust suits were filed against the Standard by various states' attorneys general, and in late 1906 the United States Bureau of Corporations filed its own enforcement suit, triggering the case that eventually led to the breakup of the Standard five years later.

By the time the case got to the Supreme Court in 1910, the record, in the Court's words, was

> inordinately voluminous . . . aggregating about 12,000 pages, containing a vast amount of confusing and conflicting testimony relating to innumerable, complex, and varied business transactions, extending over a period of nearly forty years. . . .

---

*Oliver Wendell Holmes, Jr., in a well-known dissent in *Northern Securities,* zeroed in on the logical weakness of the tight/loose distinction. The government finally abandoned it, and the antitrust division now reviews proposed mergers for their anticompetitive effect regardless of their legal form.

Both as to law and as to the facts, the opposing contentions pressed in the argument are numerous, and in all their aspects . . . irreconcilable.

Thus on the one hand, with relentless pertinacity and minuteness of analysis, it is insisted that the facts establish that the assailed combination took its birth in a purpose to unlawfully acquire wealth by oppressing the public and destroying the just rights of others . . . .[with the result that the Standard] is an open and enduring menace to all freedom of trade, and is a byword and reproach to modern economic methods. . . .

On the other hand, in a powerful analysis of the facts, it is insisted that . . . [the Standard is] the result of lawful competitive methods, guided by economic genius of the highest order, sustained by courage, by a keen insight into commercial situations, resulting in the acquisition of great wealth, but at the same time serving . . . to widely extend the distribution of the products of petroleum at a cost largely below that which would have otherwise prevailed.

(The Court neatly ducked deciding between those polar positions, basing its breakup ruling merely on the fact that the Standard had achieved a practical monopoly.)

Unlike the Court, many historians appear to take the government's anti-Standard case as proven, although the actual record is not nearly so clear. One of the major threads in the government's case, for example, was the charge of predatory pricing, or below-cost price strategies to drive specific independents out of business. When the historian John McGee examined *every* alleged case of predatory pricing, however, he could not find "a single instance in which the Standard used predatory price cutting." While there were a few cases that remained ambiguous, most stemmed merely from regional price differences, which McGee found almost always justified by local economics. In several cases where there had been price wars, they had been initiated by the complaining independents. Another major line of pricing charges involved a Standard experiment with self-service wholesale distribution centers for retailers, which local jobbers charged was a predatory attack on their businesses. But the Standard didn't change its prices; rather, it set up stations where retailers could come and fill kerosene cans at the same prices charged to local middlemen—possibly an instance where the Standard was picking up distribution tricks from the meatpackers. The complaints, moreover, were often enough successful oilmen. Lewis Emery, for example, who later was a fiery anti-Standard Pennsylvania state legislator, made a career out of starting oil companies and selling them to the

Standard; the Standard even provided start-up financing for one of his companies.* At the time of his complaint, Emery was a primary investor in the Pure Oil Co., one of the most successful of the independents. Jeremiah Jenks, the staff director for the 1899 Industrial Commission hearings, examined Standard pricing practices and concluded that "many instances" of arbitrary price shifting to disadvantage competitors "may be considered as established," although in the one case he examined in detail he found that the facts did not support the charge.

There were also many complaints of discriminatory use of the Standard's powerful position in pipelines. But until the law was amended in 1906, pipelines were clearly *not* a common carrier under the Interstate Commerce Act, which covered only "the transportation of passengers or property wholly by railroad, or partly by railroad and partly by water." And the suspicions of collusion with railroads and the payments of illegal rebates never died. Archbold, in the Industrial Commission hearings, freely admitted that the Standard had negotiated many varieties of rebates before they were outlawed by the Interstate Commerce Act, but had not done so since, producing letters from all the leading railroad presidents attesting to the truth of his assertion. But the charges persisted, most sensationally in a case brought by the government in 1906 that resulted in the Standard being assessed, in the words of Ron Chernow, "the largest fine in corporate history for a practice it supposedly had given up long before." The case bears examining in some detail.

In its suit, the government alleged that Standard Oil of Indiana had received a discounted rate of six cents per one hundred pounds, instead of the tariff rate of eighteen cents, on oil shipped from its Whiting, Indiana, refinery by the Chicago and Alton Railroad. After a jury had found for the government, the district court judge, Kenesaw Mountain Landis (later a famous reforming commissioner of baseball), determined that 1,462 carloads of oil had been shipped during the three-year period covered by the charge (1903–05) and imposed a penalty of $20,000 per carload, or $29,240,000, which he calculated to be about a third of the net worth of the parent, the Standard Oil Co. of New Jersey.

---

*Some of these judgments are, obviously, in the eye of the beholder. Another analysis, based on the same data, suggests that Emery may have been a "serial squeezee" rather than a willing serial seller, although it does not address the fact that the Standard was also an Emery investor.

According to the case record, the Alton had filed an 1895 commodity shipping tariff for eighteen cents per one hundred pounds; the tariff included a long list of covered commodities, but did not mention oil. A subsequent ruling by an Illinois commission, however, determined that oil came within one of the 1895 tariff's classifications. In testimony that was excluded by Landis, the Standard freight manager said that when he inquired as to oil freight rates at the Alton, he was handed a headquarters freight sheet showing the six-cent rate, and a copy of the tariff application to the ICC. The railroad traffic agent, in testimony that was also excluded, confirmed the Standard manager's account and said he had never known of another rate. Apparently in consequence of a clerical mistake, however, the six-cent oil tariff was not actually filed until after the period in question.

The primary Standard defense was that it had reasonably relied on the railroad's representation, and it also pointed out that the only other railroad serving that route, the Eastern Illinois, also charged the six-cent rate. But Landis found the Eastern Illinois's rate also to be improper. The Eastern Illinois, after joining with the Alton in the original 1895 commodity tariff filing, had indeed filed a separate six-cent oil tariff a month later. In 1903, however, it had issued another tariff "confirming" the eighteen-cent tariff in the original 1895 filing. Apparently realizing that the new filing arguably conflicted with the separate 1895 oil tariff, the railroad issued an amendment the next day, reconfirming the six-cent oil tariff. But the Eastern Illinois failed to complete the filing of that amendment until after 1905. Landis ruled that it was the Standard's responsibility to determine whether railroad tariffs were properly filed, and since there were no mitigating factors, he imposed the largest possible fine permitted under the law.

The Standard's position in Indiana is relevant to understanding the case. The Whiting refinery was the largest in its system, and was the largest in the world when it opened in 1890. It was very much of a personal Rockefeller project, and the Standard's dominant position in the Indiana–Illinois area could be considered his last great bequest to his company. Oilmen had long known of large Midwest crude reserves, but it was high-sulphur "sour" oil, unusable for any commercial purposes. Rockefeller always worried about declining production from Pennsylvania wells, and pressed for major Midwest acquisitions to secure a continuing crude supply. At one point, after his partners had voted against the acquisitions, he announced that he would proceed with his own money. (They subsequently changed their

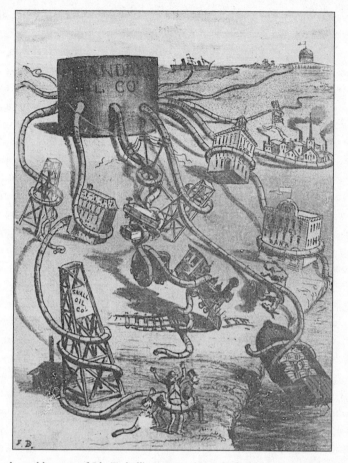

After the publication of Ida Tarbell's *History of Standard Oil,* the company became the country's prime trust-busting target. Ironically, Rockefeller profited mightily from the breakup as the shares of all the separate companies soared.

minds.) After securing his midwestern crude base, it was Rockefeller who drove the creation of the Standard's petroleum research laboratory, and recruited Herman Frasch, a German chemist and later a pioneer in the American chemical and sulphur mining industries, who, in the mid-1880s, came up with a practical and inexpensive desulphurizing process.

During the period covered by the suit, the Standard controlled about 70 percent of the region's crude production, and there was effectively no local refining competition. Since its desulphurizing patents still had several years to run, the few independents were forced to concentrate on higher-cost niche products. The city of Whiting, like the Pennsylvania oil towns, had grown up around the refinery and its employees. The refinery's output was shipped over a complex network of railroad connections, Rockefeller pipelines, and mostly Rockefeller-owned steamship lines. No other refinery or oil shipper was serviced by the two roads in question.*

An obvious question is why did the government focus on this case? And how did it come to light in the first place? The alleged violation was subtle in the extreme. The crucial Alton tariff had to be "deciphered," in the words of the court of appeals, since it had to be cross-referenced with material from the State of Illinois to determine whether it even applied to oil, and there was substantial evidence that the violation, if there was one, was inadvertent. There was no other shipper to complain of discrimination, and the money involved was modest; the alleged twelve-cent undercharge, over the entire three years, would have been worth about $91,000, or 0.03 percent of Landis's fine, during a period when the Standard earned more than $200 million.

The clear impression is that prosecutors had trawled through years of tariff filings searching for possible Standard violations, however technical. In short, it looks like harassment—an impression that is reinforced by the government's request on retrial, after the case was thrown out on appeal, to present a separate evidential argument for each of the 1,462 carloads. Historians have frequently commented on the barely concealed scorn Archbold and Rogers sometimes displayed at government tribunals. Their lack of diplomacy was an expensive form of self-indulgence, unworthy of such senior executives, and damaging to the public perception of the company. The Indiana case, however, suggests that they may have had considerable provocation.†

The apparently trumped-up character of the Indiana charges, of course,

---

*The lack of competing refiners in the region may explain the railroads' paperwork snarls. The record showed that the Alton maintained 386 current commodity tariff filings—each a longish legal document. Testimony showed that the six-cent oil rate had been quoted for a number of years, while a subsequent hearing before a federal examiner also showed that six- to seven-cent commodity rates were common in the area. With no need to keep a community of customers regularly updated on rates, oil tariff filings may have been pushed to the bottom of the in-box.

†Landis's decision was reversed on appeal. After the evidence had been presented in the retrial, the judge directed a verdict for the Standard, in effect, ruling that the government had failed to make a triable case.

doesn't demonstrate the company's innocence. Archbold, for example, was embarrassingly exposed paying "retainers," i.e., bribes, to, among others, a U.S. senator, a congressman, and a Pennsylvania legislator. But still it is noteworthy that even as late as the 1910 Stanley Committee hearings, hundreds and hundreds of pages of testimony mostly rake over decades-old material, like the South Improvement Company and the 1880s pipeline wars. And the very substantial government resources devoted to the Indiana case lend plausibility to McGee's conclusions on the flimsiness of the "predatory pricing" allegations.

The Standard, indeed, had every incentive for behaving as a law-abiding corporate citizen from at least the closing years of the nineteenth century. At a time when it was anxious *not* to increase its market share, predatory tactics against independents like the Tidewater and Pure Oil would have made no sense. And the company was by no means free of competition. As one of the first integrated global businesses, 70 percent of its sales were overseas. Its period of global monopoly ended when the formidable Nobel brothers opened the Russian Baku fields in the early 1880s, built railroads and pipelines into Europe, and patented refining technology arguably superior to the Standard's. About the same time, Royal Dutch Shell made major new strikes in the East Indies and invested heavily in ocean tanker technology. All critics admitted that the Standard's prices fell steadily for the entire period after Rockefeller achieved his dominant industry position, and even the very hostile Bureau of Corporations acknowledged that it was the most efficient of the American producers.

At the same time, especially under Archbold, there are clear signs that the company was beginning to settle in to enjoy its quasi-monopoly position while it lasted—at least domestically—for the Standard consistently charged lower prices in hotly contested foreign arenas than it did at home. Profits and dividends also rose quite sharply. From 1883 through 1896, under Rockefeller, average earnings on book equity were a healthy, but not unreasonable, 14.9 percent; from 1900 through 1906, they jumped to 24.5 percent; dividends over the same periods went from an average 10.1 percent of book equity to 16.4 percent (see Appendix II).

The sharp jump in earnings is perfectly consistent with the evidence that the Standard of the early 1900s was rapidly *losing* its competitive edge. The political analyst Charles Ferguson has pointed out that it is not the aggressive, efficient monopoly that is most to be feared. Far greater economic costs are inflicted by complacent, dead-weight, monopolistic incumbents. For a modern example, just consider the explosion of communications that followed in the wake of the 1984 breakup of AT&T; and even today, a company like Verizon is notably more responsive and technically advanced in its competitive businesses, like wireless, than it is in traditional telephony. Signs of monopolistic complacency at the Standard came as early as the 1880s, when it tried to impose a "gummy, slow-burning" lamp oil on the European market. A groundswell of complaints was met with the bland response that customers were using the wrong wicks. The company reluctantly addressed the problem only after a "bitter" mass meeting by its European marketing representatives—although the completion of the Nobels' trans-Caucasian/Baku railroad undoubtedly helped to concentrate minds.

"Administrative fatigue," as one historian put it, seems to have begun setting in, especially after Rockefeller's departure. By the time of the breakup, despite its profitability, the Standard's competitive outlook was ominously clouded. The center of crude production had shifted from its base in Pennsylvania and the Midwest to Texas, where it had no presence, and to the midcontinent (Kansas through Colorado) and California fields, where its position was weak. Gulf Oil, Texaco, Sun Oil, and California's Union Oil were emerging as far more formidable independents than Tidewater and Pure Oil had ever been. Although the Standard displayed considerable inventiveness in wringing more production out of declining fields, the vast investment in eastern and midwestern extraction and distribution facilities began to be something of an albatross. As the British had discovered to their grief in steel, it is almost impossible to maintain a technology edge amid declining production, and the huge new refineries and pipelines in Texas and California were inevitably a generation ahead of the Standard's. By the time the breakup order was finalized, the Standard's alleged "90% share" of domestic refining was closer to 65 percent and falling, while its position in other industry sectors was much lower than that. Worst of all, its central business premise was crumbling with frightening speed. The accelerating spread of electricity was clearly going to obliterate the kerosene market, and the company had been late to appreciate the opportunity in automobiles.

Trustbusters thought they were slaying a dangerous monster when the Standard was broken up in 1911; instead, they were doing the shareholders, and especially John Rockefeller, a large favor. Once the stock of the individual companies were listed in their own names, and they could compete freely, their market values multiplied many times over, and Rockefeller's wealth ballooned to levels that even Andrew Carnegie had never dreamed of.

The "Good" Tycoon

Ironically, whenever an official body wanted to point to an honest, competitive industrialist to contrast with robber barons like Rockefeller, they would hold up the example of Andrew Carnegie. By any measure, however, the record of all the steel companies, including Carnegie's, in the wake of the Interstate Commerce and Sherman Antitrust Acts was one of persistent, flagrant law-breaking.

For years Carnegie had assailed the Pennsylvania's practice of charging higher rates to Pittsburgh steel mills than to their competition around Chicago and the Great Lakes. He finally caught their attention by starting his own railroad out of Pittsburgh in 1896, and extracted major rebates—precisely one of the very few practices clearly forbidden under the ICA. The arrangement came undone when A. J. Cassatt assumed the presidency of the Pennsylvania in 1899 and ended all rebates.* Carnegie was outraged, threatening a barrage of countermoves, undeterred by a somewhat shocked message from a Cassatt intermediary that the company was not *allowed* to provide rebates—Carnegie surely understood that "the rebates you were getting were not only unlawful but if [Cassatt] had continued them after he knew all about them, he would have been committing a criminal offense." Of course Carnegie understood that, but it counted for nothing when profits were at stake.

Board minutes from June 1900 include a clear case of rebate laundering. Carnegie Steel had an ore freight contract providing for a 40 percent

---

*Frick Coke was also a major rebate recipient, and Cassatt's action cut deeply into its earnings. Frick's attempt to raise coke prices in 1899—which precipitated the break with Carnegie—was probably motivated by the lost rebates. Carnegie had not previously known the extent of the coke company's rebates, and was furious when he learned of them—not because they were illegal but because they had not been paid to the steel company.

rebate on posted shipping rates, but the railroad was worried about paying it in violation of the law. Since the road had recently been acquired by Federal Steel, Carnegie Steel—working directly with Elbert Gary—devised a window-dressing long-term shipping contract that provided rebate-equivalent payments from Federal Steel for shipments over the ore line, in order, as the minutes bluntly put it, "to avoid the appearance of rebating freight."

Similarly, among the few practices clearly forbidden by the Sherman Act were price-maintenance pools among competitors. But Carnegie and his fellow steel executives assiduously created such pools throughout the 1890s: there were contractual pricing and market-sharing arrangements covering rails, tin plate, hoops, and wire, as well as multiple other "associations" for pig iron, billet makers, and others, all of which had some element of price maintenance. Carnegie, notwithstanding his frequent public statements against pooling, entered them as readily as the next executive, reaping high profits when times were good. His main distinction was his willingness to break pooling arrangements; ever the devotee of "running full," he quickly deserted pools when markets turned flat. (The pools were openly reported in *Iron Age,* but a congressional committee professed to be shocked when they were revealed a decade later.)

Most egregious was the collusion with Bethlehem Steel on ship armor contracts. Bethlehem once had the armor business entirely to itself, but the Carnegie company gained entrance in 1890, in part by securing advance copies of confidential bidding documents. After some head-banging, the two companies reached a market-sharing agreement in 1893 that was followed "with arithmetic precision" for the next decade. (In 1895, when the companies were charging $600 a ton to the government, Bethlehem was caught selling the same product to Russia for $250.) The shamelessness of the horse-trading is captured by a proposal from a third company, Midvale Steel, which was hoping to enter the business in 1900. As Schwab summarized it for the Carnegie Steel board: "the proposition was that they were to have 3/4 of the forgings made in this country, whether for guns or otherwise, and, in addition, $2,000,000.00 in cash. If their proposition was accepted they would not bid on armor." Several years later, the three companies instead agreed to allocate a fixed amount of business to Midvale: as a Bethlehem memo put it, "Probably the least suspicious procedure would be if Carnegie and Bethlehem were to follow the general practice of each bidding the same price for the entire tonnage, and letting [Midvale] cut under to the extent of a few dollars per ton to secure the 2060 tons referred to above." Bid rigging produced extraordinary margins: in the late 1890s the companies collected $345–420 per ton of armor (a compromise after the Russia–Bethlehem embarrassment) against production costs of perhaps $150. With that kind of money at stake, what patriot could pass up the chance to defraud his fellow citizens?

· 8 ·

THE AGE OF MORGAN

$\blacktriangledown$

Pierpont Morgan's yacht, the *Corsair,* was half the length of a steel battleship and designed for speed; with its black hull, its black and gold silk upholstery, and its raked stacks, it had an intentionally racy look. The name itself spoke volumes of Morgan's view of the modern banker. (Jay Gould built an even bigger yacht, but he was not admitted to the New York Yacht Club because of his "robber baron" notoriety.)

On a warm July morning in 1885, the *Corsair* took Morgan and his friend Chauncey DePew, president of the New York Central, and later a U.S. senator, to a Jersey City pier where they picked up George Roberts and Frank Thomson, the two top executives of the Pennsylvania Railroad. The four spent the rest of the day beneath the yacht's gaily striped deck awnings, cruising up and down the Hudson as they discussed selling out Andrew Carnegie. Morgan was the New York Central's primary banker and a company director, while the Pennsylvania's banking requirements were handled by his partner, Tony Drexel. (It did not seem to matter that Carnegie was also a long-time client and was numbered among the "friends of the firm" at Junius's London office.)

At issue was a budding war between the two roads, egged on and partly financed by Carnegie. After years of fuming impotently over the Pennsylvania's policy of price gouging its Pittsburgh-based customers, Carnegie had

finally found a way to strike back—through the agency of William Vanderbilt, principal owner of the New York Central. Vanderbilt had mostly stayed
clear of battles with the Pennsylvania, since the two lines had few overlap-
ping territories. But the Pennsylvania had quietly backed the revival of a
moribund line, the West Shore, to attack the heart of the New York Central
franchise up the Hudson to the Great Lakes. Infuriated, the usually irenic
Vanderbilt had ferreted out a dormant railroad charter of his own. As
luck would have it, it was for a line that could connect from Carnegie's steel
plants across the Alleghenies to the Philadelphia & Reading, breaking
the Pennsylvania's monopoly on cross-state traffic. The line would be
expensive—at least $15 million—and involved difficult mountain terrain,
but as soon as Carnegie heard of it, he organized a pool of Pittsburgh manufacturers for a third of the capital. By the time of the *Corsair* excursion,
work on the road was proceeding apace. Twenty-six workers had died, but
the mountain tunnels were blasted, the artificial gorges cut, the piers
placed for river bridges, and the rails ordered—all to an *obbligato* of impa-
tient urgings from Carnegie.

But what Pittsburgh manufacturers saw as a bright new day of fairer
rates and better service looked like unmitigated catastrophe to Pierpont and
Junius Morgan. Like most of the day's bankers, they used the words
"ruinous" and "competition" as if they were hyphenated. After overshooting
in the market runup of 1879–82, railroad security prices had fallen sharply
in the short 1883 recession, and the last thing bankers wanted was lower
fares.* The energies Junius and Pierpont devoted to heading off a confrontation underscore the importance they attached to it. When Vanderbilt
had been in Europe in the spring, Junius did his best to dissuade him from
his Pennsylvania venture. Failing that, he leaned on his client, Cyrus Field,
the cable tycoon and a major investor in the new line, to delay a scheduled
bondholders' meeting, just so Pierpont could rush to Europe in time to
accompany Vanderbilt on the sail back home.

Few men could stand up to a full week with Morgan, and Vanderbilt had
never been overendowed with spine. By the time they docked the deal was
cut. If the Pennsylvania would agree, the two roads would buy out each

---

*Bankers loved America's dominance of world grain markets and the consequent strength of the
greenback, but didn't seem to connect them to the dirt-cheap freight rates and pell-mell western
railroad construction of the previous two decades.

other's new line; since there were legal obstacles to a direct Pennsylvania purchase of the cross-Allegheny line, the Morgans would buy it for them and exchange it for equivalent securities at some later time. Getting the Pennsylvania to sign on took a full day of DePew's eloquence on the *Corsair*—Pierpont mostly glowered and waved his cigar—and the deal was agreed only when they landed in the evening. (The Morgans had made it so attractive that Roberts was suspicious.) Carnegie had no inkling of what was going on until he got a cryptic note from Vanderbilt that construction on the new road had been suspended. Both of the roads abandoned their new acquisitions, throwing away millions in investment. The Allegheny mountain cuts and tunnels, built at such a cruel human cost, were left to disappear in the forest undergrowth until they were delightedly discovered a half century later by engineers laying out the Pennsylvania Turnpike.

Andrew Carnegie posed in front of a tunnel cut for the railroad that Morgan forced him to abandon in 1885, wasting a multi-million-dollar investment. The tunnel was later used for the Pennsylvania Turnpike.

Morgan was among the first generation of bankers whose clients were primarily private corporations instead of governments, but there were substantial continuities in approach. His mediations among the railroad barons were very much in the tradition of the supranational financial/diplomatic service operated by the Rothschilds and the Barings in midcentury Europe. Despite their occasional huge profits from war finance, the great banking houses detested war: the business disruptions were simply not worth it. The lead partners were in close touch with all the main ministries of the continent, regularly called upon the royal families, and while they never exercised the near-dictatorial powers of legend, they could withhold finance from bellicose rulers, and occasionally even brokered trades of ports or railroads to head off a fight. Morgan played much the same role his entire career, with the difference that he was heading off warfare among competitive private companies.

The *Corsair* deal was an important milestone in Pierpont's ascendance to the leadership of the Morgan banking interests. It came at a time when Junius was steadily reducing his day-to-day involvement in the firm, although Pierpont continued to keep him closely informed and regularly sought his advice. By the time Junius died of a carriage accident in 1890, and Tony Drexel, the nominally senior partner of Drexel, Morgan, died in 1893, Pierpont—fifty-six and at the peak of his powers—was already the bank's acknowledged leader on both sides of the Atlantic. The New York firm was renamed J. P. Morgan & Co. in 1894, with a branch in Philadelphia (Drexel & Co.) and another in Paris (Morgan, Harjes). J. S. Morgan & Co. remained a separate partnership in London, with Pierpont as its senior.

By the turn of the century Morgan was arguably the leading banker in the world, and no other firm even came close to the authority he exercised in the United States. He not only mediated substantial changes in the profile of American business, but, given America's shameful lack of grown-up financial institutions, served as its *de facto* central banker as well.

"Jupiter"

Edward Steichen's famous 1903 portrait-photograph of Morgan captures him as the "Jupiter" of the markets—the massive, smoldering presence; the glowering inarticulateness; the barely restrained explosiveness. People were in awe of Morgan—he had "the driving power of a locomotive," according to one commentator—or were simply afraid of him. His power was real, grounded in his unique role in channeling the ballooning trove of American

The World's Banker: J. P. Morgan, as photographed by Edward Steichen in 1903.

savings. One way or another, through control of boards, investment partnerships, or just implicit understandings that a bank's or an insurance company's investment committee would follow Morgan's lead, he and his partners disposed of perhaps 40 percent of the liquid industrial, commercial, and financial capital of the United States, by far the largest pool of money in the world.

Roughly from the turn of the century to the start of World War I, every American financing of more than $10 million was handled either by Morgan or one of just four other firms: two Boston firms, Kidder, Peabody and Lee Higginson; National City Bank; and Kuhn, Loeb, the first of the great American Jewish banking houses. All of them acknowledged Morgan's primacy. As Jacob Schiff, the top partner in Kuhn, Loeb, once remarked as he declined a railroad deal, "That is J. P. Morgan's affair. I don't want to interfere with anything he is trying to do."

Unlike the sprawling bureaucracies of a modern bank, the Morgan bank's power was also very personal. During Morgan's career, there were never more than twelve or thirteen partners at any one time, nor more than about eighty employees altogether. If you walked through the office, you could see Morgan's desk arrayed along with the other partners' in glass enclosures in full view from the floor. The senior partners often had great discretion to complete their own deals, but "Mr. Morgan's" word on almost anything was final. Even the top men did not like to argue with him, or ask for another hearing once he had said "No."

The bank's high reputation in Europe was a key to its position in America. Europeans remained major buyers of American stocks and bonds throughout the nineteenth century, and clearly preferred paper with Morgan's name on it. As Pierpont would have been the first to acknowledge, that respect was tribute to Junius's many decades of solid, conservative banking performance. A signal indicator of the bank's global stature came in 1890 when the Barings banking house nearly failed after a disastrous gamble on Argentinian bonds. With most London firms running for cover, the Bank of England turned to Pierpont to lead the Barings rescue: for nearly five years Morgan was effectively Barings' receiver, making him an important player on the London exchanges.

At home, Morgan was primarily a railroad banker through the mid-1890s, and was the dominant figure in restructuring railroad finances after the crash of 1893–94. Financial headlines had blared "Panic" in the 1870s, and again in 1883, but those crises were mostly financial markets phenomena with relatively mild effects in the real economy. The break in 1893–94, however, was a different story; the 6.5 percent drop in output in 1894 is by far the worst performance of the entire nineteenth century outside of the Civil War years. In the wake of the 1893–94 crash, some 192 railroads, with 41,000 miles of track and a market capitalization of $2.5 billion, or about a fourth of the entire rail system, were in various stages of bankruptcy.

By the late 1890s, American railroads had more or less coalesced into a half dozen loosely connected systems, held together by stock ownership or networks of common directors, and Morgan was a primary figure in four of them. He served as the banker for three major networks—the Pennsylvania's, the Vanderbilt lines, and James J. Hill's in the West and Northwest—and he controlled outright another substantial group of lines through his power to appoint their finance committees. The two remaining networks, that of George Gould, Jay's son, who had succeeded to his father's empire, and E. H. Harriman's, were not under Morgan's direct influence, and his relations with them varied from antagonistic to the merely correct. Although Gould did a good job of shepherding his father's lines through the 1890s downturn, he was otherwise an inattentive manager who left little mark on the industry. Harriman came late to the railroad business, but by the turn of the century had emerged as one of the first of the great modern railroad executives.

Morgan's restructuring of the Philadelphia & Reading in 1885, one of his earliest, is a prototype for his operations in the 1890s. Although it lived in the shadow of the Pennsylvania, the Reading was one of the country's major railroads and one of the largest coal operators. Its principal partner, Franklin Gowen, mercurial, bellicose, and with a flair for publicity, had been a central actor in the bitter Pinkerton–Molly Maguire coal field wars of the mid-1870s, and again in the lethal railroad strikes of 1877. He had also been the railroad partner in the Tidewater pipeline's attempt to undercut the Standard Oil–Pennsylvania oil shipping franchise, just as he was the key partner in Vanderbilt and Carnegie's new railroad—the Reading would have provided the linkage to the coast, once the road crossed the Alleghenies. The Reading was also in receivership, in great part from the lingering strains of losing the pipeline war. It can hardly be a coincidence that Morgan agreed to take the line out of receivership just a few months after the *Corsair* agreement, on the express condition that Gowen step down. In the Rothschilds' European territorial settlements, they always went to great lengths to tie up all the potentially disruptive elements. Gowen would have been outraged at Morgan's quashing his railroad deal with Vanderbilt and Carnegie, so the Reading's sudden emergence as a Morgan client, and the quick departure of Gowen, looks like another example of a diplomat-banker locking up a deal.

Nineteenth-century restructurings operated pretty much like restructurings today. A troubled company's balance sheet is a palimpsest of past business reverses and managerial misjudgments—the layers of debt and preferred stock pile up like scar tissue as the company is forced to go back to investors again and again for the cash to navigate through yet another bad patch. In the hard-asset-oriented nineteenth century, "floating," or unsecured, debt meant that a company had no hard assets left to mortgage—a sure sign of terminal trouble. The Reading was deep in floating debt, ripe for a dose of Morgan's purgatives. Previous layers of debt and preferred stock were wiped out and replaced with common stock at a fraction of the previous valuations (today we call it "cramdown" stock). A simplified structure of debt and preferred stock for new investors brought interest and dividends down to manageable levels. The Reading's voting stock was placed in a trust under Morgan's control for a period of five years—another standard Morgan condition—and financial covenants were enforced through regular, audited, statements of account. Morgan's fees for his trouble were very high, almost always at least 5 percent and sometimes as much as 10 percent of the new money raised. In fairness, he usually took most of it in stock so that his interests were aligned with those of his investors.

The Reading restructuring was one of the first to be managed by Charles Coster, a new Morgan partner who was to become the era's greatest financial engineer, a veritable walking spreadsheet. Coster became very wealthy from his work at Morgan, but had little time to enjoy it. The market analyst John Moody described him as "a white-faced, nervous man, hurrying from meeting to meeting and at evenings carrying home his portfolios." Morgan relied on him for the analytics and pricing on all of his railroad deals, and Coster sat on dozens of finance committees and boards until he died in 1907, still in full harness at fifty-six. Although his death was ascribed to an untreated cold, few doubted that it was the consequence of years of overwork.

The denouement of the Reading refinancing, however, was a salutary lesson in the limits of banker power. The restructured property naturally remained a Morgan banking client, and as the road appeared to make a strong recovery, it was released from the voting trust requirement in less than two years. A few months later, in the spring of 1888, the Philadelphia and London houses proudly issued two new tranches of Reading debt, prompting a warm encomium from Morgan to the new Reading management. Astonishingly, hardly a year and a half after *that*, the Reading was once again on the brink of insolvency, prompting howls of outrage from the London investors. The anger in London is understandable; that the Morgan bank did not see it coming is less so. The new management had embarked on an aggressive expansion program, including the unpardonable sin of challenging another of Morgan's troubled roads, the New Haven—in other words, precisely the behavior that the oversight mechanisms and reporting requirements were supposed to flag.

It took almost five years to work out yet another restructuring. When the Reading proposed a new bailout on lenient terms, Morgan would have nothing to do with it; but the Philadelphia branch eventually arranged several tranches of tide-over financing, which were embarrassingly difficult to place. If the 1893 market panic wasn't enough to eliminate any disposition toward leniency, Tony Drexel's death that same year certainly did—the Drexels were Philadelphia stalwarts, and had long been identified with the Reading. Morgan finally took over the deal himself and eventually forced a harsh restructuring, including a wholesale replacement of the offending managers and strict terms of parole. The word that Morgan was managing the transaction himself was enough to attract investor interest, and as the economy ticked back up, the road embarked on a long period of stability.

The Reading's difficulties were just one more confirmation of Morgan's settled conviction that reckless expansion was the root of all railroads' troubles. Morgan was a bull on the United States; he was an early backer of Thomas Edison, and a primary banker to the nascent telephone industry, so he was no Luddite. Intellectually he fully understood that disruptive price and technology competitions expanded markets and speeded growth. But given a choice, he came down on the side of cartels and stability every time.

The Unbearable Elusiveness of Peace

We still struggle with the challenge of managing competition among essential high-fixed-cost industries. The core problem is that a railroad, a telephone company, or an airline must invest huge amounts of capital before it can earn a dime. Then once the infrastructure is in place, it makes sense to sell services at almost any price to help cover the fixed-cost overhang. Free competition therefore quickly leads to cutthroat pricing and financial turmoil, as in the scorched-earth competition among AT&T, Worldcom, and MCI in the 1990s, or the continuing wave of bankruptcies in the airline industry. Unfortunately, the uniformly dismal experience with regulated monopolies makes the nasty Darwinism of unfettered competition almost attractive. Just consider the appallingly bad performance of regulated companies like the electrical utilities on almost any measure.

Our own murky understanding of the dynamics of big business competition, despite the doctrines du jour generated by consultants and academics, should temper our judgments of Morgan and his contemporaries. In the 1960s and 1970s, for example, the business historian Alfred Chandler and others noted the remarkable stability of the ranks of big American companies over the previous half century. He and his students identified the large, stable, perennial leaders as "Center" firms, with common characteristics: they were "integrate[d] vertically" and enjoyed "lower unit costs achieved through long production runs," as one 1984 study had it. That statement, unfortunately, was published at a time when American long-production-run companies were being thoroughly routed by the Japanese rapid model change style of manufacturing. The long production run, it turns out, was an Achilles' heel, a lazy adaptation to the days of consumer scarcity, when everyone was happy with one black phone, and overseas competitors were regularly destroyed by war. Its last redoubts today are in Russia and the state-owned companies of China. Twenty years later, the largest American company, with a quarter *trillion* dollars in annual sales, is Wal-Mart, which is neither vertically integrated in Chandler's sense nor has any production runs. America's fastest growing steel company, with a market value about twice that of U. S. Steel, is Nucor, a company that expressly eschews vertical integration. Finally, who would have guessed in 1984 that a small Seattle-area software contractor would soon pose one of the gnarliest of global monopoly challenges? In short, if Morgan didn't always get it right, he's since acquired a lot of company.

By the late 1880s, even Jay Gould was showing signs of exhaustion from twenty years of unrelenting railroad warfare—although in Gould's case the exhaustion was abetted by a losing, if carefully concealed, battle with tuberculosis. But the fact remains that even so intrepid a warrior as Gould was attracted by the notion of a large-scale cartel. Just then he also happened to be on relatively good terms with Morgan. Morgan had managed the sale of the Baltimore & Ohio's telegraph company to Gould, and he sat on Gould's Western Union board. He was also a director and occasional banker for Gould's Manhattan street railway interests, and helped broker Gould's dramatic reemergence as the control party of the Union Pacific in 1890.

The day's leading thinker about regulatory issues was Charles Francis Adams, Jr., brother of the historians Henry and Brook, and descendant of the two presidents. After serving with distinction as a wartime Union officer, and with no necessity of earning a living, Adams cast about for something useful to do and finally settled on railroads. His 1869 magazine article, "Chapters of Erie," is still the classic retelling of the Erie railroad wars, and a main source of the dark legend of Jay Gould. Adams was a primary force in the creation of the Massachusetts Railroad Commission that same year, serving a full decade as a commissioner, and later as a director of the eastern railroad rate-setting pool run by Albert Fink, whom he greatly admired. Close to the Boston Ameses, who were still major shareholders in the Union Pacific, he had been a government director of the UP and was elected to the board in his own right in 1883. That was just about the time Gould and Sidney Dillon, Gould's partner and the UP president, were withdrawing from the UP to concentrate on their southwestern lines. With the strong backing from the Boston shareholders, and his outstanding reputation for integrity, Adams was the natural choice for the UP presidency in 1884.

Adams was the quintessential rational man; his faith in the power of information and the intelligence of elites anticipated the Progressive reformers of the early twentieth century. Although he worried about the unsupervised power of large corporations, he accepted that railroads were probably a natural monopoly, and was intrigued by the challenge of constructing an effective supervisory regime. His preferred solution, and the model for the Massachusetts body, was the "sunshine commission." Collect good data, be sure that everyone is working from the same base of information, and the fairest and most efficient solutions will inevitably suggest themselves. He once commented that if all railroad presidents lived on the same street and walked to work together each morning, they would not embark on their wasteful wars. Nor, presumably, would they ever have built the gross over-capacity so uniformly lamented by the wisest contemporaries and by generations of subsequent scholars.

Adams and Gould detested each other, so their working together to rein in the railroad wars attests to the importance they attached to it. It was Gould who made the first moves. In 1888, he and Collis Huntington, the powerful western railroad magnate, with whom he had long had a kind of scorpions in a bottle working truce, worked out a tentative clearinghouse arrangement to allocate traffic and regulate rates among the western roads. But they hoped to go even further and create a true joint executive authority over the roads. Gould deferred the initiative to Morgan as the honest broker, and Morgan convened all the western railroad leadership at his house in New York late in the year. Together, Adams and Gould pushed a plan that Adams called the "Interstate Commerce Association," a cartel arrangement that he hoped would operate with the express cooperation of the new Interstate Commerce Commission.* Morgan did his best, but after considerable haggling he was able to cobble together only the weakest of pools. Gould was very disappointed, but still signed on in the spring, when the pool was already collapsing. He inquired of one of his executives whether they should attend the next meeting, or "simply send flowers for the corpse?"

The competitive landscape shifted dramatically when Gould returned to the control of the Union Pacific in 1890. Adams's tenure had been a rocky one; all of his theories ran aground on the same financial shoals that had sunk his predecessors. A stock market break after the Barings crash in 1890 found both Adams and his road badly overextended. To everyone's astonishment, Gould used the opportunity to snap up large blocks of shares in the UP and other western roads. Headlines blared: "JAY GOULD ONCE AGAIN THE MASTER SPIRIT IN WALL STREET." Morgan went to see Gould about his intentions, and brought the bad news to Adams that he was

---

*The puzzling feature of Adams's Interstate Commerce Association is that the plain language of section 5 of the Interstate Commerce Act prohibits pools. The railroad leadership, it seems, was so convinced of the importance of reaching some kind of rate-stabilizing agreements that they assumed, possibly correctly, that the commissioners would go along with it.

expected to hand over the line. When they met to seal the bargain, Gould, as always, treated Adams with impeccable manners, while Adams, with his Adams-centric view of the world, could interpret Gould's maneuvering only as an instance of the lower classes striking back at their betters. Not knowing that Gould was dying, he noted that he looked,

> Smaller, meaner, more haggard and lined in the face, and more shrivelled up and ashamed of himself than usual;—his clothes seemed too

An exhausted-looking Jay Gould, not long before his death in 1892. After twenty years of triggering railroad wars, Gould spent his last years trying to broker a peace.

big for him, and his eyes did not seek mine, but were fixed on the upper buttons of my waist-coat. I felt as if in the hour of my defeat I was over-awing him,—and as if he felt so, too.

Although Gould must have enjoyed seeing off the pompous Adams, he wasn't indulging in a personal vendetta. Instead, he was strengthening his position in the hope of forcing a concordance among the western lines. It was the first order of business he turned himself to, and he prevailed upon Morgan to sponsor another assembly of railroad presidents late in the year, only to be disappointed again when the gathering quickly collapsed into bickering. It was Gould's last important appearance on the railroad stage. The tuberculosis was already in a critical stage; his capacity for work declined steadily throughout the next year, and he died in 1892.

For Morgan's part, the failure of the rate-setting forays soured him on the usefulness of pools, and from that point the stock merger became his preferred route to market rationalization. What all the cartel plans overlooked— which is surprising for Gould, if not for Adams—is the essential streak of irrationality in the entrepreneurial mind. The fact that railroads had so irra-tionally spread themselves over the empty plains, in stark defiance of every tenet of conventional economics and common sense, was a major factor in the explosive rate of American growth. That lesson was brought home yet again by E. H. Harriman, whose meteoric career in the first decade of the twentieth century—he died of cancer in 1909—establishes him as the nat-ural heir to Gould. As much as anyone, he completed the rail network that Gould had originally laid out. Like Gould, he was usually at odds with Mor-gan, and was on the other side of the table in Morgan's biggest rail merger, the Northern Securities Co.

Harriman and Morgan

Edward Henry Harriman—his friends called him Henry—was a highly suc-cessful stockbroker who became fascinated with railroads after serving on several railroad boards and executive committees. But he was fifty before he actually managed a road. As the economic recovery began to gather steam in the late 1890s, and the pace of western development noticeably quick-ened, he had identified the Union Pacific, in receivership after Gould's death, as one of the most undervalued of American roads. A bantam of a man, tough and athletic, with an abrasive personality and a lightning-quick mind, Harriman acquired enough UP stock to leverage himself into the reorganization process, and as his talents became obvious, became chief executive when the road emerged from bankruptcy in 1898. Crucially for Harriman, given his relationship with Morgan, Morgan had lost interest in the UP and was happy to cede the business to Jacob Schiff.

Harriman was one of the first to divine that the plague of overcapacity so loudly lamented by all knowledgeable railroad managers and bankers was about to be swept away by a surge of new development. One of his first acts on assuming the UP presidency was to push through a $25 million improvement program, in an era when bankers regarded $1 million as a large sum to spend on a recently insolvent road. As the investment quickly paid for itself with much higher volumes, lower rates, and excellent profits, Harriman and Schiff used the resulting cash flow and Harriman's growing reputation for profitable operations to "Harrimanize" an ever-wider swathe of western roads. Together, they lavished sums on a scale that Gould had never dreamed of: $160 million on the Union Pacific in the decade after he took over in 1898, then a quarter billion dollars on the Southern Pacific in just eight years after 1901—representing annual spending rates up to twenty times higher than ever before. For the most part, he was not building new lines but investing in heavier rails, better grades, stronger bridges, and the giant new locomotives and freight cars needed to meet the demands of the high-intensity western development—development that would have been years behind if the roads had not been waiting for it. By 1903, as he expanded his railroad interests into steamships and other enterprises both at home and abroad, he controlled the largest transportation empire in the world. By the time of his death, at only sixty-one, he had invested more than a half billion dollars to bring his roads to the highest of current standards. He was also a superb manager, and more than any other individual he was responsible for the first-class national system that the country enjoyed at the eve of World War I.

The Northern Securities Co. grew out of a fight for control of the rail traffic in the Pacific Northwest between Harriman's UP and two Morgan lines, James Hill's Great Northern and the Northern Pacific, Jay Cooke's old line, all of them running essentially parallel routes from the Great Lakes to the Washington and Oregon coasts. When the Morgan lines attempted to squeeze out Harriman, he quietly mounted a very Gouldlike, heavily camouflaged attack on the Northern Pacific. As Harriman and Schiff approached a control position in the Northern Pacific, their purchases led to large fluctuations in railroad securities, but they masked their moves so well that Wall Street assumed that it was the UP that was under attack. Since the Northern Pacific was controlled through a Morgan voting trust, the Morgan bank itself was unwittingly making large sales to Harriman and Schiff.

But just as Harriman was on the point of winning control, he may have been betrayed by Schiff, who was very worried about a direct confrontation with Morgan. Extraordinarily, Schiff disclosed Harriman's strong position in the Northern Pacific to Hill, who had had no idea what was afoot. The very next day it dawned on Harriman, who was home sick with a cold, that his stock position wasn't yet invulnerable. He owned enough preferred stock to control management, but still needed a majority of the common, since they could remove management rights from the preferred. He was only 40,000 shares short of a common majority, however, so he called Schiff's office and ordered the purchase. It was Saturday and Schiff was at synagogue. When an associate tracked him down to sign off on the order, Schiff told him not to proceed, that he would take responsibility. By that time an anxious Hill had warned a Morgan partner, who cabled Morgan in Europe for authority to defend the Northern Pacific. The cable reached Morgan only on Sunday, which would have been too late if Schiff had not held up Harriman's order.

On Monday, the Morgan bank launched an all-out buying campaign in competition with Harriman and a now-panicked Schiff. Both sides had almost unlimited war chests, and by midweek, Northern Pacific shares had jumped from the low 100s, which was already very high, to more than 1000. Since no one but the principals knew what was going on, many brokerage houses sold the Northern Pacific short, only to realize to their horror that Morgan and Kuhn, Loeb had locked up literally *all* the outstanding shares. With no way to cover their shorts, firms up and down Wall Street faced bankruptcy, as did the banks who had been financing their positions; Harriman had no choice but to back off the fight, so Morgan and Schiff could unwind their positions and forestall a crash. The eventual compromise was the Northern Securities Co., a New Jersey corporation to hold the shares of the contested roads; Harriman had board seats, but Hill was left in control. When the Supreme Court declared the arrangement to be a violation of the Sherman Antitrust Act, Hill and Morgan used the subsequent dissolution process to exclude Harriman almost completely.

Harriman came out the loser in the Northwest, but it was one of his rare setbacks—and even in this case, he eventually made a killing on the stock he retained from the dissolution. As he steadily expanded his very profitable position through the center of the country, he became not only the most powerful railroad magnate but arguably also the country's most important railroad banker, with major positions in a host of other lines. Less adept at politics than at railroading, he fell afoul of Theodore Roosevelt, and became a major target of Roosevelt's trust-busting forays. As much as anything, it was Harriman's burgeoning power that led Congress to expand the Interstate Commerce Commission's enforcement authority in 1906, and to bring rate-setting within its purview. Harriman was already dead by the time the commission began to experiment with its new powers; but by that time even Morgan had become resigned to the fact that it was time for the government to have a try at delivering the "stability" he had so signally failed to create by persuasion.

The Accidental Central Banker

Morgan's role as de facto central banker for the United States was a consequence of the ignorant destruction wreaked by Andrew Jackson on the superb financial infrastructure bequeathed by Alexander Hamilton. Civil War–era reforms patched over some of Jackson's depredations, but as America's economic power mounted, the lack of a central banking authority became both glaring and dangerous. It is testimony to Pierpont Morgan's immense personal prestige that in two perilous instances of American institutional failure—the gold panic of 1893–95 and the stock market panic of 1907—he was able to assume the role we currently expect of a strong Federal Reserve or SEC chairman, and did so without a shred of legal or institutional authority.

The gold panic was a case of lagging overseas perceptions of American economic strength, abetted by the dithering of the new Cleveland administration. Foreigners, who had been unnerved by Democratic wavering on the gold standard during the 1892 election, began dumping gold-based railroad bonds after the 1893 Wall Street crash.* Speculative selling increased as U.S. gold reserves plummeted toward the $100 million mark, the minimum safety reserve informally promised upon resumption of specie payments. This was the sort of crisis that competent central bankers could have resolved with a few days of cables—the British had every interest in maintaining the greenback's convertibility, and the Bank of England could have readily set up defensive credit arrangements to calm investors. The problem was that there was no one to talk to on the American side. The new men at the U.S. Treasury had doubts about their legal authority to act at all, and particularly wanted to be seen as independent of the bankers. Their initial stratagem—to sell gold bonds directly from the Treasury—actually increased the pressure on the gold reserve, since their network tapped primarily domestic buyers who had to convert paper assets into gold before they could take up the new bonds.

At the outset of the crisis, Morgan privately proposed to the Treasury that he arrange a $100 million gold loan in conjunction with the Rothschilds. He calculated that a loan of that scale would end the speculation, especially if at least half of it were placed abroad. In private, he had considerable misgivings, and his insistence on managing the whole transaction through the two houses reflected his quite reasonable conviction that no other banks could pull it off. The administration refused the offer, proceeding with sporadic measures of its own through 1894, even as American reserves continued their alarming downward spiral.

The Treasury finally asked Morgan and the Rothschilds for their help early in 1895. After a series of rapid-fire negotiations, Morgan cabled London that he had worked out a salable package. To his shock, he received word the next morning that the Treasury would pass up the deal, preferring to manage the sale on its own. Morgan telegraphed the Treasury that he was coming to Washington and requested that they hold up the announcement. The next day's scenes are among the most priceless from the Morgan gallery. Cleveland said he wouldn't see him, but Morgan still bulled his way into the president's office, where a meeting on the crisis was in progress, and spent most of the

---

*Republicans had reason to grumble that it was all Carnegie's fault. Without the disaster at Homestead, they might have held the White House, and foreigners would have had no cause to worry about the American commitment to gold.

day smoldering in a corner, smoking cigars, as dire reports flowed in. Finally in the afternoon it was reported that the Treasury held only $9 million in gold. Morgan gruffly announced that his office held a $10 million gold draft due that day. Were the gentlemen prepared to discuss his proposal?

The final terms that Morgan hammered out with the Treasury included commitments that any banker would have considered foolhardy—the loan would not only be smaller than he thought necessary but he also promised that there would be no further runs on the gold reserve through the fall, when earnings from crop exports would relieve the pressure. In effect, Morgan was promising to manage the greenback–sterling exchange rate,* which required entering foreign exchange markets to buy greenbacks, or sell sterling, any time the greenback wobbled. This is a classic central bank function—extremely risky for a private partnership with no call on public resources, and an unseemly delegation of government power. The White House's procrastinations out of fear of appearing in the bankers' thrall, in other words, had brought matters to the point where the bankers, or at least one them, actually *were* running American monetary policy. In any event, both the loan and the exchange syndicate were carried off successfully, although not without some strain.

Twitches of the gold scare persisted through 1896, the summer of William Jennings Bryan's "Cross of Gold" speech. Morgan brokered another large loan—Cleveland admitted he should have gone for the bigger deal in 1895—and created another exchange management syndicate to keep the greenback steady through the 1896 election. By that point the gold securities sold under duress the year before were commanding such spectacular premiums that the bankers were accused of profiteering.

In truth, the 1890s attacks on the greenback were the last spasmodic kicks from an ancien régime that had yet to grasp how the fulcrum of world economic power was shifting. America first achieved a goods export surplus when railroads opened up the western grain trade in the 1870s. Export surpluses grew steadily thereafter, but were overbalanced by large investment inflows. But America's savings were also growing rapidly, so American capital *out*flows, combined with exports, were gradually pushing the accounts into overall balance. The peak year of the greenback attack, in 1895,

*Sterling served as the equivalent of gold, much as the dollar did after World War II. So long as the greenback retained a solid parity with sterling, investors would have no reason to undertake the expense and inconvenience of holding gold.

The benevolent figure of Morgan, depicted as a stork, restores fresh confidence to Wall Street after the 1907 market crisis.

marked the last external American deficit until the modern era. During the decade beginning in 1897, the American trade surplus in goods averaged about $600 million a year, while its overall balance—including trade, tourism, services, investment flows, and so forth—consistently showed a surplus of around $400 million. The backlog of foreign claims built up since the country's inception peaked at $3.3 billion in 1896 and fell steadily thereafter. Within twenty years, Europe needed to come to America to borrow the money to fight its Great War.

Morgan assumed the management of the gold crisis interventions at a time when he was at the peak of his powers; but the second occasion when he was forced to take command of America's finances, in the aftermath of the 1907 Wall Street crash, came when he was seventy, semiretired, and in indifferent health. The market break was extremely severe: the year-over-year decline in the Dow Jones average is still the second largest on record. Wags blamed the government for rattling investors: a long-running investigation of New York's life insurance industry had disclosed disgraceful self-dealing among executives, and Roosevelt was in full-throated cry against the trusts, although his rhetoric was much fiercer than his actions. In fact, a correction was long overdue; the markets had been frothy for several years, buying on margin was overdone, and banks were overextended on brokers' loans. The absence of meaningful financial regulation—overseeing the quality of bank lending, reining in credit during easy times, checking on the honesty of corporate reports—virtually assured that market swings would be wide and disruptive.

The 1907 crash cascaded so fast throughout the financial community that it threatened a systemic thrombosis. A number of trust banks came close to failing, several big brokerages were on the brink, there was a run on New York banks, and both the City of New York and the New York Stock Exchange were temporarily insolvent. Morgan was called to take the helm, almost by acclamation, after lesser figures had failed to restore order. For nearly a month Morgan held court in the library of his home on Madison Avenue, acting as chairman of an informal steering committee of himself, James Stillman, head of the National City Bank, and George Baker of the First National. Benjamin Strong, the youthful head of Bankers' Trust and later the first and long-serving head of the Federal Reserve, acted as secretary to the committee, in effect serving an apprenticeship for his future post.

Despite his age, Morgan put in twelve- to fifteen-hour days, often working until three in the morning, brusquely summoning the trust company presidents, the brokerage chairmen, the clearing bank members, banging heads to shore up that day's weakest links, meting out the attendant punishments and rewards. It was an extraordinary demonstration of sheer personal authority. The secretary of the treasury played hardly more than a supporting role, and even the Bank of England and Banque de France were assigned bit parts in the drama. No one refused a call from Pierpont Morgan, or argued long over his assignment. Even the president cheerfully agreed that U. S. Steel could buy an iron and steel company out of a failing brokerage's portfolio without triggering an antitrust inquiry.*

---

*This purchase, of the Tennessee Coal and Iron Co. from an insolvent brokerage, was later subject of a noisy congressional investigation, and is the most frequently cited instance of taking advantage. Accusations that U. S. Steel virtually stole the company, or masterminded the attack on the brokerage, aren't supported by the evidence. The steel company may have wanted the property to enhance its control over iron reserves, but Morgan would not have been involved in that level of fine-grained strategizing. The brokerage needed to be saved, and TC&I was its largest asset, so Morgan asked Elbert Gary, the chairman of U. S. Steel, and Frick, who was on its board, to take a look at it. Frick didn't like the deal, but Gary said he would buy it if the government cleared it in advance.

When the crisis passed, and the news of what Morgan had accomplished sunk in, the public reacted with something like shock. There were many suggestions that the bankers, or even Morgan personally, had engineered the crisis to enrich themselves. All shakeouts rearrange the pecking order on Wall Street, and there is no doubt that the sharpest financiers came out of the crisis better off than they went in; but there is no basis for accusations that the crisis was contrived, or that Morgan's own actions were based on anything other than a sense of public duty. But the sense of shock was still well placed; regardless of whether one thought Morgan was patriot or plutocratic puppeteer, this was no way to run a country. If nothing else, the 1907 crisis was an important factor in building a legislative consensus for the creation of the Federal Reserve system in 1913.

The Great Merger Movement

It was the vast burst of merger activity around the turn of the century that triggered Teddy Roosevelt's trust-busting campaigns and great outpourings of anxiety in the national press. But the merger boom itself evidenced the country's growing comfort with the notion of very large companies. After all, it was hard to imagine how a *little* company could service an area the size of the Union Pacific's, or achieve the fabled management efficiencies of the Pennsylvania, or the global dominance of a Standard Oil. Many Americans doubtless took patriotic pride in the fact that Carnegie Co. was wresting world steel leadership from the British, or that a newcomer like American Telephone & Telegraph was running the world's biggest telephone network. By 1900, in any case, some 425,000 people worked for the biggest companies. That was a small percentage of the working population, but still too large a voting bloc to alarm with job-disrupting political moves. The AFL's Samuel Gompers had much the same view of big companies as Morgan: they were "an advance over small, ruinously competitive companies." Social Darwinists went even further: rather than shameful monuments to large-scale brigandage, big companies were a higher order of human achievement—the cathedrals of a Machine Age. Roosevelt took pains to stress that he wasn't opposed to big companies, only to monopolies; in the eyes of the Supreme Court, not even the giant U. S. Steel qualified under that standard.

One careful listing of large-scale mergers counted 157 separate transactions between 1895 and 1904 (excluding railroad transactions). Two-thirds of them were concentrated in just three years, 1899 to 1901, with sixty-three major transactions in 1899 alone. Except for the brief and ill-starred conglomerate movement of the 1960s and 1970s, no period of intense merger activity has involved such a large number of companies. In recent years, for example, there has been intense merger activity in banking, airlines, and pharmaceuticals, but typical deals involve just two or three companies. The 1899 tin plate merger, however, involved some forty separate firms. Possibly 1,800 companies disappeared in the 1895–1904 consolidations. The firms that emerged also generally had substantial market power. Of ninety-three deals for which market share data are available, seventy-two of them absorbed at least 40 percent of their industry, while forty-two ended up with at least 70 percent. In short, the great turn-of-the-century merger movement fundamentally changed the structure of the country's biggest industries.

There was a quasi-spontaneous aspect to the merger boom. The big investment banks, like Morgan, were involved in only a handful of the biggest deals. The rest were mediated by stock brokerages and commercial banks, or by specialist merger-and-acquisition groups, like that of the Moore brothers, whom Carnegie so despised. William Rockefeller and Henry Rogers, the erstwhile distillation chemist who had risen to the highest levels of the Standard, also emerged as important independent financiers, and had a splendid time playing the deals game with the characteristic Rockefeller blend of shrewdness and abandon. The Amalgamated Copper consolidation of 1899 was a Rockefeller deal. Rockefeller and Rogers were also major railroad investors, often in conjunction with Harriman, and they participated in Morgan's pre-U. S. Steel iron and steel deals. (John D. was not much involved; he worried about Rogers's judgment, and was a cautionary restraint on William.)

The "Great Merger Movement" was mostly about reining in price competition. The Morgan gospel of replacing "ruinous competition" with "cooperation" had clearly found a wide and receptive audience. In Lincoln's day, when business was mostly a local affair, many companies enjoyed modest minimonopolies. But when railroads, telegraphs, and mail-order houses nationalized markets, competition grew long claws, and the competitive wars of the 1880s and 1890s were unusually fierce.

The typical company swept up in the merger mania, according to a profile developed by the historian Naomi Lamoreaux, was a medium-sized business in an industry with modestly high fixed costs and rapid growth. Papermaking is a good example. The explosion of print media in the 1880s and 1890s, and modern Fourdrinier papermaking machines, created mouth-watering opportunities for ambitious entrepreneurs. But the machines were almost too affordable—right in the gray area where a midsize business could buy one, but then couldn't afford to let it sit idle. The result was a deadly cycle of temporary scarcities, waves of new competitors, price wars and competitive shakeouts, followed by another round of scarcity, and another wave of entrants.* Wire and nail makers and makers of tin plate (coated sheet steel for tin cans and roofing material) showed an almost identical pattern. In the case of tin plate, the market was driven both by the boom in canned goods and by a stiff tariff against British tin plate in 1890.

After a sequence of especially vicious price wars during the 1893–94 downturn, a wide range of industries tried to organize cartels. None of them succeeded. The wire and nail makers' cartel was one of the most effective, lasting for about eighteen months, but it broke down when steady profits drew in other companies, including some big steel firms. It was the failure of the cartels that led to the mergers. The tin plate makers, after failing to get a cartel off the ground, invited the Moores to act as their agent in 1899, resulting in the American Tin Plate Co., with about 90 percent of national capacity. The Moores went on to create three more steel consolidations—the American Sheet Steel Co., the American Steel Hoop Co., and National Steel, a primary steelmaker like Carnegie Steel. John W. Gates, who started his career as a barbed-wire salesman, organized the American Wire & Steel Co. in 1898, which started with about a dozen companies, comprising about 70 percent of the wire capacity and 55 percent of nails; then, over the next year, he managed to bring in almost everybody else. International Paper, an 1898 merger of seventeen paper mills with about 60 percent of the newsprint market, was one of the few consolidations to launch without

---

*Not unlike the modern software industry (although software cycles turn on obsolescence, not scarcity). Although Microsoft has managed to achieve "discipline," in Morgan's sense, in personal computer software, there is no clear leader in business software. Software is deceptively easy to enter, but fixed costs can be quite high (for testing, documentation, maintaining cross-platform compatibility, the required stream of new features, etc.), so each stage of product innovation is usually marked by a cycle of cutthroat competition and a nasty shakeout. Computer *hardware* is already approaching a state of nearly frictionless economic pricing. Even the biggest and most successful companies have no margin for stumbles—vide the swift demise of Compaq.

the help of a merger specialist—the companies just worked it out among themselves.

Executing a merger was primarily a paper-shuffling transaction; few of them required large amounts of outside financing. (The $1.4 billion U. S. Steel deal involved only $25 million in new cash; the rest was just the nominal value of the paper issued in exchange for the securities of the merger participants.) The job of promoters like the Moores was to mediate the selection of participants, work out an equitable method for allocating ownership, supervise the legal work, and create a business plan. Would they consolidate operations or remain separate units? How would they handle marketing and branding? If the participants couldn't put up the required working capital, he would arrange a financing, either from a bank or possibly through a security offering. When the deal closed, the participants took stock in the amount of their ownership. Senior securities went to outsiders who put up working capital. Larger deals, like Gates's American Steel & Wire, which needed to finance a major operations restructuring, listed their shares on the national exchanges.

Contemporaries were frequently shocked by the extreme overcapitalization of the companies and by the huge fees earned by the promoters, up to 10 percent, or even more, of the deal value. Both complaints are overdrawn. Promoters like the Moores typically took their pay entirely in common stock. If the deal was a success, the Moores stood to make a lot of money; if it wasn't, they had wasted months of hard work—and hammering out a consensus on valuation and business strategy among dozens of prickly former competitors *was* hard work, with lots of nasty travel, long nights, and execrable meals. The impression of overcapitalization stems mostly from the nineteenth-century insistence on setting a par value for the common shares. (A few contemporaries, like Charles Francis Adams, had begun to realize that par values were meaningless. Today, virtually all new stock issues are no par or at "peppercorn" par valuations for both preferred and common.) Overcapitalization is a problem if it entails mandatory interest or dividend payments, but the sheer *number* of shares is of no effect, since they quickly reprice to reflect the company's true worth. The Moores' fees, of course, diluted the ownership interests of the consolidators, but the effect in individual cases was negligible.

Alfred Chandler famously argued that the entities that survived the Great Merger Movement—about a third failed within just a few years—did so because they achieved significant operational efficiencies through vertical integration. In some instances, that is certainly true, as in the DuPonts' rollup and rationalization of the national explosives industry. But in most cases, the evidence for efficiency is ambiguous at best. The surviving entities certainly used lots of competitive techniques that had little to do with efficiency, like achieving raw material monopolies, buying out competitors, or using market power to punish distributors who carried competitive products. In the case of U. S. Steel, however, even Chandler conceded that the combination had nothing to do with efficiency.

The Birth of Big Steel

Morgan came late to industrial securities. His relation with Thomas Edison led him to sponsor the 1892 General Electric consolidation,* but that was exceptional. The Morgan bank was completing its first two steel deals when Henry Frick floated the idea of a Carnegie Steel buyout in late 1898, but Morgan chose to pass on the opportunity. He must have kicked himself, for he ended up paying twice as much a little more than two years later.

A 1911 congressional investigation accurately summed up the U. S. Steel transaction: "[T]he United States Steel Corporation, in buying the Carnegie Company, paid not only for tangible assets, but also—and very liberally—for earning power, and, perhaps more important still, for the elimination of Mr. Carnegie." The three primary steel makers (rails, beams, and unfinished steel) in the U.S. Steel consortium were Carnegie, Federal, and National. Carnegie had about 42 percent of their combined capacity, while Federal and National roughly split the remainder. But the final deal

---

*General Electric was a merger between Edison Electric and Thomson-Houston, primarily to clear up patent disputes. Edison had resisted the Westinghouse/Thomson shift toward AC power, which could be transmitted over long distances, insisting on sticking with DC power, which required networks of small generators. The deal started as a takeover of Thomson-Houston by Edison, but when Coster realized how poorly the Edison company was managed, he and Morgan insisted that the Thomson-Houston management take control of the new firm. The spectacular Cataract project at Niagara Falls demonstrated the feasibility of long-range commercial electrical power generation in 1896. Electricity permitted efficient decentralization of manufacturing facilities, and spread first in industry. But only about 5 percent of American factories had been electrified by 1900, and electricity did not come into widespread residential use until the 1920s. Edison greatly resented the Thomson-Houston takeover, although it made him wealthy. He hated losing the DC versus AC argument, and he missed his name on the signplate.

valued each ton of Carnegie Co. capacity at $105, compared to $55 for Federal and only $31 for National. More than 60 percent of the Carnegie purchase price, moreover, was paid in first mortgage gold bonds, whereas shareholders in all the other companies got only stock. Since the bonds traded at a much higher price than the stock, the true per-ton consideration paid for Carnegie was six times that paid for Federal and nine times the price for National. There was no way to justify that premium, the committee staff suggested, except as "the price of peace"—in effect as a bribe to get Andrew Carnegie out of the business.

Elbert Gary, the corporate lawyer who ran U. S. Steel, freely conceded the point. Gary had been counsel to Illinois Steel, Carnegie Steel's largest competitor during the 1897–98 rail price war, and became president of Federal Steel, a Morgan consolidation that included Illinois, after impressing Morgan with his work on the merger. Harking back to the searing experience of the rail war, Gary said:

> I believe, perhaps, if unrestricted and unchecked destructive competition had gone on, the Illinois Steel Co. would undoubtedly have been driven out of business, and perhaps, I might say more. I do not say it with a view of casting any reflection upon anyone's management, but it is not at all certain that if the old management or the management which was in force at one time had continued the Carnegie Co. would have driven entirely out of business every steel company in the United States.

The U. S. Steel deal, he summed up, was a necessary action to "prevent utter demoralization and destructive competition such as used to prevail."

Carnegie, in fact, had not started the 1897 price war—a smaller rail maker, Lackawanna Steel, had—but Carnegie needed little excuse to go to war since he had long been restive over Frick's and Schwab's willingness to abide by pool arrangements. Through 1897 Carnegie Steel drove rail prices down to their lowest level ever, below most other steel companies' production costs, and *still* made record profits. A strong railroad recovery, however, spurred a wave of new construction; steel prices and volumes rose very strongly for the next two years, bailing out the whole industry, and leading to the reinstatement of the pool.

To Carnegie's dismay, almost all of the companies used their boom profits to make major plant investments. Walter Scranton, the head of Lackawanna, called the rail fight "an object lesson" and built a brand-new plant on the Buffalo lake shore. John W. Gates, then president of Illinois Steel, told his shareholders in 1898 that the company could no longer "do business on the basis of large profits for comparatively small tonnage. . . . We must meet competition and reduce the cost of production to the minimum." By joining in the Federal Steel merger, Illinois Steel also acquired substantial ore and transport resources to cut further into the Carnegie cost advantage. Carnegie himself lamented in 1899: "The autumn of last year seemed as good a time to force [a list of steel companies] out of business as any other. It did not prove so. The boom came and cost us a great deal of money." Available data and other reports suggest that by then Federal Steel, and several others, like Jones & Laughlin, were catching up to Carnegie in the productivity race.

Rising volumes and soaring prices and profits brought peace to the steel industry in 1898 and 1899, until a sharp market break in 1900 triggered the events that led to the formation of U. S. Steel. But this time the battle would be over *finished* steel products, not primary steel, and once again it was Carnegie's competitors who threw down the gauntlet, leaving him little choice but to respond.

Morgan's National Tube merger in early 1899 rolled up 85 percent of the country's steel tube and pipe makers and, along with the rapid-fire mergers in hoops, tin plate, sheet steel, and wire and nails, completely changed the profile of finished steel-making. All of the big new combines were near-monopolies, but none was as powerful as it looked on paper. The nineteenth-century "axiom" (Schwab's word) that bigger was always more efficient was approximately true in only a handful of the biggest industries. Finished steel wasn't one of them: economies of scale in wire-making, or hoops, or tin plate weren't nearly sufficient to lock out new price-cutting market entrants. It was mostly *primary* steelmaking that enjoyed big economies of scale, because of the huge fixed cost of continuous-process integration of the ore to steel cycle. It is no accident that the few finished products that required massive investment, like rails, ship plate, and structural beams, were all made by the primary steel companies.

To protect their near-monopolies in finished steel, therefore, all the consolidations felt pressured to integrate backward into primary steel. National Steel was organized by the Moores expressly to feed their three finished steel companies; Gates had planned his own steel production for his wire and nail combine from the start; and National Tube started laying out its own steel plants as soon as it built its massive new tube works. In the meantime, in view of the financial relationships among Gates, the Moores, and Morgan, all of the combines made either National or Federal Steel their primary steel vendors of choice. Every one of these moves cut into Carnegie Steel's order book; in short, apparently without giving the matter much thought, Morgan and the Moores had positioned themselves as Carnegie's biggest and most aggressive competitors.

The strategy was grossly misconceived on almost every count. Given the relatively modest investment required to enter most finished steel businesses, it would always be easier for the primary steel companies to integrate forward into wire, hoops, or tubes. And by using their new finished lines to sop up surplus primary steel capacity, they would have the luxury of selling below cost and killing off independents at will. (It was very expensive to idle a blast furnace, but a tin plate "dippery" could be turned on or off any time.) The notion that nail-makers or pipe-makers could compete by integrating backward was, frankly, nuts—the more so since the post–1897 boom in steel plant investment had left the country with surplus capacity.* Charles Coster and Robert Bacon were the Morgan partners driving the strategy, but Morgan himself was very involved. One historian called National Tube his "favorite child."

Worse than thoughtless, the challenge to Carnegie was sloppy. When the British expert, Stephen Jeans, toured American steel facilities at the turn of the century, he was extremely impressed with most of the works he visited. But he made a notable exception of Morgan's National Tube works—although it was the largest tube works in the world "by far," he thought it lacked "that method and order" he expected in a modern plant. Similarly, the Moores' National Steel consolidation appears to have been far less efficient than either Federal or Carnegie Steel, and was assigned a correspondingly low price in the U. S. Steel rollup. These were lambs fecklessly poking sticks at a lion, and had only themselves to blame if they were eaten.

---

*Integrating backward is not always and everywhere impossible. Armco (originally steel building materials) and Inland Steel (agricultural equipment) both took advantage of the shift to open-hearth rails in the early 1900s to integrate backward into steel-making. But they clearly knew what they were doing. The railroads' growing preference for open-hearth had created a shortage of open-hearth rails. The U. S. Steel combine provided a generous pricing umbrella, and was anxious not to appear the predatory monopolist. Carnegie was under no such constraints.

As the boom rolled into 1900, Carnegie Steel's order books were so full that Carnegie could do little but grumble about Morgan's and the Moores' moves. But the market break in the spring put him on the war path. The distractions of the Frick ouster were over, and with Schwab in charge, and the boom ending, it was time to teach the world another lesson about competition. Receiving a pessimistic note on new business from Schwab in early June, Carnegie responded by urging a start on a tube plant: "Your cable of 2nd did not surprise me. It seems to me that . . . a struggle must ensue among producers for orders. . . . The sooner you scoop the market the better." Schwab was ready; as he reported to the board the next month:

> I do not see that there is anything left for us to do but to build a hoop and wire mill. The American Steel & Wire Co. have served notice on us for cancellation of their contract with us. The American Steel Hoop Co. are buying but little from us. With the loss of customers we have sustained it will leave us in a position to have no four inch billets to make. There does not seem to be any other place at present to place them. . . . [W]e formerly sold to the constituent companies of American Steel & Wire Co. and the American Steel Hoop Co. from 30,000 to 35,000 tons of billets a month.

Carnegie wanted to push ahead on every front, even if it meant giving up the interest payments on his bonds. What really excited him was the tube plant, to be built at Carnegie Steel's Lake Erie ore port facilities at Conneaut on the Pennsylvania/Ohio border. Designed by Schwab for continuous process flow from the ore dock to the finished product, it promised to be the most advanced finished steel operation in the world. Not only would he get maximum efficiency in ore and coke handling, and exploit a brand-new tube-making technology, but he could fully utilize his large Pittsburgh-Great Lakes railroad investments. Even better, fifteen years after the fact, Carnegie could finally get even with Morgan for the *Corsair* insult, for he had worked out a deal with George Gould, Jay's son, for a competitive rail line from Carnegie's Lake railroad to the east coast. Crushing Morgan's steel combines and striking a blow at the hated Pennsylvania at the same time! Heaven rarely gift-wrapped such opportunities.

Here's how Carnegie described Conneaut to the investigating committee on steel a decade later (picture him perched at the witness table, savoring the moment, glowing with red-cheeked good humor):

Mr. Carnegie: [I]t did not require much consideration to let us see that if we . . . put a modern steel plant there, the ore would come there and be dumped from the boat right in the furnace yard. And Mr. Schwab drew up plans. The mill was 1,100 feet long . . . with all new, modern machinery, no men hardly, all rolls conveying the masses without hand labor, all that. . . . [A]nd I said: "Schwab, what difference can you make?" and he said, "Mr. Carnegie, not less than $10 a ton. . . ."*

The Chairman: Was anything ever said about this great steel plant . . . and the tremendous advantages you had?

Mr. Carnegie: We bought the land and that was known.

The Chairman: And you knew what you were going to do.

Mr. Carnegie: Yes; indeed we did. [Laughter]

The Chairman: There has been some intimation that, even with your sanguine temperament, and your long experience, that the Carnegie works, like Napoleon at Waterloo, were face to face with a combination so extensive, so manned by men so experienced and sustained by resources so tremendous . . . that perhaps you escaped destructive competition by retiring from the field. Was it possible for Carnegie Co. to have met these combined forces?

Mr. Carnegie: Nonsense. [Laughter] Why did Morgan send word to me that he would like to buy me out?

The Chairman: I understand that he was uneasy about the condition of your health, and gave that as a reason.

Mr. Carnegie: I was still able to take sustenance. [Laughter]

The board of Carnegie Co. voted to proceed with the Conneaut plant at a meeting on November 12, 1900. Carnegie attended in person—a rare event in those days—presumably to shore up any waverers. And there were indeed some waverers, especially among the old-timers, who had thought that the reorganization as Carnegie Co. barely eight months past had finally brought them to port, into the long-promised land of dividends and honey; yet here was the old man once more, competitive juices in full sap, ready to

---

*That would have been a crushing advantage. A reasonable steady-state price for tubes was $45–50 a ton. Picking up $10 would have probably let Carnegie price under the National Tube cost of production.

plunge them into a world of spending and strife. Schwab was an enthusiast, at least openly—as he wrote Carnegie on January 24, 1901:

> I really believe that for the next 10 years the Carnegie Company will show greater earnings than will the others together. A poor plant makes a relatively better showing in prosperous years. Then we will advance rapidly—Others will not. I shall not feel satisfied until we are producing 500.000 tons per month [about double their 1900 rate] and finishing same. And we'll do it within 5 years—Look at our Ore & Coke as compared with the others. If you continue to give me the support you have in the past we'll make a greater industry than even we ever dreamed of.—Am anxious to get at Conneaut—Are finishing plans rapidly & will be ready for a start in the spring.

When Morgan heard what Carnegie was up to, he glumly remarked that "Carnegie is going to demoralize railroads just as he has demoralized steel."

Pierpont Morgan's buyout of Carnegie and the organization of U. S. Steel is an oft-told story. Although steel and railroad men clamored for Morgan's intervention, he did not make a direct approach to Carnegie, possibly because he expected a hostile reception. Historians have speculated that the Carnegie-Schwab competitive flurry was partly maneuvering to extract a blockbuster offer from Morgan. But if anyone was playing a double game it would have been Schwab: he had shown himself as more than a little two-faced during Frick's ouster, brimming with unctuous compliments and gratitude toward Frick one day, and voting for his ouster the next, albeit with profuse apologies.

The catalytic event was a speech Schwab gave at the University Club in New York on December 12, 1900. Morgan was in attendance, as was Carnegie, although Carnegie left early. Schwab laid out a blueprint for a future steel industry that could be taken as a leitmotiv for the new century, an intellectualist vision of a vast, unified machinery for making and delivering steel products—one of the first fully worked out conceptions by a knowledgeable insider of the organizational ideals that inspired Socialists, Progressives, and technocrats, and obviously some leading businessmen, at the hinge of the new century. Schwab envisioned a top-down rationalization of the entire industry "in a scientific manner,"* eliminating competition, and

---

*There was no transcript of Schwab's talk, although he described it some years after the fact. But he laid out a similar vision in a *North American Review* article published just after the U. S. Steel deal was closed, which is quoted here.

assigning all production among specialist factories distributed for least-distance transport of ore, coke, primary steel, and finished product. No wasteful competition or duplication of effort, just pure, frictionless efficiency.

Morgan loved it. For his entire career he had pursued a barely articulated ideal of "cooperation," some workable alternative to a perpetual state of "ruinous competition"; and here, rather than just a glimpse of light through a keyhole, was the vision whole. He spoke briefly to Schwab and asked for a later meeting, which turned out to be an all-nighter at Morgan's house shortly after the new year. Besides Morgan and Schwab, there were Gates and Bacon, so Schwab was clearly consorting with the enemy. They apparently worked out the outline of a deal, and, a few days later, Schwab gave Morgan a detailed memorandum on the targets for the merger, and the prices that should be paid. "I knew exactly what each one was worth," he later recalled. "Nobody in the world helped me with that list." Morgan was ready to go, so long as Schwab could reel in Carnegie. On the question of Schwab's capacity for dissimulation, note that his January 24 letter to Carnegie about crushing the competition came more than two weeks *after* his meeting with Morgan.

Schwab first conferred with Carnegie's wife, who advised him to broach the question on the golf course, when Carnegie was always in a good mood, and he put the proposition to Carnegie at the end of January. Carnegie thought about it overnight, and said he wanted $400 million—$160 million in gold bonds for the Carnegie Co. gold bonds, plus $240 million in U. S. Steel stock for the $160 million of Carnegie stock—a 1.5/1 exchange. Thinking about it some more, he added $80 million for "Profit of past year and estimated profit of coming year," bringing the total to $480 million.* He penciled those numbers on a notepad and gave them to Schwab to bring to Morgan.

There was more than a little flummery in the profit forecast. Carnegie had fully expected to make $40–50 million in steel profits in 1900; being Carnegie, he bragged widely of the prospect, and enshrined the $40 million profit claim in his *Autobiography*. The "$80 million" seems strongly to imply that the company had made $40 million in 1900 and would again in 1901, and historians have repeated the $40 million for 1900 ever since. In actual-

---

*Carnegie, his wife, his sister, and his cousin were paid entirely in first mortgage gold bonds. The other Carnegie Co. shareholders got mostly stock, but at a better ratio than Carnegie's. Details are in the the chapter Notes.

ity, the company made between $29 million and $31 million in 1900. (There are gaps in the second half data for some of the non-steel holdings; see Appendix I.) More important, its second half earnings slumped to only about $6 million. In effect, Carnegie was forecasting $50 million in earnings for 1901, which from a half-year base that low was absurd. Carnegie's exaggerations once again highlight the ambiguous position of Schwab, who obviously knew the correct numbers. Psychologically, at this point, his allegiance must have already shifted to Morgan. One cannot imagine that when he transmitted Carnegie's note he did not disclose the real state of affairs, if indeed he had not yet done so. Morgan wouldn't have cared. The U. S. Steel deal was about fending off catastrophe—better to get cheated than to die. And in any case, Morgan and Schwab would have assumed that once they controlled the industry, they could set prices to generate whatever profits they needed.

And Then There Was Rockefeller . . .

Morgan still had another tycoon to deal with. Gary and the Moore brothers insisted that the combine needed to secure its ore and ore shipping capabilities. The Carnegie holdings were a good start, but the dominant owner of the indispensable Great Lakes ore and related steamship transport was John D. Rockefeller. As Gary later recounted it to Ida Tarbell:

"How are we going to get them?" demanded Morgan.

"You are going to talk to Mr. Rockefeller."

"I would not think of it."

"Why?"

"I don't like him."

The feeling was reciprocated. Rockefeller had no reason to think highly of financiers. In his experience, they were functionaries, rather like plumbers. If you needed cash to buy a refinery, or make a settlement with Tom Scott, you told them how much, and they scrambled to get it for you. Henry Rogers and William Rockefeller both knew Morgan well, however, and William had once introduced Morgan to his brother. John later recalled:

> We had a few pleasant words, but I could see that Mr. Morgan was very much—well, like Mr. Morgan; very haughty, very much inclined to look down on other men. I looked at him. For my part, I have never been able to see why any man should have such a high and mighty feeling about himself.

Allan Nevins comments, quite acutely: "There is a world of meaning in those four words: 'I looked at him.'"

But there was a deal to be done, so Morgan ate a bit of crow, just as he had with Carnegie. After he had accepted Carnegie's price for his company, he proposed that Carnegie come to his office to finalize the deal. Carnegie remarked that his house was about as far from Morgan's office as Morgan's office was from his house. Morgan took the point and made the call on Carnegie. Essentially the same exchange was repeated with Rockefeller, and Morgan, rather morosely one imagines, came calling upon Rockefeller. Rockefeller treated it as a social call, and when Morgan asked him for a "proposition," replied that he was no longer active in business, and that his son, John D., Jr., and Frederick Gates handled his investments. Henry Rogers thereupon mediated a trip by young John to Morgan's office, where Morgan tried some of the "Jupiter" treatment. He left Rockefeller sitting there, without acknowledging his presence, while he completed other business, then turned to him with his thunderous glare and a fierce "Well, what's your price?" With great aplomb the young man answered, "Mr. Morgan, I think there must be some mistake. I did not come here to sell. I understood you wished to buy." Rogers intervened with a proposal that Frick be called in to set a price, and a deal was quickly made. Rockefeller Sr. and Rogers were made directors of the new combination, although Rockefeller never attended a meeting. He resigned his seat in 1904, and was replaced by John D., Jr.*

U. S. Steel opened for business on April 1, less than three months after Schwab's first nighttime meeting at Morgan's house. At $1.4 billion final capitalization, it was by far the biggest company in history, and in real (dis-inflated) dollars, would remain the largest merger until the RJR Nabisco deal in 1987. The new entity comprised Carnegie Co., Federal Steel, and National Steel; all the finished steel combines in tubes, tin plate, sheet steel, and wire and nails; a national bridge-construction combine; and both the Rockefeller and Carnegie Lake Superior ore reserves and ore transport. Pulling that many entities together, as well as lining up the three hundred-member investment syndicate in such a short space of time, still stands as one of history's great feats of investment banking. As Peter Finley Dunne's Mr. Dooley put it:

> Pierpont Morgan calls in wan iv his office boys, th' president iv a national bank, an' says he, "James," he says, "take some change out iv th' damper an' r-run out an' buy Europe f'r me," he says. "I intend to re-organize it an' put it on a paying basis," he says. "Call up the Czar an' th' Pope an' th' Sultan an' th' Impror Willum, an' tell thim we won't need their savices afther nex' week," he says. "Give thim a year's salary in advance. An', James," he says, "ye better put that r-red headed book-keeper near th' dure in charge iv the continennt. He doesn't seem to be doin' much," he says.

Schwab was president of the new company, while Gary was chairman of the board and chairman of the executive committee. Schwab's tenure was not a happy one, and he was gone by 1903. Although he made some progress on rationalization, and made rather larger plant investments than Morgan had hoped, he was constantly at odds with Gary, who was really the boss. Gary made it plain that the purpose of U. S. Steel was to stabilize prices and profitability, not to pursue technocratic Edens. The Conneaut

---

*The relationship between Morgan and the senior Rockefeller was better in 1907. While Morgan was struggling to pilot the country through the market crash, Rockefeller made a point of calling on him at his office and pledging half his fortune if it were required. The news report itself had a calming effect.

tube plant, of course, was summarily scrapped—why would anyone want to lower tube prices? The price of steel rails was frozen at $28 a ton and remained unchanged for fifteen years. It is hard to point to a single new technology initiative that emerged from U. S. Steel for the next thirty years. The Pennsylvania Railroad, indeed, set up its own laboratories to pursue steel innovations, which were passed on to U. S. Steel as product specifications. The stock opened with a burst of enthusiasm, but traded well under par for most of the 1900s, until wartime and reconstruction opened up a long era of complacent dominance by American steel companies, and by U. S. Steel in particular. Gary and Morgan had brilliantly succeeded in winning their peace, although it occasionally looked like the peace of the tomb.

Assessing Morgan

Pierpont Morgan was the greatest banker of his age, occupying a world stage at the start of the new century much as Nathan and James Rothschild did in the old one. The walruslike figure of Morgan's later years has provided the cartoon image of the "Banker" ever since. The gruff taciturnity, the direct stare, the resolute focus on facts and numbers, the crusty insistence on sticking by your word, all went to the very essence of banking. Morgan's personal prestige and his enormous range of connections in global finance made it easier for the British chancellor of the Exchequer, despite xenophobic qualms at the Bank of England, to turn to Morgan when England was suffering its own gold reserve problems in the midst of the Boer War. The dollar would have emerged as the world's dominant currency without Morgan—by 1915 America was sitting on the world's largest gold reserve—but Morgan's reassuring presence at a crucial period during the gradual, invisible, but ineluctable, passing of the financial scepter helped make the process more natural and less painful than it otherwise might have been.

Morgan's microlevel behavior, however, was often oddly inconsistent with his image. Louis Brandeis was no admirer of Morgan but, unlike many of Morgan's critics, had a thorough understanding of corporate finance. He once expressed puzzlement, with Morgan predominantly in mind, that bankers were credited with being a "conservative force in the community," since in his experience they were so often associated with "financial reck-lessness."

Brandeis was specifically referring to the New York, New Haven, & Hartford Railroad, which was not only a "Morgan road" but one of Pierpont's favorite properties—his grandfather had been among the original investors and it had been one of Junius's first directorships. Pierpont joined the board in 1891, and was its principal banker thereafter. He hand-picked the president in 1903, a Charles Mellen, who had managed the Northern Pacific under the Morgan voting trust; and Morgan strongly supported an aggressive expansion program in New England rail and steamship properties. Brandeis, sometimes as a representative of the public, sometimes on his own, challenged Mellen at every step, charging that the road was excessively indebted and maintained its dividends only through concealed borrowings, which was illegal. After a decade-long fight, it finally became clear that Brandeis had been right all along. Mellen was forced out, and the Morgans had to finance an expensive rescue operation substantially on their own. There is no possible justification or explanation for Morgan's failure to supervise Mellen. A director might plausibly claim he was relying on the advice of the executive, but the Morgan bank underwrote the road's securities all those years and made materially inaccurate representations to purchasers, which was either incompetent or fraudulent.

The International Mercantile Marine (IMM) was another fiasco. A standard scholarly account is that it demonstrated "how even a combination of even the world's most astute bankers and shipping men could be misled in analysis and held powerless to affect their own destiny by the march of economic and political events." A less charitable reading would be that Morgan, who more or less managed the deal himself, behaved either venally or like a naïve rookie.

Morgan agreed to broker a merger of two American mercantile freight companies, Atlantic Transport and the International Navigation Co. (INC), in 1900. The Morgan bank held some of INC's bonds, and also, in cooperation with another bank, extended a credit of $11 million to Atlantic Transport to upgrade its fleet. There was an expectation that Congress would approve an operating subsidy to assist the American merchant fleet, but the record is unclear on whether that was an important consideration. At some point, Morgan, INC, and Atlantic Transport agreed that the merged entity would be stronger if it included key British competitors. Preliminary talks were held with Cunard; White Star, a very profitable line; and Leyland, a family firm run by a canny financial operator named John Ellerman. Cunard dropped out, but Morgan proceeded with Leyland and White Star. His preliminary term sheet, for the two American and two British companies, envisioned an all-stock transaction of just under $75 million, including $60 million for the stock purchases, plus initial working capital, fees, and a takeout of the $11 million advance to Atlantic Transport.

Those terms quickly unraveled. The Leyland purchase had been penciled in as a buyout just of Ellerman's position, which was enough for control. But Ellerman insisted that all shareholders participate equally, and that the purchase be in cash, not stock, raising the price from $3.5 million in stock to $11 million in cash. Then White Star insisted on $32 million instead of Morgan's projected $24 million, and topped that off with an extra $7 million in cash to reflect their blowout profits in 1901. And so it went. At no point, it seems, did the "Jupiter" of the markets look his clients in the eye and say, "Sorry, gentlemen. This has gotten out of hand." The term sheet ballooned from $75 million in stock to $115 million of stock plus $50 million in cash, with projected interest and dividend payouts absorbing the lion's share of very optimistic earnings projections. And the subsidy bill failed to get out of Congress.

With Morgan's name on the deal, IMM had a boffo initial reception—until investors realized that the company didn't have a chance. IMM opened for business with an illiquid balance sheet: current liabilities (the obligations that were due within a year) were about 1.5 times current assets. A healthy company would have had perhaps a 2:1 ratio the other way. In addition, it was saddled with almost $64 million in gold bonds and $52 million in preferred. The financial press had warned all along that the very high 1901 shipping earnings were an aberration, and they turned out to be right, leaving the underwriting syndicate to eat some $80 million of unsold paper. IMM also owned the *Titanic*, which didn't help, but it was doomed from the start, and was in and out of bankruptcy for the rest of its days.

Why did Morgan do it? Perhaps he had caught the deals fever. IMM has many of the hallmarks of the stretched to the limit leveraged buyouts of the late 1980s; and, indeed, the 1903 "rich man's panic" on Wall Street has many parallels with the 1989 junk bond crash. Or perhaps he just wanted to recover his $11 million advance to Atlantic Transport. The Morgan bank was not a deposit-taking entity and, unlike a National City or an Equitable Life, didn't have access to hundreds of millions in deposits or insurance premiums, so an advance of that size was a lot to carry. Since the IMM securities were almost all distributed among his syndicate partners, Morgan's loss on the underwriting was only $2 million to $3 million, a small enough price perhaps. Neither interpretation is in keeping with the portrait of Morgan as a pillar of conservatism and rectitude.

It in no way diminishes Morgan's achievements to say that he never transcended his milieu or its assumptions, or seems to have been possessed of a single original insight even in his own field of finance. He had little feel for the country's political pulse. (See the wonderful comment to Roosevelt upon the announcement of the antitrust challenge to Northern Securities: Morgan visited the White House and told the president, "If we have done anything wrong, send your man to my man and they can fix it up.") His industrial financings mostly followed the crowd; they were just bigger, because he was Morgan. The one discernible principle from a lifetime of railroad and industrial banking was avoiding "ruinous competition." Morgan also never understood the need for external regulation after finance capitalism had burst the bonds of the tight family-based networks that prevailed in his father's day. Later events showed that he had vastly overestimated the integrity and honesty of his business colleagues.

The 1911 "Pujo" investigations attempted to expose the machinations of the "money trust," which was simply the Morgan network. As Brandeis described it:

> J. P. Morgan (or a partner), a director of the New York, New Haven, and Hartford Railroad, causes that company to sell to J. P. Morgan & Co. an issue of bonds. J. P. Morgan & Co. borrow the money with which to pay the bonds from the Guaranty Trust Co., of which Mr. Morgan (or a partner) is a director. J. P. Morgan & Co. sell the bonds to the Penn Mutual Life Insurance Company of which Mr. Morgan (or a partner) is a director. The New Haven spends the proceeds of the bonds in purchasing steel rails from the United States Steel Corporation, of which Mr. Morgan (or a partner) is a director. The United States Steel Corporation spends the proceeds of the rails in purchasing electrical supplies from the General Electric Company, of which Mr. Morgan (or a partner) is a director . . . [and much more in this vein].

But the central claim of the investigations—that the Morgan bank used its power to exploit its clients—was never effectively established. A long list of alleged blue-chip victims assured the committee that they were proud to be Mr. Morgan's clients, and that their companies were better for it.

Twenty years later, however, the Pecora investigation, in the wake of the 1929 crash, demonstrated that the men of Morgan's circle had proved themselves disgracefully devoid of ethics or conscience when it came to disposing of the savings of working people. National City Bank's investment trusts give some of the flavor. The bank routinely bundled bad loans and securities on its books into mutual funds that were sold to retail investors, pumped up the funds' nominal assets with borrowed money, and engaged in deceitful trading operations to drive up their prices. The same example would be multiplied many times throughout the Wall Street community, and was an important factor in the 1929 crash. Whatever sense of honor such men had in their dealings with each other clearly did not extend beyond their class.

Morgan spent his career working on the canvas his father left him, although on a scale Junius could never have imagined. That he did it so well was a massive achievement in itself, and signally important for his country. Given the remarkable new phenomenon unfurling itself in America, it was Morgan's very lack of originality, and his solid roots in the world of European banking, that allowed him to play such a crucial mediating role in the immense power shift that was under way.

· 9 ·

AMERICA RULES

N̲atty" Rothschild, the head of the family's London branch, and grand-
son of old Nathan, the London house's founder, was close to Cecil Rhodes,
and was the primary financier of Rhodes's DeBeers Diamond Co. True to
the family tradition, he abhorred Rhodes's provocative military free-lancing
against the Boers and local tribes, and devoted much of his energies
through the 1890s trying to avert a South African war. When the Boer War
finally broke out in 1899, however, he fully expected his government to
honor the second leg of family tradition and place its war financing through
the Rothschild bank. He was therefore less than pleased to discover that
the Exchequer planned to grant half the financing mandate to an American
syndicate led by Morgan. Recriminations by Rothschild and other City
leaders forced the government to restrict the Morgan bank to a very minor
role during the first tranche of fund-raising. But as drawn-out war pressured
British gold reserves, the Exchequer had no choice but to give Morgan an
equal role. Perhaps out of pique at the government's dithering on the first
round of financing, Morgan insisted on, and got, a commission twice as
high as the British consortium's. It had been more than a century since
Great Britain had to borrow from a foreign power to finance a war within its
own empire. The historian of the Rothschild family, Niall Ferguson, writes,
"It was an early sign of that shift in the centre of financial gravity across the

Atlantic that would be such a decisive—and for the Rothschilds fateful—feature of the new century."

The raw numbers tell the story: well before the end of the nineteenth century a tidal surge of American growth carried it soaring past the older industrial powers. In 1800, the output of American factories and mines was only a sixth that of Great Britain; by 1860, it was a third, and by 1880, two-thirds. America pulled ahead of Great Britain sometime in the late 1880s; by 1900, its industrial output was a quarter larger, and by the eve of the World War, 2.3 times larger. In 1860, Great Britain accounted for about 20 percent of world industrial output, and the United States only about 7 percent; by 1913, the American share was 32 percent, while Great Britain's had slid to 14 percent.

Strikingly, despite rapid growth in population, per capita industrial production also grew faster in the United States than anywhere else in the world. Industrial output per head grew sixfold in the United States from 1860 to 1913, compared to only 1.8 times in Great Britain. Only Germany among the major powers showed per capita growth rates (5.6 times) comparable to that in America, and the Germans started from a much lower baseline: on the eve of the Great War, British per capita output was still about a third higher than that of the Germans. For the total period from 1870 to 1913, American industrial output grew at a compound annual rate of 4.9 percent, Germany's at 3.9 percent, and Great Britain's at 2.2 percent. As for the other Great Powers, France steadily lost ground to both Great Britain and Germany, while Russia remained a sink of despondency.

Even per capita comparisons understate the American performance, for some 40 percent of its workforce was still engaged in agriculture, so the industrial output measures are spread over a larger population base. American industrial workers used twice the capital and twice the energy as British workers, had 50 percent higher wages, and produced up to five times the value added. American manufacturing productivity consistently doubled Great Britain's throughout the nineteenth century. By the end of the 1870s, America also dominated international trade in grain—in most years accounting for 30–50 percent of the Western world's available grain crops—and enjoyed a near monopoly of the world meat trade, with a 70–80 percent share.* The American growth rates are the more impressive when

---

*Overall American agricultural productivity after the Civil War was actually lower than Great Britain's, due to the dismal productivity in the American South and to the typically low output of

one considers that Americans' incomes may have surpassed English incomes as early as the 1820s. The very high rates of growth in the second half of the century, that is, took off from a very high base; by century's end, the United States was in a league of its own.

What Happened to England?

Late nineteenth-century British savants were mesmerized by the relentless American advance. A near-obsessive search for the causes of the relative British decline spurred a century's worth of economic history on both sides of the Atlantic that offers a superb lens for tracing the sources of American advantage. The divergent paths followed by the American and British steel industries have been perhaps the most intensively researched and are a rich source of insights.

Loss of leadership in steel was especially painful for Britons. Steel was the foundation industry for the late-Victorian period, much as information technology is today. Military power, high-technology capital equipment, and mass production of consumer goods, all depended on steel, and British steel had been the global benchmark literally for centuries. America was not even a player in steel at the outset of the Civil War; although its crafts-men were forced to use local steel during wartime import interruptions, they quickly switched back to British suppliers when imports resumed. Sheffield steel set the quality standard for the world, and its crucible steel had almost the status of a semiprecious metal. Nor did there seem to be any question of Great Britain's technological leadership. Almost all the era's steel-making advances came from the United Kingdom—the hot-air blast furnace; the Bessemer process; the Thomas-Gilchrist "basic" lining, enabling

---

first-generation western settlers. Midwestern "factory farming" did not move into full swing until the 1880s, about the same time as the spread of railroads and the telegraph brought transport and utility services to a level comparable with Britain's. Banking and other financial services lagged well behind Britain's into the twentieth century. Comparisons between the United Kingdom and the United States in the 1870s and 1880s are therefore much like those between the United States and Japan in the 1970s and 1980s, when Japan's stunning productivity advantage in man-ufacturing was more than offset by lagging productivity in services and agriculture. By the 1890s, however, across-the-board United States productivity had surpassed that in the United Kingdom, which was still the highest in Europe. A recent review of the data concludes that by 1910 the United States had a total productivity advantage over the United Kingdom of about 25 percent, and a correspondingly greater advantage over the rest of the world.

the use of high-phosphorus ore. Charles Siemens, whose open-hearth furnace eventually supplanted the Bessemer process, was German, but he spent much of his career in England.

The suddenness of the American challenge therefore made it all the more astonishing. Stephen Jeans, secretary of the British Iron Trade Association, and the steel engineer Frank Popplewell both wrote book-length surveys around the turn of the century seeking the reasons for the American success. As Jeans put it, just the *increase* in the American output over the six years from 1895 "is considerably larger than the total output of steel of all kinds throughout the world in any one year prior to 1890, and is about half a million tons more than the total make of steel in Great Britain in any two years prior to 1897." It was also "more than three times the total steel output of the United States so recently as 1887, and more than nine times as much as the total output of any one year up to and including 1880." Jeans glumly noted that American annual steel and pig iron output was already twice as large as Great Britain's, and greater than the total of Great Britain and Germany combined. By this time, the German industry was advancing as rapidly as the American. The prospect of steel juggernauts to both the west and the east was a source of much disquiet among knowledgeable Britons.

Popplewell and Jeans each make it clear that the American advantage involved no fundamental breakthroughs, but was rather about methodologies, work organization, and, above all, mechanization. Popplewell's list of the characteristic features of an American plant were all in place at Carnegie's Edgar Thomson Works by the early 1880s, most of them incorporated in the original design. There were some splendid British steel plants—Holley, indeed, had extolled several as models for the United States. After Americans invented a new kind of high-speed tool steel in the early 1900s, for example, the leadership in producing the new tool steels quickly migrated to Sheffield. But the British industry had many more older, and smaller, plants than did America, a lower degree of mechanization and continuous processing through the entire ore to steel cycle, and less recourse to the most expensive equipment, like the "chargers" that injected the various chemical and mineral additives into the converter mechanically rather than by hand. American rail and rod mills routinely produced three times the output of British mills with fewer than half the men; it was

Popplewell who commented on the "very conspicuous absence of labourers in the American mills."

The cost advantage once enjoyed by the British industry from its conveniently located ore and coal supplies gradually disappeared as Americans mechanized ore mining and transport through the 1890s. Great Lakes Mesabi Range ore was surface-mined with giant steam shovels, and Popplewell was awestruck at Lake port ore handling—huge mechanical clamshell shovels unloaded 5,000-ton oreboats into moving lines of freight cars, at rates over 1,000 tons an hour. There was hardly a laborer in sight, and none of the shovelers or wheelbarrow handlers who worked the British loading docks. Carnegie Steel's own Pittsburgh to Erie railroad, with some of the largest cars and the most advanced loading facilities, had driven ore transport costs to just pennies a ton. At the same time, American product standardization facilitated very large production runs, while British manufacturers were plagued by a multiplicity of product designs. Some of the British diversity stemmed from perverse pride in local idiosyncrasy, but it was also an inevitable consequence of serving a very diverse export market. In America, by contrast, Carnegie Steel, as Jeans noted, could "act for the steel trade generally." Its structural steel handbook defined construction beam sections, and with the help of the burgeoning professional engineering associations, similar standards had been worked out for axles, plates, rivets, and rails.

The British still led the world in the scale and quality of their ship plate production and in other very high-end products, and no other country, Jeans felt, could match the British in ultralarge steam forges for ship components. Although American locomotives from Baldwin were spreading throughout the world, Jeans did not think they came up to the British quality mark, but conceded that they were cheaper. British workers were much better treated than those in America, he thought, and typically worked eight-hour days rather than the American twelve, and he was appalled by conditions in the American steel towns. By this time, with very strong growth in American factory wages through the late 1890s and early 1900s, American steel wages were half again as high as in Great Britain. But the late-Victorian era in England was a time of major public investment in working class housing, transportation, and other amenities, like parks and seaside resorts, so British workers probably did enjoy more pleasant lives.

Jeans's overall conclusion—that American steel "can compete with Great Britain and Germany in the leading markets of the world"—was sugarcoating for his parliamentary audience. The scale, the aggressiveness, the modernity of the American plants that he so painstakingly documents leave little doubt that the contest was over. Indeed, just about the time Jeans completed his review, Great Britain was transmuting from the world's dominant steel producer into the largest steel *importer*. Both American and German steel, it seemed, were underselling Great Britain in its home market.

But *why* did Great Britain lose its leadership? The menu of causes cited by Jeans, Popplewell, and other contemporary commentators is much like that of modern scholars, although debate continues on which factors were most important.

Britain, first of all, suffered the disadvantages that accrue to any pathbreaker. By the time American and German competitors appeared on the scene, the structure of the British industry already had a long-settled character. The prevalence of smaller companies, many specializing just in iron, or just in steel, made continuous-flow processing from blast furnaces to steel converters less widely practicable. British railroads were designed for densely populated areas, and were smaller-scale, with tighter turns, so their speed and efficiency couldn't match those in America. The list of locked-in early-generation adverse choices could go on and on. Overcoming problems like these would have required changes *all the way through*—a whole-scale reorganization and resizing; but the highly decentralized, laissez-faire economy that was the glory of the Victorians was a poor environment for a ground-up restructuring. Market signals actually added to the confusion. An orgy of American railroad building in the late 1870s and early 1880s drove British steel exports and profits to record levels. In an era of chestpuffing success, the Cassandras' warnings of the looming American threat—and there were more than a few—were dismissed out of hand.

The machine tradition that played such a central role in the growth of American manufacturing prowess somehow never took hold in Great Britain. At the 1851 Crystal Palace Exhibition, British industrialists had been dazzled when Robbins and Lawrence technicians disassembled a stack of rifles, mixed up the parts, and reassembled working rifles. More than a half century later, British industrialists were *still* amazed when Cadillac engineers performed the same feat with three cars at a Royal Automobile Club exhibit. Despite the early success of the Enfield armory, it took another forty years for American machine methods to gain a foothold—1890s bicycle manufacturers may have been the first commercial adopters. In contrast to the big American plants, British steel-making stayed resolutely craft-oriented. Jeans noted that three-quarters of British steelworkers were in skilled crafts categories, few of which still existed at American plants.

Mechanization, moreover, was hindered by the smaller scale of British plants. Mechanical furnace chargers and automated rolling mills were too expensive for any but the largest works. The enormous size of the American home market readily conduced to very large plants that could fully exploit scale economies; German plants were similarly of very large scale. The slowdown in British steel itself created problems. Both Popplewell and Jeans noted that the high growth rate of the American industry created a continuous demand for new plants, so the average works was much newer than its British competitors. The high rate of growth in Germany would have had the same effect.

Finally, a long finger of suspicion points at both British workmen and British managers. Most fair-minded observers conceded that American and German workers and bosses were better educated and more open to scientific advances than their British counterparts. Worker recalcitrance and union resistance were a major obstacle to mechanization at all British plants. As early as the 1870s, Capt. Bill Jones had warned his Carnegie bosses that they "must steer clear as far as possible from Englishmen, who are great sticklers for high wages, small production, and strikes." The insistence on traditional craft practices, much as in small-arms making, tilted toward more specialized, small-market products. Some contemporaries even worried that British workers were a "distinctly deteriorated race." But if that was true, British managers played a big role in the deterioration. The entrepreneurial drive of the 1840s and 1850s had markedly ebbed. Old-school managers, consciously or not, connived with their workers to stick with what they knew—the smaller plants, the old methods, the clubman's version of genteel competition. While geography undoubtedly constrained the efficiency of the railroads, they were also badly organized, with lots of empty runs. As one expert put it, "outside England people say, 'What is the saving?' In England, the first question is, 'What is the cost?'" A sympathetic American was struck by the "pessimism and lack of courage" among British iron and steel men.

The same slippage can be seen throughout British industry. In midcentury, Great Britain led the world in inorganic chemicals (ammonia, caustic soda, sulfuric acid), but failed to adjust when the new Solvay technology emerged in the 1870s; within a decade German and Belgian manufacturers had perhaps a 20 percent cost advantage, with far less environmental damage. The Americans came on very strongly in the late 1890s, starting with the Solvay process and the even newer electrolytic technology. Similarly, in electrical power generation, the steam turbine engine, one of the critical enabling technologies, was invented by an Englishman, Charles Parsons, in 1884. But the industry was quickly dominated by America's General Electric and Westinghouse and Germany's Siemens. The small field systems of British agriculture, laid out, like its rail network, for a densely populated country, could not adapt to the mile-long harvester runs that were standard on American factory farms. And some failures seem cultural. In reaction to a wave of machine-made American shoe imports in the early 1900s, British industry switched to American shoe-making machines, yet somehow never realized American productivity levels.

Finally, there is another factor in the relative British decline: the very aggressive use of the protective tariff, especially in steel, and especially by America and Germany, against a British nation that, despite some wavering, steadfastly refused to deviate from its free-trade principles.

The Tariff Question

Over a fifteen-year period beginning with Robert Peel's repeal of the protectionist Corn Laws in 1846, Great Britain steadily dismantled all restrictions on trade. By the end of the American Civil War, Great Britain had become perhaps history's purest example of a free-trade nation, a posture which it maintained, except during the Great War, until 1931. The free-trade movement was rooted in an ideological grab bag of Reform Protestantism (tariffs interfered with the workings of Providence); antigovernment libertarianism (indirect taxation fostered big government); and "Manchester school" liberal economics. By the high Victorian and Edwardian eras, free trade had hardened into religion, with the reformer Richard Cobden its patron saint, and devotion rewarded by the prosperity of the Victorian era. Aggressive protectionism in both Germany and the United States, especially in steel, put that commitment to a severe test in the early 1900s. German and American policies were quite different, however, and their interactions with the British free-trade regime shed light on policy issues that are still controversial today.

The United States used tariffs as a primary revenue source from the beginning of its existence, but its powerful merchant and planter interests forestalled blatant protectionism. Alexander Hamilton famously made the "infant industry" argument, but his 1792 tariff schedule, which extended the list of protected goods and increased most levies, was still, on average, only about 10 percent of import prices. It was only when the northern manufacturing interest won control of the Congress in the Civil War era that American policy turned protectionist. Throughout the rest of the nineteenth century, American tariffs were very stiff, and in iron and steel, blatantly exclusionary. The tariff on steel rails, for example, was set at 45 percent in 1864, and converted to a flat $28 a ton in 1870. Since rail prices were falling, the flat $28 impost became a bigger and bigger barrier, rising to a range of 70–100 percent of British export prices.

But while post–Civil War U.S. policy was protectionist, it was not *predatory*. Since the ravenous demand for steel at home left little surplus capacity, high domestic prices weren't used to finance below-cost export drives ("dumping"). Modest quantities of American steel don't appear in the export data until the mid-1890s, much of it going to Canada and Latin America, and Carnegie Steel did not seriously enter world markets until 1900. That year's sudden steel depression in the United States prompted a big jump in exports, which quickly fell as the American railroad recovery gathered steam. A systematic attempt to increase the American share of world markets came only with the advent of U. S. Steel. American steel exports grew steadily in the years before the Great War, and American export prices were frequently lower than those at home.

German policy, on the other hand, was determinedly predatory and clearly targeted against Great Britain. Bismarck's newly unified Prussian-German state emerged as the most formidable of the continental powers, and the only one with a steel industry that matched the American in scale and efficiency. Its steel policy in the 1880s and 1890s looks much like the Japanese assault on the semiconductor industry a century later. Production was concentrated in a few large cartelized firms with close ties to the government, while high domestic prices financed cut-price sales volume drives abroad. Domestic German rail prices, for example, averaged some 25–30 percent more than export prices through most of the period. In the classic cartel pattern, as Germany began to achieve dominance in its continental markets, the price gap steadily narrowed.

Great Britain found itself squeezed from both west and east. American protectionism gradually evicted the British from the big North American market, while German predation and locational advantage cut a deep swathe through traditional British customers in Europe and Russia. By 1900, German steel production was already about 30 percent greater than Great Britain's, and America's was more than twice as large. Between then and 1913, American and German production both tripled, while Great Britain's grew by only 63 percent. On the eve of the war, German exports were nearly double Great Britain's, and nearly equal to Britain's and America's combined. Much of the British export trade, moreover, was in finished products made from primary steel imported from Germany, or increasingly from America, while sales were disproportionately oriented toward the empire. In modern jargon, the prewar years saw the "hollowing out" of British steel. Something similar happened with the smaller, but still important, British chemical industry. After the 1897 Dingel tariff, for example, British exports of soda ash to the United States dropped to less than a fifth of their pre-tariff level.

It is all the more remarkable, therefore, that the British political and business establishment emphatically rejected a return to protectionism in the early 1900s, even though it was couched only as a tit for tat retaliation against predators—so-called "fair trade." The rejection was partly a matter of self-interest—textile manufacturers feared losing access to their raw materials if a trade war broke out; British finished steel makers liked importing primary steel at cut-rate prices; and labor unions had long linked free trade with cheap food. But to a striking degree, the rejection was also based on deeply engrained ideology, supported by a web of purely intellectual and highly abstract arguments. As the London *Times* put it, "Protection . . . brings its own punishment. Nature will retaliate upon France whether we do or not." The flower of the British economics establishment, the legendary professors Marshall, Pigou, and Jevons, all pronounced on the folly of trade restriction, insisting that the British industry was merely undergoing a "natural" adjustment. Winston Churchill worried how ministries

and parliament, "hitherto chaste because unsolicited," might behave once
the protectionist bawd ran free.

The Cambridge steel historian, D.L. Burn, in an exhaustive review of
the fair trade debate on steel, written in the late 1930s, subjects the intellectual argument to a withering analysis, not because it was wrong but
because it was either ignorant, or willfully ignored facts that conflicted with
its theoretic presumptions. It was simply not true, as the professors
claimed, that Britain no longer had access to low-cost ore or that British
steel plants had reached optimum size; and their denial that Germans were
dumping—because theory said it was irrational—flew in the face of available data.

Burn does not oppose the basic free trade position. Rather he attacks
the smug certitudes of the professoriat, their carelessness with facts, and
their complacent conviction that the Germans would eventually realize that
predatory trade was against their own interests, which was hardly obvious.
At the same time, he leaves no doubt that the core problem was still the
slack response of British steel-makers to the German assault. To exploit
Britain's reserves of low-cost ore, for example, would have required a comprehensive resizing and restructuring along American and German lines,
and it is doubtful that British steel men had the stomach for it. While Burn
speculates on the feasibility of using tariffs to shield an industry reorganization, he concedes his own doubts that it could have succeeded. The subsequent history of "temporary" periods of protection both in the United
States and Europe bears out his skepticism.

The German-British competition in steel, in fact, is a poor fit for the
free-trade paradigm. The basic premise of classic trade theory—David
Ricardo's principle of "comparative advantage"*—is that trade policy aims
at maximizing national income. But Bismarckian Germany, like post–World

---

*"Comparative advantage" was first set out rigorously by Ricardo in 1817. It shows that total wel-
fare (i.e., production) is maximized if each trading partner specializes in its own highest productivity industry. In his famous example of England and Portugal producing wine and cloth, he
shows that even if Portugal could produce *both* wine and cloth more efficiently than England, both
countries would be better off if Portugal concentrated on wine and traded for cloth, and vice versa,
provided only that England was better at cloth than wine, and Portugal better at wine than cloth.
It didn't matter that Portugal was also better at cloth than England, if it was comparatively even
better at wine. Ricardo's "comparative advantage" is both more general and less intuitive than
Adam Smith's "absolute advantage," which would reach the above result only if England was better at cloth than Portugal.

"The Original Coxey's Army." With Andrew Carnegie in the lead, American fat cats arrive at the Capitol in their Pullman parlor cars to plead for tariff protection.

War II Japan, was bent on optimizing specific strategic industries. Germany was force-feeding steel for military conquest, and Japan its semiconductors for industrial conquest—*even if* total national output and income suffered as a result. In both cases, the quasi-command organization of the economy intentionally obstructed the operation of corrective market mechanisms: high domestic prices did not call forth domestic competition since entry was restricted by the cartel. Taking the regime objectives on their own terms, both policies were arguably effective. The German rise was checked only by war, and the Japanese takeover of semiconductors primarily by a competing cartel in Korea.

The American nineteenth-century trade experience fits much more within the Ricardian paradigm. When Andrew Carnegie defended steel tariffs, it was always as a time-limited "infant industry" exception to the fundamental theory—that America, and total welfare, would benefit *in the longer run* if a period of protection first permitted the creation of sufficiently robust home-grown competition. There was, of course, a good dollop of hypocrisy in Carnegie's free-trade pose, for American steel tariffs were continued far beyond the time when its industry could conceivably qualify as "infant." But the fundamental question is still of interest to economic historians: Was the infant industry justification warranted in the case of the United States?

The 1890 American tin plate tariff is perhaps the case most often cited in support of early-stage protective tariffs. Tin plate is used primarily in tin cans and roofing material. Under a Treasury interpretation, the post–Civil War tariff legislation did not cover tin plate,* and the American market was dominated by low-cost Welsh producers. Imposing the 1890 tariff was a close-run thing. There was formidable opposition, not only from the food industry, but also from Standard Oil, the world's largest tin plate user, whose blue five-gallon kerosene cans were ubiquitous throughout the tropics and Asia. (The American Treasury, however, paid "drawbacks," or rebates, of tariffs paid on reexported goods.) The law passed the House only by a single vote, and only with a proviso that it would lapse unless domestic production

---

*The interpretation was almost certainly incorrect. The original legislation read: "On tin plates, and iron galvanized or coated with . . ."; the Treasury, probably through a misunderstanding, moved the comma so it read: "On tin plates and iron, galvanized or coated with. . . ." Since tin plate was never galvanized or coated, it was held not to be covered by the legislation.

reached certain minimum production thresholds; it was, in any case, halved in 1894 as part of a broader tariff-reducing initiative.

The economist Frank Taussig, writing in 1915, found the evidence from the tin plate episode, while mixed, "not unfavorable to the protectionist." Almost as soon as the tariff was passed, the American price rose to the Welsh price plus the tariff premium and production jumped remarkably; within a very few years, the Welsh industry had been decimated and imports had almost ceased. (Large segments of the Welsh industry emigrated and set up shop in the United States.) High domestic tin plate profits evoked a rash of new competition, and the American price premium quickly dropped to about half the tariff rate, and kept dropping even after the tariff was reduced in 1894. As Taussig points out, however, the primary factor in the continuing price reduction was falling material prices. Steel billets, from which the sheet was rolled, accounted for about 60 percent of the price of tin plate, and was subjected to very high tariffs. American tin plate, that is, wouldn't have needed the tariff if billets hadn't been protected. Falling billet prices from growing domestic capacity explained much of the increased tin plate production.

That happy progression was abruptly interrupted by Judge Moore's 1898 tin plate merger, confirming "Sugar King" H. O. Havemeyer's dictum that "the Mother of all trusts is the custom tariff law." The new Tin Plate Co. pushed prices back up very near the tariff premium, and the combination of high tin plate and falling billets generated spectacular profitability. But it was precisely the very shaky prospect of maintaining such socko profits against a surge of new entrants, including the formidable Carnegie Steel, that led to the formation of U. S. Steel. After the consolidation, the Steel combine stabilized prices at about half the tariff premium, although it continued to lose domestic share to new competition, and the domestic price gradually drifted down to international levels. By 1910, Standard Oil, surely one of the shrewdest of cost managers, dropped its tariff drawbacks and switched to domestic suppliers. By that time, U. S. Steel was a substantial exporter of tin plate, usually at prices lower than it charged at home. Superficially, at least, it looks like the tariff worked. Although it took almost two decades, excess protected profits evoked a horde of competitors, and the United States eventually emerged with a large industry and competitive prices.

The economist and historian Douglas Irwin has recently reanalyzed the episode to try to tease out a clearer picture of the tariff's effects. The mere fact that domestic production flourished under the initial tariff regime does not by itself justify the tariff; the real question is how does that experience compare with what would have happened *without* the tariff. From the available data, Irwin develops a model for how the American industry responded to changes in the economic environment—to growth in demand, to changes in the tariff, to billet prices, and to improvements in technology. Contrafactual exercises are, of course, inherently speculative and often highly sensitive to initial specifications, but they do force specificity and spotlight the relevant variables.

Irwin's study underscores the "commodity" character of the tin plate industry—low margins, minimal capital costs, and short learning curves, with little basis for quality differentiation from one producer to the other. With few barriers to entry, excess profits quickly elicited new competition. Irwin's model shows that the steady drop in billet prices would have eventually created a domestic tin plate industry without tariff protection, although the 1890 tariff accelerated its development by as much as a decade. But the additional costs to tin plate consumers under all of Irwin's scenarios exceeded tariff revenues and excess producer profits, so the net income effects were negative. In short, Irwin's model says that the country would have been better off without the tin plate tariff.

What about the broader question of nineteenth-century iron and steel tariffs? While they clearly damaged Great Britain's industry, did they help or hinder American growth? While there can be no definitive answer, there is a good case that, largely because of the presence of Andrew Carnegie, the tariffs were a good deal for America.

The Carnegie Effect

Almost all historians agree that the United States would have had a large iron and steel industry with or without a tariff. With such a rich endowment of inexpensive coal and iron ore, coupled with such a pervasive commitment to rapid growth, it is hard to imagine how it could be otherwise. And almost no one disagrees that the presence of the tariff accelerated the industry's growth. The first cost sheets for the Edgar Thomson Works that Andrew Carnegie and Alexander Holley brought to Junius Morgan in 1874 projected very high profits. But by the time the plant was up and running, rail prices had fallen and margins were only $4–8 a ton, even including the $28 per ton tariff-based price umbrella. Without the tariff, the ET could never have gotten off the ground. Later, in 1882, the ET's accounts show average steel production cost of $43 a ton, or about $10 more than British export prices. Since ET's costs were quite likely the lowest in the industry, American steel obviously still needed protection, although not $28 worth.

The $28 tariff impost, however, grossly overstates its burden on American consumers, since competition within America almost always prevented steel companies from pricing up to the full tariff premium. During the frenzied rail boom of 1880 and 1881, American prices were marked up almost exactly $28 over British export prices ($61 a ton in 1881 versus the British $32.75, pre-shipping), and British rail exports to America broke all records. But those were the only instances of full-premium pricing in the entire period from 1880 through 1901. The next highest premium was $15 in 1887, another strong year for British exports. But excluding 1880 and 1881, the average premium over the two decades was only about $5. Even during the heyday of the rail price pool from 1893 through 1896, the premium was very modest, varying between $4–7. By the time of the rail price war of 1897–98, Carnegie Steel was making record profits at sales prices well under those of the British, although it may have been the only American company that could do so. When the pool was reestablished in 1899, the American price was set at just 12 percent, or $3, over the British export price, which is probably not far from the "relationship" premium a stateside steel vendor might normally command. (Rational buyers frequently pay premiums to lock in an accessible vendor who can work out flexible supply arrangements, help with technical issues, or possibly help them win orders.) The next year, 1900, American and British prices were virtually identical.

By the time of the formation of U. S. Steel, in other words, the Americans could easily undersell the British, and the tariff had become an irrelevance. The new steel consortium fixed American rail prices at exactly $28, or far above the cost of production, but roughly equal to British export prices. It was the high cost of British steel, not the tariff, that set the price ceiling for the Americans.

A substantial share of the credit for keeping the tariff burden so low must go to Andrew Carnegie. The deadweight costs of a protected cartel are some of the most destructive consequences of a high-tariff regime. But Carnegie never behaved like a rational cartelizer. Although he consistently earned the highest profits in the industry, he paid the smallest dividends, choosing instead to plow earnings back into better plants, more mechanization, and larger output. Falling prices were just opportunities to take share— the Carnegie companies increased their market share in every recession. John W. Gates's 1898 comment, amid the wreckage of the late-1890s rail price war, says it all: Carnegie's savage price-cutting meant that the days of "large profits for comparatively small tonnage" were over; Gates's Illinois Steel was going to have to spend millions to get more competitive. Among America's wannabe cartelizers, like Gates and Elbert Gary, Carnegie was a "bull in a china shop," bent on driving "entirely out of business every steel company in the United States."

American steel producers enjoyed great natural advantages in their vast coal reserves and the nearly infinite, low-cost Great Lakes ore ranges. But it required huge investments to bring that potential to fruition. Cost-effective use of Mesabi ore came only with the advent of large-scale surface mining machines, mechanized loading and unloading docks, massive ore boats, and purpose-built railroads, like Carnegie's Pittsburgh and Bessemer line. The Carnegie companies took the pole position in most of those investment initiatives, they set the steel price caps for their competitors, and since they reinvested so much of their earnings, they forced copycat investment on everyone else.

American steel tariffs may be the unusual case where the excess earnings were intelligently used. There is no way to quantify the impact of Carnegie. There were other men of energy and invention in the nascent American steel trade—the Fritz brothers at Cambria and Bethlehem, for instance—but none had his drive, ambition, or subversive instincts. Absent Carnegie, the "Fathers" of the Bessemer Association, America's original steel cartel, could more easily have maintained their cautious, controlled development strategy; the genius of Alexander Holley might never have been given full play; men on the cut of a Gates and a Gary would have been in control from the start. Without the tariff, in short, the American industry might have evolved more like that of Great Britain, and one of the earliest, and the most dramatic, examples of the highly mechanized, mass-scale, intensely driven industrial machine that was a hallmark of the American advance might have been delayed too long to make a difference.

What Was Special about America?

The quite different development paths of the American and German steel industries offer insights into America's uniqueness. Superficially, on the eve of the World War, they appeared very similar—both were highly mechanized, with very large-scale plants, and the Germans especially impressed with their immaculate work organization. The difference lay in how they used their production. Since Germany exported a far higher proportion of its steel, its per capita domestic steel consumption was less than two-thirds that in America, and the difference is greater still when one considers the very substantial share of German domestic production devoted to military purposes. Per capita military spending was some four times greater in Germany than in America, and, as in the naval arms race with Great Britain, was very steel-intensive. Even nominally nonmilitary German spending, moreover, was tilted to military ends; its heavy industry and the military were united in the *Wehrverein*, the union of defense, and German railroad and telegraph development was partially subordinate to military requirements; the Railway Section was one of the more important of the General Staff departments.

The remarkable feature of nineteenth-century American development, in short, is not just the staggering size of the gap it opened up over the rest of the world but the fact that it was so overwhelmingly directed to private purposes. The historian David Landes has pointed out the uniqueness of the western European commitment to private enterprise, and its consequent hyperrational, contract-centered ordering of affairs. The commercial focus of European society, he argues, gave it a "tremendous advantage in the invention and adoption of new technologies." If that was true, America was Europe on steroids, for its settlers were the people who found Europe confining and repressive.

In America, moreover, the world's most energetic people were paired with the most boundless trove of natural resources, resources that were as close as ever to being free, so long as you had the will to go get them. Lincoln's claim that the average man "labors for wages a while, saves a surplus with which to buy tools or land, for himself . . . and at length hires another new beginner to help him," was sufficiently true that it became the standard to judge oneself by. De Tocqueville was struck by Americans' restless mobility, their unrootedness in place or class, the fevered striving, the obsession with money. How could they be otherwise? The prize was never so achievable, or so palpable. The very speed of the race evoked the common-sense, straight-at-them, unadorned American style. The craftsmen who decorated the great palaces of Europe could not be hired in America; Americans were too busy making and selling useful things.

A land of abundance was the perfect incubator for a machine-based business culture—with free resources, any method of accelerating output built wealth. As a Crystal Palace commentator said in 1851, the American approach to technology was ideal for "increasing the number or the quantity of articles suited to the wants of a whole people, and adapted to promote the enjoyment of that moderate competency which prevails among them." Even in the 1850s, rural factories were machine-producing a hundred doors a day, just as machines let scattered farm families open large new tracts of land to commercial farming. Well before the Civil War, Americans, at least outside the South, had more goods and more food more equitably distributed than any people in history.

Andrew Carnegie, John D. Rockefeller, and Jay Gould, the archetypes for the megatycoons that dominated the second half of the century, all arrived just at the cusp of the fateful post–Civil War transition from artisanal to big-business forms. All three came from modest circumstances, and while they were all men of great intelligence and lightning commercial reflexes, they separated themselves by the boundlessness of their ambition and their instincts for disruption. The economist Joseph Schumpeter spoke of progress as "creative destruction." These three were walking whirlwinds: over some twenty-five years they forced the pace in all the critical underpinnings of the modern industrial state—steel, oil, railroads, coal, telegraphs—constantly driving to larger scales and lower costs, constantly attacking the comfortable settling points where normal businessmen paused to enjoy their success.

Cheap national distribution combined with machine-based production created the world's first mass consumer culture, the vast outpouring of "good-enough" products that filled the households, if never quite satisfied the wants, of the first-ever middle-class nation. The steady drop in prices through the second half of the century was not mostly about currency adjustments. Rather it appears that most goods actually were cheaper in a real sense, much as the real price of computer power has dropped so amazingly in our own day. *Scientific American* noted in 1904 how steel fishing rods were sweeping away the old bamboo versions. They were lighter, more durable, more easily weighted, more sensitive to the touch—and they were turned out by factories instead of by craftsmen, so ordinary people could buy them.

Other nations, including even the "cousins" in England, who had the closest relations, were late to realize the stunning scale and breadth of the American boom. That was partly because America was such a voracious consumer of its own manufacturing; as far as export markets were concerned, Americans produced mostly food products and oil. The immense power of the American economy instead made itself felt as a kind of natural storm system, a "vast but unpredictable bellows" that, for no apparent reason, might suddenly blow hot winds or icy gales through the entire world. Londoners grew cynical at Wall Street's recurrent crashes. When the 1907 crash hit, the *Economist* wrote wearily, "The collapse in New York, so long anticipated, has at last come to pass." Although there was absolutely nothing wrong with the British economy, or with America's either, in the British view, the force of the contraction was so great that the Bank of England had almost to quadruple its bank rate, to a punishing 7½ percent. It was "all very violent and primitive and annoying to Londoners."

Perceptive financiers, however, understood how the force fields lay. A senior Barings partner, Gaspard Farrar, surprised his colleagues in 1904 by remarking "that it cannot be very long before New York is the financial centre of the world; but I fear for our sakes that it is coming too quickly." One of Pierpont Morgan's great roles, besides imposing a semblance of order on finances at home, was to mediate the cohabitation between the more settled financial systems of the Old World and the often chaotic arrangements of the New.

The same mixture of irritation and concern greeted the United States's hesitant emergence in world affairs. European countries did not upgrade their American ministries to full ambassador status until the 1890s. The sudden war with Spain seemed to have sprung more from the rantings of American press barons than from considerations of policy. What John Hay intended by his 1900 "Open Door" policy in China was a puzzle to other statesmen. Yet the British carefully backed away from a potential confrontation with the United States in Latin America. There was nothing to be gained from goading adolescent giants.

European elites were struck by America's rawness, its tawdriness, its half-finished character. Much of Henry James's work digs after the micropoints of intersection between the Old and the New Worlds. In his last novel, *The Golden Bowl* (1904), a beautiful, accomplished, young American woman, Charlotte, who has been living on the fringes of English society, marries a widowed American tycoon who is on a "collecting" tour. Charlotte's older Englishwoman friend contemplates her return to America with horror, for her fate is the pointedly named "American City": "I see the long miles of ocean and the dreadful great country, State after State—which have never seemed to me so big or so terrible. I see *them* at last, day by day and step by step, at the far end—and I see them never come back."

James, the expatriate Londoner, does not elaborate on Charlotte's future, nor offer more than a scrap of description of American City, for his readers, both English and American, know it will be dreadful. But his tycoon, Adam Verver, is still by far the most formidable character in the novel, a man of great power and quiet confidence, with an ear for emotional nuance and an eye for Damascene tiles.

The impecunious Italian prince who marries Verver's daughter recognizes that he is being collected, along with other artworks, and his resolve to live up to the bargain underscores his fundamental decency. This somewhat etiolated aristocrat, an habitué of crumbling palaces, understands in all sincerity that this American tycoon is "the best man I've ever seen in my life."

The surge of raw power at the commencement of a great empire can sustain expansionist momentum long after its internal dynamism flags. A telltale sign of ebbing energy is when intellectual elites start constructing imperial narratives. The tale spinners of Augustan Rome were priests and poets; in the twentieth-century empire of American business, they were pundits and professors.

THE WRONG LESSONS

First, a multiple choice test. Consider the following two men.

We have met Alexander Holley many times in this book. He brought modern steel technology to America, and more than anyone else, created, and then steadily improved, the highly mechanized, labor-saving American system of steel manufacture. Holley's work greatly expanded the reach of the Connecticut Valley machine tradition, and was the definitive demonstration of the characteristically American style of driving productivity through advanced technology.

A quarter century after Holley laid out his great steelworks, Frederick W. Taylor solved the problem of hand-loading pig iron into freight cars. By his account, after much research and analysis, he and his assistants worked out optimum weight loads and walking speeds, and minutely calculated the precise physical motions for an ideal result. His "scientific" samplings were actually almost all based on a single man, the wiry, vigorous Henry Noll, who Taylor later immortalized as the stupid immigrant "Schmidt." Noll, it seems, loved heavy labor and often ran a mile home after work, but even Noll could not consistently keep up with Taylor's standards. Since Taylor used his standards for piecework pay rates, almost all the pig loaders had their wages cut.

The challenge for the reader is to guess which of these two men would be anointed by intellectuals and business school professors as "the Father of Scientific Management." Which would be hailed by no less an eminence than the management guru Peter Drucker for "the most powerful as well as the most lasting contribution America has made to western thought since the Federalist papers"? Which man, in a 1977 survey of professors and historians to choose the most important contributors to management thought and practice, would crush all other contenders, including Andrew Carnegie, John D. Rockefeller, Alfred Sloan, and Henry Ford? Those who picked Holley may go to the back of the class.

Taylor's real lifework was as an innovator in machine shop technology, where his contributions were sufficiently important that he could fairly be dubbed "the father of modern machine shop management." But the work that he himself claimed as the central feature of "scientific management" was the organization and engineering of manual operations, like his "science of shoveling" or his "law of heavy labor," which lays down that a "first-class" man carrying ninety-two-pound weights needs to be load-free 57 percent of the work day, but only 46 percent if the load is reduced by half. (Yes, it's nonsense.) But even if Taylor's claims could be taken at face value, their essential triviality is astonishing. There is a place in industry for engineered manual operations. But when presented with a problem like loading pig iron, an Alexander Holley or a Henry Ford would first ask, why on earth are you doing it by hand? And before looking more closely at Taylor's work, we must first ask why on earth did people think his claims were so important?

The answer is wrapped up in the way American opinion-makers came to terms with the immense new power centers that the tycoons left behind them. In part the process entailed taking at face value Morgan's assurance that the great new combines were designed to domesticate taloned predators like Carnegie Steel and to reestablish "orderly" competition. In part it was the relief of knowing that "business," rather than an endless waste of eye-gouging warfare, was just another topic that could fit on a professor's blackboard. Especially for the growing American upper-middle classes, who were investing so heavily in their children, it was a comfort to know that the first step toward success in business, just as in law or medicine, was simply doing well in school. And, finally, the notion that business was, after all, just a science like any other reassured intellectuals that they might still have something to say about the course of affairs.

Intellectuals Discover the Machine

Consider the aging Henry Adams, historian and descendent of presidents, standing agape before a giant electrical dynamo at the Paris Exposition of 1900, ready to fall on his knees "bewildered and helpless, as in the fourth century, a priest of Isis before the Cross of Christ." Adams's distress typified the severe intellectual crisis suffered by American elites around the turn of the century. A generation before, even secularists implicitly believed in the providential nature of the American adventure: the glow around the City on a Hill no longer emanated from God, perhaps, but they could still see it. For a while, providentialism survived the encounter with Darwin—the textbook evolutionary tree, after all, usually showed a white European male perched on top. But by century's end, elites had begun to understand evolution's essential randomness; if the only criterion for "fitness" was survival, the future might well belong to beetles and rats. One by one the old verities crumbled: radioactivity put the lie to the permanence of matter, while Freud's expeditions into the darker recesses of the mind exposed the pretensions of the Rational Man. Karl Pearson's 1892 bestseller, *The Grammar of Science,* stressed the probabilistic character of physics, and its agnosticism toward the reality of entities like force. *The Education of Henry Adams* mocked its author's plight:

> To Thomas Aquinas, the universe was still a person; to Spinoza, a substance; to Kant . . . a categorical imperative; to Poincaré, a convenience; to Pearson, a medium of exchange. The historian never stopped repeating to himself that he knew nothing about it. . . . He saw his education complete, and was sorry he ever began it. As a matter of taste, he greatly preferred his eighteenth-century education when God was a father and nature a mother, and all was for the best in a scientific universe.

America's raucous economic successes were not much consolation. As a youthful Walter Lippmann put it, modern industry "is the great fact in our lives, blackening our cities, fed with the lives of our children, a tyrant over men and women, turning out enormous stocks of produce, good, bad, and horrible." And although all Americans on each Fourth of July duly celebrated "the huddled masses yearning to breathe free," that same "wretched refuse" from distant teeming shores was clearly making a terrible mess of big eastern cities. The crime rates and disease in Boston's and New York City's slums were horrific.

But a deus ex machina, quite literally, was on hand for the rescue. When U. S. Steel was founded, Charles Schwab stressed that the biggest companies were run by specialist managers trained in "the science of business": "Nothing is left to chance. Every step of the process is carefully worked out in advance. All waste is cut off." Lippmann, who was a reliable weathervane of the period's intellectual fads, enthusiastically echoed Schwab: "American business has been passing through a reorganization so radical that we are just beginning to grasp its meaning. . . . The scope of human endeavor is enormously larger, and with it has come . . . a general change in social scale." But the "new business world has produced a new kind of business man. For it requires a different order of ability to conduct the Steel Trust, than it did to manage a primitive blast-furnace." Trust-busters, Lippmann said, failed to understand that the right size for a business was a matter for "experts in the new science of administration. . . . The fact is that administration is becoming an applied science, capable of devising executive methods capable of dealing with tremendous units." In Edward Bellamy's utopian 1887 novel, *Looking Backward,* social strife disappeared once all production was put in the hands of a "single syndicate. . . . The Great Trust."

From a chair in academia, or from a journalistic desk, giant corporations like Standard Oil or U. S. Steel took on the polished, quietly humming appearance of the awesome Corliss engine that had towered like a brooding god over the Philadelphia Exposition a generation before. The scientific approach to business was underscored by the star attraction of the 1904 St. Louis Exposition, the Pennsylvania Railroad's display of a working locomotive testing plant. Mammoth overhead cranes could swing even the largest locomotive onto mechanical rollers, where it would power up and roar away at top speeds—schedules would announce when visitors could watch a locomotive running at, say, seventy miles per hour—while teams of technicians carefully measured temperatures, fuel consumption, tractive resistance, and pulling power, stopping the run from time to time to change a part or adjust a setting.

The notion of businessman-as-scientist flowed directly from Pearson's insistence, in his *Grammar of Science,* that science was primarily about *method.* The scientist strove for pure objectivity, impersonal, value-free. He proceeded by "the careful and often laborious classification of facts, in the

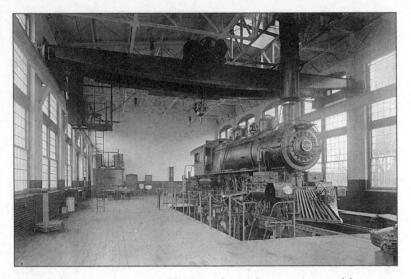

Scientific Management in action: The Pennsylvania's locomotive testing laboratory at Altoona, Pennsylvania. Previously, it had been an exhibit at the 1904 St. Louis Exposition.

comparison of their relationships and sequences, and, finally, in the discovery . . . of a brief statement, or a *formula,* which . . . is termed a scientific law." Science-as-method, Pearson wrote, "claims that the whole range of phenomena, mental as well as physical—the entire universe—is its field. . . . every phase of social life, every stage of past or present development is material for science." There was, in short, no need to jettison the promise of Progress and American exceptionalism, but the path to the shining City, instead of being lighted by God, would be revealed through Science.

This was heady stuff. The success of marginalist economics seemed to buttress Pearson's claim. Just as a few simple laws choreographed the freely colliding molecules of a gas, correct prices arose from the activity of countless atomized market participants obeying simple canons of self-interest. The fledgling study of sociology jumped on the statistical dogcart; when the American Sociological Society was founded in 1905, it was open only to "scientific" practitioners. Sociology was expressly framed as a science of "social control," teasing out the laws of individual interactions that created a "social equilibrating apparatus."* Even Henry Adams tried his hand at a "Dynamic Theory of History," hopeful of discovering the tidal laws governing the rise and fall of nations. John Dewey was confident that schools could be run like "great factories" to churn out the self-reliant citizens to people his vision of a liberal democracy.

The cult of the expert was born. Dewey said that science aimed at "the transformation of natural powers into expert, tested powers." The Pennsylvania Railroad's publicity material at St. Louis emphasized that the test routines were rigidly specified and minutely directed by a Purdue professor, one F. M. Goss. There was a core of truth here: many big companies were indeed building research laboratories and driving toward scientific quality control and product development; but the relationship between businessmen and scientists—even at the Pennsylvania—was arm's length and prickly, as it largely remains today. For journalists and intellectuals, however, who often knew little about business and less about science, the scientific expert transmuted into a kind of wizard. The historian Theodore Porter has noted that the Pearsonian version of science was "ideally suited to American democracy. Social scientists . . . could disarm suspicion that their advice was self-interested by intoning the phrase *scientific method*."

So when Frederick W. Taylor proclaimed that he had discovered the principles of "Scientific Management," his audiences went into a collective swoon.

What Did Taylor Do?

Frederick Winslow Taylor, born to a wealthy Philadelphia family in 1856, was a prodigiously gifted young man, vigorous and outgoing, a natural leader, and a good student with a strong bent for mathematics and physics. He was also a superb athlete, for he and a friend won the U.S. Open tennis doubles championship in 1881. After graduating from Phillips Exeter Academy, he passed up college to become an apprentice machinist in a local

---

*Immigrants tended to come off badly in these exercises. True to the Pearsonian ideal of cold adherence to (apparent) facts, the scientists tracked immigrants' assimilation, measured their skulls, and generally pronounced them inferior. Race protection was one of the era's important subthemes. Pearson himself was a strong advocate for race-based eugenics.

company owned by a friend of the family. After four years learning his trade—a period which he later claimed gave him special insight into the minds of ordinary workers—Taylor became a subforeman at Philadelphia's Midvale Steel in 1878. He proved to be a hard "driver" style of manager, imposing monetary fines for ruined work or waste, and experimenting with various piece rate pay systems. He spent more than ten years at Midvale, rising through series of promotions to chief engineer, while he earned his mechanical engineering degree at night. Most of the basic themes of his subsequent work can be traced directly to his Midvale experiences, including his lifelong hostility to "soldiering"—the tactic of manual workers to settle into comfortable group-enforced output norms. He also proved to be a brilliant mechanic, and was awarded a number of patents for improved machine tool designs.

The years Taylor was at Midvale, roughly the decade of the 1880s, marked a pronounced business scale shift from local toward regional or national organization modes. Railroads led the way, in the process surmounting management challenges of an entirely new scale—thousands of miles of roads, millions of shipments, far-flung construction and maintenance activities, tens of thousands of employees. The railroads' drive to standardization, cost management, and quality control forced comparable adaptations at their suppliers, like Carnegie Steel, Westinghouse Airbrake, Baldwin Locomotive, and Pullman Sleeping Car. Holley evangelized the steel industry on the heavy costs of sloppy control—the unscheduled shutdown of a big blast furnace could cost a small fortune—while Carnegie methodically mechanized away most of the old steel craft trades. Comparable developments took place in other railroad-enabled industries, like flour, sugar, and chemicals, and in the new mass distribution companies, like Montgomery Ward, the food store chains, and the big department stores. As operating scales outran the personal reach of top managers, there was a proliferation of paper-based control systems—departmental cost-tracking, standard paying and receiving systems, data tabulation and performance reporting. Office furniture, filing systems, forms, and typewriters became important industries, and office towers recarved urban skylines.

But outside of the biggest or most advanced companies, the penetration of systematic management was spotty at best, and more often almost non-existent. Especially in midtechnology mechanical industries, operations were typically a mess. The manufacturer and reformer Henry Towne, in

1886, told the American Society of Mechanical Engineers (ASME) that "the management of works is unorganized, is almost without literature, has no organization or medium for the interchange of experience. . . . The remedy . . . should originate from engineers." The typical manufacturer often had minimal local competition, was rarely held to exacting quality standards, and had grown mostly by hiring more and more craftsmen in the old artisanal tradition. Internal contracting, or the use of independent contractors within the factory on a fixed piecework basis, was still common. And even in bigger, well-managed companies, midsized craft operations, like the machine shop in a steel plant, still often ran as if they were independent companies. Shop operations were Taylor's sweet spot, especially the job shop, where there was likely to be considerable variation from one job to the next.

There was an obsessive streak in Taylor, much like John Hall's. A half century before, Hall had spent years on the challenge of machining interchangeable precision parts, driving down to each microlevel obstacle, and attacking and mastering them one by one. Taylor took on shop management in much the same way. Getting control implied standardizing every aspect of production—the quality of the machines and the cutting tools, the speed of the tool, the depth of the cut, the rate of the feed, the sequence of operations—details that Midvale, like most shops, left up to the foremen or the individual machinists. Step by step, Taylor isolated the critical performance variables and drove to a best-practice standard. As his system took shape, cutting tools were maintained in a central tool room, a specialist team oversaw the belting,* a planning group laid out production schedules, jobs were allocated with an instruction card that specified machining sequences and tolerances, materials were charged out to each job, and job and time cards tracked each machinist's performance. The last step in the process was a piece rate, with the punitive feature that the piece rate *dropped* at lower levels of production. To set the rates, Taylor introduced stopwatch timing of the detailed operations. If Taylor's subsequent practice is any guide, he confined his time study to the best men, and his timing was

---

*In a steam- or water-driven factory, power was transmitted through shaft-and-belt systems. Loose or lightweight belts could have a drastic effect on performance, so consistent belt maintenance paid large productivity dividends. Belt-driven machines disappeared with the spread of electric motors toward the end of the century.

approximate at best. In one Midvale example that survives, the men would have had to nearly double their production to earn their former wage.

Taylor's obsessiveness was matched by a streak of grandiosity. Once he had the machine shop in order, he pushed to apply the same techniques to the entire company. A sparse record suggests that outside of the machine shop he worked only with laboring units, and, since there was no machinery involved, concentrated only on time studies and piece rates. At some point, he became enamored of the idea that *all* human actions could be engineered like a machine. As he put it some years later, "every single act of every workman can be reduced to a science." But it required trained experts:

> [A] man who is fit to handle pig iron as a regular occupation is . . . so stupid and so phlegmatic that he more nearly resembles in his mental makeup the ox than any other type. . . . He is so stupid that he . . . must consequently be trained by a man more intelligent than himself into the habit of working in accordance with the laws of this science before he can be successful.

Even the most intelligent workers needed the help of experts, however:

> [I]n the higher classes of work, the scientific laws which are developed are so intricate that the high-priced mechanic needs (even more than the cheap laborer) the cooperation of men better educated than himself in finding the laws . . . and training him to work in accordance with them. . . . [I]n practically all the mechanic arts the science which underlies each workman's act is so great and amounts to so much that the workman who is best suited to actually doing the work is incapable, either through a lack of education or through insufficient mental capacity, of understanding this science.

Which reveals another of Taylor's traits, a penchant for pompous mystification. One imagines that old "Big Bill" Rockefeller, John D.'s medicine man dad, would have saluted a kindred spirit.

After Taylor left Midvale in 1889, he bounced from job to job for another decade—a paper company, a ball bearing company, the Cramp shipyard (that built Pierpont Morgan's *Corsair*), an electric motor business, then back to the ball bearing company. He consistently proved himself an outstanding plant manager, mostly through hard-driving piece rate systems and ruthless winnowing of workers who didn't perform at the top level. (In his own favorite example of pig iron loaders, he set the piece standard so high that only one of every eight men could meet it. So he got rid of the rest and replaced them with far fewer "first-class men.") Along the way he continued to polish up his ideas for shop management, which, although always intelligent, tended toward the fussy and overcomplicated. In his ideal machine shop, for instance, a machinist would report to *eight* different functional foremen. His presentations at the ASME, especially on piece rates, began to attract a small band of acolytes, including Henry Gantt, creator of the famous "Gantt chart,"* who joined his team at Midvale.

One of his new assistants was Sanford Thompson, whom Taylor had met at the paper company and whom he hired to pull together his Midvale time studies for publication. (Taylor was wealthy enough to pay for staff out of his pocket; besides his family resources, he was earning a growing royalty stream from his tool inventions.) When Thompson discovered how rudimentary and inconsistent Taylor's time studies had actually been, he and Taylor agreed that he should start over from scratch. Over the next six years Thompson performed detailed time analyses of construction site workers in eight trades running from "excavation" through "rock quarrying."

Thompson's results, together with a manual of timing techniques (including how to conceal the stopwatch from workers), form a major section of Taylor's 1903 text, *Shop Management*. It is a splendid example of sham science and spurious specificity run riot. In the "barrow work" subtrade, the dirt-moving planner could assume that it would take a man 1.948 minutes to load a barrow with loosened clay, at a rate of 0.144 minutes per shovelful, while sand required only 1.240 minutes at a rate of 0.094 minutes per shovelful. Starting the barrow took 0.182 minutes, wheeling it 50 feet on level ground 0.225 minutes, and dumping and turning 0.172 minutes. And so on. Those results are reduced to a "general formula for barrow work" where "a = time filling a barrow," "b = time preparing to wheel," etc., to arrive at:

$$B = (p+[a+b+c+d+f+(\text{distance hauled}/100)(c+e)]27/L)(1+P)$$

---

*A Gantt chart is a visual representation of project tasks as a series of time bars; they are still a standard output of project planning software packages.

There are additional formulae for filling the shovel and throwing the material, or filling the shovel, walking, and *then* throwing the material, and helpful tables for calculating throwing time based on the distance and the height thrown. Where the vertical throwing distance is four feet, and the horizontal five feet, it takes 0.073 minutes to fill the shovel and 0.031 minutes to throw the material. Throwing time rises to 0.043 minutes (or by seven-tenths of a second) if the vertical is increased to six feet while holding the horizontal constant. Taylor points out that the time for filling a shovel is independent of the distance thrown, but does vary with the kind of material, so the tables provide different values for various earth types. There is also a handy table of equations for deriving times of operations that are too quick to capture with a stopwatch, but for the equations to work "the number of successive elements observed together must be prime to the total number of elements in the cycle." Clearly, any shoveler who aspired to become a supervisor had a lot of book work ahead of him.

The silliness of it all is betrayed by the capital P, the last term in Taylor's long formula above. The P represented the time a worker needed to rest, or was consumed by something other than full-bore production. It was always a large, round number. In one extensive assignment covering many different jobs, the P ranged from 25 percent to 75 percent, obviously overwhelming the three-decimal time-study tables. Where did the P come from? In fact, it was a best guess, but when pressed, Taylor fiercely stuck to his guns: P was never arbitrary, but was based on "scientific investigation, a careful, thorough, scientific investigation of the facts." When a congressman suggested that traditional piece rates were also based on a foreman's long observations, Taylor insisted that "The one is guesswork, while the other is a careful scientific experiment."

Taylor's first and only full-time consulting assignment came in 1898 at Bethlehem Steel, which was experiencing serious production problems in its armor business. One of the Bethlehem senior executives had worked with Taylor at Midvale and admired his piece rate ideas, and so arranged for a presentation to Bethlehem management. Taylor stressed that it could take up to two years to install a full-blown piece rate system, because all the other elements had to be in place before he could conduct useful time studies. The board was enthusiastic, and Taylor began work in the spring. On its own terms, the engagement was a failure, and Taylor was fired two years later. Ironically, it was also the occasion of his greatest contribution to machining technology, the discovery of high-speed tool steel.

Ship plate and ship cannon production required very large-scale planing and boring operations, so Taylor immediately focused on the machine shop, introducing the full panoply of his management ideas. By the second year of the engagement, however, although the shops were running more smoothly, managers complained that they weren't actually *producing* any more than usual. To their irritation, they discovered that Taylor had still not begun work on the time studies and piece rate systems, which was the main reason he had been hired.

The fact is, Taylor had found something more interesting to do. For some twenty years he had been gnawing at the problem of optimizing machining operations, along the way experimenting with a great variety of cutting tool steels. Early in the Bethlehem assignment, he recommended a favorite tool steel from Midvale, and was embarrassed when it performed badly in a bakeoff with other steels. Checking further, he found that when it was forged, the toolsmith had overheated it to "dull cherry" (steel heat was still measured by color), which, as the smith should have known, made it soft and crumbly under pressure. Taylor had wangled a full-scale lab setup at Bethlehem, so he did some experiments on his own, corroborating that the Midvale steel got very hard just below cherry, but lost its integrity above that point. Then, to his amazement, he discovered that as he increased the heat through "salmon" to "yellow," the steel went through yet another phase change and got *super* hard.

That was a big deal, and Taylor knew it. With the assistance of Maunsel White, the Bethlehem metallurgist, he spent much of the next year on a model set of empirical experiments that completely specified the detailed processes for making the new steel. Along the way, experimenting with the newly invented pyrometer, they succeeded in replacing all the color-based heat descriptions with precise temperatures, so "light cherry" became "845°C." Centuries of lore, and the traditionalists' beloved color categories, were swept away into the attics of industrial museums.

The performance of the new tools was startling: they typically ran at double or triple the speed of standard tools, heating all the way to "cherry" (about 1000°C) without any loss of cutting efficiency. A spectacular Taylor-White tool exhibit at the 1900 Paris Exposition got the attention of the entire industry—it was a giant lathe cutting at high speed, and positioned in semidarkness to highlight the cherry-red glow of the tool and the blue glow of the stream of hot chips. High-speed steel swept through the industry, and by 1902 machine makers were creating entirely new lines of equipment to take advantage of the new tools. (But it took some years to take full advantage of them. Re-gearing motors to triple the speed of the cutting tool was easy enough, but it was much harder to redesign, say, a heavy planing table to feed three times as fast, and still stay true.) Although the Taylor-White patents secured his fortune, Taylor, ever the obsessive, downplayed their importance, insisting that they were just a *component* of the comprehensive "Taylorized" shop system. He was even disappointed at the rousing reception accorded his 1906 ASME presidential address, "On the Art of Cutting Metals," because the audience focused only on the new tools, ignoring the functional foremen, the stopwatch timing, the piece rates, and the rest of his apparatus, which he regarded as equally fundamental.*

After Taylor was ushered out of Bethlehem—he had managed to antagonize a remarkable number of people, from top management down to the shop floor—he effectively retired from active business, building a large house near Philadelphia, working hard at his golf game, and serving as a kind of mountaintop guru for the cause of "scientific management." He frequently played host to small groups of businessmen, treating them to lunch and a Taylor disquisition. Taylor could be a mesmerizing speaker, and his stories and successes steadily improved with each re-telling; as one biographer delicately put it, "potential dramatic appeal . . . outweighed any consideration of historical accuracy." The day would wind up with a tour of a local factory run by a friend and admirer, James Dodge, who had installed one of the few examples of a pure Taylorized operation. Many of those tours resulted in consulting assignments, which he parceled out among a still small but growing band of disciples.

And there, under normal circumstances, Taylor's story would have

---

*His address was followed by a metallurgist's presentation that specified the detailed composition of the new steels. Taylor, whose science was in the older empirical tradition, pooh-poohed the metallurgical results; but his failure to specify the metallurgy caused him to lose his patents in 1909. The patents were difficult to defend under any circumstances, and Taylor went to ingenious lengths to conceal the underlying (and relatively simple) processes that they entailed. The small community of cutting toolmakers, still concentrated in Sheffield, had duplicated Taylor's results by the middle of the decade.

ended. Although he was little known outside of professional circles, his machining contributions would have warranted a special note in industrial histories. One imagines that the ASME might have honored him with a statue, much as they did Holley. What happened instead is that in 1910, Louis Brandeis decided to take up the cudgels for Taylorism.

Enter Mr. Brandeis

We last met Brandeis as the sworn opponent of reckless financial management at Pierpont Morgan's New York, New Haven & Hartford Railroad. In the midst of that long struggle, all the major eastern railroads made application to the Interstate Commerce Commission for a 10 percent tariff increase based on rising wages and other operational costs. The subsequent hearings, in the so-called 1910 *Eastern Rate* case, were a major event, and Brandeis leveraged himself into the role of public representative.

Brandeis was a matchless advocate—a brilliant lawyer, unusually thorough in his preparation, and with a lethal flair for publicity. He heard of Taylor's little band of efficiency gurus through a factory-owning friend and, after some inquiry, decided it was a promising line of attack. Brandeis thereupon plunged into an immersion-style education, meeting several times with Taylor, spending time at Dodge's model factory, and organizing a group of Taylor's disciples as advisers and witnesses. Besides Gantt and Dodge, there was Horace Hathaway, another Midvale veteran, and two more recent adherents, Harrington Emerson and Frank Gilbreth. Emerson was a former language professor, and a born promoter who, after an indifferent business career, had read Taylor's books and become a management consultant. Gilbreth was a building contractor, who had made a fetish of "motion studies." Where Taylor had considered an action like "filling a shovel" an elementary task, Gilbreth used a high-speed camera to analyze micro-motions, which he called "therbligs"—for Gilbreth spelled backward—insisting that the therbligs were "the same whether a hand held a scalpel, a trowel, or a monkey wrench."*

---

*Gilbreth was the model for a novel by two of his children that later became the movie *Cheaper by the Dozen* (1950). He is, albeit affectionately, portrayed as something of a fool. His wife, Lillian, was actively involved in his consulting work, and they both constantly motion-studied their kids.

Brandeis carefully scripted the order and style of their presentations. He wanted the Taylorites to project dogmatic certainty and absolute consistency (Taylor must have loved it), and he wanted a headline-grabbing name for what they did, and midwifed the selection of "Scientific Management." At the hearings, Brandeis posed a seemingly innocent set of questions to a series of executives. They ran more or less:—"What is the cost of [some railroad activity]?"—"I'm afraid I can't answer that."—"Is it performed efficiently?"—"Of course."—"How can you be sure?"—"Well, through the long experience of our managers." His traps laid and sprung, Brandeis then trundled out his parade of Scientific Management witnesses, who announced that since the executives did not practice Scientific Management, they couldn't possibly know what they were talking about.

Gantt declared that management's transition to a "science" was "very recent; not more than three or four years at the most." While "systematized management" imposed order on routine tasks, Scientific Management was based on a "scientific investigation in detail of each piece of work and the determination of the best method and the shortest time in which the work can be done." As Gilbreth put it: Scientific Management "separated the planning from the performing. Put that in writing in the form of an instruction card . . . [So a man says:] 'That is the way the scientists have found out that this can be done the best.'" It had taken him many years to find the best way of carrying bricks, Gilbreth said, but he never despaired because "in the process of scientific management that fact was prophesied, that we would be able to do it as surely as the position of one of the outer planets was prophesied by mathematics." Hathaway said that with Scientific Management the workman "no longer trudge[d] alone in darkness afoot through a sandy road."

All of the time-honored claims were trotted out—quadrupling pig iron loaders' output, tripling shovelers'. Gilbreth claimed to have reduced bricklayers' motions from eighteen to only four and a half—all bricklayers had once tapped their bricks with their trowels after placing them, for instance, and by eliminating such useless motions, he had tripled their output. And all the witnesses agreed that Scientific Management put an end to labor difficulties. Gantt said that Scientific Management gives the workman "pride in his work and [he] soon distinctly improves in personal appearance." The improvement was even more marked in "girls than in men, for the girls invariably acquire a better color and improve in health." The journalist Ray

Stannard Baker wrote, "Few of those present had ever heard of scientific management, or of Mr. Taylor, its originator, and the testimony, at first, awakened a clearly perceptible incredulity," which was swept away by "the extraordinary fervor and enthusiasm expressed by every man who testified. Theirs was the firm faith of apostles."

Emerson trumpeted the success of a consultancy with the Santa Fe Railroad* where he claimed to have halved the turnaround times for locomotive repairs. When Brandeis asked him how much the railroads could save if they all followed his advice, Emerson averred that it was at least $1 million a day, extrapolating his Santa Fe experience across all the nation's roads. The other witnesses had done their independent calculations, which remarkably enough, all came within a few percentage points of Emerson's. It was a sensation. The *New York Times* headlined

ROADS COULD SAVE $1,000,000 A DAY
Brandeis Says Scientific Management Would Do It
Calls Rate Increases Unnecessary

Brandeis won his rate case, and Taylor was suddenly a celebrity. "Weeding Waste Out of Business Is This Man's Special Joy," the *New York Tribune* headlined. He found himself beset by interviews, magazine profiles, pilgrims to his home; his name was spread over the Sunday supplements. "Taylorism" was suddenly a household word, and there was a rash of "time-and-motion" cartoons, including a spoof "The Fifteen Unnecessary Motions of a Kiss." Pressed to produce a popular version of his teachings, Taylor rushed to produce *Principles of Scientific Management*. To his irritation, the ASME, which had sponsored his other work, refused to publish it, because they did not believe management was a "science."† Harpers was happy to, however, and gave it much greater exposure. Gilbreth, Emerson, and others all rushed into print with their own Scientific Management manuals.

---

*In private, Emerson was refreshingly frank about his work. When he had arrived at the Santa Fe, he said he was "entirely ignorant as to workings of such a plant . . . and had to be cautious about opening my mouth, lest I put my foot in it. By saying nothing, I was credited with deep knowledge." What was his method? "Every employee is strictly instructed to heed my requests . . . and then I sail around and find all the fault I can and propose various improvements."

†Even James Dodge, his good friend and disciple who chaired the ASME editorial committee, balked at Taylor's claims, pointing to the unscientific designation of "first-class" workers, and the arbitrary P factors in Taylor's time studies.

Gilbreth's, with a preface by Brandeis, was framed in a question-and-answer format that perfectly captures the quasireligious, catechizing spirit of Taylorism. Samples:

> **Why is Scientific Management not called "the Taylor System"?**
> [It] *should* . . . and *would* . . . be, but for the personal objections of Dr. Taylor.
>
> **At what speed does Taylor's plan expect any man to work?**
> . . . At that speed which is the fastest at which he will be happy and at which he can thrive continuously.

As the nation's pundits were swept up in an "efficiency craze," Taylor did his best to feed their ambitions. The coda to his *Principles* stated:

> [S]cientific management . . . may be summarized as:
> Science, not rule of thumb.
> Harmony, not discord.
> Cooperation, not individualism.
> Maximum output, instead of restricted output.
> The development of each man to his greatest efficiency and prosperity. . . .
>
> Scientific management will mean, for the employers and workmen who adopt it . . . the elimination of almost all causes for dispute and disagreement between them. What constitutes a fair day's work will be a question for scientific investigation, instead of a subject to be bargained and haggled over. . . .
>
> [Scientific management] means increase in prosperity and diminution in poverty . . . for the whole community. . . .
>
> Is not the realization of results such as these of far more importance than the solution of most of the problems which are now agitating the English and American peoples? And is it not the duty of those who are acquainted with these facts, to exert themselves to make the whole community realize this importance?

That swelling peroration fed into a growing consensus that the future belonged to technocrats and engineers. Comfort Adams, a professor of electrical engineering at Harvard, asked an audience of engineers in 1908: "Are there no laws in this other realm of human relations which are just as

"Scientific Shoveling" clearly required "Scientific Shovels." This advertisement takes for granted that its customers will know about Frederick W. Taylor's work and "Scientific Management."

inexorable as the physical laws with which we are so familiar?" Much like
Taylor, many leading engineers were convinced that there were "scientific
laws" that would provide the permanent solution to knotty problems like
railroad rate setting or labor problems, finally illuminating "the sane middle
ground between grasping individualism and Utopian socialism." All that
was required was "placing engineers in all responsible positions in these
great industries," a sentiment that was loudly cheered by technocratic
groupies like Lippmann. This "new professional class with special skills to
solve socio-industrial problems" readily discovered that Taylorism was the
ideal banner for their cause, and, until the 1920s, Taylorites dominated
most of the professional engineering societies. Herbert Hoover may have
been the greatest representative of the tradition.

In the meantime, the eponymous hero of the shining new cause found
his cup of victory laced with bitterness. There was a strong reaction against
his theories on the part of unions and other worker advocates, and he was
given decidedly rough treatment by a 1912 congressional committee investigating a job action at a "Taylorizing" federal arsenal.* Nearly two years of
lionizing may have disarmed Taylor, for he made his appearance as almost a
regal figure, delivering an initial statement that consumed more than seven
hours and two committee sessions. To his dismay, he then found himself
politely skewered for another two full sessions, especially by the chairman,
a canny old miner named William Wilson, who drilled relentlessly at the
holes in his theories, like the "scientific" definition of a "first-class man,"
and the large arbitrary fudge factors in his time studies. Taylor never bore
up well under attack, and finally fell back on abject logic chopping—it was
impossible for Scientific Management to be abused, he stubbornly insisted,
for if it was abused, it was no longer Scientific Management. Thereafter
Taylor sharply limited his public appearances, pleading that an ill wife

---

*Taylor was not directly involved in the engagement, but had been its impresario, and had picked
the consultants. The machine shop engagement went smoothly, as usual, but foundry workers
objected to stopwatch timing. Later, they secretly shadow-timed operations being tracked by a
time-study "expert," a Taylor associate named David Merrick, not realizing that Merrick counted
only "productive" time instead of the total elapsed time. When he came up with only twenty-four
minutes for a task they timed out at fifty, they assumed he was lying. But when Merrick was later
pressed on the point, he conceded that he knew nothing about foundry work, and was "very confident that I didn't get a true observation. . . . I felt that 30 minutes was too long a time for it, so I
made a guess at 24 minutes." Taylor himself had shocked the head of the arsenals, William
Crozier, a true-believing Taylorite, when he suggested that they could install piece rates just by
making "a rough guess" at the times.

required his full-time attention. (She was very demanding, it seems, but a Taylor biographer, Robert Kanigel, wonders if he was using her as a shelter.) The less he said in public, perhaps, the better. In one of his few appearances, before the U.S. Industrial Relations Commission in 1913, he proudly declared, "We never take a human instrument that is badly suited for its work. . . . We take a proper human animal, just as we would take a proper horse to study."

Taylor died in 1915, at only fifty-nine years of age. To the last, he remained obsessively vigilant against imputations that Scientific Management might have had a history before his work at Midvale, and came down like avenging thunder on any of his acolytes who deviated from the pure doctrine.

Taylor and the Intellectuals

Brandeis's publicity fireworks for Taylorism seems to have ignited a long-smoldering, vaguely defined, and highly protean intellectualist fantasy of Scientific Management as a kind of philosopher's stone capable of unlocking secrets of great power. When Taylor speaks of laws "so intricate" and science "so great," he sounds like a Grand Master Mason claiming the runic keys to a mystic kingdom—in this case, the secret path to Edward Bellamy's managerial utopia, or John Dewey's Republic of Experts, or Walter Lippmann's blessed state of "Mastery." More recent scholarship, in contrast to the unabashed Taylor idolatry of a generation or so ago, takes a more skeptical tone. But there is still much tiptoeing around the legend, even though it requires a violent reordering of the evidence to conflate Taylor's work with the broad upgrade in business practice that was in full flood when he was still in high school.

The curt summary by the historian Phillip Scranton—that Taylor was "a batch and specialty shops veteran obsessed with eradicating variation and uncertainty"—has it exactly right. It is not true that Henry Ford's Model T factory was just a special case of Taylorism, as Alfred Chandler would have it, or Taylor himself claimed. Taylor's machine shop work was aimed at increasing the production of skilled machinists making variable goods with general-purpose machines. The Ford factory, by contrast, was the apotheosis of the Armory tradition of making interchangeable parts with single-purpose machines operated by unskilled labor. Instead of devising standardized instructions for machinists, as Taylor did, Ford *eliminated* machinists in favor of machine tenders. If a part needed the slightest fitting by a skilled machinist, the line would have broken down. Inspiration for the line itself came from canning, flour, and meat-packing factories, industries that Taylor knew little or nothing about. Similarly, materials management in a large, fast-moving, mass-production factory like Ford's was on a different planet from the ticket-based stores tracking systems Taylor used in his shops. The only overlap between Taylorism and a Ford factory is that the Ford engineers conducted what they later called time and motion studies to work out the speed of the line and the best layout for assembly materials. They may have gotten those ideas from Taylor—although Ford said not— but it's hard to imagine they couldn't have come up with them independently. Canning factories had long dealt with the same problems, and even the first department stores had quickly realized that a well laid-out work area let a salesclerk handle more customers.

Attempts to stamp the Taylorist label on the multi-division corporate management systems worked out early in the century, by Gerard Swope at General Electric and Hamilton Barksdale at DuPont, are similarly unconvincing. DuPont's paint, varnish, dye, and dynamite lines were all flow-process businesses on the model Rockefeller had pioneered at Standard Oil, while Barksdale's ingenious blend of centralized control systems and decentralized product divisions was wholly outside Taylor's experience. General Electric, whose major product early in the century was consumer lightbulbs, had much more to learn from Ford and the sewing machine industry than from Taylor, while Swope's control systems, like Barksdale's, were of a scale and breadth Taylor had never dealt with. It seems that only Taylor and his acolytes, and, inexplicably, several generations of business historians, could nurture the delusion that he was the discoverer of planning and schedules. Taylor implicitly undercut his own claims when he cautioned Gantt and others against accepting engagements from well-managed companies, where they were not likely to make much difference.

Railroads were naturally incensed at the notion that Taylorism was the solution to their budget problems. A riposte to Emerson's claims at the *Eastern Rate* hearings was published the following year in the *Quarterly Journal of Economics*. While accepting all Scientific Management claims at face value, the author, an economist named William Cunningham, quite correctly pointed out that its methodologies were designed for job shops or manual laborers, and had limited applicability to railroads. Railroads, in any case, had been the pioneers of the scheduling and control systems at the heart of Scientific Management. Emerson's specific claim that he had reduced Santa Fe locomotive repair times from sixty to thirty days actually came off badly in comparison with the Harriman lines' average of fifteen days. The Santa Fe, in fact, was below average on virtually all cost and performance indicators, and so was a poor exemplar for global industry cost reductions.

It was still true, however, that run-of-the-mill American enterprises, in contrast to the railroads and other big companies, were typically badly managed. With the sea change in the scale and tempo of American business since the 1880s, many companies were struggling to cope and sorely needed help installing basic management processes. Business consultancy was becoming an industry in its own right about the time that Taylor died. As the former band of Taylorists built profitable businesses, their practical eclecticism caused much friction with Taylor, especially between Taylor and Gantt, his very first disciple. Preaching a "Taylor system" was great for marketing, but in their day-to-day work the disciples quietly dropped "system" pretenses in favor of selling solutions that fit their clients' circumstances.*

The phenomenon of Taylorism, in any case, had little to do with bread-and-butter management consulting, for practical businessmen quickly learned to pick and choose among consultants' offerings without falling victim to -isms. The true audience for Taylorism was rather America's new intelligentsia—journalists, professors, and pundits. The essence of Scientific Management, Taylor preached, was to remove "all possible brain work" from the practical men in the shops, whose sole job would be to see that "operations planned and directed from the planning room are promptly carried out." Now *that* was a sentiment intellectuals could rally behind. For the

---

*Gantt had been Taylor's first choice for the Watertown Arsenal assignment, but he scandalized his old mentor by pointing out that the client had asked only for a foundry piece rate system, which he could install in a couple of months. Taylor insisted on a three-year Scientific Management engagement that began in the machine shop. Had he taken Gantt's advice, he might have saved himself much grief in his last years. Gantt was the only member of the Taylor coterie with experience in foundries, and was especially good at avoiding the kind of worker disaffection that led to the Watertown job action.

"chattering classes," as we now call them, Scientific Management seemed to open a path to the "social control" they so ardently desired.

. . . And There Were Consequences

Taylorism says more about its devotees than about Taylor. Taylor himself was a narrow-minded obsessive, a hard-driving plant manager, and a snob. While he made important contributions to machining management and technology, his conviction that there was a science that would allow planners to determine the "one best way" for every task was statistically dubious and wrong in practice. But it had immense, if short-lived, resonance for opinion leaders.

The first rush of enthusiasm for Taylorism arose because it offered a path for coming to terms with the awesome new corporate power centers. Instead of impotently ruing the might of the trusts, intellectuals could celebrate big companies as triumphs of American enterprise, with the comfort of knowing there was a technology for controlling them. As the faith in technocratic Progressivism began to wane in the 1920s, however, pundits lost interest in Taylorism, although its appeal to European and Soviet planners* lasted some years longer. In the public mind, the name of Taylor came to be associated with the semi-comic figure of the time-and-motion man—the 1954 musical *The Pajama Game* is a typical spoof.

Aspects of Taylorism, however, especially the *attitudes* of Taylorism, took root in the business schools and continued to exert a subtle, but deep, influence on the intellectual assumptions of an increasingly professionalized cadre of managers. Three path-breaking books by Alfred Chandler—*Strategy and Structure* (1962), *The Visible Hand* (1977), and *Scale and Scope* (1990)—offer the canonical account of the rise of the American managerial tradition. Chandler's approach to history has been called "teutonic"; his account, indeed, is of a dialectical progression, a kind of triumphal

---

*Time-and-motion studies were enthusiastically incorporated into the Soviet Union's Five-Year plans. By 1930, the Rates and Norms Bureaus had set some 232,000 separate norms, derived from the "science of biomechanics" and covering about 70 percent of all workers. Metals trades were reclassified from twelve categories into 176. The blizzard of statistics perfectly suited careerist managers and bureaucrats in a system in which most factories were idle much of the time for a lack of equipment and supplies.

Hegelian unfolding of management consciousness, from the small, single-unit enterprise of the era of family capitalism through "administrative coordination" of the multi-unit business, to the large, vertically integrated company and the discovery of "the economies of speed," and, finally, in the highest realization of the industrial Spirit, the vertically integrated, hierarchical, multi-divisional, broadly owned and professionally managed "modern industrial enterprise." Those "Center" companies, as Chandler called them, produced many different products, controlled almost all their essential resources, and were marked by long-run, high-speed production lines and clear managerial stratification. "[M]anaging and coordinating the processes of production and distribution" was the job of middle managers, while "the top managers concentrated on evaluating, planning, and allocating resources for the enterprise as a whole." Chandler's top management was the central intelligence that energized the whole organization, the hot star at the heart of the corporate galaxy. It is, in fact, just a colossal version of Taylor's Planning Room, the place where the "brainwork" happened.

The new business schools evangelized a highly intellectualized "professional" version of management, which is faithfully reflected in Chandler. It is striking, for example, how little attention Chandler pays to production technology, or to technology in general; instead, it appears in his story almost as an exogenous variable. The companies he admires all have research laboratories, but they are black boxes on a chart, intermittently producing recommendations to be mulled by the philosopher-kings at the top. In the Harvard Business School's maiden (1908) curriculum, of fifteen course choices only two—railroad operations and municipal administration—dealt explicitly with management. The remainder were spread among accounting, commercial law, investment, organization, economics, insurance, and the like, as if the school's management hatchlings would skip right by gritty plant-level problems into the top management orbit. In fact, from the beginning, the school's graduates have overwhelmingly gravitated to finance and consultancy.

The business school's founders had actually considered whether to include a manufacturing curriculum, but decided against it, since it appeared that Taylor and his disciples had exhausted the topic; so as a compromise they engaged Taylor as a guest lecturer. There was evidently little further thought on the subject, for a half century later, Chandler noted that post–World War II plant managers "had plenty of information to go on, for it was on this lowest administrative level that Frederick W. Taylor, Frank Gilbreth . . . and other advocates and practitioners of 'scientific management' concentrated their energies."

The remoteness of the business schools is unwittingly demonstrated by Chandler's *Strategy and Structure*. It is a fine book, the first to explore the evolution and implications of the centralized/decentralized organization blend pioneered at companies like Dupont, and it triggered a vast amount of spin-off research, if mostly of the anecdotal variety. What is striking, however, is that Chandler's book appeared *forty years* after the multidivisional organization became widely adopted in business—Chandler's case studies are mostly from the 1920s. Imagine if engineering professors at MIT first noticed the integrated circuit only in 2002 or so.

The disconnect had real consequences. Consider just one arcane, but important, episode—the search for the EOQ, or the Economic Order Quantity, the mathematically optimized solution to the very practical, and very challenging, business problem of setting the "right" amount of inventory. The research, which consumed quite formidable amounts of brainpower

An abandoned steel mill, about 1980, detritus from the cataclysmic failure of a complacent, "professionalized" American management cadre. The jury is still out on whether America has regained its competitiveness in basic industry.

throughout the post–World War II era, proceeded from three apparently incontrovertible axioms:

a) At some point, the cost of eliminating additional defects starts rising, and becomes prohibitive.

b) Unplanned stops in a high-speed production line are catastrophically expensive.

c) Unit production costs fall with longer production runs, because setup and changeover costs are spread over the larger volume.

The EOQ, or right inventory level, is the one that optimizes within those constraints—that is, you need just enough inventory to replace the economically optimum level of defective parts; enough to cover for a botched assembly operation to avoid stopping the line; plus the temporary overages that result from optimum-length production runs. EOQ-style problem solving was a deeply engrained characteristic of the American managerial psyche, a milestone toward the ideal of a professionalized Scientific Management that inspired Taylor and was celebrated by Chandler.

The 1970s/1980s sweep-the-board triumph by Japanese companies in nearly every important mass-production industry shocked and demoralized American executives. It was not just the humiliation of catastrophic defeat but the stomach-wrenching discovery that fundamental compass points, like the EOQ axioms, were utterly, and disastrously, wrong.* The most famous of the Japanese paradigms, the "Toyota system," developed over more than twenty years under the leadership of Taiichi Ohno, was a direct refutation of the EOQ logic. Costs *fell* with zero defects. The right amount of inventory was *none at all*. One *always* stopped the production line to prevent a defect (or else it would always recur). Long production runs *always* produced wasteful amounts of inventory. (The solution was to reduce the cost and time of changeovers to near zero.) Ohno's system emphasized close

---

*As part of my business activities, through most of the 1980s I spent a substantial amount of time with manufacturing companies. It was the period of a determined, almost frenzied, top-to-bottom effort to rethink every basic plant assumption. A senior manufacturing manager at Cummins Engine, one of the most effective of the early responders, repeated to me several times, almost in awe, that "all the textbooks were wrong."

contact between top management and the plant floor, and a deep respect for workers—in contrast to the quite open disdain that pervaded Taylorism. The American "pursuit of quantity and speed," Ohno suggested, produced only "unnecessary losses." Vertical integration was usually wasteful; it was more efficient to develop stable supply relationships with specialist contractors (in contrast to the adversarial American contracting culture).

American managers naturally came in for widespread and well-deserved criticism. One of the earliest, and most scathing, "Managing Our Way to Economic Decline," was published in 1980 by two Harvard Business School professors, Robert Hayes and William Abernathy. It attacked American executives for "priz[ing] analytical detachment and methodological elegance over insight based on experience" and "the false and shallow concept of the professional manager, a 'pseudo-professional' really." The professors' attack is right on target, but comes with rather poor grace, for there is no wisp of recognition that their own institution had spent three quarters of a century drilling precisely those values into American business elites. Robert McNamara, after all, was the paragon of the business school's generalist manager tradition, and his meaningless body-count database in Vietnam the perfect expression of its Taylorist genes.

At the conclusion of *The Visible Hand,* Chandler remarks that "the businessman of today [the 1970s] would find himself at home in the business world of 1910." Indeed he would have, which is testimony not only to the greatness of the original tycoons but to the inordinate length of time we lived off their capital.

The Carnegie Company's 1900 Earnings

The price set by Andrew Carnegie for Carnegie Co. in the run-up to the U. S. Steel merger included $80 million for "Profit of past year and estimated profit of coming year." Early in 1900, the company had confidently expected to earn $40–50 million for the year. James Bridge, who had good inside sources, stated in his 1903 *Inside History of Carnegie Steel* that the company earned $40 million in 1900, and Carnegie repeated the claim in his *Autobiography.* Bridge is the source for Carnegie Co. background in the Stanley Committee's 1911 U.S. Steel investigation, and the $40 million number is cited by virtually all subsequent historians. While the records are insufficient to pin down a precise number, the $40 million is far too high.* (Since total second half earnings were only about $6 million, Carnegie's implicit forecast of $50 million for 1901 seems clearly to be a misrepresentation.)

The Carnegie Co. was a holding company formed in April 1900, comprising:

---

*I assume Bridge got the number from Frick, who was a major source for his book. Frick wasn't speaking to Carnegie, but probably got it from Schwab.

- The Carnegie Steel Co., its dominant property, plus other holdings previously held on the books of the Steel Co., including:
- The Frick Coke Co. The Steel Co. previously held a 29.55% interest in the Coke Co., but the Carnegie Co. bought out the other shareholders shortly after it was organized, so its interest increased to 100%.
- A five-sixths interest in the Oliver Mining Co., which held large ore leases in the Mesabi ore range.
- A variety of railroads, steamship lines, and Great Lakes docks, many of them newly developed and used primarily by the Carnegie subsidiaries.

The Steel Company's Earnings

Steel Co. earnings grew very strongly throughout the 1890s. Carnegie Steel was so much more productive than the competition that it was able to fight a rail price war in 1897, take significant market share, and still rack up record earnings, even as most of its competitors were booking losses. The earnings below include the Steel Co.'s earnings from its 29.55% share of the Coke Co. and from its other subsidiaries. For reference, the Coke Co.'s 1899 earnings were a record $4.2 million, of which $1.25 million accrued to the

· TABLE 1 ·

Annual Earnings—Carnegie Steel Co.

1893	$3,000,000
1894	4,000,000
1895	5,000,000
1896	6,000,000
1897	7,000,000
1898	11,500,000*
1899	21,000,000

Source: ACLC

*1898 earnings are often reported as $16 million. The higher number includes several extraordinary items—a $2 million right-of-way payment over one of the railroads, plus a collection of estimated market value writeups on subsidiaries (none of which was publicly traded). The company rounded its earnings by drawing from/paying to a contingency fund depending on whether the figure was being rounded up or down.

Steel Co.'s account. Earnings from the twelve other subsidiaries taken together were lower than from Coke.

The U. S. steel market grew at a 20–25% annual clip in 1898 and 1899, and steel prices rose sharply. In the first quarter of 1900, Carnegie was confidently forecasting $40–50 million *steel* profits for the year. But growth turned down in the second quarter, and the market virtually collapsed in the third quarter.

Annual financials for 1900 for either Carnegie Co. or the Steel Co. do not seem to have been preserved, but Steel Co. monthly earnings for the first eleven months of the year can be documented from board-level reports, while the missing December number can be inferred from Carnegie's personal financials.

· TABLE 2 ·

Monthly Earnings, 1900—Carnegie Steel Co.

Jan	$3,638,642
Feb	3,541,679
Mar	4,700,032
Apr	3,219,879
May	2,381,127
Jun	1,850,047
Jul	978,102
Aug	641,662
Sep	470,441
Oct	940,446
Nov	361,857
Dec	1,046,086
Total	23,770,000
Average	1,980,833

Source: ACLC; author's calculations

The Coke Co. was transferred to the Carnegie Co.'s (the holding company's) books in April 1900. The Steel Co.'s earnings in Table 2 therefore reflect its 29.55% share of the Coke Co.'s earnings, or $511,600, only through March.

As the table shows, there was a dramatic profit collapse in the second half of the year. Total Steel Co. second half earnings were only $4.4 million, down from $19.3 million in the first half. The Homestead Works, which by itself booked almost $4 million earnings just in the first quarter, ran a *loss* of $160,000 in the four second half months for which there are plant-level figures. It might be noted that the Homestead losses were policy-driven, in the sense that a decision was made in July that, except for rails, they would "take all the business going at low prices."

The 1900 Steel Market Break

The earnings outcomes are consistent with the very sharp break in the steel market during 1900. Table 3 shows Pittsburgh steel prices for a selection of standard products. Prices roughly doubled during 1899, stayed more or less steady at the outset of 1900, then gave up most of the 1899 increases by the third and fourth quarter. (All data from *Iron Age*.) The price collapse was apparently steeper than even these prices suggest. *Iron Age* noted in June 1900 that despite the "nominal Pittsburgh prices . . . the market is now an open one and . . . Pig Iron and Steel are both being offered at much lower prices." In its year-end review, *Iron Age* summed up 1900 as a year with "long stretches of dullness . . . serious diminution of consumption . . . labor troubles of a most vexatious kind . . . and a sharp decline in prices." A measure of the severity of the second half market break is that, after growing 24.8% in 1898 and 19.1% in 1899, and despite blistering growth for the first several months of 1900, total steel output *declined* by 4.2% over the full year.

· **TABLE 3** ·

Selected Pittsburgh Steel Price Quotes

	Jan-99	Jan-00	Feb-00	Mar-00	Apr-00	May-00	Jun-00	Jul-00	Aug-00	Sep-00	Oct-00	Nov-00	Dec-00
Steel billets	$16.25	$35.00	$33.00	$33.00	$33.00	$30.00	$28.00	$25.00	$19.00	$18.00	$16.50	$18.00	$19.75
Wire rods	22.25	50.00	50.00	50.00	50.00	48.00	48.00	35.00	35.00	33.50	33.00	33.00	33.00
Steel bars	1.00	2.20	2.20	2.25	2.25	1.95	1.80	1.40	1.00	1.10	1.05	1.10	1.25
Beams	1.30	2.25	2.25	2.25	2.25	2.25	2.25	1.90	1.90	1.50	1.50	1.50	1.50

Source: Iron Age

Commentary at Carnegie Steel Co. board meetings underlines the seriousness of the crash. (Peacock and Bope are sales executives.)

May: (Operating Committee) "[Peacock] stated that Jones & Laughlin are practically shut down. The Illinois Steel Co., aside from the rail mill, are shut down. The National Steel Company are running about one-half of their different plants."

June: (Schwab) "As near as I can find out there is no new business coming up in the Pig Iron or Steel business. All manufacturers that have talked with [me] tell me they have nothing to do and that things are too rapidly approaching a standstill."

July: (Peacock) "Pig Iron Association says they have sold practically no Pig Iron for the past two months."

September: (Peacock) "Bars are selling as low as 37½ cents per hundred pounds and plates are as low as we have ever known or heard them to be."

October: (Bope) "As to general market, conditions are unchanged. It is a waiting market and not a great deal of business is being placed."

Rail orders were so low that the board discussed shutting down the Edgar Thomson Works in November. Schwab merely cautioned to be sure that they had exhausted all their rail orders before they did so. Total Rail Pool allocations had shrunk two-thirds. I could not find a date for a shutdown, but there was a note in a December minute that the rail mills had "reopened" on December 5, when markets were showing signs of recovery. On July 28, Carnegie asked whether they should consider delaying interest on Carnegie Co. bonds to finance his investment program. Schwab thought that was not necessary.

Carnegie's Personal Balance Sheet

The eleven-month numbers retrievable from board reports track with Carnegie's personal account statement for 1900, which shows an item "Earnings of Carnegie Steel" at $12.87 million. His custom in previous years was to book his equity share of Carnegie Steel's earnings as personal earnings. At the start of the year, he held 58.5% of the company. Subtracting his transfers of shares to Schwab and several of the other partners, he would have been left with 54.14%, which suggests total earnings of $23.77 million for the year (and $1.05 million in earnings in December, which is consistent with the recovery getting under way at that time. I use that number in Table 2). Properly speaking, he shouldn't have made that booking, since he had exchanged his shares for holding company shares, which did not flow through equity-method earnings. But this is a personal account, not a company account, and Rockefeller followed a similar practice, even after the 1911 Standard breakup.

The Carnegie Company's Other Properties

I found a report listing the first half earnings of the holding company's properties. It is not an earnings booking, but just an informational report, and includes 100% of the Coke Co. earnings, and those of other subsidiaries, for the first quarter (i.e., prior to their acquisition). They are set out in Table 4.

Carnegie Co. was the holding company, and did not flow through the earnings of its subsidiaries, instead reporting just dividends and interest accrued and received. (Corporate lawyers advised maintaining the fiction that the holding company did not exercise management control.) Since this document is obviously just a background document, it includes all earnings for the listed companies, including for periods prior to their ownership by the Carnegie Co., and there is, additionally, a certain amount of double-counting in the presentation. Since we also know the Steel Co. H2 earnings, I applied the H1 steel/non-steel earnings ratio to those to produce a first-order estimate of the full-year earnings for the entire company. (The Steel Co. was the primary, or sole, customer for all the other subsidiaries.) Some notes on the details follow:

1. Frick Coke included four subsidiaries—the Youghiogeney Railroad and the three water companies. The total of the Q1 Frick Coke entries and the four subsidiaries multiplied by the 29.55% Carnegie Steel ownership percentage produces the $511,601, already included in the "Frick" amount shown in the Carnegie Steel entries.

· TABLE 4 ·

Six-Month Earnings of Carnegie Co. Holdings, 1900*

	Jan.	Feb.	Mar.	Apr.	May	June	Total
Carnegie Steel	$3,638,549	$3,591,365	$4,700,244	$3,219,872	$2,387,455	$1,823,241	$19,360,726
HC Frick Coke	687,061	593,066	428,946	803,373	700,250	647,305	3,860,001
Youghiogeney RR	2,388	2,475	3,006	3,766	2,987	2,626	17,248
Mt Pleasant Water	2,359	2,297	2,308	2,264	2,178	2,038	13,444
Youghiogeney Water	927	822	907	772	796	669	4,893
Trotter Water	1,720	1,510	1,513	1,566	1,440	1,322	9,071
Union Supply	29,824	46,421	29,728	30,648	30,692	28,125	195,438
Carnegie Natural Gas	80,162	71,094	82,607	103,061	103,082	91,897	531,903
Union RR	−41,687	−79,405	−65,573	−5,176	39,528	73,202	−79,111
Pitts, Bess, and L Erie RR	−56,594	−63,866	−33,893	−46,113	74,518	85,774	−40,174
Pitts Steamship	0	0	−431	−12,813	119,885	75,068	181,709
Pitts and Conneaut Dock	−5,874	−4,215	−892	−9,610	71,407	39,652	90,468
Pitts Limestone Co.	4,229	3,200	2,595	2,531	2,337	2,039	16,931
Oliver Iron Mining	500,000	500,000	500,000	500,000	500,000	500,000	3,000,000
Totals	4,843,064	4,664,764	5,651,065	4,594,141	4,036,555	3,372,958	27,162,547

Source: ACLC

*There are minor discrepancies between the Steel Co. numbers reported here and those in Table 2, doubtless due to closing adjustments. Since they are immaterial, I let them stand.

All of the Q1 Frick and subsidiary earnings in the table, therefore, should be excluded from Carnegie 1900 earnings, since the owned portion has already been counted.

2. The remaining entries for the first quarter, except for the Oliver earnings, are all also included in the Carnegie Steel entries. They are, in any case, slightly negative (by $2,570). Taking the Oliver numbers at face value (but see my reservations below), they should be reduced by the 16.7% held by outside shareholders, or by $250,500. Adding the net Oliver to the Carnegie Steel entries produces Q1 earnings of $13.18 million.

3. Q2 I simply take as presented, less the $250,500 for external Oliver ownership, which produces a total of $11.75 million, for a total net first half of $24.93 million.

4. Including net Oliver and all Frick (and eliminating the $511,601 Frick double-count in the Steel Q1 earnings), the ratio of non-steel to steel earnings in the first half is 38.7%.
5. Second half steel earnings were $4.44 million. Assuming non-steel earnings in H2 were in the same ratio as in H1 produces an additional $1.72 million for a total of $6.16 million—or a grand total of $31.09 million for the year.

Having said that, I remain extremely skeptical of the claimed Oliver earnings, the more so since they look like a "plug" entry. The Steel Co. did not include Oliver earnings in its monthly profit bookings. I did find a year-end Oliver entry, for 1898. It was an estimated booking for the Steel Co.'s share of Oliver earnings for the year. Oliver had estimated its 1898 earnings to be $800,000, which the Steel Co. reduced to $600,000 "to be safe" (making an entry of $500,000 to reflect its 83.3 percent share). Even at the $800,000 figure, however, the ratio of ore to steel earnings was only half that suggested by Table 4. In addition, in 1899 the contract between Oliver and the Steel Co. was revised so non-Bessemer ore was transfer-priced at cost. That should have accounted for at least half of the Steel Co.'s output, which would have commensurately reduced Oliver's earnings.

Furthermore, there are several other spring 1900 accounting entries that may shed light on the ore figures:

1. There are two offsetting entries of approximately $20 million increasing both payables and inventory for "ore at mines." These are apparently related to a discussion at the board about Oliver's problems with customers who were deferring shipments of previously ordered ore. The Steel Co., as a precedent for other Oliver customers, agreed to be invoiced for ore at an earlier stage, instead of waiting until the ore had been delivered to a Lake dock. Oliver presumably booked the invoices as a sale, which would have inflated its earnings. (It would have had the effect of advancing future earnings into the current period.) Modern Profit-and-Loss accounting would have reduced Carnegie Steel's earnings by a commensurate amount, since the invoice would be treated as an expense. But nineteenth-century companies did not keep P&Ls, but reported only balance sheets and balance-sheet changes. Since monthly Steel Co. earnings seem to track sales during

this period, I strongly suspect that the big receivable increase at Oliver was not offset by an expense at Steel, which would have artificially inflated the total earnings of the holding company.

2. A further entry in May 1900 increases March steel earnings from the $4.7 million shown in this table and in previous board reports by about $350,000. That is the same way the ore earnings were booked in 1898, as a post-close item when Oliver got around to reporting them. If this number represents the Steel Co. share of Q1 Oliver earnings (I can't think of what else it could be), it would be much closer to, although somewhat lower than, the 1898 ratio. (But that would be consistent with the transfer pricing of non-Bessemer ore.)

Since there seem to be good grounds for skepticism of the ore earnings, I make an alternative estimate simply by applying the 1898 ratio of ore to steel earnings, net of the amount held by external investors, ignoring the apparent agreement to transfer-price non-Bessemer ore. That would reduce projected full year ore earnings by $2 million.

Conclusion

Depending on which Oliver estimate is used, the range of 1900 earnings of the constituent entities of the holding company would be:

• TABLE 5 •

Estimated 1900 Earnings, Carnegie Steel and Carnegie Co.
($ in millions)

	High Oliver	Adj. Oliver
Carnegie Steel	23.77	23.77
All Other	7.27	5.27
Total Carnegie Co.	31.04	29.04

Source: ACLC; author's calculations

Either number is consistent with a private note from Carnegie to his cousin and director, George Lauder, that 1900 earnings were "30 millions or thereabouts" (January 24, 1901, ACLC).

Some Additional Questions

Did Carnegie Co. Pay Dividends and Interest Due in 1900?
For the nine months of 1900 following the recapitalization, Carnegie was entitled to receive $3.6 million in interest and a similar amount in preferred dividends. His income statement, however, shows only $2.2 million in interest received and no dividends.

There was clearly enough money to pay both interest and dividends. Even with the terrible second half, the Steel Co.'s spectacular first half fully covered the holding company's obligations. In addition, Carnegie Co. operations reports for the first five months following the recapitalization, i.e., through September, show that it collected an additional $2 million of Coke Co. dividends.

On the other hand, Carnegie might have been uncomfortable with distributing all that cash on the eve of what was shaping up as another all-out price and investment war. Carnegie's income statement has no supporting detail, so it must be interpreted with caution. It may support an inference that Carnegie himself deferred his interest and dividend payments in order to support the investment program. I did not find any discussion of the question in the board minutes except for Carnegie's July suggestion to withhold interest and dividend payments. The board rejected the idea, but earnings were still relatively strong at the time. Some board minutes from 1900, however, were doctored after the fact, and some seem to have been removed, so if there were such references, they may have been expunged.

Depreciation Accounting
Carnegie Steel and its predecessors consistently overstated profits by failing to expense plant depreciation. Andrew Carnegie's practice was always to invest most of his cash flow in new plant investment. The failure to expense depreciation therefore had the effect of treating plant investment as a free good. (But as Carnegie's partners could bitterly attest, it was coming out of their profits.) The book value of Carnegie Steel's plant, property, and equipment was about $59 million in the spring of 1900. Assuming a ten-year plant life, which was probably realistic, there would be an additional $5.9 million charge against earnings (or $2.95 million if a twenty-year schedule

is used). Note that this practice would benefit Carnegie companies in comparison with competitors that raised their investment capital through borrowings, since they would be carrying an explicit cost of capital expense. The failure to expense depreciation was a common practice at the time, for there were no settled accounting rules for noncash expenses. (Standard Oil maintained depreciation accounts in the first couple decades of its existence, but for some reason dropped the practice about 1893.)

Efficiency Indices
The table below shows earnings per ton of steel at Carnegie Steel in 1899 and 1900, stripping out all non-steel earnings, compared to estimated 1900 earnings per ton at Federal Steel and National Steel.

· TABLE 6 ·

Comparative Earnings per Ton of Steel

Year	Company	Tons (000s)	Earnings per Ton
1899	Carnegie Steel	2,664	$7.41
1900	Carnegie Steel	2,970	$7.83
1900	Federal Steel	1,225	$8.16
1900	National Steel	1,400	$5.71

Source: ACLC; author's calculations

The 1900 estimates for Federal Steel and National Steel were made by Schwab in early 1901. (The earnings per ton are perhaps deceptively precise, because his earnings estimates, $10 million for Federal and $8 million for National, are clearly round numbers.) Note also that the conventional assumption that Carnegie earned $40 million in 1900 produces the spectacular profitability figure of $13.47 a ton, which so amazed later congressional investigators. There are reports that John W. Gates, a major shareholder in Federal Steel, was irritated that Morgan was effectively paying six times the price per ton of capacity for Carnegie Co. as he was for Federal. On these numbers, he had cause to be upset.

Federal was the product of a Morgan merger that also included ore, coke, and railroad properties, so the $8.16 is doubtless inflated by some non-steel earnings. But Federal's subsidiary holdings were not nearly so large as Carnegie's, and they had been investing heavily in their steel plants since the rail price war, so it is not surprising that they had attained approximate parity. *Iron Age* also claimed that Jones & Laughlin could match anyone on price by 1900.

Finally, the convention followed by many historians of reporting earnings as a percent of nominal capital is not a useful measure, since private companies, like Carnegie Steel, either kept their nominal capital constant from year to year, or else wrote it up in the occasional huge swoop, as they did in 1900. The statement by Carnegie biographer Joseph Frazier Wall, for example, that Carnegie Steel's 1899 earnings were "more than an 80% return on capital" is meaningless. Allan Nevins slips into the same gee-whiz tone with Standard Oil's late 1890s returns, which were running at the 50-percent-plus level on nominal capital. Using a more sensible basis of book equity (net hard assets and retained earnings, less liabilities), Carnegie Steel's 1899 return was 28%,* a very good, but not astonishing outcome, and lower than that if depreciation is properly accounted for. Standard's earnings ratios were roughly comparable, as shown in Appendix II.

---

*The 1899 capital base includes $15 million in securities held for investment, almost all of which were transferred to the holding company in the spring of 1900. I included them in the 1899 base, since they represent accrued equity stemming from Steel Co. earnings. (But I took out the $2.5 million 1898 write-up, so they are comparable with other investments.) The 1899 book equity was therefore $71.5 million.

Standard Oil Earnings

$\mathcal{S}$tandard Oil was a far larger and more profitable company than Carnegie Steel. The data below were revealed as part of the discovery material for the government's 1906 breakup suit. Dividends were obviously very high, especially after Archbold took control in the mid-1890s and apparently began to monetize the Standard's market power to a greater extent than Rockefeller had done. Until the breakup, however, the company stubbornly maintained its nominal capital at $100 million, even though proper accounting shows that book equity was from two to three and a half times higher. Historians, including Allan Nevins, tended to report earnings and dividends as percentage of nominal capital; in 1900, therefore, earnings and dividends would be reported as 55.5% and 46.7% of capital, respectively, instead of the numbers in the table, which are robust enough, but not quite so outrageous.

• TABLE 1 •

Standard Oil Book Equity, Earnings, and Dividends
($ in millions)

Year	Book Equity	Net Earnings	Earnings/Equity	Dividends	Divs/Equity
1883	$72,869,596	$11,231,790	15.4%	$4,268,086	5.9%
1884	75,858,960	7,778,205	10.3%	4,288,842	5.7%
1885	76,762,672	8,382,935	10.9%	7,479,223	9.7%
1886	87,012,107	15,350,787	17.6%	7,226,452	8.3%
1887	94,377,970	14,026,590	14.9%	8,463,327	9.0%
1888	97,005,621	16,226,955	16.7%	13,705,505	14.1%
1889	101,281,192	14,845,201	14.7%	10,620,630	10.5%
1890	115,810,074	19,131,470	16.5%	11,200,089	9.7%
1891	120,771,075	16,331,826	13.5%	11,648,826	9.6%
1892	128,102,428	19,174,878	15.0%	11,874,225	9.3%
1893	131,886,701	15,457,354	11.7%	11,670,000	8.8%
1894	135,755,449	15,544,326	11.5%	11,670,000	8.6%
1895	143,295,603	24,078,077	16.8%	16,532,500	11.5%
1896	147,220,400	34,077,519	23.1%	30,147,500	20.5%
1897–99	N/A	N/A	N/A	N/A	N/A
1900	205,480,449	55,501,775	27.0%	46,691,474	22.7%
1901	210,997,066	52,291,768	24.8%	46,775,390	22.2%
1902	231,758,406	64,613,365	27.9%	43,851,966	18.9%
1903	270,217,922	81,336,994	30.1%	42,877,478	15.9%
1904	297,489,225	61,570,111	20.7%	35,188,266	11.8%
1905	315,613,262	57,459,356	18.2%	39,335,320	12.5%
1906	359,400,195	83,122,252	23.1%	39,335,320	10.9%

Note: N/A = not available.
Source: Allan Nevins, John D. Rockefeller

According to newspaper reports, dividends for the years 1897 through 1899 totalled $96 million. Assuming that the years 1907 through 1910 were roughly at the 1900s average, and that Rockefeller owned about 25% of the Standard throughout this period, his total dividends received would have been about $170 million from 1883 until the breakup, or perhaps $175–180 million over the life of the company.

According to Nevins, Rockefeller's personal net worth several years after the breakup was just short of $1 billion, and would have easily exceeded $1 billion except for a number of large gifts. I suspect that is an understatement. In the personal balance sheets that I was able to examine through 1915, Rockefeller still maintained his Standard holdings as a single unit— as if there had been no breakup—credited with a total nominal capital of $200 million. While he had doubled the nominal valuation from the pre-breakup $100 million, his valuation basis was still far too low, at just over half of the real book value of the company as early as 1906. On a market valuation basis, especially after breakup, Rockefeller was undoubtedly a billionaire several times over.

Notes

Abbreviations

The Andrew Carnegie Papers, Library of Congress (ACLC)
Carnegie Steel Company Records, Historical Society of Western Pennsylvania (HSWP)
The Pierpont Morgan Library, Syndicate Books (PML)
John D. Rockefeller Papers, Rockefeller Archive Center, Sleepy Hollow, New York (RAC)

Preface

All material in this section is sourced in the notes to the main text.

1. Prelude

The details of Lincoln's funeral and the funeral journey are drawn from Ralph G. Newman, "'In this Sad World of Ours, Sorrow Comes to All': A Timetable for the Lincoln Funeral Train," *Journal of the Illinois State Historical Society* (Spring 1965), 9–20; Dorothy Meserve Kundhardt and Philip B. Kundhardt, Jr., *Twenty Days* (North Hollywood, Calif.: Newcastle Publishing Co., 1985); and the contemporary accounts in *The New York Times* and the *New York Tribune*. There are minor differences among all sources.

On the Brink

Besides the sources cited above, I used: For the early oil fields, Harold F. Williamson and Arnold R. Daum, *The American Petroleum Industry: Vol. I, The Age of Illumination, 1859–1899* (Evanston, Ill.: Northwestern University Press, 1959), pp. 117–35. For Philadelphia industry and the Franklin Institute, Philip Scranton, *Endless Novelty: Specialty Production and American Industrialization, 1865–1925* (Princeton, N.J.: Princeton University Press, 1997), pp. 52–56, 61–64; for New York, Thomas Kessner, *Capital City: New York City and the Men behind America's Rise to Economic Dominance, 1860–1900* (New York: Simon and Schuster, 2003), pp. 48–55.

For New York's farmers, Donald H. Parkerson, *The Agricultural Transition in New York State: Markets and Migration in Mid-Nineteenth-Century America* (Ames, Iowa: Iowa State University Press, 1995), and Nancy Gray Osterud, *Bonds of Community: The Lives of Farm Women in Nineteenth Century New York* (Ithaca, N.Y.: Cornell University Press, 1991). The "trumpery" quote is in Parkerson, p. 10. Additional detail is from Donald E. Sutherland, *The Expansion of Everyday Life—1860–1876* (Fayette, Ark.: University of Arkansas Press, 2000), especially pp. 53–78. For growing regional specialization, Nathan Rosenberg, "Technological Interdependence in the American Economy," *Technology and Culture* (January 1979), 25–38. For evolution of Midwestern farming, and role of Chicago, Paul David, "The Mechanization of Reaping in the Ante-Bellum Midwest," in Henry Rosovsky, *Industrialization in Two Systems: Essays in Honor of Alexander Gerschenkron by a Group of His Students* (New York: Wiley, 1966), pp. 3–39. For the Pullman contribution, see Scott D. Trostel, *The Lincoln Funeral Train* (Fletcher, Ohio: Cam-Tech Publishing, 2002), pp. 84–85. Description of railroad penetration is from the fine maps in "Railway Statistics," from Thomas M. Cooley, ed., *The American Railway: Its Construction, Development, Management, and Appliances* (New York: Scribner's Sons, 1889), pp. 385 ff.

For the decline of independent farming in the South, see the essays in Mary Beth Pudup et al. (eds.), *Appalachia in the Making: The Mountain South in the Nineteenth Century* (Chapel Hill, N.C.: University of North Carolina Press, 1995), especially Dwight B. Billings and Kathleen M. Blee, "Agriculture and Poverty in the Kentucky Mountains," 233–69, and Mary Beth Pudup, "Town and Country in the Transformation of Appalachian Kentucky," in *ibid.*, 270–96. Details on gauges and ferrying are in Carl Bateman, *The Baltimore and Ohio Railroad: The Story of a Railroad that Grew with the United States* (Baltimore, Md.: The Baltimore and Ohio Railroad Printing Plant, 1951), pp. 16–20. For the frenetic scheming after riches, see the Colonel Sellers character in Mark Twain and Charles Dudley Warner's *The Gilded Age: A Tale of Today* (1873) and Anthony Trollope's Hamilton Fisker and Augustus Melmotte of *The Way We Live Now* (1873) from an English perspective.

The Artisanal Eden of Abraham Lincoln

The Lincoln "best for all" quote is in Reinhard H. Luthin, *The Real Abraham Lincoln* (Clifton, N.J.: Prentice-Hall, 1960), p. 129. The discussion of the Republican party follows Eric Foner, *Free Soil, Free Labor, Free Men: The Ideology of the Republican Party before the Civil War* (New York: Oxford University Press, 1970), especially pp. 301–17 for the connections between antislavery and prodevelopment positions. For the deplorably low level of investment and development in the South, see Eugene D. Genovese, *The Political Economy of Slavery: Studies in the Economy and Society of the Slave South* (New York: Vintage Books, 1965), pp. 55–61. For the 1860 nomination, David Potter, *The Impending Crisis, 1848–1861* (New York, Harper & Row, 1976), pp. 422ff. For Lincoln's law cases, I used Luthin and Stephen B. Oates, *With Malice toward None: A Life of Abraham Lincoln* (New York: HarperPerennial, 1994). The quotes on the patent laws and "Discoveries and Inventions" quote are from Roy P. Basler, ed., *The Collected Works of Abraham Lincoln*, 9 vols. (New Brunswick, N.J.: Rutgers University Press, 1953–55), III:361, 363. Lincoln wrote a version of the "Discoveries" talk in the spring of 1858, then redrafted it for his 1859 speaking tour, and gave it several times in the first months of his tour. For the revised historiography of the causes of the war, see Foner, *op. cit.*, and also his "The Causes of the Civil War: Recent Interpretations and New Directions," *Civil War History*, vol. 20 (September 1974), pp. 197–214. The Webster quote and "two profoundly" are from Foner, *Free Soil*, pp. 15, 9–10. Quotes from Lincoln's Wisconsin speech are in Basler, *op. cit.*, pp. 478–79. The "mean duties" quote is in Foner, *Free Soil*, p. 66. The speaker was South Carolina senator James Hammond; the talk, called his "mudsill" speech, was well known at the time. For the explicit antagonism between slavery and white egalitarianism, William W. Freehling, *The Road to Disunion: Secessionists at Bay, 1776–1854* (New York: Oxford University Press, 1990), pp. 450 and ff.; it is a major theme of Freehling's treatment of the 1850s. For Lincoln's Chicago speech, Basler, *op. cit.*, II:499–500.

The "second American Revolution" quote is in James M. McPherson, *Battle Cry of Freedom: The Civil War Era* (New York: Oxford University Press, 1988), p. 452. As an example of the war's overshadowing Lincoln's domestic program, the otherwise excellent Oates biography omits any mention of the Homestead, Morrill, or Pacific Railway Acts. For the text of the second inaugural address, I used Ronald C. White, Jr., *Lincoln's Greatest Speech: The Second Inaugural* (New York: Simon and Schuster, 2002), pp. 18–19. For the long political preponderance of the South and uniqueness of the North, see McPherson, *op. cit.*, pp. 859–61.

Young Tycoons

CARNEGIE

The sketch of Carnegie follows Joseph Frazier Wall, *Andrew Carnegie* (Pittsburgh, Pa.: University of Pittsburgh Press, 1989), supplemented by Peter Krass, *Carnegie* (Hoboken, N.J.: John Wiley and Sons, 2002). For the two "Scott's Andy" and the "devil" quotes, Wall, pp. 121, 125, 126; "the reward," "alas," and "Kind master" in Andrew Carnegie, *The Autobiography of Andrew Carnegie* (Boston: Northeastern University Press, 1986), pp. 82, 223.

ROCKEFELLER

The Rockefeller sketch is drawn from Ron Chernow, *Titan: The Life of John D. Rockefeller, Sr.* (New York: Random House, 1998), Allan Nevins, *John D. Rockefeller: The Heroic Age of American Enterprise*, 2 vols. (New York: Charles Scribner's Sons, 1940), and Harold F. Williamson and Arnold R. Daum, *The American Petroleum Industry: Vol. I, The Age of Illumination, 1859–1899* (Evanston, Ill.: Northwestern University Press, 1959), especially pp. 27–114 for early history of the industry.

On John's father, the "long, mysterious" quote is from Nevins, I:89, who also has him eventually disappearing "beyond the Mississippi" (I:79). Chernow has the full story on William, pp. 57–59 and 192–94. Since William's double life was reported in the press, it is astonishing that previous biographers either missed it or chose not to report it. The "*very large*" quote is in Chernow, p. 77, "soul of a bookkeeper" in Nevins, I:111. The Bryce quote is from James Bryce, *The American Commonwealth*, 2 vols. (New York: Macmillan, 1923), II:164.

GOULD

The sketch of Gould's early life and career follows Maury Klein, *The Life and Legend of Jay Gould* (Baltimore, Md.: Johns Hopkins University Press, 1986). The Adams quote is from Charles Francis Adams, Jr., and Henry Adams, *Chapters of Erie* (Ithaca, N.Y.: Cornell University Press, 1956), p. 105; the Drew quote is in Klein, p. 3. The battle headline and the credit report are from Klein, pp. 60, 72. The quote "probably the most" is from Julius Grodsinsky, *Jay Gould: His Business Career, 1867–1892, The Expansion of America's Railroad Empire* (Philadelphia, Pa.: University of Pennsylvania Press, 1957), p. 450.

MORGAN

The sketch of J. P. Morgan follows Vincent P. Carosso, *The Morgans: Private International Bankers, 1854–1913* (Cambridge, Mass.: Harvard University Press, 1987) and Jean Strouse, *Morgan: American Financier* (New York: Random House, 1999).

For the Hall carbine affair, see R. Gordon Wasson, *The Hall Carbine Affair: A Study in Contemporary Folklore* (New York: Pandick Press, 1948), although Wasson (and Carosso) would have it that Morgan did not know that the rifles were being resold to the government, which is implausible. For the muckraker version of the affair, see Matthew Josephson, *The Robber Barons: The Great American Capitalists* (New York: Harcourt, Brace and World, 1962), pp. 60–61. The "first rate" quote is Carosso, *ibid.*, p. 104. The "gentlemen pay their debts" is my characterization, not a direct quote. Gary's "bitter" and "demoralization" quotes are in U.S. House of Representatives, *Hearings before the Committee on Investigation of United States Steel Corporation (Stanley Committee)*, 8 vols. (Washington, D.C.: U.S. Government Printing Office, 1912), I:122–23. For the middle-class character of pioneers, Eric Foner, *Free Soil*, p. 14.

2. "... glorious Yankee Doodle"

The *America's* Cup account is from David Shaw, *America's Victory* (New York: The Free Press, 2002); the "Is the ..." quote is from p. 213. (After the queen's party left, the wind died, and the much lighter *Aurora* almost made a race of it, but *America* still finished comfortably ahead.) For Crystal Palace details, I consulted multiple Web sites devoted to the exhibition, supplemented by Nathan Rosenberg, ed., *The American System of Manufactures* (Edinburgh: Edinburgh University Press, 1969), pp. 2–19. Quote "overrun" is from Rosenberg, p. 3; "wood pigeons" from Shaw, p. 184; Hobbs episode, McCormick reaper *Times* quotes, Colt exhibit and speech, "prairie" and "magnificent," Rosenberg, pp. 9–12, 8, 15–17, 7; first *Punch* quote from Shaw, p. 155; and "Yankee Doodle" from Rosenberg, pp. 18–19. The Rosenberg book compiles the reports of a parliamentary committee of inquiry and of two separate British delegations that toured American factories in the immediate aftermath of the Crystal Palace revelations about American manufacturing prowess. Rosenberg's extended Introduction (pp. 1–89) is a superb summary of the rise of the "American System of Manufacturing," while David A. Hounshell's *From American System to Mass Production, 1800–1932: The Development of Manufacturing Technology in the United States* (Baltimore, Md.: Johns Hopkins University Press, 1984) is the basic text. An extremely valuable overview of the "American System's" evolution, much of it based on interviews with craftsmen in the more important manufactories, was compiled by Charles H. Fitch, a Census Office agent, as part of his work on the 1880s Census of Manufactures. See his *Fire-Arms Manufacture 1880: Report on the Manufactures of Interchangeable Mechanisms* (Bradley, Ill.: Lindsay Publications, 1992) (reprint of 1883 Census Office Report) and "The Rise of a Mechanical Ideal," *Magazine of American History,* 11 (June 1884), 516–27. Many of the priorities he assigns to specific innovators, mostly derived from interviews, have been corrected by subsequent researchers, but Fitch's pieces remain a key source for drawings, machine specifications, and the development sequences.

Rise of the Nerds
The Blanchard story follows Asa H. Waters, *Biographical Sketch of Thomas Blanchard and His Inventions* (Worcester, Mass.: L. P. Goddard, 1878). Waters knew Blanchard and is the primary source on his life; he produced several accounts, which all differ slightly from each other. See also Carolyn C. Cooper, *Shaping Invention: Thomas Blanchard's Machinery and Patent Management in Nineteenth-Century America* (New York: Columbia University Press, 1991), who is particularly good on the history of lathes. (She makes the excellent point that the key innovation in the stocking machine was the independently driven cutting wheel.) The "royal" quote is from Cooper, p. 75; "glanced," "Well," "whole principle," "I've got," "I guess," from Waters, pp. 5–7. My appreciation to the staff of the American Precision Museum in Windsor, Vermont, for their careful explanations. The eulogy is Waters's, *op. cit.*, p. 1. For Springfield's interest, and the history of Blanchard's contract, besides Cooper, I used Merritt Roe Smith, *Harpers Ferry Armory and the New Technology: The Challenge of Change* (Ithaca, N.Y.: Cornell University Press, 1977), pp. 124–38. Smith's work is based on extensive analysis of the Springfield and Harpers Ferry archives.

Valley Guys
The Connecticut River Valley description from this period is a collective portrait from Felicia Johnson Deyrup, *Arms Makers of the Connecticut Valley: A Regional Study of the Economic Development of the Small Arms Industry, 1798–1870* (Northampton, Mass.: Smith College Studies in History, vol. 33, 1948), an important source; Constance McLaughlin Green, *Holyoke, Massachusetts: A Case Study of the Industrial Revolution in America* (New Haven, Conn.: Yale University Press, 1939); and Vera Shlakman, *Economic History of a Factory Town: A Study of Chicopee, Massachusetts* (Northampton, Mass.: Smith College Studies in History, vol. 20, 1935). The quote "[T]here is not" is from Nathan Rosenberg, *American System*, p. 204. For the influence of Gribeauval and Blanc, see David Hounshell, *From American System,* pp.

25–26, and Merritt Roe Smith, *Harpers Ferry*, pp. 88–89. The accounts of the venture groups follow Constance McLaughlin Green, *Holyoke, Massachusetts*, pp. 19–63 and Vera Shlakman, *Economic History*, pp. 24–80. For a discussion of "enabling technologies," see the collection of papers by Nathan Rosenberg in his *Exploring the Black Box*, especially his "The Historiography of Technical Progress," pp. 3–33, and "Marx as a Student of Technology," pp. 34–51.

The Quest for the Holy Grail

For the modern view of Whitney's contribution, see Robert S. Woodbury, "The Legend of Eli Whitney and Interchangeable Parts," *Technology and Culture* (Summer 1960), 235–53; the standard account is in Constance McLaughlin Green, *Eli Whitney and the Birth of American Technology* (Boston, Mass.: Little, Brown, 1956). For Colt pistol interchangeability, see David Hounshell, *From American System*, pp. 48–49. The best sources on Hall are Merritt Roe Smith, *Harpers Ferry*, especially pp. 184–251, and R. T. Huntington, *Hall's Breechloaders: John H. Hall's Invention and Development of a Breechloading Rifle with Precision-Made Interchangeable Parts and Its Introduction into the United States Service* (York, Pa.: G. Shumway, 1972), which has extensive selections from Hall's correspondence and various official reports on his rifles. Certain specialized works were also helpful, like Robert S. Woodbury, *History of the Milling Machine* (Cambridge, Mass.: The Technology Press, 1960). The pamphlet quotation is from John H. Hall, "Remarks upon the Patent Improved Rifles Made by John H. Hall of Portland, ME" (pamphlet) (Portland: F. Douglas, 1816); it is a composite from pp. 1, 5. For Thornton background and involvement with Fitch, I used James Thomas Flexner, *Steamboats Come True: American Inventors in Action* (Boston: Little, Brown, 1978), pp. 177–84. Thornton's involvement with the federal city is in Dumas Malone, *Jefferson and the Rights of Man* (vol. 2 of *Jefferson and His Times*) (Boston: Little, Brown, 1951), pp. 385–87. The quote on his patents is from the Web-based *American National Biographical Dictionary*. The quotes "Upon" and "It would" are in Huntington, pp. 3, 4. When scholars exhumed the Thornton patent episode, it explained a long-standing puzzle. The patent submission included an oddly dysfunctional flint lock on the side of the rifle that appears in no known Hall firearm. It appears this is the one "improvement" contributed by Thornton. Smith has identified the firearm displayed to Hall by Thornton as a Ferguson, an English gun dating from 1776 (*Harpers Ferry*, p. 186). The "bullet-proof" and Thornton quatrain are in Huntington, pp. 12, 27. Hall's "very guarded" is from Smith, p. 196; "*of infinite*," "I was not aware" are in Huntington, pp. 305, 17; "the manner," "waste," are from Smith, pp. 200, 201.

The 1827 military board and manufacturing reviews are reprinted in full in Huntington, pp. 306–23. The quoted sections are on pp. 311, 319–20, 323. Fitch, in his "The Rise of a Mechanical Ideal," agrees that Hall had "achieved practical conformity in large lots of arms," but with the reservation that "the joints between the interchangeable parts were by no means fine"; but he concedes that Hall's work had clearly passed the "severe tests" that the inspectors had used, although it would not have met 1880s standards (pp. 516, 519). The quote ". . . by 1820" is from Constance McLaughlin Green, *Eli Whitney*, p. 139.

The American Machine Tradition

For Colt history, besides sources previously cited, I used William Hosley, *Colt: The Making of an American Legend* (Amherst, Mass.: University of Massachusetts Press, 1996) and Paul Uselding, "Elisha K. Root, Forging, and the 'American System,'" *Technology and Culture* (October 1974), 543–68. The "highest-paid" and "[C]redit for" quotes are from Uselding, 563, 543. "[I]t is impossible" from Nathan Rosenberg, ed., *The American System*, p. 46. Colt's British factory was not a success, and closed in 1856. Colt placed the blame on British labor, but England may not have been ready for mass-produced guns. Outside of the military, the most important weapons buyers were upper-class sportsmen who, for instance, liked their rifle stocks custom-made for arm lengths and shoulder fit. It wasn't just craftsmen's recalcitrance but also the nature of demand that determined British production preferences. For Alexander Holley, see chapter 5 and sources therein. The quote "very conspicuous" is from Frank Popplewell, *Some*

Modern Conditions and Recent Developments in Iron and Steel Production in America (Manchester: University Press, 1906), p. 103. The synopsis of state of consumer manufacturing is drawn primarily from David Hounshell, *From American System,* which is generally organized by dates and product types.

The British Reaction

Nathan Rosenberg's Introduction to *American System* surveys the British gun manufacturing industry and the parliamentary debates leading up to the decision to proceed with Enfield. The quotes "produced a very impressive," "[I]n the adaptation," "In no branch," and "The American machinery" are from *ibid.,* pp. 43–45, 128–29, 343–44, and 65–66. Whitworth stressed, however, that Great Britain was still ahead in general-purpose machines, and, indeed, the great British machine-tool makers had a lead of many decades over Americans especially in the very advanced tooling for manufacturing large steam engines, ship plate, and similar products. From the start, Americans were more oriented toward mass production of consumer or similar end-products. That may reflect both the nature of British demand—in the absence of a broad middle-class market—but also the fact that they began during a somewhat earlier phase of industrialization. See Abbott Payson Usher, "The Industrialization of Modern Britain," *Technology and Culture* (Spring 1960), 109–27, especially pp. 120–21.

What Made America Different?

For wood manufacturing and Sheffield steel, see Kenneth D. and Jane W. Roberts, *Planemakers and Other Edge Tool Enterprises in New York State in the Nineteenth Century* (Cooperstown, N.Y.: New York State Historical Association, 1971), especially pp. 1–12; for wartime steel supplies and imports, see Felicia Johnson Deyrup, *Arms Makers,* pp. 80–81, 179. For American income and production, see David S. Landes, *The Wealth and Poverty of Nations: Why Some Are So Rich and Some Are So Poor* (New York: W. W. Norton, 1999), pp. 232, 300. Whitworth on "cheap press" is in Nathan Rosenberg, *American System,* p. 389. For farm mechanization, see Paul David, "The Mechanization of Reaping in the Ante-Bellum Midwest," in Henry Rosovsky, *Industrialization in Two Systems: Essays in Honor of Alexander Gerschenkron by a Group of His Students* (New York: John Wiley, 1966), pp. 3–39. The *Scientific American* quote is on p. 7. For Nathan Rosenberg on role of natural resources, see his *Exploring the Black Box,* pp. 109–20, an extremely intelligent analysis of what was different about America. For antebellum educational spending, see Albert Fishlow, "The American Common School Revival: Fact or Fancy?" in Henry Rosovsky, *Industrialization in Two Systems,* pp. 40–67. Apparently, public agitation for better schooling started in the 1820s, but didn't translate into greater investment until the 1840s, when it began to rise very strongly. The quotes ". . . the Englishman," "In America," and "The absence" are from Nathan Rosenberg, *American System,* pp. 15, 14, and 7n. The Oliver Evans drawing and quote are in a one-page news-sheet advertisement, "Improvements on the Art of Manufacturing Grain into Flour or Meal" (Patent Licensing Announcement, c. 1791, Rare Books Division, New York Public Library). Improvement in British textile machine designs is from David S. Landes, *The Wealth,* p. 300. The two Lincoln quotes are from Roy P. Basler, ed., *The Collected Works,* III:361, 478. The "I should not" quote is from Felicia Johnson Deyrup, *Arms Makers,* p. 95.

3. Bandit Capitalism

For the river episode, see W. A. Swanberg, *Jim Fisk: The Career of an Improbable Rascal* (New York: Scribners, 1959), pp. 47–48, and Maury Klein, *The Life and Legend of Jay Gould* (Baltimore, Md.: Johns Hopkins University Press, 1986), p. 83. For foreign investment in America, see United States Bureau of the Census, *Historical Statistics of the United States, Colonial Times to 1970* (vol. 2) (Washington, D.C.: U.S. Government Printing Office, 1975), Series 1–25. Gladstone's economic policies are in Roy Jenkins, *Gladstone: A Biography* (New York: Random House, 1997), especially pp. 137–57.

Opéra Bouffe

For Gould, Fisk, and the Erie wars, I used Maury Klein, *Life and Legend;* Julius Grodinsky, *Jay Gould: His Business Career, 1867–1892, The Expansion of America's Railroad Empire* (Philadelphia, Pa.: University of Pennsylvania Press, 1957); Charles Francis Adams, Jr. and Henry Adams, *Chapters of Erie* (Ithaca, N.Y.: Cornell University Press, 1956); Edward Harold Mott, *Between the Ocean and the Lakes: The Story of Erie* (New York: John S. Collins, 1898); W. A. Swanberg, *Jim Fisk;* and Bouck White, *The Book of Daniel Drew: A Glimpse of the Fisk-Gould-Tweed Régime from the Inside* (Garden City, N.Y.: Doubleday, 1911). Klein is the premier Gould scholar, and his book is marked by common sense and good judgment throughout. The Adams essays are the most colorful, and very well researched. The Mott book is the most detailed history of the Erie; it is crisp, thorough, and sardonic, and includes a rich sampling of relevant documents (it is an old book and hard to find; it warrants a reprint edition). The White book on Drew purports to be a diary, but is almost certainly a fabrication, and is best read as a popular biography of Drew, unfortunately disguised as a memoir.

The legality of the convertible issuances was precisely the kind of shadow land where Gould was at his best. The Erie's capital structure under its legislative charter arguably did permit issuance of convertibles, and there was some precedent for it. (See Julius Grodinsky, *Jay Gould*, p. 41.) The journal of "legal" expenses is from Assembly of the State of New York, *Report of the Select Committee Appointed by the Assembly, March 11, 1873, to Investigate the Alleged Mismanagement on the Part of the Erie Railway Company, Together with the Testimony Taken Before Said Committee* (vol. 6, no. 98) (Albany, N.Y.: Argus, 1873), pp. 336–37. The *Report* may be the richest source of details on the Erie wars.

Railroad Privateer

"Airplane-seat pricing" is just a special case of industries, including railroads, with heavy fixed and low variable costs, where competitive pressures lead to "marginal cost pricing," charging at or slightly above the variable cost. Memory chip factories, another example, cost $1 billion or more to build, but the labor and materials cost of each chip is only about twenty-five cents or so. The desperate hunt for revenues to recover the factory investment inevitably triggers savage chip price wars. The Japanese solution was a government sponsored chip cartel in the 1970s and 1980s, eventually broken by the Koreans. Recent OPEC history also exemplifies the challenges of keeping cartels intact. Gould's acquisition drive was born of his perception that it was foolish to expect independent companies to subordinate their competitive instincts to a cartel agreement; J. P. Morgan proved the soundness of that instinct over some thirty years of futile cartel construction.

Julius Grodinsky, *Jay Gould*, pp. 57–69; 73–74 has a clear description of Gould's acquisition strategy. For the Pennsylvania reaction, Maury Klein, *Life and Legend*, pp. 93–95; "state mercantilism" is in James E. Vance, Jr., *The North American Railroad* (Baltimore, Md.: The Johns Hopkins University Press, 1995), p. 89. The most detailed account of the Albany & Susquehanna–Erie struggle is in Charles and Henry Adams, *Chapters*, pp. 137–90, written by Charles, which omits any mention of Morgan (who was not a significant figure when Adams wrote it). For Morgan's role, see Vincent P. Carosso, *The Morgans: Private International Bankers, 1854–1913* (Cambridge, Mass.: Harvard University Press, 1987), pp. 121–23.

The Gold Corner

The best short accounts of the Gold Corner are Maury Klein, *Life and Legend*, pp. 100–15; and Charles and Henry Adams, *Chapters*, pp. 101–36. (The Gold Corner story was written by Henry, and is the best of the three sections of *Chapters*.) The best overall source is U.S. House of Representatives, Committee on Banking and Currency, *Report no. 31, Gold Panic Investigation*, 1870 (reprinted: New York: Arno Press, 1974). The hearings open with extensive groundlaying testimony that fully explains the operations of the Gold Exchange, hedging practices, and other essential background. For general background on the postwar currency system, see Irwin Unger, *The Greenback Era: A Social and Political History of American Finance, 1865–1879* (Princeton, N.J.: Princeton University Press, 1964).

Modern trading markets differ only in detail from Gould's day. The kind of hedging operation described here is now normally accomplished in the futures markets—selling an uncovered futures contract is functionally equivalent to taking a short position, and futures cash margin requirements work in essentially the same way. Although markets are now much deeper and more liquid, and there are much tighter controls over trading positions, trading fiascos still occur like clockwork, especially after the introduction of some new product or trading efficiency. In addition, we tend to look more benignly on "speculation" as an essential part of the price-discovery process.

Quotes: Gould's "fictitiousness" is from *Gold Panic Investigation*, pp. 153–54; Adams's "worthy" from Charles and Henry Adams, *Chapters*, p. 119; Corbin's "only for the sake of," *Gold Panic Investigation*, p. 253; Gould on purpose of gifts, and "I did not," *ibid*., pp. 163, 135; "Delivered" versions, *ibid*., p.174 and Klein, *Life and Legend*, p. 106; Gould's "What put gold," and "undone," *Gold Panic Investigation*, pp. 135, 256. Fisk to Speyers, *ibid*., p. 64; "crazy," Klein, *Life and Legend*, p. 112. Fisk on Butterfield tip, *Gold Panic Investigation*, p. 181; Fisk on the Corbins, *ibid*., p. 176.

Ouster

The most thorough account of Gould's unseating is Assembly of the State of New York, *Report*, which I use for the summary here. The English shareholders' complaint against Gould was summarized in a 101-count pleading that, although obviously partisan, is an excellent—and it appears mostly accurate—time line of the Gould-Fisk reign. It is reproduced in full at *Heath et al. v Erie Railway Co. et al.* 11 Federal Cases, 976 (April 27, 1871). The Stevens quote is in Assembly of the State of New York, *Report*, p. 310; the Bischoffheimer deal, the Gould settlement, and "raise the cry" are from *ibid*., pp. 35–38, 314–15, and 746. Gould's settlement was later reopened and he was forced to disgorge some additional money; but by that time he was once again very rich. On the valuations of the Gould package, the English shareholders' complaint (Count 57) listed the Opera House at a value of $700,000 (to argue the enormity of the Fisk-Gould embezzlements), but the settlement accounting valued it at $1.5 million. Peter Watson was an investor in, and later president of, the westernmost of the "lake shore" routes, the Michigan & Southern, and had held other positions within that network. His appointment to the Erie board signaled Vanderbilt's temporary preeminence, since the lake shore routes were now firmly within the Commodore's control. In the New York Assembly hearings referred to above, Watson patiently explained basic concepts like expenses, capitalized expenditures, depreciation, net earnings, and the priorities between interest and dividends. See, for example, his testimony, pp. 188ff.; the committee's own summary demonstrates considerable confusion on all these issues. The "gigantic offspring" quote is in Chester McArthur Destler, "The Standard Oil, Child of the Erie Ring, 1868–1872: Six Contracts and a Letter," *Mississippi Valley Historical Review* (June 1946) 89–114, at p. 100.

The First Oil Baron

The basic story triangulates the accounts in Ron Chernow, *Titan: The Life of John D. Rockefeller, Sr.* (New York: Random House, 1998), pp. 129–55; Allan Nevins, *John D. Rockefeller: The Heroic Age of American Enterprise* (New York: Charles Scribner's Sons, 2 vols.), I:217–346; Ida M. Tarbell, *The History of the Standard Oil Company* (New York: Macmillan, 1925, 2 vols.), I:38–103; and Harold F. Williamson and Arnold R. Daum, *The American Petroleum Industry: Vol. I, The Age of Illumination, 1859–1899* (Evanston, Ill.: Northwestern University Press, 1959). Williamson, pp. 170–201, 297–308, has a crisp, accurate account of the early evolution of the competition between the trunk lines; comparative mileage data are from p. 300. Refining technology is from *ibid*., pp. 202–51. Rockefeller's "running scared" is based on Allan Nevins, *op. cit.*, I:279–81, who relied on interview data, long after the fact, but it fits everything else we know. The details of the 1868 deal between the Erie lines, the three refineries, and the pipeline are from the original documents reprinted in Chester McArthur Destler, "The Standard Oil," pp. 103–14. Destler finds the contract reprehensible.

Crisis and Consolidation

Oil price data is from the table in Harold F. Williamson, *The American Petroleum Industry,* p. 360. The annual reports of Andrew Carnegie's Columbia Oil Co. list ten years of monthly average sale prices per barrel. The variations within each year are quite wide, and the price collapse in 1873 is apparent. Columbia generally suspended operations when prices fell to a dollar. (HSWP, Box 20, folder 1)

	High	Low
1864	13.00	4.00
1865	9.25	4.00
1866	5.00	1.65
1867	4.00	1.50
1868	5.00	1.80
1869	7.00	4.25
1870	4.00	2.75
1871	5.15	3.40
1872	4.60	3.00
1873	1.05	1.00
1874	1.90	0.65

For Standard's capitalization, see the table on page 344. A comment: Nevins (Allan Nevins, *John D. Rockefeller,* I:292) seems to imply that the initial $1 million represented new cash—"each incorporator taking his own allotment and paying for it"—but the partnership of Rockefeller, Andrews, and Flagler would have been dissolved at the same time; instead of distributing the assets, they would have been converted into shares of the new entity. The reorganization was much more about flexibility than about raising money, although there was one new investor. Nevins, *ibid.,* then assumes that the Cleveland bankers invested just before the capitalization increase of January 1872. Nevins makes polemical use of that assumption, see *infra,* but absent more evidence, his inferences seem unwarranted. The table on page 344 summarizes the capitalization changes over this period. Altogether, they seem quite normal for a two-year period, comprising merely the sale of the original 1,000 treasury shares, some reallocations of Rockefeller's shares, and a sale of part of Jennings's stake. BP America, a successor to part of the Exxon archives, was the custodian of the 1870s minute books, the capitalization source for Nevins and Chernow, but the files were transferred a few years ago, and are now missing, so I could not determine the precise dates of the transfers (if, indeed, the minute books show them). I do appreciate the assiduous search by Sarah Howell, at BP's public relations firm, and Tom Pardo, of the BP staff, to track them down. Shortly before I commenced the research for this book, Exxon transferred its early-period files to the University of Texas. Whether they would shed further light on this period I don't know, but they will be closed until 2006 or so until the cataloging is complete.

Nevins argues (Allan Nevins, *John D. Rockefeller,* I:306–37) that Rockefeller was poised to commence his Cleveland consolidation before he heard of the SIC, and only went into it as a second-best option. His primary evidence is that Rockefeller had expanded the company's capitalization before he heard of the SIC and that the merger with Payne was independent of the SIC. Neither argument is convincing. He did not increase, but only rejiggered, the Standard's capitalization in the two years after 1870, and it strains credulity that the Payne merger and Payne's taking shares in the Standard and SIC on successive days, all within about two weeks, were unrelated transactions. The stock table is reconstructed from Nevins's narrative, I:290–337.

Standard Oil Stock Tables, 1870–1872

	Jan. 10, 1870	Dec. 31, 1871	Change	Jan.1, 1872 Dist. to Shlders (13)	Jan.1, 1872 New Issue (14)	Jan. 2, 1872 New Issue	Total	% Owned
John D. Rockefeller	2,667	2,016	–651	806	3,000		5,822	16.6%
William Rockefeller	1,333	1,459	126	584			2,043	5.8%
Henry Flagler	1,333	1,459	126	584	1,400		3,443	9.8%
Samuel Andrews	1,333	1,458	125	583			2,041	5.8%
Stephen Harkness (1)	1,334	1,458	124	583			2,041	5.8%
O. B. Jennings (2)	1,000	500	–500	200			700	2.0%
Rockefeller, Andrews, & Flagler (3)	1,000	0	–1,000	0			0	0.0%
Amasa Stone (4)		500	500	200			700	2.0%
Stillman Witt (5)		500	500	200			700	2.0%
T. P. Handy (6)		400	400	160			560	1.6%
Benjamin Brewster (7)		250	250	100			350	1.0%
Clark, Payne (8)					4,000		4,000	11.4%
Jabez Bostwick (9)					700		700	2.0%
Joseph Stanley (10)					200		200	0.6%
Peter Watson (11)					500		500	1.4%
J. D. Rockefeller as agent (12)					1,200	10,000	11,200	32.0%
Total	10,000	10,000	0	4,000	11,000	10,000	35,000	100.0%

1. An in-law of Flagler
2. William Rockefeller's father-in-law
3. Former partnership name; shares held for future distribution
4,5,6. Cleveland bankers and businessmen
7. Entrepreneur/investor
8. Acquisition of refinery
9. Acquisition of refinery/marketing/distribution business
10. Acquisition of refinery
11. President, South Improvement Company
12. Treasury shares, held for future acquisitions
13. Shares awarded pro rata, presumably in lieu of cash dividend
14. New Rockefeller/Flagler shares purchased; remainder for acquisitions and Watson grant, in addition to new treasury shares

Quote "alias" from Ida M. Tarbell, *History,* I:99. Industry margin changes calculated from the table in Harold F. Williamson, *The American Petroleum Industry,* p. 360.

The Muckrakers' Case against Rockefeller
Ron Chernow, *Titan,* pp. 435–61, has a fine background essay on Tarbell, supported by work in her personal papers and notes. Quotes "unjust and illegal" and "swift and ruddy" from Ida M. Tarbell, *History,* I:101, 36–37. Harold F. Williamson, *The American Petroleum Industry,* pp. 170–89, has a lucid discussion of the positioning of the railroads, and on pp. 287–301, of the respective advantages and disadvantages of the different refining centers; and on pp. 344–46, the secondary, albeit important, character of petroleum freight compared to the grain trade. Export data are from United States Bureau of the Census, *Historical Statistics,* vol. 2, Series U, pp. 274–94.

For a recent neo-Tarbellian argument, see Elizabeth Granitz and Benjamin Klein, "Monopolization by 'Raising Rivals' Costs': The Standard Oil Case," *Journal of Law and Economics*, 39:1 (April 1996), 1–47. They argue that the real monopoly belonged to the three railroads—the Erie, the Central, and the PRR—and that they built up the Standard to act as the policeman and the freight evener over their cartel. While the argument is ingenious, it suffers from many of the same flaws as Tarbell's. An essential premise, as it was for Tarbell, is that there were no efficiencies of scale in refining, so they assume all refineries were making about the same returns, which is patently wrong. Only by that assumption can they conclude that, absent railroad collusion with the Standard, it would make no sense for other refiners to sell out, instead of holding on and enjoying a "free rider" price increase when Rockefeller achieved his near monopoly. Returns to scale, in fact, seem to have been quite high during this period, as evidenced by the rapid move to scale on the part of all the best refiners—besides the usual processing and capital efficiencies, scale allowed better exploitation of the nonkerosene fractions. And in Rockefeller's case, he moved much faster than the rest of the industry to exploit both tiny scale efficiencies in refinery management—like his own barrel shop—and the very large ones to be gained from moving into distribution. Granitz and Klein are correct that in the decade before the long-distance pipeline, the Standard emerged as the evener of railroad freights, but that seems the natural *consequence* of its market power. Granitz and Klein would have it the other way, that the railroads *bestowed* that power on the Standard, but fail to explain why the roads would have picked Rockefeller as their savior before he had market power—a problem they also share with Tarbell. The authors also have considerable difficulty fitting the very nasty 1877 Standard/PRR war (see chapter 5) into their framework. One of their primary pieces of evidence for a conspiracy, finally, is that the Standard did not fully exploit its market power in exacting lower freight rates from the railroads. But that is perfectly consistent with Rockefeller's normal behavior; he was almost always happy to allow modest extra premiums to keep important vendors contented and loyal.

The only explicit mention of the use of rebates to pump up the railroad revenue line for bondholders is in Allan Nevins, I:262, where a contemporary explains them as a device "to satisfy the stockholders on the one side, and prevent competition on the other." It is normal behavior for early investors in a high-growth industry to focus on revenue growth and market share rather than profits. As an example of free discussion of rebates, see the testimony of Peter Watson and O. H. P. Archer, at the time respectively president and vice president of the Erie, Assembly of the State of New York, *Report*, pp. 417–19, 299–302. For a near-contemporary argument on the virtues of rebates, see Guy Morrison Walker, *Railroad Rates and Rebates* (New York: privately published, 1917). This is an advocacy paper, but argues, I believe correctly, that rebates were typically the leading edge of general rate reductions. The pattern of steady rate reductions ended with regulation, to be succeeded by a long period of rising rates and improved profits.

On Standard and rebates, John Archbold insisted to an 1889 congressional committee that the Standard took no rebates after they were outlawed in 1887, producing letters from presidents of all the major railroads confirming his statement—U.S. House of Representatives, *Investigation of Certain Trusts: Report in Relation to the Sugar Trust and Standard Oil Trust by the Committee on Manufactures* (Washington, D.C.: U.S. Government Printing Office, 1889), p. 514ff. Chernow, *op. cit.*, p. 252, tells us that although Rockefeller (much later) said that the Standard did not receive rebates after *1880*, the practice continued "well into the 1880s," citing a case from 1886, which was, of course, before they had been outlawed. (Rockefeller was probably confused on the dates, but Chernow, like Tarbell, seems to believe that rebates were always and everywhere illegal.)

The quotes in the text and in the footnote on the common law and restraints of trade are from Tony Allan Freyer, *Regulating Big Business: Antitrust in Great Britain and America* (New York: Cambridge University Press, 1992), pp. 127, 24. Even to speak of a British common law of railroads is misleading, since the roads were governed by highly specific statutory enactments from the earliest days—some nine hundred railroad acts were passed in the 1840s and 1850s alone. See Edward Cleveland-Stevens, *English Railways: Their Development and Relation to the State* (New York: Dutton, 1915). Data on legislation are on p. 25. Parliamentary rate regulation tended to focus on maximum rates, and seem rather more focused on passenger provision than American initiatives. In an important case from the early 1840s, the Lord Chancellor refused to prohibit differential rates, saying that the court "would not interfere unless it were clear that the public interest required it, and that in this case, it being admitted that the higher charge was not more than the Act permitted, it did not appear that the public were prejudiced by the arrangement" (p. 46n). The quote "undue or unreasonable" is from a comprehensive 1854 Act that attempted to codify the previous legislative scheme, *ibid.*, p. 193.

For the reception of the common law into American antitrust doctrine, see Rudolph J. R. Peritz, *Competition Policy in America, 1888–1992: History, Rhetoric, Law* (New York: Oxford University Press, 1996), pp. 13–38. The "[A]t a very" quote is from *Standard Oil Co. of N.J. v. U.S.* 221 U.S. 1 (1911), 52. The Supreme Court refrained from finding that any *specific* acts of the Standard were illegal, and concurred with the lower court that acts alleged to have been in restraint of trade which took place before the passage of the Sherman Act could not have been illegal. But the court found that the Standard had achieved such thoroughgoing control of the industry as to amount to a monopoly, which was by definition an "undue restraint on trade." The behavioral history, whether the individual acts were legal or not, was held to be relevant to the question of whether the Standard *intended* to take over the industry—which could hardly be disputed. For common law and Progressives, see the first three chapters of Edward A. Purcell, Jr., *Brandeis and the Progressive Constitution: Erie, the Judicial Power, and the Politics of the Federal Courts in Twentieth-Century America* (New Haven, Conn.: Yale University Press, 2000).

For Tarbell on region refiner rollup, Ida M. Tarbell, *History*, I:154–60. Chernow, *Titan*, p. 150, suggests that Rockefeller was driven to the consolidation by his "outsized debt," which is highly doubtful. Rockefeller borrowed almost solely from banks, who were almost exclusively short-term lenders at this period. A bank letter quoted by Nevins, I:274, stipulates that in the previous year (1869) Rockefeller's balance sheet varied between high levels of debt and large cash surpluses, which is what one would expect of a short-term working capital borrower. Compared to the railroads, refining was not especially capital intensive, and new facilities were brought on line very rapidly. The Standard managed to reconstruct virtually the entire Cleveland refinery industry in 1872–73, and still keep production flowing, apparently profitably. The large dividends the company paid would also be inconsistent with a company straining under a debt load. Chernow, 151, also says that noncompetition agreements with acquirees' managers would be "outlawed as a restraint of trade" today. In fact, they are standard in takeover agreements—I have signed several—although modern courts would not enforce the ten-year terms of the Rockefeller agreements, and some state courts usually refuse to enforce them except in exceptional circumstances.

Carnegie Chooses a Career

The summary of Carnegie's multiple enterprises follows Joseph Frazier Wall, *Andrew Carnegie* (Pittsburgh, Pa.: University of Pittsburgh Press, 1989), pp. 192–306. For the St. Louis Bridge, see Robert W. Jackson, *Rails across the Mississippi: A History of the St. Louis Bridge* (Urbana, Ill.: University of Illinois Press, 2001); the Sullivan quote is from Carl W. Condit, "Sullivan's Skyscrapers as an Expression of Nineteenth Century Technology," *Technology and Culture* (Winter 1959), 62–83, at 67. Both Jackson's book, and David G. McCullough, *The Great Bridge* (New York: Simon and Schuster, 1972), on the Brooklyn Bridge, have excellent descriptions of the pneumatic caissons. (The bends are a common hazard for scuba divers. Recreational divers go as deep as 120 feet without special precautions, except for limiting bottom time and ascending slowly. The problem at the bridges was the rate of the men's ascents, not the depth itself.) Morgan's quote on delays is from Robert W. Jackson, *Rails*, p. 135; his "Think Mr. Gould" and "somewhat less" are from, respectively, Vincent P. Carosso, *The Morgans: Private International Bankers, 1854–1913* (Cambridge, Mass.: Harvard University Press, 1987), p. 244, and Julius Grodinsky, *Jay Gould*, p. 340.

The Pennsylvania crackdown on its executives is detailed in *Report of the Investigating Committee of the Pennsylvania Railroad Company* (Philadelphia, Pa.: March 10, 1874), a strikingly thorough and professional document. For the evolution of conflict of interest rules, see Steven W. Usselman, *Regulating Railroad Innovation*, especially pp. 65–82, which focuses on the Pennsylvania. For the footnote on insider dealing in this era, see Naomi Lamoreaux, "Information Problems and Banks' Specialization in Short-Term Commercial Lending: New England in the Nineteenth Century," in Peter Temin, ed., *Inside the Business Enterprise: Historical Perspectives on the Use of Information* (Chicago, Ill.: University of Chicago Press, 1991), pp. 161–205.

4. Wrenchings

The main sources for the strikes are Philip Foner, *The Great Labor Uprising* (New York: Monad Press, 1977); J. A. Dacus, *Annals of the Great Strikes in the United States* (New York: Burt Franklin, 1969) (reprint of 1877 edition); along with reports in the *Commercial and Financial Chronicle*. Quotes "saturnalia" and "bungling" from the *Chronicle*, July 28, 1877; "peace everywhere" (actually *Pax semper et ubique*) in Foner, *op. cit.*, pp. 200–201. The "long and merciless" quote is from Allan Nevins, *John D. Rockefeller: The Heroic Age of American Enterprise* (New York: Charles Scribner's Sons, 1940 (2 vols.), I:444.

The Crash of 1873

Jay Cooke's career and banking failure are drawn primarily from Henrietta M. Larson, *Jay Cooke, Private Banker* (Cambridge, Mass.: Harvard University Press, 1936), supplemented by contemporary reports in the *Chronicle*. Quotes "received with," "Jay Cooke panic," and "Since" from the *Chronicle*, September 20, 1873; railroad default count, *Chronicle*, October 10, 1874. After his bank collapsed, Cooke, rather than stiffing his creditors à la Jay Gould, spent three years working out settlements, emerging, if not actually poor, with sharply constrained means. Within a few years, he made a second fortune in silver mining, and before his death, had the pleasure of seeing the Northern Pacific live up to his most expansive forecasts. Duluth built a statue in his honor, and the railroad made him their guest on a special train for the full trip to Puget Sound.

The bank squeeze follows accounts in the *Chronicle*, as well as Frederick J. L. Edwards, "Some Economic Effects of the Depression of the 1870s in the United States" (master's thesis, Columbia University, 1951), and Milton Friedman and Anna Jacobson Schwartz, *A Monetary History of the United States, 1867–1960* (Princeton, N.J.: Princeton University Press, 1963), pp. 76–77. The Friedman and Schwartz chapter "The Greenback Period," pp. 15–88, is a very crisp roundup of the era. The crop turnaround between 1872 and 1873 was extremely large— exports to Great Britain, the United States' primary customer, jumped from 12 million bushels in 1872 to 26 million in 1873, far higher than any previous year, *Chronicle*, September 12, 1874.

A Most Peculiar Decade

A good summary of the reconstructive work is Paul W. Rhode, "Gallman's Annual Output Series for the United States, 1834–1909," *National Bureau of Economic Research, Working Paper* 8860 (April 2002), which includes an updated set of Gallman tables, as well as Gallman's own unpublished corrections and adjustments. The original Gallman tables are in Robert E. Gallman, "Gross National Product in the United States, 1834–1909," in Dorothy Brady, ed., National Bureau of Economic Research, *Output, Employment, and Productivity in the United States after 1800* (New York: Columbia University Press, 1966), pp. 3–75. Also see Simon Kuznets, "Notes on the Pattern of U.S. Economic Growth," in Edgar O. Edwards, ed., *The Nation's Economic Objectives* (Chicago, Ill.: University of Chicago Press, 1964). The year-to-year growth rates are 4.5 percent from 1869 to 1879, and 6.0 percent from 1870 to 1880 (1880 growth was very strong); Kuznets's five-year arithmetic averages give an annual rate of 4.95 percent. Gallman does not estimate data for the 1859–68 decade because of the war disruptions, although Kuznets does. Comparing the five years from 1869–73 to 1879–83 gives 6.1 percent.

The "more recent" higher growth calculation is cited in Michael D. Bordo and Angela Redish, "Is Deflation Depressing? Evidence from the Classical Gold Standard," *NBER Working Paper 9520* (Cambridge, Mass.: National Bureau of Economic Research, February 2003), p. 15. Friedman and Schwartz, based on their monetary analysis, think that the Kuznets data may be too high, but stress that even their lowered estimate "confirms one striking finding of the Kuznets estimates, namely that the decade from 1869 to 1879 was characterized by an extraordinarily rapid growth of output: at a rate of 4.3 or 4.9 per cent per year in total output, and 2.0 or 2.6 per cent per year in per capita output."

Commodity and physical output data, except as noted, are from Robert S. Manthy, *Natural Resource Commodities—A Century of Statistics: Prices, Output, Consumption, Foreign Trade, and Employment in the United States, 1870–1913* (Baltimore, Md.: Johns Hopkins University Press, 1978), see Tables N–1, 2, 4, and 5; MC–11, 20, and MO–3; for food, Tables AC–11, 12, 9, and 10. There are no comprehensive data on railroad loadings for this period, so I took a sample of large roads from the relevant *Poor's Manual of Railroads* (Henry V. Poor) (New York: Poor's Publishing Co., annual from 1869). For the Chicago, Burlington, and Quincy; Lake Shore and Michigan and Southern; New York Central; Pennsylvania; and Union Pacific, from 1871 (1872 for Union Pacific) to 1877, freight tonnage rose, respectively, 135%, 46%, 40%, 47%, and 89%, which is roughly consistent with the increases in commodity output. Immigration data are from United States Bureau of the Census, *Historical Statistics of the United States, Colonial Times to 1970* (2 vols.) (Washington, D.C.: U.S. Government Printing Office, 1975), Series C 89–119.

For U.K.-U.S. steel production, Peter Temin, "Relative Decline of British Steel Industry, 1880–1913," in Henry Rosovsky, ed., *Industrialization in Two Systems: Essays in Honor of Alexander Gerschenkron by a Group of His Students* (New York: John Wiley, 1966), pp. 140–55, at p. 143. The "awful" quote and Frick coke volumes are from Kenneth Warren, *Wealth, Waste, and Alienation: Growth and Decline in the Connellsville Coke Industry* (Pittsburgh, Pa.: University of Pittsburgh Press, 2001), pp. 34, 32. For employment, I use Stanley Lebergott, "Labor Force and Employment, 1800–1960," in Dorothy Brady, ed., *Output, Employment, and Productivity*, pp. 117–204, with the railroad adjustments from Albert Fishlow, "Productivity and Technological Change in the Railroad Sector, 1840–1910," in *ibid.*, pp. 583–646. The quote "the wage-earning" is cited in Thomas Kessner, *Capital City: New York City and the Men behind America's Rise to Economic Dominance, 1860–1900* (New York: Simon and Schuster, 2003), p. 191. The data for the footnote on unskilled labor is from Edith Abbott, "The Wages of Unskilled Laborers in the United States, 1850–1900," *The Journal of Political Economy*, vol. 13, no. 3 (June 1905), 321–67, at 363.

The overview of hardship follows, except as noted, Samuel Reznack, "Distress, Relief, and Discontent in the United States during the Depression of 1873–1878," *Journal of Political Economy* (December 1950), 494–512. The "20%" quote is on p. 496. The "much-cited" contemporary analysis is quoted at length in Reznack; I could not track down a copy of it, but the description seems to make clear that it is following price data (which Friedman and Schwartz also surmised, *op. cit.*, p. 43n). For commodity volumes, see *supra*; merchandise exports are given only in current prices in United States Bureau of the Census, *Historical Statistics*, Series U, 1–25. The half million unemployed was a contemporary estimate from the Massachusetts labor commissioner, Carroll Wright, extrapolating from his Massachusetts count (Reznack, *op. cit.*, p. 498), while the five million, the highest I've seen, is from Philip Foner, *The Great Labor Uprising of 1877*, p. 24, but no source is given. (Wright's estimates perhaps gain some credibility from his later incarnation as the pioneer of comprehensive labor statistics at the federal level.) For concentration of employment in small and medium businesses, see Stanley Lebergott, "Labor Force," pp. 118–20; and also Harold F. Williamson, Ralph L. Andreano, and Carmen Menezes, "The American Petroleum Industry," in Dorothy Brady, ed., *Output, Employment, and Productivity*, pp. 349–403, at p. 377. *Chronicle* job loss estimate is from issue of August 22, 1874. Possibly the largest ever American railroad building crew was the roughly 6,000 men that the Union Pacific employed in crossing the Rockies. (The Chinese crews on the Central Pacific were even bigger, but no one would have counted them in unemployment data.) The UP crew, however, was virtually a moveable city, with huge numbers of wagonmen carting supplies into a still relatively unexplored wilderness, cattle herders, loggers and sawyers so they could harvest ties and poles from passing forests, plus equipment for the massive cuts and trestles to go through or over mountain passes. See Maury Klein, *Union Pacific*, vol. 1 (New York: Doubleday, 1987), pp. 165–69. Normal crews, in settled areas, would have been in the hundreds. For perspective, by the 1870s, a single crew readily laid five miles a day; in a good year, the industry added 5,000 miles of new track. The post-crash job loss in steel is from Thomas J. Misa, *A Nation of Steel: The Making of Modern America, 1865–1925* (Baltimore, Md.: Johns Hopkins University Press, 1995), p. 31.

For other manufacturers, see David A. Hounshell, *From American System to Mass Production, 1800–1932: The Development of Manufacturing Technology in the United States* (Baltimore, Md.: Johns Hopkins University Press, 1984), pp. 89 (Singer), 147 (Studebaker), and 174–76 (McCormick); Philip Scranton, *Endless Novelty: Specialty Production and American Industrialization, 1865–1925* (Princeton, N.J.: Princeton University Press, 1997), pp. 90–91 (Philadelphia) and 109 (Providence). The "Despite" quote in the note is from Scranton, *ibid.*, p. 91. For acreage and mechanization, William Parker and Judith L. V. Klein, "Productivity Growth in Grain Production in the United States, 1840–1860 and 1900–1910," in Dorothy Brady, ed., *Output, Employment, and Productivity*, pp. 523–82, at pp. 542–43. For the shift of capital formation away from "extensive" additions, like clearing more land, to "intensive" investments, like mechanization in the 1870s, see Robert Gallman, "The United States Capital Stock in the Nineteenth Century," in Stanley Engerman and Robert Gallman, eds., *Long-Term Factors in American Economic Growth: National Bureau of Economic Research Studies in Income and Wealth*, vol. 51 (Chicago: University of Chicago Press, 1986), pp. 165–214.

Pennsylvania finances are from *Report of the Investigating Committee of the Pennsylvania Railroad Company* (Philadelphia, Pa.: March 10, 1874). National railroad earnings are from *Poor's Manual of Railroads*, 1877–78 (which has a ten-year table). Revenues rose about 30 percent from 1871 to the banner year of 1873, then fell about 10 percent from 1873 to 1877, while operating margins to revenues rose from 35.1 percent in 1871 to 36.2 percent in 1877. The only year that margins fell below 35 percent was in 1873 when, presumably, gross earnings were so good that the roads could afford to get a little sloppy. The *Sun* quote is from Foner, *op. cit.*, p. 34; *Chronicle* editorial, July 28, 1877.

Supply Shock?

The discussion of the greenback is drawn mostly from Irwin Unger, *The Greenback Era*, and Milton Friedman and Anna Jacobson Schwartz, *A Monetary History*. The *Chronicle* quotes are from the issues of May 23, 1874, and March 27, 1875. See Michael D. Bordo and Angela Redish, "Is Deflation Depressing?," which argues the case for a "supply shock." For the development of the bill of lading and car accounting, Alfred D. Chandler, Jr., *The Visible Hand: The Managerial Revolution in American Business* (Cambridge, Mass.: The Belknap Press of Harvard University Press, 1977), pp. 128–29. The "Prices," "overwhelming," and "the wails" quotes are from A. E. Musson, "The Great Depression in Britain, 1873–1896: A Reappraisal," *Journal of Economic History* XIX (June 1959), 199–228, at 199–200. S. B. Saul, *The Myth of the Great Depression, 1873–1896* (Basingstoke, Hampshire, U.K.: Macmillan, 1985), is a book-length treatment of the same issues that broadly agrees with Musson.

The Birth of the Factory Farm

My main source for the bonanza farm is Hiram A. Drache, *The Day of the Bonanza: A History of Bonanza Farming in the Red River Valley of the North* (Fargo, N.D.: North Dakota Institute for Regional Studies, 1964). Other useful material includes Jeremy Atack, Fred Bateman, and William N. Parker, "The Farm, The Farmer, and the Market," in Stanley Engerman and Robert Gallman, eds., *The Cambridge Economic History of the United States, Vol. II, The Long*

Nineteenth Century (Cambridge, U.K.: Cambridge University Press, 2000), pp. 245–84; for a shorter version that covers much of the same material, see Jeremy Atack and Peter Passell, *A New Economic View of American History* (New York: W. W. Norton, 1994), pp. 402–26. For details on particular farms, there is an assembly of materials at www.fargo-history.com. Farm operations are drawn from Hiram A. Drache, *The Day of the Bonanza*, pp. 91–120; for productivity data, see Jeremy Atack, et al., "The Farm," pp. 258–63; Jeremy Atack and Peter Passell, *A New Economic View*, pp. 280–81. For the growth of grain exchanges, see Alfred D. Chandler, Jr., *The Visible Hand: The Managerial Revolution in American Business* (Cambridge, Mass.: The Belknap Press of Harvard University Press, 1977), pp. 209–15. The Kansas Board of Trade, one of the earliest wheat exchanges, also has useful historical material available on its Web site.

The Disassembly Line

My main sources for ranching and meatpacking are Jimmy M. Skaggs, *Prime Cut: Livestock Raising and Meatpacking in the United States, 1607–1983* (College Station, Tex.: Texas A&M University Press, 1983), pp. 50–89 (ranching) and 90–129 (meatpacking); and Robert Adudell and Louis Cain, "Location and Collusion in the Meatpacking Industry," in Louis P. Cain and Paul J. Uselding, eds., *Business Enterprise and Economic Change: Essays in Honor of Harold F. Williamson* (Kent, Ohio: Kent State University Press, 1973), pp. 85–117. Both sources are data rich and substantially in agreement. Adudell and Cain make some interesting competitive points. Local butchers could compete so long as they were within 100–300 miles of their beef supply—i.e., lower transportation costs made up for the lack of scale. On the other hand, the authors argue that the 1890s meatpacking plants were too big. Economies of scale flattened out as production hit about one hundred carcasses a day. (Packing houses still had to work one steer at a time, whereas steel plants could install ever bigger furnaces or rolling mills.) Rational behavior would have led to much more decentralized plants to capture transportation economies earlier in the chain. Adudell and Cain suggest that the rampant collusion that characterized the industry from the mid-1880s on was necessary to protect outsized packing house investments. The industrialists' mantra at this time was that bigger is always better—Andrew Carnegie was among the most vocal on this point—but in fact the appropriate scale depends on the process being rationalized. The extractive and infrastructure industries, like oil and steel, just happened to be ones where the appropriate scale was very large. The "Yesterday was" quote is from Robert W. Jackson, *Rails across the Mississippi: A History of the St. Louis Bridge* (Urbana, Ill.: University of Illinois Press, 2001), pp. 152–53. For Jay Gould and southwestern railroads, see Julius Grodinsky, *Jay Gould: His Business Career, 1867–1892, The Expansion of America's Railroad Empire* (Philadelphia, Pa.: University of Pennsylvania Press, 1957), pp. 252–67.

The brief section exploring the discord between contemporary perception and the generally accepted economic data is obviously speculative, but would be consistent with episodes of rapid change in our own time, especially in rapidly developing countries. Frank Norris's novels about the grain trade, *The Octopus* (1901) and *The Pit* (1903), treat the market almost as a vast natural storm system with no human elements. The American ideology of always getting ahead and moving on probably made the transition to modernity far more compressed and less painful than in many other countries. For the Grangers, I used Solon Justus Buck, *The Granger Movement: A Study of Agricultural Organization and Its Political, Economic, and Social Manifestations* (Lincoln, Neb.: University of Nebraska Press, 1963; reprint of 1913 Harvard University Press edition). The "Granger Laws" are at the center of an important line of Supreme Court cases, upholding the right of states to regulate businesses infused with a "public interest" even in areas where the federal government had a superior regulatory claim. *Munn v. Illinois*, 94 U.S. 113 (1877) is the leading case. It upheld state grain elevator regulation, which was a harder case than railroads, since they were not on public land. For the higher cost of short-term rail routes, Stanley Lebergott, *The Americans: An Economic Record* (New York: Norton, 1984), pp. 290–91. On foreclosure rate, *ibid.*, p. 306. In one instance where there are good records—for the Davenport banking family covering 1869–1900—there were foreclosures on only nineteen out of 1,380 loans; also see Jeremy Atack and Peter Passell, *A New Economic View*, pp. 412–14.

5. Mega-Machine

For a fine description of the Philadelphia Exposition, see William Dean Howells, "A Sennight of the Centennial," *The Atlantic Monthly* (July 1876), 92–107, and also Donald E. Sutherland, *The Expansion of Everyday Life—1860–1876* (Fayette, Ark.: University of Arkansas Press, 2000), pp. 263–70. The quote "Dear Mother" is in Sutherland, p. 264. The Howells quote is from *op. cit.*, p. 96. For George Corliss and his engine, see Louis C. Hunter, *A History of Industrial Power in the United States, 1780–1930, Vol. II: Steam Power* (Charlottesville, Va.: The University Press of Virginia, 1985), pp. 251–300. There is an extended note on the Exposition engine itself on p. 293. Corliss may have been the greatest of the American contributors to steam engine technology. The Exposition engine, despite reports to the contrary, was not the largest ever built, but was close. When the Exposition closed, the engine was purchased by the Pullman Company, and powered one of its car factories until it was replaced by a turbine in 1910. For an assessment of railroads as an economic driver, see Albert Fishlow, "Internal Transportation in the Nineteenth and Early Twentieth Century," in Stanley Engerman and Robert Gallman, eds., *The Cambridge Economic History of the United States, Vol. II, The Long Nineteenth Century* (Cambridge, U.K.: Cambridge University Press, 2000), pp. 543–642, especially pp. 609–23. This essay pulls together a great deal of Fishlow's previous work, and is for now the last word on a sometimes excessively controversial subject.

The Edgar Thomson Works

The description of the ET works is primarily from A. L. Holley and Lenox Smith, "American Iron and Steel Works, No. XXI, The Works of the Edgar Thomson Steel Company (Limited)," *Engineer* (London), April 19, 1878, 295–301; April 26, 1878, 313–17; May 17, 1878, 381–84. (The quotes are from 313, 383, and 295.) I also used Joseph Frazier Wall, *Andrew Carnegie* (Pittsburgh, Pa.: University of Pittsburgh Press, 1989), pp. 309–22 and Thomas J. Misa, *A Nation of Steel: The Making of Modern America, 1865–1925* (Baltimore, Md.: Johns Hopkins University Press, 1995), pp. 23–28. The "English expert" is Frank Popplewell, *Some Modern Conditions and Recent Developments in Iron and Steel Production in America* (Manchester, U.K.: University Press, 1906), in which he specified six characteristically "American" features, one of which, the fifth, applies to the Siemens open-hearth technology, not the ET's Bessemer process. They are: "(1) the close combination between pig-iron and steel smelting plants, (2) the employment in Bessemer converters and open-hearth furnaces of molten pig-iron direct from the blast-furnace, (3) the equalization of composition of the products of a number of furnaces effected by means of a pig-iron mixer, (4) ingot-casting on cars, (5) the employment of mechanical charging-machines for open-hearth furnaces, and (6) the large replacement of hand labour by machinery in rolling-mills." Items 4 and 6 were in place from the start, and the integration of iron and steel manufacture with the ET's own blast furnaces by 1879. The blast furnaces were linked directly to the converter by 1882, with the final step in a completely continuous process, the "Jones mixer," in place in 1887, Misa, *op. cit.*, pp. 27–28, and Peter Temin, *Iron and Steel in Nineteenth-Century America: An Economic Inquiry* (Cambridge, Mass.: The MIT Press, 1964), p. 157. The quote "Where" is from Wall, *op. cit.*, p. 320. The ET's profits are in ACLC, vol. 73. They were 22.9 percent (on $750,000 capitalization) in 1876; 19 percent (on $1 million capitalization) in 1877; and 29 percent (on $1.034 million average capitalization) in 1878. The capitalization was raised from $1 million to $1.25 million on November 11, 1878 (ACLC, Vol. 4), which I average over the year.

Steel Is King

In addition to the material cited for the previous section, D.L. Burn, *The Economic History of Steelmaking, 1867–1939: A Study in Competition* (Cambridge, U.K.: Cambridge University Press, 1940) offers an excellent lens on the American industry from a British perspective, with much detailed information on comparative practices. The technology development narrative is drawn primarily from Thomas Misa, *Nation of Steel*, and Peter Temin, *Iron and Steel*. The "onions" quote is from Misa, p. 176. The definitional controversy, in its first phase, was about whether carbon contents by themselves were determinative of steel or nonsteel or whether process steps were also required—especially very high heats to ensure a more homogeneous product than typical low-carbon irons. Increased specificity of chemistry and, over time, the replacement of chemistry-based definitions with ones based on molecular structures gradually achieved consensus. Misa, pp. 31–39, has a good discussion. My appreciation of Holley's contribution to the American industry was greatly deepened by a collection of his reports and speeches in HSWP, Box 36B. For the initial reception of "American practice" in Great Britain, see D. L. Burn, *Economic History*, pp. 47–51. The "subsidy" to the Vulcan works may have been a payment to defer entering the rail business; for a discussion, see Peter Temin, *Iron and Steel*, pp. 176–78.

King of Steel

Unless otherwise noted, the narrative follows Joseph Frazier Wall, *Andrew Carnegie*. Carnegie's quote "A man who" is from *ibid.*, p. 319. His 1873 balance sheet is from HSWP Box 20, Folder 2. The cash balance showed only $4,708 at the end of the year, plus $66,327 in bills receivable. More than half of the assets were in Carnegie company shares and other interests, which were not liquid. The companies had also borrowed heavily to finance the Lucy furnace, and Carnegie was further strained by some foolish speculation by Andrew Kloman. Kloman had not realized that by investing in a mining partnership, he had placed his Carnegie, Kloman shares within reach of the partnership's creditors. Carnegie had to intervene to prevent the shares falling into outside hands. The story of the Bessemer "Fathers" meeting was actually told in 1928, or fifty-three years after the event. The quote "I shall" is from Wall, *op. cit.*, p. 331. There is no way Carnegie could have produced 19 percent of the industry's output from the outset. Steel production in 1876 was 533,000 tons; 19 percent would have been 101,000 tons. Carnegie probably produced about half that much, and almost all in rails. A 19 percent share of just steel *rails* would have required about 70,000 tons of rails, or about 40 percent more than his actual rail production. Production data from Peter Temin, *Iron and Steel*, "Appendix C: Statistics of Iron and Steel," pp. 264–85.

For the structural steel handbooks, Thomas J. Misa, *Nation of Steel*, pp. 71–74. The quote "When demand" is from D. L. Burn, *Economic History*, p. 283; "[e]xcepting" from A. L. Holley and Lenox Smith, "American Iron and Steel Works," April 26, 1878, p. 313. Captain Jones's letters are in HSWP, Box 71, Folder 1; the dates of the letters quoted are May 6, 1878, May 7, 1881, and November 2, 1883. The reports referenced are in *ibid.*, Box 72, Folder 5. The "very sad" and "Two courses" quotes are from Wall, *op. cit.*, pp. 351, 349. For "hard-driving" see Peter Temin, *Iron and Steel*, pp. 160–63. The Pennsylvania order is noted in "The Pennsylvania Railroad, No. LVIII, Maintenance of Way," *Engineer* (February 8, 1878), 100; the item also noted that 79 percent of the Pennsylvania's rails were steel by that point. The Garrett negotiation is in Steven W. Usselman, *Regulating Railroad Innovation: Business, Technology, and Politics in America, 1840–1920* (New York: Cambridge University Press, 2002), p. 89.

Gould, Back from the Grave

The account of Gould's involvement with the Union Pacific triangulates those in Maury Klein, *The Life and Legend of Jay Gould* (Baltimore, Md.: Johns Hopkins University Press, 1986); Maury Klein, *Union Pacific* (New York: Doubleday, 1987, vol.1); and Julius Grodinsky, *Jay Gould: His Business Career, 1867–1892, The Expansion of America's Railroad Empire* (Philadelphia, Pa.: University of Pennsylvania Press, 1957). The quotes "steal" and "the elevation" are from Maury Klein, *Union Pacific*, p. 308.

For the Crédit Mobilier scandal, besides the sources above, I used Robert W. Fogel, *The Union Pacific Railroad: A Case in Premature Enterprise* (Baltimore, Md.: Johns Hopkins University Press, 1960) and J. B. Crawford, *The Credit Mobilier of America: Its Origin and History* (Westport, Conn.: Greenwood Press, 1969; reprint of 1880 edition). There is a careful account of Garfield's involvement in Allan Peskin, *Garfield: A Biography* (Kent, Ohio: Kent State University Press, 1978), pp. 359–62, 412–13. Oakes Ames was clearly financing purchases of UP stock in a rising market for selected congressmen. They didn't put up any money; he just entered the supposed purchases in his book and later on wrote them a check for their profits. Garfield rather lamely said he thought his check was a loan. But while Garfield had the good sense to make an excuse, however lame, Colfax embarrassed everyone by insisting he had behaved properly, so he was punished more severely. Ames said that the verdict reminded him of "the man in Massachusetts who committed adultery and the jury brought in a verdict that he was guilty as the devil but that the woman was innocent as an angel" (Peskin, *ibid.*, p. 362).

The quote "The surest" is from Maury Klein, *Life and Legend*, p. 141; "magical wand" from Julius Grodinsky, *Jay Gould*, p. 129; and "will play us" from Klein, *Life and Legend*, p. 145. The improvement in the UP's 1874 and 1875 earnings are from reports in the *Commercial and Financial Chronicle*, June 6, 1874, and October 2, 1875. (The road's fiscal year ended in June.) The best account I found of Tom Scott's role in the 1877 political crisis is in C. Vann Woodward, *Reunion and Reaction: The Compromise of 1877 and the End of Reconstruction* (Boston: Little, Brown and Company, 1966), see especially pp. 101–22, but the story is marbled throughout the entire book, since Scott played such a central role in the Southern strategy. There is a shorter account in T. Lloyd Benson and Trina Rossman, "Re-Assessing Tom Scott, the 'Railroad Prince,'" *Paper Presented at Mid-America Conference on History, September 16 1995* (available at http://alpha.furman.edu/~benson/col-tom.html).

Gould (Almost) Conquers All

The quotes "But straightaway," "The yacht," "I am so," and "I never" are from Maury Klein, *Life and Legend*, pp. 196, 307, and 258. The first *Times* quote is from 1875, which suggests how fast Gould's reputation recovered after his departure from the Erie. For Fink, see Alfred D. Chandler, Jr., *The Visible Hand: The Managerial Revolution in American Business* (Cambridge, Mass.: Harvard University Press, 1977), pp. 116–17 and 138–48. The "hand over" quote is from Julius Grodinsky, *Jay Gould*, p. 281; Klein's "was no" is from his *Life and Legend*, p. 382. The Schumpeter quote is from Nathan Rosenberg, *Exploring the Black Box: Technology, Economics, and History* (New York: Cambridge University Press, 1994), p. 66. "The brokers" is from Grodinsky, *op. cit.*, p. 326. For the early profitability of eastern railroads (in footnote) see Albert Fishlow, *American Railroads and the Transformation of the Ante-bellum Economy* (Cambridge, Mass.: Harvard University Press, 1965). For all practical purposes, save for a few short, isolated lines, there were no railroads west of the Mississippi before the Civil War. Perkins's "economical maintenance" is from Steven W. Usselman, *Regulating Railroad Innovation*, p. 182.

Rockefeller's Machine

As in previous chapters, the narrative of the Standard triangulates the accounts in Ron Chernow, *Titan: The Life of John D. Rockefeller, Sr.* (New York: Random House, 1998); Allan Nevins, *John D. Rockefeller: The Heroic Age of American Enterprise* (New York: Charles Scribner's Sons, 1940, 2 vols.); and Ida M. Tarbell, *The History of the Standard Oil Company* (New York: Macmillan, 1925, 2 vols.). The Garland and Stowe comments on kerosene lighting are from Harold F. Williamson and Arnold R. Daum, *The American Petroleum Industry: Vol. I, The Age of Illumination, 1859–1899* (Evanston, Ill.: Northwestern University Press, 1959), p. 339. Rockefeller's statements of personal wealth are in RAC, Series F, "Trial Balances, 1875 and 1897" and "Trial Balances, 1890–1915." The quote "from 90" is in Nevins, *op. cit.*, I:486. The Archbold letters are in RAC, Series B; all the letters were written between December 1877 and February 1878. The A. J. Cassatt quotes are from U.S. House of Representatives, *Investigation of Certain Trusts: Report in Relation to the Sugar Trust and Standard Oil Trust by the Committee on Manufactures* (Washington, D.C.: U.S. Government Printing Office, 1889), pp. 178–79, 177. For the friction over storage after the Bradford production boom, the best detail is in Williamson, *op. cit.*, pp. 189–94 and 383–90; and for Tidewater and the implications of long-distance pipelines *ibid.*, pp. 430–62.

Running the Machine
The quote is from Ida M. Tarbell, *The History of the Standard Oil*, II:234–35.

6. The First Mass Consumer Society

Wanamaker's opening is in Thomas J. Schlereth, *Victorian America: Transformations in Everyday Life, 1876–1915* (New York: HarperCollins, 1991), pp. 146–47. The best history of the growth and culture of department stores is Susan Benson Porter, *Counter-Cultures: Saleswomen, Managers, and Customers in American Department Stores, 1890–1940* (Urbana, Ill.: University of Illinois Press, 1986); also see Alfred D. Chandler, Jr., *The Visible Hand: The Managerial Revolution in American Business* (Cambridge, Mass.: Harvard University Press, 1977), pp. 224–29. The history of Ivory soap and Procter & Gamble is available at the company's Web site, www.pg.com. My appreciation to Ed Rider of P&G Corporate Archives for estimates of P&G's late nineteenth-century earnings. Pharmacist's comment is Alfred Smetham, F.C.S., "Soap Manufacture and the Soap of Commerce," *American Journal of Pharmacy*, vol. 56, no. 3 (March 1884), 7–12. The quote is on 8.

The New Middle Class
The Whitman quote is in Stuart M. Blumin, *The Emergence of the Middle Class: Social Experience in the American City, 1760–1900* (New York: Cambridge University Press, 1989), p. 1. The account in this section for the most part follows Blumin, supplemented as noted. The de Tocqueville quote is from Alexis de Tocqueville, *Democracy in America* (New York: Alfred A. Knopf, 1945, 2 vols.), I:53. Potter quote is from David Potter, *People of Plenty* (Chicago: University of Chicago Press, 1954), p. 96. The discussion of inequality and occupational mobility in the next two paragraphs follows Clayne Pope, "Inequality in the Nineteenth Century," in Stanley Engerman and Robert Gallman, eds., *The Cambridge Economic History of the United States, Vol. II, The Long Nineteenth Century* (Cambridge, U.K.: Cambridge University Press, 2000), pp. 109–42.

A common index of wealth and income inequality is the "Gini coefficient." The degree of inequality is measured on a scale of 0–1. (At 1, one household owns everything.) Gini coefficients were between 0.81–0.83 in 1860 and 1870, and was 0.78 in 2003 (all very high inequality scores), compared with only 0.66 in 1774. The richest 1 percent owned 26 percent of all wealth in both 1890 and 1962, but 34 percent in 2003. Wealth concentration in the top 10 percent of households, however, is 72 percent in 1890, 62 percent in 1962, and 69 percent in 2003 (i.e., the 2003 data show a top class even more skewed toward the top 1 percent). Income is usually about half as concentrated as wealth, but nineteenth-century income data are too sketchy for the analysis. For details on Gini coefficients, see Vincenzo Quadrini and José-Victor Rios-Rull, "Understanding the U.S. Distribution of Wealth," *Federal Reserve Bank of Minneapolis Quarterly Review*, vol. 21, no. 2 (Spring 1997), 22–36.

The 1887 *Harpers* article, data on white-collar growth, and account of Tailer are in Blumin, *op. cit.*, pp. 274, 267, 112–14. Zunz clerical data are from Olivier Zunz, *Making America Corporate, 1870–1920* (Chicago: University of Chicago Press, 1990), pp. 127–31. The Boston study, ethnicity, and discussion of artisan/businessman status are from Blumin, *op. cit.*, pp. 271, 291, and 134–37.

For developments in housing, Donald E. Sutherland, *The Expansion of Everyday Life—1860–1876* (Fayetteville, Ark.: University of Arkansas Press, 2000), pp. 27–41, has a good discussion, as does Blumin and Richard L. Bushman, *The Refinement of America: Persons, Houses, Cities* (New York: Alfred A. Knopf, 1992), pp. 238–79. For living conditions on early nineteenth-century farms, see Jack Larkin, *The Reshaping of Everyday Life, 1790–1840* (New York: Harper & Row, 1988), especially pp. 124–30. The quote "piggery" is from Sutherland, *op. cit.*, p. 69. For water-borne diseases, see David Cutler and Grant Miller, "The Role of Public Health Improvements in Health Advances: the 20th Century United States," *NBER Working Paper 10511* (Cambridge, Mass.: National Bureau of Economic Research, May 2004). Isabel

March's quote from *A Hazard of New Fortunes* is on pp. 44–45 of the Modern Library Paperback Edition. Quote "much larger" is from Stuart M. Blumin, *The Emergence*, p. 155. For education reform, see Donald H. Parkerson and Jo Ann Parkerson, *Transitions in American Education: A Social History of Teaching* (New York: RoutledgeFalmer, 2001); the quote "the student should" is from pp. 156–57.

Things

The piano and related quote are from Montgomery Ward & Co., *Catalogue and Buyer's Guide, Spring and Summer, 1895* (New York: Dover Publications, 1969, facsimile edition), pp. 238–39; the Sears items are from Sears Roebuck & Co., *1897 Sears Roebuck Catalogue* (New York: Chelsea House Publishers, 1968, facsimile edition), "Drug Department" (pages not numbered). And see Bloomingdale Brothers, *Bloomingdale's Illustrated 1886 Catalog* (New York: Dover Publications, 1988, facsimile edition). History of mail order draws from W. L. Brann, *The Romance of Montgomery Ward & Co.* (New York: Campbell, Starring & Co., 1929); Boris Emmet and John E. Jeuck, *Catalogues and Counters: A History of Sears, Roebuck and Company* (Chicago: University of Chicago Press, 1950); Cecil C. Hoge, *The First Hundred Years Are the Toughest: What We Can Learn from a Century of Competition between Sears and Wards* (Berkeley, Calif.: Ten Speed Press, 1988); and Gordon E. Weil, *Sears Roebuck U.S.A.: The Great American Catalog Store and How It Grew* (New York: Stein and Day, 1977). Wanamaker quote is from Emmett and Jeuck, p. 13.

The section on consumer items, except as noted, is from Thomas J. Schlereth, *Victorian America*, pp. 141–67; immigrant mother's quote is on p. 167. The Heinz sign is from James Traub, *The Devil's Playground: A Century of Pleasure and Profit in Times Square* (New York: Random House, 2004), p. 44; the grocer doggerel from Otto L. Bettmann, *The Good Old Days— They Were Terrible!* (New York: Random House, 1974), p. 117.

Armory Practice Redux

This section draws primarily from David A. Hounshell, *From American System to Mass Production, 1800–1932: The Development of Manufacturing Technology in the United States* (Baltimore, Md.: Johns Hopkins University Press, 1984), especially pp. 189–215, 67–123. For Pope, in addition to Hounshell, see Stephen B. Goddard, *Colonel Albert Pope and His American Dream Machines: The Life and Times of a Bicycle Tycoon Turned an Automotive Pioneer* (Jefferson, N.C.: McFarland, 2000). The quote "father" is from p. 190. For Cleveland, see Naomi R. Lamoreaux, Margaret Levenstein, Kenneth L. Sokoloff, "Financing Invention during the Second Industrial Revolution: Cleveland, Ohio, 1870–1920," *NBER Working Paper 10923* (Cambridge, Mass.: National Bureau of Economic Research, November 2004). The Sears executive's "money, organization" and brains is from Boris Emmet and John E. Jeuck, *Catalogues and Counters*, p. 4.

Anxiety

The de Tocqueville quote is from *op. cit.*, II:106. The Beecher quote is from Karen Halttunen, *Confidence Men and Painted Women: A Study of Middle-Class Culture in America, 1830–1870* (New Haven, Conn.: Yale University Press, 1982), p. 23; for his shopping addiction, Daniel Horowitz, *The Morality of Spending: Attitudes toward the Consumer Society in America, 1875–1940* (Chicago: Ivan R. Dee, 1985), p. 11. Halttunen has a fine discussion on sources of class anxiety; see pp. 191–97 for a summary. The discussion on population trends and contraceptive practices relies on Jenny Bourne Wahl, "New Results on the Decline in Household Fertility in the United States from 1750 to 1900," in Stanley Engerman and Robert Gallman, eds., *Long-Term Factors in American Economic Growth: National Bureau of Economic Research, Studies in Income and Wealth*, vol. 51 (Chicago: University of Chicago Press, 1986), pp. 391–438; and Paul A. David and Warren C. Sanderson, "Rudimentary Contraceptive Methods and the American Transition to Marital Fertility Control, 1855–1915," in *ibid.*, pp. 307–90. The quote on modern China is from *The Economist*, November 20, 2004.

7. Paper Tigers

The *Tribune* quote is available on the extensive Fire Web site maintained by the Chicago Historical Society at http://www.chicagohs.org/fire/. For the "Chicago school," I follow Carl W. Condit, *The Chicago School of Architecture: A History of Commercial and Public Building in the Chicago Area, 1875–1925* (Chicago: University of Chicago Press, 1964). The quote "Bearing in mind" from John Root, of Burnham and Root, is on p. 49. For a discussion of Chicago's leading role in steel-frame architecture, especially compared to New York, see Thomas J. Misa, *A Nation of Steel: The Making of Modern America, 1865–1925* (Baltimore, Md.: Johns Hopkins University Press, 1995), pp. 63–69. For the creation of a paper management industry, see JoAnn Yates, "Investing in Information: Supply and Demand Forces in the Use of Information in American Firms, 1850–1920," in Peter Temin, ed., *Inside the Business Enterprise: Historical Perspectives on the Use of Information* (Chicago: University of Chicago Press, 1991), pp. 117–60.

The Conquest of the Clerks
There are good discussions of the different filters used by economic and business historians in Peter Temin, ed., *Inside the Business*. See especially the essay, Daniel M. G. Raff and Peter Temin, "Business History and Recent Economic Theory: Imperfect Information, Incentives, and the Internal Organization of Firms," pp. 7–40. A key difference is that economists tend to treat the "firm" as a kind of rational monad, like the "consumer," while business historians try to deconstruct the monads, especially to illuminate the nonrational parts. For a highly intelligent discussion on these issues, related to the history of the steel industry, see Thomas J. Misa, *A Nation of Steel*, pp. 270–82.

The description of Holley's exhortations is based on the collection of his reports and speeches in HSWP, Box 36B, including "Report to the Bessemer Steel Company Limited, No. 1, 1880: The John Cockerill Works, Practice and Costs, at Seraing, Belgium"; "Report to the Bessemer Steel Company Limited No. 3, 1880: The Rail Mill and General Plant and Practice at the Wilson, Cammel & Co."; "Report to the Bessemer Steel Company Limited, No. 2 1881, Krupp's Practice and Plant"; "On American Rolling Mills," *Journal of the Iron and Steel Institute*, No. II, 1874; reprinted by Bessemer Council; and "Address of President A. L. Holley before the American Institute of Mining Engineers, October 26, 1874." The crisis in heavy rails is in Steven W. Usselman, *Regulating Railroad Innovation: Business, Technology, and Politics in America, 1840–1920* (New York: Cambridge University Press, 2002), pp. 223–39; and in structural steel, Thomas J. Misa, *A Nation of Steel*, pp. 60–83. For the increased links between science and business, and the data on professional sciences and university development, see Olivier Zunz, "Producers, Brokers, and Users of Knowledge: The Institutional Matrix," in Dorothy Ross, ed., *Modernist Impulses in the Human Sciences, 1870–1930* (Baltimore, Md.: Johns Hopkins University Press, 1994), pp. 290–307.

For industrial securities, I used Thomas R. Navin and Marion V. Sears, "The Rise of a Market for Industrial Securities, 1887–1902," *Business History Review* 29:1 (Spring 1955), 105–38; and Gene Smiley, "The Expansion of the U.S. Securities Market at the Turn of the Century," *Business History Review* 55:1 (Spring 1981), 75–85. For Samuel Dodd and the Standard, see Allan Nevins, *John D. Rockefeller: The Heroic Age of American Enterprise* (New York: Charles Scribner's Sons, 1940, 2 vols.), I:603–17. The quotes "the receipt," "the trusts," and "merely" are from U.S. House of Representatives, *Investigation of Certain Trusts: Report in Relation to the Sugar Trust and Standard Oil Trust by the Committee on Manufactures* (Washington, D.C.: U.S. Government Printing Office, 1889), pp. II, 300. Rockefeller's 1896 stock holdings are from RAC, Series F, "Trial Balances, 1890–1915." The Carnegie accounting example is David Brody, *Steelworkers in America: The Nonunion Era* (New York: Russell and Russell, 1970), p. 19.

For changing context of management-labor relations, see David Brody, *Steelworkers in America*, and David Montgomery, *The Fall of the House of Labor: The Workplace, the State, and American Labor Activism, 1865–1925* (New York: Cambridge University Press, 1977). Bruce Laurie, *Artisans into Workers, Labor in Nineteenth-Century America* (Urbana, Ill.: University of

Illinois Press, 1997) is a fine survey with an extensive discussion of Homestead. For the effects of technology improvements on mill operations, I generally follow the excellent discussion in Brody, pp. 7–79. The "have to be" quote is from p. 34.

Homestead

The basic narrative follows the accounts in Kenneth Warren, *Triumphant Capitalism: Henry Clay Frick and the Industrial Transformation of America* (Pittsburgh, Pa.: University of Pittsburgh Press, 1996), pp. 63–97, and Joseph Frazier Wall, *Andrew Carnegie* (Pittsburgh, Pa.: University of Pittsburgh Press, 1989), pp. 537–82. The Carnegie labor quotes are in Joseph Frazier Wall, *Andrew Carnegie,* pp. 525–26, the "young & rather," p. 575. The Jones quotes on wages are in HSWP, Box 71, Folder 1; his "entirely out of" is in Wall, *op. cit.,* p. 521. The story of Carnegie's use of Pinkertons at the ET is in James Howard Bridge, *The Inside History of the Carnegie Steel Company, A Romance of Millions* (New York: Aldine, 1903), pp. 189–90. Wall oddly omits the Pinkertons, instead following an account in Burton J. Hendrick, *The Life of Andrew Carnegie* (Garden City, N.Y.: Doubleday, Doran, 1932, 2 vols.), I:388–403, a hagiographic work, which in turn cites only Carnegie's "own relation" many years later to a congressional committee. Warren, a careful scholar, follows Bridge. The two quotes are Bridge's. The Gates quote and "patronizing" examples in the footnote are from Kenneth Warren, *Triumphant Capitalism,* pp. 120, 136, 211, and 185. The quotes "Amalgamated placed," "foolish . . . repugnant," "long and," "Matters at," and "I do not" are from Joseph Frazier Wall, *Andrew Carnegie,* pp. 579, 574, 541, 561, and 563; "something of," Kenneth Warren, *op. cit.,* p. 89; "These are," Wall, *op. cit.,* p. 624.

The one-fifth reduction and the 58 pages of footnotes are in David Brody, *Steelworkers,* pp. 45, 53. The Jones cost reduction and data for my earnings impact calculation are from HSWP, Box 72, Folder 5. And see the table in Kenneth Warren, *Triumphant Capitalism,* p. 110. For "dismal labor policies," Thomas J. Misa, *A Nation of Steel,* p. 270. The quote "agreed with practically" is in U.S. House of Representatives, *Investigation of Certain Trusts,* p. 29. "The Works are" from Wall, *op. cit.,* p. 575. For the Ludlow story in the footnote, I used Ron Chernow, *Titan: The Life of John D. Rockefeller, Sr.* (New York: Random House, 1998), pp. 578–85. The Garland account is in Hamlin Garland, "Homestead and Its Perilous Trades, Impressions of a Visit," *McClure's Magazine,* vol. III, no. 1 (June 1894), 3–19, on p. 3. Jones and Schwab could always rev up competitions with other mills and men would work willingly till they dropped. The quote "a good deal" is from J. Stephen Jeans, ed., *American Industrial Conditions and Competition: Reports of the Commissioners Appointed by the British Iron Trade Association to Enquire into the Iron, Steel, and Allied Industries of the United States* (London, 1902), p. 329. "If Pittsburgh is" is quoted in Kenneth Warren, *Triumphant Capitalism,* pp. 111–12. For Jeans's wage mystification, J. Stephen Jeans, ed., *op. cit.,* pp. 316–17. Carnegie's "to rake up," "neither the power," "ability, fairness," "thought the three," "Kind master, tell," and "alas" are in Joseph Frazier Wall, *Andrew Carnegie,* pp. 576–77, 568, and Andrew Carnegie, *The Autobiography of Andrew Carnegie* (Boston: Northeastern University Press edition, 1986), p. 223; The *St. Louis Post-Dispatch* editorial, Wall, pp. 572–73.

The Creation of the Carnegie Company

The sequence of events here follows Kenneth Warren, *Triumphant Capitalism.* The "Mr. Carnegie" and "A. C. must have" quotes are from pp. 217, 218; "every movement of," James Howard Bridge, *Inside History,* p. 274. For Schwab, see Robert Hessen, *Steel Titan: The Life of Charles M. Schwab* (New York: Oxford University Press, 1975). See Joseph Frazier Wall, *Andrew Carnegie,* pp. 600–12, for the ore deals with Rockefeller. Rockefeller's "astonished" quote is from Allan Nevins, *John D. Rockefeller: The Heroic Age of American Enterprise* (New York: Charles Scribner's Sons, 1940, 2 vols.), II:399. The financial data for the valuation discussions are all from ACLC; the calculations are mine. The quotes "with great" and "his oldest" are from Kenneth Warren, *Triumphant Capitalism,* p. 230. Gary's "received no encouragement" is in U.S. House of Representatives, *Hearings before the Committee on Investigation of United States Steel Corporation (Stanley Committee),* (Washington, D.C.: U.S. Government Printing

Office, 1912, 8 vols.), I:205. Quote "making securities" is in Kenneth Warren, *op. cit.,* p. 232. Wall has a somewhat different account of Moore's option from Warren's (Wall, *op. cit.,* pp. 728–32, although in the note on p. 1094 he concedes that the episode is murky). Wall has Carnegie asking for $2 million pro rata for the partners. The $1,170,000 would have represented his 53 percent, while the other partners consented to waive their shares. The *Iron Age* quotes, "not one," "attention to" are from Warren, *op. cit.,* pp. 234–35, 237. Carnegie's note confirming his intent to return the $170,000 is reproduced in James Howard Bridge, *op. cit.,* p. 320; the Frick/Phipps cable describing their bonus is in Wall, *op. cit.,* p. 730. "Declaration of," "For years" are from Warren, *op. cit.,* pp. 245, 257. "The Directors have" quote is from a letter from Phipps to Carnegie, April 21, 1900, ACLC, vol. 75. The details of the 1898 profits numbers are in ACLC, vol. 61; an analysis of actual earnings in 1900 is in the next chapter and Appendix I. Carnegie's proposal to delay bond interest was in a cable for the directors' meeting on July 28, 1900, ACLC, vol. 76. The Phipps offer is in Schwab to Carnegie, February 3, 1900, ACLC, vol. 72.

Note on Frick's performance: Carnegie Steel's first full year was 1893. Profit tabulations below for pre–1893 period consolidate Carnegie Bros., which owned the ET, and Carnegie, Phipps, which was formed to acquire the Homestead Works. See ACLC, vol. 61 and vol. 73.

Year	Profit	Firm
1886	2,925,350	C, Ph/CB
1887	3,441,887	C, Ph/CB
1888	1,941,555	C, Ph/CB
1889	3,540,000	C, Ph/CB
1890	5,350,000	C, Ph/CB
1891	4,300,000	C, Ph/CB
1892	4,000,000	C, Ph/CB
1893	3,000,000	C. Steel
1894	4,000,000	C. Steel
1895	5,000,000	C. Steel
1896	6,000,000	C. Steel
1897	7,000,000	C. Steel
1898	11,500,000	C. Steel
1899	21,000,000	C. Steel

Frick took over just Carnegie Bros. in 1889. Wall, Carnegie's biographer, says of Frick's performance: "In the year that he had been in charge of Carnegie Brothers, the profit had nearly doubled, from $1,941,555 to $3,540,000" (p. 535). That would indeed have been spectacular, but Wall is giving Frick credit for all the profit improvement, while he was actually in charge of only half the business. (Wall was probably misled by a table in ACLC 61 that allocates all steel earnings to Carnegie Bros., when it obviously includes both of the companies.) Wall further exaggerates, however, because 1888 profits were seriously affected by the five-month strike at the ET in which Carnegie resorted to the Pinkertons. As can be seen, 1889 profits were essentially the same as in the pre-strike year of 1887. In other words, fairly compared, there was arguably no improvement at all, and to the extent that there was, only a portion of it can be assigned to Frick.

Profits really took off in 1896 and 1897, which is when Carnegie waged a scorched-earth rail price war, reaping huge profit gains while other companies were driven to the wall. That degree of productivity advantage takes a long time to create, and probably owed much to Frick's unification and systematization of the company's operations. The elevation of Schwab must also have had an effect—he was very close to factory operations and was the best technologist in senior management—but Frick had created the unified machine for Schwab to exercise his skills upon. The even bigger jumps in 1898 and 1899 were mostly the consequence of very rapid price increases in most product lines, especially rails, assisted by the high-margin armor business. Even with all qualifications, Carnegie's internal campaign against an executive with such a record looks like sheer, petulant destructiveness.

Trust-Busting

The more important works I used in this section include, among others, Rudolph J. R. Peritz, *Competition Policy in America, 1888–1992: History, Rhetoric, Law* (New York: Oxford University Press, 1996); Tony A. Freyer, *Regulating Big Business: Antitrust in Great Britain and America, 1880–1990* (New York: Cambridge University Press, 1992); "Business Law and American Economic History," in Stanley Engerman and Robert Gallman, eds., *The Cambridge Economic History of the United States, Vol. II, The Long Nineteenth Century* (Cambridge, U.K.: Cambridge University Press, 2000), pp. 435–82; and Richard Hofstadter, "What Happened to the Antitrust Movement?: Notes on the Evolution of an American Creed," in Robert F. Himmelberg, ed., *Antitrust and Business Regulation in the Postwar Era, 1946–1964* (New York: Garland Publishing, 1994). The quotes "way of life" and "farmers and small-town" are from Richard Hofstadter, *ibid.*, pp. 74, 75.

For the political and business interests in railroad rate regulation see Albro Martin, "The Troubled Subject of Railroad Regulation in the Gilded Age—A Reappraisal," in Robert F. Himmelberg, ed., *The Rise of Big Business and the Beginnings of Antitrust and Railroad Regulation* (New York: Garland Publishing, 1994), pp. 231–64. Joshua Bernhardt, *The Interstate Commerce Commission: Its History, Activities, and Organization* (Baltimore, Md.: The Johns Hopkins Press, 1923) offers the more traditional interpretation. For the shift in the Supreme Court's interpretation, see Rudolph J. R. Peritz, *Competition Policy*, pp. 9–58, and Tony A. Freyer, *Regulating Big Business*, pp. 132–49. For the *Northern Securities* background, the case itself has an excellent summary, *Northern Securities Co. v. U.S.*, 193 U.S. 197 (1904), and see Maury Klein, *The Life and Legend of E. H. Harriman* (Chapel Hill, N.C.: University of North Carolina Press, 2000), pp. 225–39, 307–16.

Spotlight on the Standard

A crisp narrative of the Standard's legal and business difficulties is in Harold F. Williamson and Arnold R. Daum, *The American Petroleum Industry: Vol. II, The Age of Energy, 1899–1959* (Evanston, Ill.: Northwestern University Press, 1963), pp. 5–19; a more detailed account is in Allan Nevins, *John D. Rockefeller: The Heroic Age of American Enterprise* (New York: Charles Scribner's Sons, 1940, 2 vols.), II:499–613. The "inordinately voluminous" quote is from *Standard Oil Co. of N.J. v. U.S.* 221 U.S. 1 (1910), pp. 48–49. For predatory pricing, John S. McGee, "Predatory Price Cutting: The Standard Oil (N.J.) Case," *Journal of Law and Economics* 1:1 (October 1958), 137–69. The "a single instance" quote is on p. 143. Also see his "Predatory Price Cutting Revisited," *Journal of Law and Economics* 23:2 (October 1980), 289–330. The differing interpretation mentioned in the note is from Elizabeth Granitz and Benjamin Klein, "Monopolization by 'Raising Rivals' Costs': The Standard Oil Case," *Journal of Law and Economics* 39:1 (April 1996), 1–47. The quotes "many instances" and "may be considered" are from the United States Industrial Commission, *Preliminary Report on Trusts and Industrial Combinations*, vol. I (Washington, D.C.: U.S. Government Printing Office, 1900), p. 17. Jeremiah Jenks was the staff director of the Industrial Commission, and organized his findings in a book, *The Trust Problem* (Garden City, N.Y.: Doubleday, Page and Co., 1914), which went through multiple editions for some twenty years after the hearings. It contains much useful information and charts the steady fall in petroleum product prices during the Standard's reign. The Archbold testimony on rebates is in United States Industrial Commission, II:516–17. The "the largest fine" quote is from Ron Chernow, *Titan: The Life of John D. Rockefeller, Sr.* (New York: Random House, 1998), p. 293.

The Indiana case details are from *United States v. Standard Oil Co. of Indiana*, 155 Federal 1st 305 (1907); *Standard Oil Co. of Indiana v. United States*, 165 Federal 1st 594, 1908; and, finally, 170 Federal 1st 988 (1909). Also see the reports in *Railway Age and Gazette* (January 31, 1908), p. 161 (for the local prevalence of six-to-seven-cent rates), and July 24, 1908, p. 594. Reversible errors were held by the court of appeals to include: the exclusion of the freight agent's and traffic manager's testimony, the failure to lay a foundation for the Standard's ability to know what the real tariff was, and the failure to lay any foundation for including the holding company as the defendant, rather than the named defendant in the case, Standard Oil of Indiana. The opinion was couched in notably acidic language. One judge remarks that reversal was "inevitable," implying that Landis intentionally wrote a sensational decision knowing it could not withstand review. Landis refused to preside over the retrial. The second judge ruled, among other things, that the Alton had never filed a "final" oil tariff, as required by the ICA, since the 1895 tariff applied to oil only by virtue of a state ruling, which could readily be changed. For the Whiting refinery background, see Allan Nevins, *op. cit.*, II:7–11. The $91,000 figure for the value of the twelve-cent premium is my calculation: the standard tank car of the period carried 190 42-gallon barrels, and I used the weight/volume conversion tables from the American Society of Petroleum Engineers (0.136 tons per bbl.). The "gummy" and "bitter" quotes are from Harold F. Williamson and Arnold R. Daum, *The American Petroleum Industry: Vol. I, The Age of Illumination, 1859–1899* (Evanston, Ill.: Northwestern University Press , 1959), p. 505. The "administrative fatigue" quote is from Harold F. Williamson and Arnold R. Daum, *op. cit.*, p. 6.

The "Good" Tycoon

The Carnegie/Cassatt episode is in Joseph Frazier Wall, *Andrew Carnegie*, pp. 775–83; "the rebates you" quote is on p. 783. All of the pools mentioned were discussed at various Carnegie Steel board meetings during 1899, ACLC, vols. 61–71. For collusion on armor, see Thomas J. Misa, *A Nation of Steel*, pp. 103–6, 125–29; "arithmetic precision" and "Probably the least" quotes are on pp. 106, 126–27; and see p. 322, n. 103, for an estimate of armor profits. The Schwab "the proposition was" is in ACLC, vol. 77.

8. The Age of Morgan

The account of the *Corsair* episode and Carnegie's railroad venture primarily follows Joseph Frazier Wall, *Andrew Carnegie* (Pittsburgh, Pa.: University of Pittsburgh Press, 1989), pp. 512–17. The death count is from the Web site of the Pennsylvania State Archives. And see Jean Strouse, *Morgan: American Financier* (New York: Random House, 1999), pp. 246–49. For Rothschild diplomacy, see Niall Ferguson, *The House of Rothschild: The World's Banker, 1849–1999* (New York: Viking Penguin, 1999), pp. 128–30.

"Jupiter"

The quotes "Jupiter" and "driving power" are from Vincent P. Carosso, *The Morgans: Private International Bankers, 1854–1913* (Cambridge, Mass.: Harvard University Press, 1987), pp. 433–34. Except as indicated, I use Carosso as the basic source for the banking transactions in this chapter. His book assigns a separate heading to each deal. The Schiff quote is on p. 387. For economic implications of crashes, I follow Paul W. Rhode, "Gallman's Annual Output Series for the United States, 1834–1909," *National Bureau of Economic Research, Working Paper 8860* (April 2002). Gallman cautioned about the accuracy of year-to-year changes, but even at the most extreme margins of error, there is no question about the severity of the 1893–94 crash.

The Unbearable Elusiveness of Peace

The quotes from "1984 study" are from Thomas K. McCraw, *Prophets of Regulation: Charles Francis Adams, Louis D. Brandeis, James M. Landis, Alfred E. Kahn* (Cambridge, Mass.: Harvard University Press, 1984), p. 75. For the Gould/Adams/Morgan search for railroad peace, I follow Maury Klein, *The Life and Legend of Jay Gould* (Baltimore, Md.: Johns Hopkins University Press, 1986), pp. 435–42 and 453–61. For Adams's background, I follow Thomas McCraw, *op. cit.*, pp. 1–56. The quotes "simply send," "Jay Gould," and "Smaller, meaner" are from Maury Klein, *Jay Gould*, pp. 440, 455, 457.

Harriman and Morgan

For Harriman, I follow Maury Klein, *The Life and Legend of E. H. Harriman* (Chapel Hill, N.C.: University of North Carolina Press, 2000). For his UP and SP investment levels, see pp. 144, 256. The Northern Securities background is clearly set out in the opinion *Northern Securities Co. v. U.S.*, 193 U.S. 197 (1904); for the atmospherics, I use Maury Klein *E. H. Harriman*, pp. 220–39, 307–16. The speculation on Schiff's motives is my own. I find it inconceivable that he would have disclosed his position to Hill if he had really wanted to win.

The Accidental Central Banker

The account here basically follows that in Vincent P. Carosso, *The Morgans*, pp. 311–49, 528–49. See also Matthew Simon, "The Morgan-Belmont Syndicate of 1895 and Intervention in the Foreign-Exchange Market," *Business History Review*, vol. 42, no. 4 (Winter 1968), pp. 385–417. (The Belmont house served as the Rothschilds' American representative); and for a careful summary of the Tennessee Coal and Iron episode, Jean Strouse, *Morgan*, pp. 582–93. Trade and current account data are from United States Bureau of the Census, *Historical Statistics of the United States, Colonial Times to 1970* (Washington, D.C.: U.S. Government Printing Office, 1975, 2 vols.) II: Series U, 1–25, 187–200.

The Great Merger Movement

The discussion here, and the statistical data, follow Naomi Lamoreaux, *The Great Merger Movement in American Business, 1895–1904* (New York: Cambridge University Press, 1985); much of the book is a reevaluation of Alfred D. Chandler, Jr., *The Visible Hand: The Managerial Revolution in American Business* (Cambridge, Mass.: The Belknap Press of Harvard University Press, 1977). See also Vincent P. Carosso, *Investment Banking in America: A History* (Cambridge, Mass.: Harvard University Press, 1970), pp. 43–46. The 1900 employment data is from Stanley Lebergott, *The Americans: An Economic Record* (New York: Norton, 1984), p. 321. The Gompers quote is in James Gilbert, *Designing the Industrial State: The Intellectual Pursuit of Collectivism in America, 1880–1940* (Chicago: Quadrangle Books, 1972) , p. 52. The reconstruction of the work Moore or other brokers undertook in these mergers is based on my own experience in deals with far fewer participants; the numbers of participants Moore managed to work with is especially impressive. For details on several deals, including instances where the promoters' interests turned out to be worthless, see Jeremiah Whipple Jenks, *The Trust Problem* (Garden City, N.Y.: Doubleday, Page and Co., 1914), pp. 88–95.

The Birth of Big Steel

The overall narrative of the U.S. Steel deal triangulates the accounts in Joseph Frazier Wall, *Andrew Carnegie*, pp. 767–93, and Kenneth Warren, *Big Steel: The First Century of the United States Steel Corporation, 1901–2001* (Pittsburgh, Pa.: University of Pittsburgh Press, 2001), pp. 7–21, supplemented by the materials in ACLC and PML. I greatly benefited from an e-mail dialogue with Professor Warren on this material.

For the electricity wars, see Jill Jonnes's fine *Empires of Light: Edison, Tesla, Westinghouse and the Race to Electrify the World* (New York: Random House, 2003). The quotes "The United States," "the price," "I believe," "prevent utter" are from *Stanley Committee*, VIII:163–64, I:220, I:253. The price calculations are in *ibid.*, VIII:161–62. The quotes "an object lesson" and "do business" are from David Brody, *Steelworkers in America: The Nonunion Era* (New York: Russell and Russell, 1970), pp. 6–7. Carnegie's "The autumn" is in Kenneth Warren, *Big Steel*, p. 11.

For the finished steel competition, "favorite child" from Joseph Frazier Wall, *Andrew Carnegie*, p. 782; Jeans's comment on National Tube, J. Stephen Jeans, ed., *American Industrial Conditions and Competition: Reports of the Commissioners Appointed by the British Iron Trade Association to Enquire into the Iron, Steel, and Allied Industries of the United States* (London, 1902), p. 154. Carnegie's "Your cable" and Schwab's "I do not see," ACLC 75, 76. Carnegie's Conneaut exposition is from *Stanley Committee*, I:116–17. Board vote and Schwab's January 24, 1901, letter in ACLC 81. Morgan's quote "Carnegie is" is in Joseph Frazier Wall,

Andrew Carnegie, p. 784. There are slight variations in all the chronologies of the U. S. Steel deal, but all follow the contours here, except perhaps John W. Gates's self-serving account before the Stanley Committee. Schwab's article is Charles M. Schwab, "What May Be Expected in the Steel and Iron Industry," *North American Review* 172 (May 1901), 655–64. The quote is on p. 656. His "I knew exactly" quote is in Robert Hessen, *Steel Titan: The Life of Charles M. Schwab* (New York: Oxford University Press, 1975), p. 117.

On the final deal proceeds allocations: to accommodate Carnegie's insistence on receiving gold bonds even for his stock, the additional $80 million (tacked on for the presumed 1900 and 1901 profits) was allocated entirely to the other shareholders. In round numbers, according to the U.S. Steel Syndicate Book in PML, the figures worked out as below:

	($ in thousands)	
	Carnegie Co.	U.S. Steel
Carnegie		
Bonds	$86,000	$226,000
Preferred	93,000	0
Minority		
Bonds	74,000	74,000
Preferred	67,000	98,000
Common	0	92,000
Total		$490,000

The final numbers reflect several minor adjustments. Carnegie's $226 million in bonds comprised a 1 for 1 swap of Carnegie bonds for USS bonds and 1.5 USS bonds for each share of Carnegie stock (1.5 x 93 = 140; 140 + 86 = 226 million). The others got $74 million in USS bonds for an equal amount of Carnegie bonds, plus 1.5 times their shares in USS preferred *plus* an additional 1.5 times their shares in USS common. Their total preferred and common shares received were thus a 3:1 multiple (67 x 3 = 200 million, which for a variety of minor reasons was adjusted down to the $190 million [98 + 92] shown on the table). The ratio of gold bonds in the total consideration was (226 + 74 = 300)/490 = 61.2%.

And Then There Was Rockefeller . . .

The account of the Rockefeller ore fields purchase follows Allan Nevins, *John D. Rockefeller: The Heroic Age of American Enterprise* (New York: Charles Scribner's Sons, 1940, 2 vols.), II:417–26. The Morgan exchange with Gary and the Moores is on p. 418. (Nevins is quoting Ida Tarbell's biography of Elbert Gary, which was written with Gary's close cooperation, so it is assumed that Gary was the source of the story. It might be noted that Tarbell greatly admired Gary, a monopolist who *raised* prices, while she reviled Rockefeller, who lowered them.) Rockefeller's quote on Morgan, and Nevins's comment, are on p. 419. The Mr. Dooley quote is from Jean Strouse, *Morgan,* p. 405.

For post–U. S. Steel sources of innovation, see Thomas J. Misa, *A Nation of Steel: The Making of Modern America, 1865–1925* (Baltimore, Md.: Johns Hopkins University Press, 1995), pp. 170–285. For the Pennsylvania's role in developing steel technology, Janet T. Koedler, "Market Structure, Industrial Research, and Consumers of Innovation: Forging Backward Links to Research in the Turn of the Century U. S. Steel Industry," *Business History Review* 67:1 (Spring 1993), 98–139.

Assessing Morgan

The Brandeis quotes "conservative" and "financial," Henry Lee Staples and Alpheus Thomas Mason, *The Fall of a Railroad Empire: Brandeis and the New Haven Merger Battle* (Syracuse, N.Y.: Syracuse University Press, 1947), p. 154. The New Haven summary follows Staples and Mason, as well as Vincent P. Carosso, *The Morgans,* especially pp. 608–12. IMM account follows Thomas R. Navin and Marion V. Sears, "A Study in Merger: Formation of the International Mercantile Marine Company," *Business History Review* 28:4 (December 1954), 291–328. The "how even" quote is on p. 291. Carosso treats it on pp. 481–86 and 491–93. The Roosevelt story is in Jean Strouse, *Morgan*, p. 441. The Brandeis "J. P. Morgan" quote is from Louis D. Brandeis, *Other People's Money: And How the Bankers Use It* (Washington, D.C.: National Home Library, 1933), pp. 36–37.

9. America Rules

For Rothschild, Morgan, and the Boer War, see Niall Ferguson, *The House of Rothschild: The World's Banker, 1899–1999* (New York: Viking Penguin, 1999), pp. 364–68. For comparative output and productivity data, I used Paul Bairoch, "International Industrialization Levels from 1750 to 1980," *Journal of European Economic History* 11:2 (Fall 1982), 269–333, and Stephen N. Broadberry and Douglas Irwin, "Labor Productivity in the United States and the United Kingdom during the Nineteenth Century," *NBER Working Paper 10364* (March 2004). The 1870–1913 growth rate calculations are from W. Arthur Lewis, *Growth and Fluctuation, 1870–1913* (London: George Allen & Unwin, 1978), pp. 17–18. S. B. Saul, *The Myth of the Great Depression, 1873–1896* (Basingstoke, Hampshire, U.K.: Macmillan, 1985), also includes a great deal of comparative data, generally consistent with Bairoch, but with a variety of additional nuances.

For background, David S. Landes, *The Unbound Prometheus: Technological Change and Industrial Development in Western Europe from 1750 to the Present* (London: Cambridge University Press, 1969), is superb. For the relative decline of British industry, see François Crouzet, *The Victorian Economy* (New York: Columbia University Press, 1982); and for the rise of America, Harold G. Vatter, *The Drive to Industrial Maturity: The U.S. Economy, 1860–1914* (Westport, Conn.: Greenwood Press, 1975). And see Paul Kennedy, *The Rise and Fall of the Great Powers: Economic Change and Military Conflict from 1500 to 2000* (New York: Random House, 1987), pp. 194–249, for a crisp assessment of turn-of-the-century Great Power economic positions.

What Happened to England?

Besides the works above, for specific comparisons of American/British prowess in steel, see D. L. Burn, *The Economic History of Steelmaking, 1867–1939: A Study in Competition* (Cambridge, U.K.: University Press, 1940), and the contemporary assessments: J. Stephen Jeans, ed., *American Industrial Conditions and Competition: Reports of the Commissioners Appointed by the British Iron Trade Association to Enquire into the Iron, Steel, and Allied Industries of the United States* (London, 1902) and Frank Popplewell, *Some Modern Conditions and Recent Developments in Iron and Steel Production in America* (Manchester, U.K.: University Press, 1906). The quotes "is considerably larger" and "more than three" are from Jeans, *op. cit.*, pp. 306–7; "very conspicuous" from Popplewell, *op. cit.*, p. 103; "act for the" and "can compete with," Jeans, *op. cit.*, pp. 257, 121; "must steer clear," "distinctly deteriorated," "outside England," "pessimism" in Burn, *op. cit.*, pp. 147, 144n, 208, 186. For Sheffield and tool steel, see Geoffrey Tweedale, *Sheffield Steel and America: A Century of Commercial and Technological Interdependence, 1830–1930* (New York: Cambridge University Press, 1987), p. 100. David Landes, *The Unbound Prometheus*, pp. 269–94, summarizes British slippage in other industries.

The Tariff Question

The history of the tariff in Great Britain follows Anthony Howe, *Free Trade and Liberal England, 1846–1946* (Oxford, U.K.: Oxford University Press, 1997), and for America, Frank W. Taussig, *The Tariff History of the United States* (New York: Capricorn Books, 1964), and Douglas A. Irwin, "The Aftermath of Hamilton's 'Report on Manufactures,'" *NBER Working Paper 9903* (August 2003). The D. L. Burn analysis is from *op. cit.* And see Peter Temin, "Relative Decline of British Steel Industry, 1880–1913," in Henry Rosovsky, ed., *Industrialization in Two Systems: Essays in Honor of Alexander Gerschenkron by a Group of His Students* (New York:

John Wiley, 1966), pp. 140–55, for the American-German squeeze on the British. For the soda ash data, see Kenneth Warren, "Technology Transfer in the Origins of the Heavy Chemicals Industry in the United States and the Russian Empire," in David J. Jeremy, *International Technology Transfer: Europe, Japan, and the USA* (Brookfield, Vt.: Edward Elgar, 1991), pp. 153–77, at p. 159. The quote "Protection . . . brings" is in Jagdish Bhagwati and Douglas A. Irwin, "The Return of the Reciprocitarians: U.S. Trade Policy Today," *The World Economy* 10:2 (June 1987), 109–30, at 113; and "hitherto chaste" from D. L. Burn, *op. cit.*, p. 312. It might be noted that selling at lower prices abroad than at home may be quite rational in an industry like steel in which increased scale can often reduce costs across the board. The larger volumes, that is, may increase profits on both domestic and foreign sales. The effect is often exaggerated, however, since scale economies tend to flatten out in all industries—i.e., big plants may be more efficient than small ones, but big, bigger, and biggest may be indistinguishable. "Dumping," strictly speaking, is selling below *cost*, which is never profitable in the short run, but may be a rational long-term strategy aimed at eliminating competition. By treaty among developed countries, such practices are now illegal; they were not in the nineteenth century. Determining what "costs" are, however, is a reliable source of annuity income for trade lawyers.

The classic statement of the rule of comparative advantage is chapter VII of David Ricardo's *Principles of Political Economy and Taxation* (Amherst, N.Y.: Prometheus Books, 1996). For the tin plate story, see Frank W. Taussig, *Some Aspects of the Tariff Question* (Cambridge, Mass.: Harvard University Press, 1915), pp. 175–85 and Douglas A. Irwin, "Did Late Nineteenth-Century U.S. Tariffs Promote Infant Industries? Evidence from the Tinplate Industry," *The Journal of American Economic History* 60:2 (June 2000), 335–60. The quote "not unfavorable" is from Taussig, *Aspects*, p. 53; and "the Mother of" is from Jeremiah Whipple Jenks, *The Trust Problem* (Garden City, N.Y.: Doubleday, Page and Co., 1914), p. 44.

The Carnegie Effect

For the discussion of American and British steel prices and margins: the Edgar Thomson margins from 1875 through 1878 are in James Howard Bridge, *The Inside History of the Carnegie Steel Company, A Romance of Millions* (New York: Aldine, 1903), pp. 94–102; Bill Jones's 1882 cost sheets for ET, Box 71, HSWP (Jones's costs cover all steel, not just rails, so the comparison is not precise, but the American cost disadvantage is very large); and for American-British price comparisons, I used the American rail prices in Peter Temin, *Iron and Steel in Nineteenth-Century America: An Economic Inquiry* (Cambridge, Mass.: The MIT Press, 1964), "Appendix C: Statistics of Iron and Steel," pp. 264–85; and the British fob rail export prices in D. L. Burn, *op. cit.*, p. 103. For Carnegie's share increases during recessions, see the table in Kenneth Warren, *Triumphant Capitalism: Henry Clay Frick and the Industrial Transformation of America* (Pittsburgh, Pa.: University of Pittsburgh Press, 1996), p. 308. Gates's "large profits" quote is in David Brody, *Steelworkers in America: The Nonunion Era* (New York: Russell and Russell, 1970), p. 7; his "bull" quote is from *Hearings before the Committee on Investigation of United States Steel Corporation (Stanley Committee)* (Washington, D.C.: U.S. Government Printing Office, 1912, 8 vols.), p. I:44, and Gary's "entirely," *ibid.*, p. I:220.

What Was Special about America?

The quote "tremendous advantage" is from David S. Landes, *The Unbound Prometheus*, p. 33; "labors for wages" from Roy P. Basler, ed., *The Collected Works of Abraham Lincoln* (New Brunswick, N.J.: Rutgers University Press, 1953–1955, 9 vols.), III:478; "increasing the number" from Nathan Rosenberg, ed., *The American System of Manufactures* (Edinburgh: Edinburgh University Press, 1969), p. 7n. The fishing rod example was in "50, 100, & 150 Years Ago," *Scientific American* (November 2004), 16. The "vast but unpredictable" quote is from Paul Kennedy, *The Rise and Fall of the Great Powers*, p. 245; "The collapse in" and "all very violent" are from J. H. Clapham, *The Economic History of Modern Britain* (Cambridge, U.K.: Cambridge University Press, 1938), vol. 3, pp. 55, 57; "that it cannot" from Philip Ziegler, *The Sixth Great Power: A History of One of the Greatest of all Banking Families, 1762–1929* (New

York: Knopf, 1988), p. 292. The Henry James quotes are from *The Golden Bowl* (New York: Penguin Classics, 1987), pp. 535, 45.

10. The Wrong Lessons

For Taylor, I follow, generally, Daniel Nelson, *Frederick W. Taylor and the Rise of Scientific Management* (Madison, Wisc.: The University of Wisconsin Press, 1980), a very clear-eyed account, supplemented by Robert Kanigel, *The One Best Way: Frederick Winslow Taylor and the Enigma of Efficiency* (New York: Viking, 1997). The Drucker quote is from Kanigel, p. 11. The quotes on the "science of shoveling" and the "law of heavy labor" and the "first-class" man are from the collection, Frederick W. Taylor, *Scientific Management: Comprising Shop Management, The Principles of Scientific Management, and Testimony before the Special House Sub-committee* (New York: Harper & Brothers, 1947), *Shop Management,* pp. 165, 57, and *Principles,* p. 65.

Intellectuals Discover the Machine

The main source for this section is Dorothy Ross, *The Origins of American Social Science* (New York: Cambridge University Press, 1991); and also see the essays in her (as editor) *Modernist Impulses in the Human Sciences, 1870–1930* (Baltimore, Md.: Johns Hopkins University Press, 1994), including her "Modernist Science in the Land of the New/Old," pp. 171–89. The quotes "bewildered and helpless" and "To Thomas" are from Henry Adams, *The Education of Henry Adams* (New York: The Modern Library, 1931), pp. 487, 456, 458. The quote "is the great fact" is from Walter Lippmann, *Drift and Mastery: An Attempt to Diagnose the Current Unrest* (Madison, Wisc.: The University of Wisconsin Press, 1985), p. 37. The Pennsylvania's St. Louis exhibit is from Steven W. Usselman, *Regulating Railroad Innovation: Business, Technology, and Politics in America, 1840–1920* (New York: Cambridge University Press, 2002), pp. 245–46; and for its subsequent history, pp. 354–57. The Charles Schwab quotes are from his "What May Be Expected in the Steel and Iron Industry," *North American Review,* no. 534 (May 1901), 655–64, at pp. 655, 661, 664. The Lippmann quotes are from his *Drift,* pp. 37–38, 41, 87, 98; the quote "single syndicate" is from Edward Bellamy, *Looking Backward* (New York: Viking Penguin, 1982), pp. 65–66. The Pearson quotes are from Theodore Porter, "The Death of the Object: *Fin-de-Siècle* Philosophy of Physics," in Dorothy Ross, ed., *Modernist Impulses,* pp. 128–51, at pp. 145–46. For the rise of sociology, see Dorothy Ross, *Origins,* especially pp. 219–56. The quotes "scientific," "social control," and "social equilibrating" are from pp. 219, 236, 238. "Dynamic Theory" from Henry Adams, *The Education,* p. 474. I used the Dewey "great factories" quote in my "It's Not The Economy, Stupid," *The Atlantic Monthly* (July 1993), pp. 49–62, but no longer have those notes and have not been able to recover its original source (the *Atlantic* vets sources carefully); Dewey's "the transformation" is from Olivier Zunz, "Producers, Brokers, and Users of Knowledge: The Institutional Matrix," in Dorothy Ross, ed., *Modernist Impulses,* p. 304; and "ideally suited" from Theodore Porter, *op. cit.,* p. 148.

What Did Taylor Do?

The quote "the management of" is from David F. Noble, *America by Design: Science, Technology, and the Rise of Corporate Capitalism* (New York: Knopf, 1977), p. 267; "every single act," "[A] man who," and "[I]n the higher" from the collection, Frederick W. Taylor, *Scientific Management, Principles,* pp. 64, 59, 97. The shoveling studies and related quotes are from Frederick W. Taylor, *op. cit., Shop Management,* pp. 150–69, 172–74. The 25% to 75% examples for *P* are from the best documented of Taylor's engagements (he was more the engagement impresario than the manager) in Hugh G. J. Aitken, *Taylorism at Watertown Arsenal: Scientific Management in Action, 1908–1915* (Cambridge, Mass.: Harvard University Press, 1960), p. 24. The Taylor quotes "scientific investigation" and "The one is guesswork" are from Frederick W. Taylor, *op. cit., Testimony,* p. 164. The account of the discovery of high-speed steel follows Thomas J. Misa, *A Nation of Steel: The Making of Modern America, 1865–1925* (Baltimore, Md.: Johns

Hopkins University Press, 1995), pp. 180–209. And see Philip Scranton, *Endless Novelty: Specialty Production and American Industrialization, 1865–1925* (Princeton, N.J.: Princeton University Press, 1997), pp. 202–4, for the challenges high-speed tools posed for machine makers. The quote "potential dramatic appeal" is from Daniel Nelson, *Frederick W. Taylor*, p. 119.

Enter Mr. Brandeis

For the Rate cases, see Louis D. Brandeis, *Scientific Management and Railroads* (New York: The *Engineering Magazine*, 1911). It includes an extended preface by the editors of the *Engineering Magazine*, Brandeis's closing statement, and the testimony of the Taylorites. The roads actually had a good case for higher rates. Blue-collar wages were rising strongly, and they were losing experienced staff; plus a radical increase in short-haul traffic density on roads like the Pennsylvania was very costly. The current tariff ideology forbade differential cost-based charging. For Gilbreth and his therbligs, Samuel Haber, *Efficiency and Uplift; Scientific Management in the Progressive Era, 1890–1920* (Chicago: University of Chicago Press, 1964), pp. 40–41. The quotes from the Taylorite testimony are from Louis D. Brandeis, *Scientific Management*, pp. 6, 7, 11, 27, 22, 39. The Emerson consulting quotes are in Daniel Nelson, *Frederick W. Taylor*, pp. 130, 128. The quote "few of those" and *Times* and *Tribune* headlines are from Robert Kanigel, *The One Best Way*, pp. 434, 433, 435. The Gilbreth text is Frank B. Gilbreth, *Primer of Scientific Management* (New York: D. Van Nostrand Co., 1914); the quotes are from pp. 6, 80. Taylor's *Principles* coda is from Frederick W. Taylor, *Scientific Management: Principles*, pp. 140–44.

The quotes "Are there no," "scientific laws" "the sane middle," and "placing engineers" are from Edward T. Layton, Jr., *The Revolt of the Engineers: Social Responsibility and the American Engineering Profession* (Baltimore, Md.: Johns Hopkins University Press, 1986), an excellent discussion of the rise and fall of engineering hubris. The quote "new professional" is from James Gilbert, *Designing the Industrial State: The Intellectual Pursuit of Collectivism in America, 1880–1940* (Chicago: Quadrangle Books, 1972). The quotes from Merrick and Taylor in the Watertown footnote are from Hugh G. J. Aitken, *Taylorism at Watertown*, pp. 147, 137. For Taylor's congressional testimony and the questioning, see Frederick W. Taylor, *Scientific Management: Testimony*. "We never take" is from Robert Kanigel, *The One Best Way*, p. 564.

Taylor and the Intellectuals

The quote "a batch and" is from Philip Scranton, *Endless Novelty*, p. 69. For Chandler on Taylor, see Alfred D. Chandler, Jr., *The Visible Hand: The Managerial Revolution in American Business* (Cambridge, Mass.: The Belknap Press of Harvard University Press, 1977), pp. 274–81. David A. Hounshell, *From American System to Mass Production, 1800–1932: The Development of Manufacturing Technology in the United States* (Baltimore, Md.: Johns Hopkins University Press, 1984), pp. 217–61, is a definitive discussion of Ford's achievements. For Taylor's reservations about working with well-managed companies, see Daniel Nelson, *Frederick W. Taylor*, p. 150. For the defense of railroad management, see William J. Cunningham, "Scientific Management in the Operation of Railroads," *The Quarterly Journal of Economics* 25 (May 1911), 539–61. Albert Fishlow's "Productivity and Technological Change in the Railroad Sector, 1840–1910, in Dorothy Brady, ed., National Bureau of Economic Research, *Output, Employment, and Productivity in the United States after 1800* (New York: Columbia University Press, 1966), pp. 583–646, shows that, in fact, productivity growth in the railroad sector was the fastest of any over that entire period.

. . . And There Were Consequences

The footnote on the Soviet version of Taylorism is from Richard Overy, *The Dictators: Hitler's Germany and Stalin's Russia* (New York: Norton, 2004), p. 320. The referenced Chandler books, in addition to *The Visible Hand*, are: Alfred D. Chandler, Jr., *Scale and Scope: The Dynamics of Industrial Capitalism* (Cambridge, Mass.: The Belknap Press of Harvard University Press, 1990); and *Strategy and Structure: Chapters in the History of Industrial Enterprise* (Cambridge, Mass.: The MIT Press, 1962). *Scale and Scope* extends the argument to the international arena, for all practical purposes excluding Japan, a significant omission by 1990 when the book was published. The "teutonic" label is from William Parker, "Business Enterprise and Economic Change," in Louis P. Cain and Paul J. Uselding, eds., *Business Enterprise and Economic Change: Essays in Honor of Harold F. Williamson* (Kent, Ohio: Kent State University Press, 1973), pp. 15–47, 24. The quotes "the economies of speed" and "[M]anaging and" are from Alfred D. Chandler, Jr., *The Visible Hand*, pp. 281, 454. For the history of the Harvard Business School, see Jeffrey L. Cruikshank, *A Delicate Experiment: The Harvard Business School: 1908–1945* (Cambridge, Mass.: The Harvard Business School Press, 1987). For "had plenty of," see Alfred D. Chandler, Jr., *Strategy and Structure*, p. 284. For EOQ, see H. Thomas Johnson and Robert S. Kaplan, *The Rise and Fall of Management Accounting* (Cambridge, Mass.: Harvard Business School Press, 1987), pp. 209–20, an important book for those who care about such things. For the Toyota system, see Taiichi Ohno, *Toyota Production System: Beyond Large-Scale Production* (Cambridge, Mass.: Productivity Press, 1988) and Japan Management Association, *Kanban: Just-in-Time at Toyota* (Cambridge, Mass.: Productivity Press, 1982). The quote "pursuit of quantity" is from Taiichi Ohno, *op. cit.*, p. 109. I wrote about the burst of reform in American factories in my *The Coming Global Boom* (New York: Bantam, 1990). The article criticizing managers is Robert H. Hayes and William J. Abernathy, "Managing Our Way to Economic Decline," *Harvard Business Review* (July–August 1980), 67–77; the quotes are from pp. 70, 74. Chandler's "the businessman of" is from his *The Visible Hand*, p. 455.

Appendix I : The Carnegie Company's 1900 Earnings

Except as noted below, all the material here is developed from the records in ACLC. For the early citations of the $40 million, see James Howard Bridge, *The Inside History of the Carnegie Steel Company, A Romance of Millions* (New York: Aldine, 1903), p. 295; Andrew Carnegie, *The Autobiography of Andrew Carnegie* (Boston: Northeastern University Press edition, 1986), p. 245; and Stanley Committee, I:161–62. In terms of subsequent citations, I have found no historian who, if he/she mentions a number, uses other than $40 million for Carnegie Co.'s 1900 profit totals. Steel pricing data are from *Iron Age*'s contemporary pricing reports; I used the weekly prices closest to the month end. Annual growth data are from the Appendix tables in Peter Temin, *Iron and Steel in Nineteenth-Century America: An Economic Inquiry* (Cambridge, Mass.: The MIT Press, 1964), "Appendix C: Statistics of Iron and Steel," pp. 264–85. The nineteenth-century error in depreciation accounting was apparently first noted by the historian Richard Brief in the 1960s, and is cited in Naomi Lamoreaux, *The Great Merger Movement in American Business, 1895–1904* (New York: Cambridge University Press, 1985), pp. 53–54.

Appendix II: Standard Oil Earnings

The table is from the breakup trial discovery data, as reported by Allan Nevins, *John D. Rockefeller: The Heroic Age of American Enterprise* (New York: Charles Scribner's Sons 1940, 2 vols.), II:719. The "book equity" in this table appears to be properly accounted for, although I don't have access to the detail. (See notes to chapter 3 for state of the Standard's archives.) The Rockefeller personal accounts are in RAC, Series F, "Trial Balances, 1890–1915."

Index

Entries in *italics* refer to illustrations.

Abernathy, William, 318
Adams, Brook, 240
Adams, Charles Francis, Jr., 240–43, 254
Adams, Comfort, 308–9
Adams, Henry, 20–21, 71, 74, 160, 240, 294, 297
advertising, *175*, 177–78
agrarian reform impulse, 216
agriculture and farming, 5–6, 67, 216
   "bonanza" and factory, 29, 109–12, *111*, 115–16, 273n, 278
   crisis of 1873 and, 101
   houses, 169–70
   mechanization and, 40n, 55
   occupational mobility and, 165–66
   New England vs. New York, 38
   productivity and, 272n–73n
   protests and, 99, 115–17
   U.S. vs. British, 278
   women and, 162–63
Alger, Horatio, 173
Amalgamated Copper, 252
Amalgamated Iron and Steel Workers, 196, 199, 202
American Federation of Labor (AFL), 196, 251
American Sheet Steel Co., 253
American Society of Mechanical Engineers (ASME), 127, 169, 299, 301, 305, 307
American Sociological Society, 296
American Steel Hoop, 253, 259

American Steel & Wire, 194, 253, 254, 259
American Telephone & Telegraph (AT&T), 191, 226, 239, 251
American Tin Plate, 194, 253
American Union, 146–47
America (yacht), 30, 31, 32
Ames, Fisher, 40
Ames, Nathan, 48, 50, 53, 59
Ames, Oakes, 137–39, 240
Ames, Oliver, 137, 139
Anderson, John, 53–54
Andrews, Sam, 18–19
antitrust law, 89. *See also* Sherman Act; trusts; *and specific companies and cases*
Archbold, John, 85, 151–53, 160, 193, 221, 224–25, 331
Armory practice, 34–37, 48–50, 53–55
   consumer products and, 180–83
   Ford follows, 311
Armour, Philip, 114–15, 117
Atlantic & Great Western Railroad, 68, 85
Atlantic & Pacific telegraph, 146
Atlantic Refining, 151
Atlantic Transport, 267–69
Autobiography (Carnegie), 262, 319
automobile manufacturing, 182, 311–12
Ayer, N. S., 177

Bacon, Robert, 258, 262
Baker, George F., 157, 250

Baker, Ray Stannard, 306–7
Baltimore & Ohio (B&O) Railroad, 2, 123, 134, 142, 146–47, 152, 154, 240
Bankers' Trust, 250
Bank of England, 235, 247, 250, 266, 290
banks and banking, 4, 231, 233
  failures of, 99–101, 104, 250
  financing of business and, 192
  mergers and, 252
  Morgan as image of, 266–67
  U.S. vs. Britain, 273n
Banque de France, 250
Barings bank, 26, 92, 100, 233, 235, 241, 290
Barksdale, Hamilton, 312
Barnard, George, 64, 78
Beard, Charles and Mary, 10
"bear raid," 21, 139n, 146–47
Beecher, Henry Ward, 183–84
Bee Line Railroad, 145
Belden, Henry, 74
Bell, Alexander Graham, 110, 119
Bellamy, Edward, 295, 311
Benson, Byron, 156–57
Berkman, Alexander, 201
Bernhardt, Sarah, 115
Bessemer, Henry, 125, 127
Bessemer process, 91, 96, 122–23, 125–29, 126, 273–74, 190
Bessemer Steel Association, 128, 131–32, 189, 287
Bethlehem Iron Company, 133
Bethlehem Steel, 128, 228–29, 287, 302–4
bicycle industry, 180–82, 277
big companies, xiii, 251–55, 295–97
Birmingham, England, steel works, 96
Bischoffheimer & Goldschmidt, 76–77
Bismarck, Otto von, 101, 279, 281
Black Friday, 74–75
Blaine, James G., 140
Blanc, Honoré, 39
Blanchard, Thomas, 33–36, 40, 42, 48, 180
  gun-stocking lathe, 34–36, 39, 52, 57–59
Bloomingdale's, 162, 174, 176
Blumin, Stuart, 164, 172
Boer War, xi, 266, 271
Bomford, George, 39, 44, 45n, 46–47
Bonsack, James, 179
boom, post–Civil War, 11, 28, 75, 115–16
Bostwick, Jabez, 84
Boucicault, Aristide, 161
Bradford, PA, oil strikes, 156n
Brandeis, Louis D., 89, 266–67, 269, 305–8, 311
brands, 177–79, 182
Bridge, James, 207, 319
bridge industry, 192, 265
British Corn Laws, repeal (1846), 278

Brooklyn Bridge, 92, 95, 104, 169
Browne and Sharpe company, 48, 181
Bryan, William Jennings, 217, 248
Bryce, Lord, 20
Buckland, Cyrus, 37, 48, 59
Bureau of Corporations, 225
Burn, D. L., 281
Burr, Aaron, 25
Burton, James H., 53
Butterfield, Daniel, 71, 73

Cabot, Samuel, 40
Cadillac automobile, 276
Calhoun, John, 44, 46
Cambria Steel Works, 128–34, 287
Camden and Amboy Railroad, 6
canning factories, 312
Carey, Henry, 8
Carnegie, Andrew, 25, 212, 252, 232, 293
  bond sales and, 192
  Carnegie Co. created by, 206–15
  character and background of, xii, 12–16, 19, 28–29, 61, 205
  early career of, 91–96
  ET works built by, 122–23
  Frick breaks with, 211–13
  Homestead strike and, 15, 196–203, 205–6, 247n
  law-breaking by, under Sherman Act, 227–29
  management style of, 135–36, 159
  mechanization and, 298
  Morgan buys out Allegheny line of, 230–32, 237
  Pennsylvania Railroad and, 14, 79
  pools and, 143
  protective tariffs and, 282, 283, 285–87
  Scott as mentor of, 13–14
  Scott break with, 130–31
  steel industry dominated by, 88n, 108, 120, 128–36, 190
  St. Louis Bridge and, 92–94, 95
  telegraph companies and, 146
  U. S. Steel merger and buyout by Morgan, 16, 256–64
  wealth of, 14–15, 130, 151n, 323–24
Carnegie, Mrs. Andrew, 16, 209, 262
Carnegie, Lucy (wife of Tom), 128n
Carnegie, Margaret (mother), 13
Carnegie, Tom, 93, 128n, 129, 130, 198, 212
Carnegie Bros., 134
Carnegie Co.
  creation of, 206–16
  earnings of, 214–15, 262–63, 319–30
  U. S. Steel buyout of, 16, 255–56, 260–66
Carnegie "Handbook," 190
Carnegie, McCandless & Company, 129, 131

Carnegie Steel, 256, 275
  consolidates properties, 132–33
  costs and productivity of, 202–3
  creation of, 199
  earnings of, 213–15, 286, 320–30
  financial systems of, 194
  Homestead strike and, 196
  integrated structure of, 207
  labor skills and, 195
  paperwork and, 188–89
  partners attempt to buy out, 209–10
  rebates and, 227–28
  ship armor contracts, 228–29
  structural steel and, 190
  U. S. Steel buyout and, 259
  world market and, 279
cartels, 238, 240–43, 253, 287
Cartwright, Samuel, 38
Cass, George, 109, 110
Cassatt, A. J., 154, 156, 227
Cass-Cheney farm, 109–10
"Cast Iron Palace," 161–62
cattle industry, 63, 112–14, 139, 144
"Center firms," 239, 315
Central Branch Union Pacific Railroad, 145
Central of New Jersey Railroad, 145
Central Pacific Railroad, 137, 140
Chandler, Alfred, 239, 254–55, 311,
  314–18
"Chapters of Erie" (Adams), 240
chemical industries, 223, 278, 280
Cheney, George, 109, 110
Chernow, Ron, 20, 221
Chicago, 6, 67, 87, 111
  architectural school, 187–88
  Exposition of 1893, 174, 178, 180, 182
  fire of 1871, 105, 187–88
  meat industry and, 114, 115
  strike of 1877, 99
Chicago and Alton Railroad, 221, 222, 224
children
  education, 171–72
  mortality rates, 185
  number of, per family, 184–85
China, xiii, 186, 290
Churchill, Winston, 280–81
Civil War, xii, 8, 10–11, 14, 42, 54, 77, 100,
  112, 137, 279
Clark, Horace, 138
Clark, James, 18–19, 83
Clark, John Bates, 217
Clark, Maurice, 17, 18–19, 83
Clark, Silas, 139
Clark, Payne oil refinery, 83–84, 90
Clay, Henry, 7
Cleveland, 5, 182
  railroads and, 79–80, 87–88

oil refineries and, 12, 18, 79–80, 82, 83–86,
  89–91, 150–52, 158
Cleveland, Grover, 201, 246–48
coal, 5, 67, 68, 99, 104, 120, 132, 163, 192, 285
  labor and, 99, 203n
Cobden, Richard, 278
coke, 102, 123, 132
Coleman, William, 129
Colfax, Schuyler, 138
Colgate, 163
Colt, Samuel, 31, 41–42, 49–51
Columbia safety bicycles, 175, 181–82
Columbus and Indianapolis Railroad, 6
Commercial and Financial Chronicle, 99, 100,
  104–7
common law, 88–89, 218
Compaq corporation, 253n
"comparative advantage," 281n
Compromise of 1877, 140
Confidence Man, The (Melville), 184
Confidence Men and Painted Women
  (Halttunen), 184
Conneaut tube plant, 259–61, 265–66
Connecticut Valley, 38–41, 48–50 53, 127,
  182, 292
consumer products and mass consumption, 5,
  49–50
  anxiety and, 183–86
  Armory standards and, 180–83
  growth and, 102, 115, 289–91
  infrastructure and, 182
  kerosene as first global, 81
  middle class and, 173–80
  supply shock and, 108
contraception, 185–86
Cooke, Jay, 99–100, 105, 109, 244
"Copperhead" Democracy, 4
Corbin, Abel, 70–72, 73, 74
Cordiner, Ralph, 158
Corliss, George, 119, 120
Corliss engine, 121, 295
Corsair agreement, 230–31, 233, 237, 259
Coster, Charles, 237, 255n, 258
cost tracking, 133–34, 189, 194, 298
cotton, 6, 25, 40–41, 54, 104
Cotton Oil Trust, 194
Crash of 1873, 96, 99–106, 120, 129–31, 136,
  150, 192, 235–36
Crash of 1883, 236
Crash of 1893–95, 194, 235–36, 238,
  246–49
Crash of 1907, 249–51, 265n, 290
Crash of 1929, 270
"creative destruction," xii 28, 289
Crédit Mobilier scandal, 137–39, 141
Crocker, Charles, 144
Crozier, William, 310n

Crystal Palace Exhibition, 30–32, 32, 35n, 37,
40n, 48, 50, 54, 56, 119, 181, 276, 289
Cunningham, William, 312–13

Dabney, Charles, 27
Dabney, Morgan & Co., 27
Dalrymple, Oliver H., 110–11, 115
Damascus Steel, 124
Darwin, Charles, 294
DeBeers Diamond Co., 271
Delaware, Lackawanna & Western Railroad,
145
Democrats, 201, 213, 246–47
Denver Pacific Railroad, 144
Denver & Rio Grande Railroad, 144–45
Denver & South Park Railroad, 144
department stores, 161–64, 163, 166–68, 298
DePew, Chauncey, 230, 232
Devereaux, J. H., 82
Dewey, John, 297, 311
Dillon, Sidney, 139, 145, 240
Dingel tariff (1897), 280
Dix, Dorothy, 180
Dodd, Samuel C. T., 193–94
Dodge, Grenville, 138n
Dodge, James, 304–5, 307n
Douglas, Stephen, 7, 9–10
Dow Jones Industrial Index, 194, 249
Draft Riots (1863), 4
Drake, Col. Edwin, 17, 150
Drew, Danniel, 21, 62–66
Drexel, Anthony "Tony," 27, 230, 233, 238
Drexel, Morgan & Co., 27, 101, 145–46, 233
Drucker, Peter, 293
Dudley, Charles, 190
Duke, James, 179
Duncan, William, 76
Duncan, Sherman & Co., 26–27, 76
Dunne, Peter Finley, 265
DuPont, 255, 312, 316
Duquesne Works, 201–2
Dwight, Edmund, 40

Eads, Capt. James, 93, 128, 129
Eastern Illinois Railroad, 222
Eastern Rate case (1910), 305, 312
Eastern Traffic Association, 217
Eastern Trunkline Association, 143
Eastman, George, 180
East St. Louis & Carondelet Railroad, 145
economies of scale, 107, 129, 257, 258
Economist, 290
Edgar Thomson Steel Works (ET), 122–23,
128–35, 192, 274, 285–86, 323
Homestead strike and, 198–206
Edison, Thomas, 119, 179, 238, 255
Edison Electric, 255n

education, 9–10, 55–56, 172–73, 184, 191
Education of Henry Adams, The, 294
Edwards, Jonathan, 25
efficiency, 255, 257, 261–62, 329–30
election of 1892, 247
election of 1896, 248
electricity, 170, 182, 255n, 278
Eliot, S. A., 40
Ellerman, John, 268
Ely, Richard, 217
Emerson, Harrington, 305, 307, 312–13
Emery, Lewis, 220–21
Empire Transportation Co., 153–56
employment, 103–5, 115, 117–18, 167, 172
Enfield, England, Armory, 53–54, 276
entertainment industry, 179–80
EOQ (Economic Order Quantity), 316–17
Erie Railroad, 81, 84, 87–88, 153, 154
Gould ousted from, 75–79, 78, 136, 138
Gould takeover of, 141, 144–45
"Wars," 61–67, 70, 82, 95, 101, 136, 240
Europe, xi, 76, 101, 113, 225–26, 235, 249,
288, 290. See also specific countries
Evans, Oliver, 57, 58
Excelsior Oil Works, 18, 19
exports, 103, 104, 248, 279, 290. See also trade

Farrar, Gaspard, 290
Federal Reserve, 250, 251
Morgan takes role of, 246, 251
Federal Steel, 228, 255–58, 265, 329–30
Ferguson, Charles, 225
Ferguson, Niall, 271–72
Ferris wheel, 178, 180
Field, Cyrus, 70, 145, 231
Field, David Dudley, 78
Fink, Albert, 88n, 142–43, 217–19, 240
firearms, 31–32, 34–40, 36, 42–55
First National Bank, 157, 250
Fisk, Jim, Jr., 60–61, 63–66, 65, 68, 70,
72–74, 76
Fitch, John, 43
Flagler, Henry, 80–85, 160n, 194
Fogel, Robert, 138n
food industry, 67, 102–3, 108–9, 115–16, 120,
177–79. See also agriculture
Ford, Henry, 115, 182, 293, 311–12
France, 39, 272
Franco-Prussian war, 101
Frasch, Herman, 223
Frémont, Gen. John C., 27
Freud, Sigmund, 294
Frick, Henry, 15–16, 102, 134, 159, 250n, 255,
256, 259, 261, 264
buyout attempt and break with Carnegie,
206–15, 319n
Homestead strike and, 197–203, 205, 206

Frick Coke Co. (FCCo), 132, 198, 211–14, 227n, 320, 321, 324–26
Fritz, George and John, 128, 287

Gallman, Robert, 102
Gantt, Henry, 301, 305–6, 312–13
Garfield, James, 137–38
Garland, Hamlin, 150, 203–4
Garrett, John, 134, 146, 147, 152
Garrett, Robert, 147
Gary, Elbert, 28, 210, 228, 250n, 256, 263, 265, 266, 287
Gates, Bill, 91, 159n
Gates, Frederick, 208, 264
Gates, John W., 199, 207n, 210, 253–54, 257–58, 262, 287, 329
General Electric, 158, 191, 255, 269, 278, 312
Germany, xi
    banking crisis of 1873 and, 101
    industry, 272, 274, 276–78
    protectionism and, 278–83
    science "stars" from, 191, 223
    steel industry, vs. U.S., 288–91
Gilbreth, Frank, 305–8, 316
Gilbreth, Lillian, 305n
Gladstone, William Ewart, 61, 203
gold
    Corner, 69–75, 106, 136, 141
    greenback exchange rate, 69–70
    panic of 1893–95, 246–49
    reserves, 247, 266
    standard, 106–7, 141, 247
Golden Bowl, The (James), 291
"Golden Spike," 137, 140
Gold Exchange, 107
Goldman, Emma, 201
Goldman, Sachs investment bank, 176
Gompers, Samuel, 196, 202, 251
Goss, F. M., 297
Gould, George, 149, 236, 259
Gould, Helen Miller, 24
Gould, Jay, 25, 65, 105, 242
    age of, ends, 150
    background and character of, xii–xiii, 12, 20–24
    big-business forms and, 120, 289
    Dillon and Sage alliance begins, 139
    Erie ouster and, 76–77, 78, 138
    Erie railroad and, 60–69, 75–76, 82, 240
    Fisk and, 65, 76
    Gold Corner and, 69–75
    illness and death of, 148–49, 240, 242, 243
    infrastructure and, 107
    post–Civil War America and, 12, 28–29
    rail network of, completed by Harriman, 243
    railroad system controlled by, 21–22, 113, 141–50

railroad trunkline battles and, 87, 88
    Rockefeller and, 79
    SIC crisis and, 85
    St. Louis bridge and, 94
    strikes of 1877, 106
    telegraph and, 141, 146–47, 148
    UP controlled by, 136–41, 241–43
    yacht of, 230
Gowen, Franklin, 157, 236, 237
grain industry, 5, 6, 105, 111–12
    shipping and, 68, 87–88, 217
    world markets and, 69, 81, 231n, 272
Grammar of Science, The (Pearson), 294–96
Granger movement, 116
Grant, Ulysses S., 2, 70–72, 101, 119, 120, 121, 137–38, 140
Grant, Mrs. Ulysses S., 74
Great Atlantic and Pacific Tea (A&P), 177
Great Britain
    common law and, 88–89
    financing of Boer War and, 271–72
    free-trade and, 278–87
    gold panic of 1893–95 and, 247
    "Great Depression" of 1870s, 108
    industry "hollowed out," 108, 280
    investment in U.S. and, 61
    precision machining and, 31–33, 37, 42, 50–55
    steel industry, 96, 102, 124–25, 127, 129, 132–33, 135, 273–74, 280
    U. S. industry surpasses, 55–59, 272–78, 290
Great Northern Railroad, 244
Great War, 249, 272, 278
greenback, 106–8, 231n, 246–49
Greenspan, Alan, 107
Gribeauval, Jean–Baptiste de, 39
grocery chains, 177–78, 298
Gurley, Phineas, 1

Hall, John, 42–49, 53, 55, 59, 180, 181, 299
    carbines case, 27, 42, 76–77
Halttunen, Karen, 184
Hamilton, Alexander, 7, 246, 279
Hammond, George, 114, 115
Hanna, Mark, 213
Harpers, 167, 171
Harpers Ferry Armory, 36–37, 45–48, 55
Harriman, Edward Henry, 219, 236, 243–46, 252, 313
Harrison, Benjamin, 201
Harvard Business School, 315–16
Hathaway, Horace, 305
Havemeyer, H.O., 284
Hay, John, 290
Hayes, Robert, 318
Hayes, Rutherford B., 107, 140
Haymarket Square bombing (1886), 196

Hazard of New Fortunes, A (Howells), 171
Henry, B. Tyler, 48
Hill, James J., 219, 236, 244–46
History of Standard Oil (Tarbell), 86, 219, 223
Hobbs, Alfred C., 31, 32, 56
Hofstadter, Richard, 216
holding companies, 194, 213–14, 218–19
Holley, Alexander, 49, 122–23, 127–34, 169,
    176, 189, 190, 274, 285, 287, 292–93,
    298, 305
Holmes, Oliver Wendell, Jr., 89, 180, 219n
Homestead Act (1862), 10, 116, 149
Homestead Steel Works, 132, 208, 322
    Strike of 1892, 15, 196–206, 247n
Hoover, Herbert, 310
Hopkins, Mark, 144
Hounshell, David, 41n
housing, 169–72, 182
Howells, William Dean, 120, 159, 171–72, 184
Huntington, Collis, 140, 143, 144, 241

Illinois Steel, 202, 256, 257, 287
immigrants, 99, 103n, 117, 166, 172–73, 297n
Industrial Commission hearings (1899), 221
industrial securities, 192–96, 255
"infant industry" argument, 279, 282, 283
interchangeability of parts, 39–42, 44–48,
    50–51, 180–81, 311–12
International Great Northern Railroad, 145
International Mercantile Marine (IMM), 267–69
International Navigation Co. (INC), 267–68
International Paper, 253–54
Interstate Commerce Act (ICA, 1887), 89,
    116n, 216–18, 221, 227
Interstate Commerce Association, 241
Interstate Commerce Commission (ICC),
    116n, 222, 241, 305
    rate-setting and, 219, 246
Iowa Pool, 144
Iowa Railroad, 145
Irish immigrants, 4, 117, 168, 172
Iron Age, 210, 228, 322, 330
Iron-Clad Agreement (1887), 135–36, 212–13
iron industry, 5, 26, 91, 99, 120, 124–25, 163
    ore, 38, 67, 68, 127, 132, 285
    workers, 104
Iron Mountain Railroad, 145
Irwin, Douglas, 284–85
Ivory soap, 162–63, *175*

Jackson, Andrew, 216, 246
James, Henry, 291
Japan, xiii, 273n, 279, 283, 317–18
Jeans, Stephen, 204–5, 258, 274–77
Jefferson, Thomas, 5, 8, 39, 43
Jenks, Jeremiah, 221
Jennings, O. B., 83

Jevons, William Stanley, 280
Johnson, Andrew, 107
Jones, Capt. William "Bill," 128–31, 133, 135,
    197–99, 202, 208, 277
Jones & Laughlin, 257, 330
J. P. Morgan & Co
    Drexel, Morgan renamed, 233
    power of, 235
    Pujo investigations and, 269–70
J. S. Morgan & Co., 26, 27, 68, 92, 233

Kanigel, Robert, 311
Kansas & Texas Railroad, 145
Kansas Pacific Railroad, 144
Kennedy, John F., 2
kerosene, 81, 86, 150, 162, 170
Keystone Bridge Co., 91, 93, 128
Kidder, Peabody banking firm, 235
Kinsey survey (1955), 185
Klein, Maury, 139, 145, 147
Kloman, Andrew, 93, 129, 130
Knights of Labor, 196
Kuhn, Loeb firm, 235, 245
Kuznets, Simon, 102

labor. *See also* employment; wages
    big companies and, 251
    bonanza farms and, 109, 111
    bosses and, 195–96
    class and, 7–10, 28, 167–68
    days off, 198n
    education and, 9
    1870s and, 103, 104
    innovation and, 55
    military draft and, 4
    productivity and wages, 272
    prosperity of, 166–67
    scarcity, 55
    Scientific Management and, 298, 318
    U.S. vs. British, 56, 275, 277
labor unions
    British, 277, 280
    Homestead strike and, 196–206
    "restraint of trade" and, 218
    rise of industrial, 195–96
    strikes of 1877, 97–99, 99, 106, 154–55
    Taylorism and, 310
Lackawanna Steel, 256–57
Lafayette and Michigan City Railroad, 6
Lake Shore Railroad, 82
Lake Superior ore reserves, 265
Lamoreaux, Naomi, 252
Landes, David, 288
land-grant colleges, 10, 111, 191
land grants, 109, 116, 140, 149
Landis, Kenesaw Mountain, 221–22, 224
Lane, Franklin, 66, 76

Lauder, George, 201, 327
Lead Smelting Trust, 194
Lee, Charles, 23
Lee, Gen. Robert E., 1
Lee, Roswell, 39
Lee Higginson firm, 235
Lehmans investment bank, 176
Leishman, John, 207–8
"Levingston, William," 17. See also Rockefeller, William (father)
Lewis, John L., 196
Leyland firm, 268
Lincoln, Abraham, 1–12, 3, 28, 57, 59, 107, 116, 118, 165, 188, 252, 288
Lincoln, Mary, 1
Lincoln, Willie, 2
Linseed Oil Trust, 194
Lippmann, Walter, 294–95, 310, 311
Lockhart, Waring, and Frew, 151
Lockwood & Co., 75
London Times, 31, 280
Looking Backward (Bellamy), 295
Lowell, Francis Cabot, 38, 57
Lucy Furnace Works, 132
Ludlow Massacre (1914), 203n

McCandless, David, 129
McClellan, Gen. George, 85
McClure's Magazine, 86, 219
McCormick, Cyrus, 6, 31, 41, 50
McCormick Reaper, 105
McCoy, Joseph, 113
McGee, John, 220, 225
McHenry, James, 76, 77
machine tradition, 31–32, 34–41, 36, 48–50, 276–77, 289, 292
McNamara, Robert, 318
McPherson, James, 11
Macy's, 162, 168
mail-order catalogs, 173–75
management. See also Scientific Management
   British vs. U.S., 277
   drive to systematic, 298–99
   failure of professionalized, 316
   consulting, 313
   tradition, rise of American, 314–18, 317
"Managing Our Way to Economic Decline" (Hays and Abernathy), 318
Mansfield, Josie, 60, 65, 66, 76, 77
manufacturing
   advanced precision, developed, 30–59, 46
   consumer products and, 180–83
   "de-skilling" and, 195
   growth of, in 1870s, 102, 105, 108
   regional development and, 4–6, 8
   steel industry and, 123
   U. S. culture and, xiii

Marshal, Alfred, 280
Martin, Albro, 217n
Massachusetts Railroad Commission, 240
mass consumer society. See consumer products
mass production, 108, 169–70, 182, 312
MCI, 239
meat industry, 6, 112–18, 144, 177, 178, 312
mechanization, 298
   U.S. vs. Europe and, 274–78
   U.S. vs. Germany, 288
Mega-Machine metaphor, 120–21
Mellen, Charles, 267
mergers, 218–19, 243–46, 251–55
Merrick, David, 310n
Mesabi ore ranges, 208, 275, 287, 320
Meville, Herman, 184
Mexican War (1846–48), 49
Microsoft, 91, 159n, 253n
middle class, 289, 293
   anxiety and, 184–85
   rise of, 164–73
   women and, 185–86
Midvale Steel, 228–29, 298, 300, 301, 303
military
   German vs. U.S. industry and, 288
   precision machining and, 36–37, 39–42
Mill, James K., 40
mills, 38–41, 56–57, 177
Missouri Pacific Railroad, 144
mobility, 165–66, 288–89
modernity
   anxiety with rise of, 183–86
   disruptions caused by, 116–18
   infrastructure of, 99
   new jobs created by, 190–91
   U.S. growth and, 276
"Molly Maguire" coal field wars, 99, 236
monopolies, 216–18, 239, 251. See also trusts
   Standard Oil as, 220, 225–26
Monroe, James, 43
Montgomery Ward, 173–74, 298
Moody, John, 194, 237, 210, 215, 252–54, 257, 258, 263
Moore, "Judge" William H., 210–11, 215, 252–54, 257, 258, 263, 284
Moore, John (brother of William H. Moore), 210
Morgan, John Pierpont, 25, 209, 232, 234, 305
   age of corporate management and, 150
   background and character of, xii, 12, 25–28
   Barings rescue and, 235
   Boer War and, 271–72
   Carnegie and St. Louis Bridge, 94, 95, 130–31
   as central banker for U.S., 246–51
   competition vs. stability and, 239–40
   conservative image vs. "financial recklessness" of, 266–70

Morgan, John Pierpont (cont'd)
  corporate finance rules set by, xiii
  Corsair deal stops Carnegie's cross-Allegheny
    railroad, 230–33
  crash of 1873 and, 101
  crash of 1893–95 and, 246–49
  crash of 1907 and, 249–51, 249, 265n
  financial systems of Old and New Worlds
    mediated by, 290
  General Electric and, 255n
  Gould and, 21, 61, 68, 75
  "Hall carbines" scandal and, 27, 42, 76–77
  leading banker in world, 233–35
  mergers, IMM deal and, 267–69
  mergers, Northern Securities and, 243–46
  mergers, U. S. Steel deal and, 16, 210,
    255–66
  mergers to regulate competition and, 121,
    143, 215, 243, 251, 252, 262, 269, 293
  post–Civil War America and, 12, 28–29, 61
  railroad restructurings and, 145, 147–48,
    235–38, 267
  railroad wars and, 230–31, 241, 243
  Rockefeller and, 265n
Morgan, Joseph, 26
Morgan, Junius, 16, 26, 27, 68, 76, 93–94,
    130–31, 145, 192, 230–33, 235, 267, 270,
    285–86
Morrill Act (1862), 10, 111, 191
Morris, Nelson, 115
Mosher, Dr. Clelia Duel, 185–86

National Biscuit, 210
National City Bank, 235, 250, 270
National Guard, 97
National Steel, 253, 255–58, 265, 329
National Tube, 194, 257, 258, 260n
natural resources, 55–56, 112, 288
Nevins, Allan, 264, 330, 331, 332
New Haven Railroad, 238
New Jersey Holding Company Act (1890),
  193
New Orleans Pacific Railroad, 145
New York, New Haven & Hartford Railroad,
  267, 269, 305
New York Central Railroad, 63, 66–68, 81,
  87–88, 145–46, 153, 154, 230–32
New York Gold Exchange, 69–70, 73–74
New York Stock Exchange, 100, 139–40, 250
New York Times, 136, 141–42, 307
New York Tribune, 307
New York World, 146
Nobel brothers, 225, 226
Noll, Henry, 292
North, Simeon, 45n, 47–48, 59, 181
North American Review, 261n
North Dakota, 111

Northern Central Railroad, 6
Northern Pacific Railroad, 99, 100, 109–10,
  116, 244, 245, 267
Northern Securities Co., 243–46
Northern Securities Co. v. U.S. (1904), 218–19,
  246, 269
Northwestern Railroad, 144
Nucor steel company, 239

Ohno, Taiichi, 317–18
oil industry. See also Rockefeller, John D.;
  Standard Oil
  antitrust and, 217
  boom, in PA, 3–4, 5, 17–18, 67
  distribution, 68, 81–82, 153–58
  growth of, 102
  modernity and, 99
  patents, 225
  Rockefeller takeover of, xiii, 12, 79, 81–91,
    150–58
  Texas and, 226
oil pipelines, 82, 153–58, 221, 224, 225
oil refineries, 79–87, 151
O'Leary, Patrick, 187
Oliver Mining co., 320, 326–27
"Open Door" policy, 290
Otis, Harrison Gray, 40

Pacific & Atlantic Telegraph Co., 92
Pacific Mail, 138–39
Pacific Railway Act (1862), 10
Pacific Road legislation, 140–41
Pajama Game, The (musical), 314
Palmolive, 163
Panic of 1903, 268
papermaking mergers, 253–54
paperwork, rise of bigger companies and,
  188–96, 192, 298
Paris Exposition
  of 1857, 36
  of 1900, 294, 303–4
Parrish, Maxwell, 181
Parsons, Charles, 278
patents, 7, 57, 59
  Blanchard and, 36, 37
  Colt and, 49
  Evans's grist mill, 58
  General Electric and, 255n
  Hall's, 42–44
  steel, 127–28, 304n
Payne, Oliver H., 83–84, 90, 151
Peabody, George, 26
Pearson, Karl, 294, 295–97, 297n
Pecora investigation, 270
Pedro, Dom, of Brazil, 119, 120
Peel, Robert, 278
Penn Mutual Life Insurance, 269

Pennsylvania Railroad, 66, 82, 105–6, 130, 134, 142, 147, 176
  Carnegie and, 13–14, 92, 95–96, 227
  corporate management, 150
  Gould and, 67–69, 75
  Morgan and, 236
  Morgan's buyout of Carnegie's cross-Allegheny line and, 227, 230–32, 232
  oil and, 79–80, 153–56
  research laboratories, 266
  science of management and, 295, 296, 297
  Scott becomes president of, 75
  size of, 251
  steel and, 123–25
  strike of 1877, 97–99, 99
Pennsylvania Steel Company, 124, 128
Pennsylvania Turnpike, 232
Peoria Railroad, 145
Perkins, Charles E., 144, 149–50
Peterson, Will, 1
Philadelphia Exposition, 295
Philadelphia & Reading Railroad, 157, 231
  Morgan restructures, 236–38
Phipps, Henry, 129, 207, 209–13, 215
Phipps, Lawrence, 214
Pigou, Arthur Cecil, 280
Pillsbury, 111, 112, 177
Pinkerton guards, 197–98, 200–201, 205, 236
Pittsburgh and Bessemer Railroad, 287
Platt, Orville, 218
Polish immigrants, 117
Poor's, 105
Pope, Albert A., 175, 181–82
Popplewell, Frank, 274–76
population growth, 102, 103
Populism, 99, 217
Porter, Theodore, 297
Potter, David, 165
Potts, Col. Joseph, 153–54, 156
Pratt, Charles, 80, 151, 160
Pratt, Zadock, 22–23
precision machining. See manufacturing
prices. See also railroad pools; rebates
  Carnegie and, xii, 134
  competition, mergers to rein in, xiii, 252–54, 256, 265–66
  fall of, 103–4, 106–9, 168, 289–90
  grain, telegraph and, 112
  railroad wars, 63, 67
  steel cartel and, 128
  trade tariffs and, 284, 286, 287
Principles of Scientific Management (Taylor), 307
printing industry, 4, 180, 253
private enterprise, 288–91
Procter & Gamble (P&G), 162, 163, 175

productive capacity, supply shock and, 107
productivity
  bonanza farms and, 111–12
  Carnegie plants and, 202, 257
  cost tracking and, 189
  U. S. vs. Britain, 55, 56, 273n, 278
protectionism, 278–81
providentialism, 294
"Pujo" investigations (1911), 269–70
Pullman Sleeping Car, 6, 91, 131, 298
  strike of 1894, 196
Punch, 32
purchasing-power parities (PPP), 171n
Pure Oil Co., 221, 225, 226

Quarterly Journal of Economics, 312
Quincy Railroad, 145

railroad pools, xiii, 67, 83, 88n, 132, 142–43, 207n, 217–19, 228, 241, 256
railroad rebates, 81, 85–86, 88–90, 157–58, 218, 221–25, 227–28
railroads, xii–xiii, 6, 8. See also Gould, Jay; rebates; and specific railroads
  anti-trust fervor and, 216
  banking crisis of 1873 and, 99–101
  competition and, 77, 239
  conflicts of interest and, 95–96
  consolidation and, 143, 149–50, 219
  construction of, 102, 105–6, 137, 140
  consumer goods and, 163, 176
  control of, by Morgan, 236
  expansion of production and, 120
  farming and, 111–14, 116
  ICC and, 219
  labor and, 104–6
  laboratories and, 190, 191
  Lincoln's funeral train, 2–7, 3
  oil shipping and rebates, 18, 79, 81–89, 153–58, 221–22, 224
  organizational controls led by, 298
  Pacific Railway Act and, 10
  rail shapes, 191
  rates, 85, 116n, 123, 134, 142–44, 191, 202, 216–18, 256
  refrigerated cars and, 114–15
  restructurings, 235–38
  revenues, 104
  routes cobbled together, 6–7
  Scott and Carnegie's start in, 13–14
  securities and, 21, 26, 103, 130–31, 138, 191–92, 194, 231–32
  steel industry and, 123–24, 134, 287
  strikes of 1877, 97–99, 140, 236
  supply shock of 1870s and, 107
  Taylorism and, 312–13
  telegraph and, 146

railroads (cont'd)
  U.S. vs. British, 276
  wars, 4, 74, 240–42
Reading Railroad, 145
Republicans, 4, 7–10, 201, 247n
research laboratories, 190–91, 223, 266, 297
"restraint of trade," 88–89, 218
retail industry, 117, 161–68, 173–76, 182, 298
Rhodes, Cecil, 271
Ricardo, David, 281, 283
RJR Nabisco deal (1987), 265
Robbins and Lawrence company, 32, 35n, 48,
  50, 53, 59, 181, 276
Roberts, George, 230, 232
Rockefeller, John D., 25, 136, 147, 293. See
  also Standard Oil
  background and character of, xii, xiii, 12,
    16–20, 155, 167
  Carnegie steel buyout attempt and, 210
  Cleveland refineries and, 79–86, 90–91,
    193
  financing and, 192
  flow-process business model and, 312
  Gould and, 79
  Indiana antitrust case and, 222–25
  labor relations and, 203
  managerial talent of, 158–60
  mergers and, 252
  Mesabi ore and, 208–9
  Morgan and 1907 crash, 265n
  oil industry consolidated by, 145, 150–58
  post–Civil War America and, 12, 28–29
  prices, markets, and profits and, 107, 143
  retirement of, 160n
  scale shift and, 120–21, 289
  SIC and, 79, 83–85
  Standard breakup and wealth of, 223,
    226–27, 331–33
  Tarbell case vs., 86–91
  U. S. Steel buyouts of, 263–65
  wealth of, 151n, 194
Rockefeller, John D., Jr., 203n, 264–65
Rockefeller, William "Big Bill" (father), 16–17,
  300
Rockefeller, William (brother), 19, 83, 153,
  156, 160n, 252, 264
Roeblings, père et fils, 92
Roebuck, Alvah, 174
Rogers, Henry, 80, 152, 160, 224, 252, 264–65
Roosevelt, Theodore, 246, 249–51, 269
Root, Elisha K., 49, 51
Rosenberg, Nathan, 55
Rosenwald, Julius, 176–77
Rothschild, James, 266
Rothschild, Nathan "Natty," 271
Rothschild family, 100, 101, 233, 237, 247
Royal Dutch Shell, 225

Russia, 272
  Baku oil fields, 225, 226

Sage, Russell, 139, 145
St. Joseph & Denver City Railroad, 144
St. Louis Bridge, 92–94, 95, 128–31, 145
St. Louis Exposition (1904), 295, 296, 297
St. Louis Post-Dispatch, 206
St. Louis Vulcan Works, 133
Sanger, Margaret, 186
Santa Fe Railroad, 307, 313
Saxe, Marshal, 44n
Scale and Scope (Chandler), 314
Schiff, Jacob, 235, 244, 245
Schumpeter, Joseph, 149, 289. See also
  "creative destruction"
Schwab, Charles, 208, 210, 212, 215, 228,
  256–57, 259–63, 265, 295, 319n, 323, 329
Scientific American, 55, 290
Scientific Management, 293, 295–317, 296, 309
Scott, Tom, 13–15, 69, 75, 82–83, 85, 87,
  92–95, 97, 99, 105, 124, 129–31, 140–42,
  153–56, 264
Scranton, Phillip, 311
Scranton, Walter, 256–57
Sears, Richard, 174, 176
Sears catalog, 174, 176, 182
semiconductors, 283
sewage systems, 170
sewing machines, 50, 180, 312
Sharps, Christian, 48
Sharps Rifle Co., 181
Sheffield steel, 96, 124, 125, 273, 274
Sherman Antitrust Act (1890), 88n, 89,
  216–18, 227–28, 246
Shinn, William, 129
Shop Management (Taylor), 301–2
Siemens, Charles, 125–26
  "open hearth" method, 125–28, 274, 278
Singer, Isaac, 41, 49–50, 180
Singer Sewing Machine, 105, 117, 181
Slater, Samuel, 38
slavery, 7–9, 103n
Sloan, Alfred, 293
small merchants, 117–18, 216–17
Smith, Adam, 281n
Smith, Henry, 73
Smith, Merritt Roe, 41n, 48
Social Darwinists, 251
sociology, 296–97
software industry, 253n
Solvay process, 278
Southern Pacific Railroad, 244
South Improvement Company (SIC), 77–79,
  83–87, 89, 90, 193, 225
Soviet Union, 314n
Spanish American war, 290

Speyers, Albert, 73, 74
Springfield Armory, 36–37, 39, 41, 46, 48, 53, 55, 59, 180
standardization, 275, 299–300. *See also* interchangeability of parts
Standard Oil Co.
  antitrust suits and breakup of, 89, 219–27, 223
  buyouts and ethics and, 151–52
  consolidates Cleveland refineries, 80–86, 89–91
  consolidates national oil industry, 150–58
  global dominance by, 251
  image of, unfair, 20
  industrial securities market and, 193–94
  integrates backwards, 158
  labor and, 203
  management of, after Rockefeller, 160
  new technologies and, 80–81, 312
  paperwork and cost tracking, 189
  profitability of, 86, 151, 225, 226, 330–33
  research laboratory and, 190–91
  Rockefeller's managerial gifts and, 158–60
  shipping and, 236
  Tarbell's case vs., 86–91
  trade tariffs and, 283, 284
Standard Oil Co. of New Jersey, 193–94, 221
Standard Oil of Indiana, 221–27
Stanford, Leland, 144
Stanley Committee hearings (1910), 225, 319
Stanton, Edwin, 1, 2, 4
Stanton, Francis, 40
steam turbine engine, 278
steel industry, 123–36. *See also* Bessemer process; Carnegie Steel; Holley, Alexander; Siemens, Charles; U. S. Steel
  abandoned mills, 316
  antitrust sentiment and, 217
  blast furnaces named after wives, 128n
  British vs. U.S., 54, 273–78, 280, 287
  cartels, xii, xiii, 16, 128
  consumer goods and, 163
  "de-skilling" of labor in, 195–96
  efficiency and, 189
  finished vs. primary, 257–58
  growth of, in 1870s and, 102, 104–5, 107–8
  heavier rail crisis, 189–90
  high-durability and slower methods, 190
  Holley vs. Taylor and, 292–93
  mergers, 202, 253. *See also* U. S. Steel
  open-hearth, 190, 208, 258n
  plant design, Holley and, 49
  process developed, 124–28
  railroads and, 68, 79
  scale shift and, 120
  structural, 189–90, 208
  Taylor's high–speed, 303–4

trade tariffs and, 279–83, 285–87
  U.S. and domestic consumption, 288–91
Steichen, Edward, 233, 234
Stevens, Simon, 27, 76–77
Stewart, A. T., 161
Stillman, James, 250
Stokes, Ned, 76
Stowe, Catherine, 150
Stowe, Harriet Beecher, 150
Strategy and Structure (Chandler), 314, 316
Strong, Benjamin, 250
Studebaker, 105
Sullivan, Louis, 92, 188
Sulzbachs investment house, 92
Sun Oil, 226
Sweeney, Peter, 66
Swift Packing Co., 114, 115, 117
Swope, Gerard, 312
système Gribeauval, le, 39

Taft, William H., 88n
Tailer, Edward, 167
Tammany machine, 4, 64
Tarbell, Ida, 19, 20, 86–88, 90, 151, 158–59, 219, 223, 263
tariffs, protective, 8, 278–87, 282
Taussig, Frank, 284
Taylor, Frederick W. (Taylorism), 292–93, 297–318
telegraph industry, xii, 56, 91–92, 107, 112, 141, 143, 146–47, 163
telephones, 2, 110–11, 238–39 251
Tennessee Coal and Iron Co. (TC&I), 250n
Texaco, 226
Texas & Pacific Railroad (T&P), 130, 140, 142, 144
textile industry, 4, 8, 38–41, 57, 105, 122, 280
Thomas-Gilchrist process, 125, 273
Thompson, Sanford, 301
Thomson, Frank, 230
Thomson, J. Edgar, 14, 75, 75, 92, 93, 95, 123–24, 129, 153
Thomson-Houston, 255n
Thorndike, Israel, 40
Thornton, William, 42–44
Tidewater pipeline, 156–57, 225, 226, 236
Tin Plate Co., 284
tin plate industry, 258
  merger of, 252–54, 257, 265
  tariffs and, 283–85
Titanic, 268
Tocqueville, Alexis de, 164–65, 183, 288–89
Towne, Henry, 298–99
Toyota system, 317–18
trade. *See also* tariffs
  deficit of 1872, 101
  "fair," 280–81

trade (*cont'd*)
  free, 278–85
  surpluses, 107, 248–49
transcontinental railroad, 94, 136–37, 138n, 140, 144
Trollope, Anthony, 7
trusts. *See also* Sherman Antitrust Act; Interstate Commerce Act
  fervor against, 216–19
  first created, 193–94
  Roosevelt vs., 246, 251–52, 269
  science of management vs., 295
  Standard Oil case, 219–27
Twain, Mark, 7, 179
Tweed, William M. "Boss," 66, 76, 78, 104

Union Iron Mills, 91, 93, 128–30, 132
Union Oil, 226
Union Pacific Railroad, 113, 251
  Carnegie and, 91, 94, 95, 207
  Gould and, 21–22, 136–41, 143–44, 146, 148–49, 240–42
  Harriman and, 243–45
United States Bureau of Corporations, 219, 225
U.S. Congress, 11, 46–47, 107, 137, 141, 213, 228, 279, 310
  antitrust laws and, 217, 225, 246
U.S. Constitution, 9
U.S. government bonds, 26
U.S. House of Representatives, 154
U.S. Industrial Relations Commission, 311
U. S. Steel, xiii, 28, 251, 279, 295
  Morgan buyout of Carnegie creates, xiii, 16, 250, 254–66, 269, 319
  prices and tariffs, 284
  Sherman Act and, 218
  unions and, 202
U.S. Supreme Court, 11, 89, 146, 218–20, 251
U.S. Treasury, 73–74, 247–48

Valley Oil Works, 152
Vanderbilt, "Commodore" Cornelius, 75, 79, 82, 83, 87, 88, 138, 143
  Erie Wars and, 60–66, 68
  SIC and, 84–85
Vanderbilt, William H., 85, 143, 145–47, 149, 231–33, 236, 237
Vandergrift, J. J., 85
Verizon, 226
vertical integration, 233, 239–40, 255, 257–58, 318
Victoria, Queen of England, 30
Visible Hand, The (Chandler), 314, 318
Vulcan Iron and Steel Works, 128, 13

Wabash Railroad, 144
Wadsworth, Decius, 39

wages, 103n, 104, 117, 172, 292
  Homestead and, 197–98, 202–3, 205
  piece rates and, 299–301, 303
  U.S. vs. British, 275
Walker, Samuel, 49
Wall, Joseph Frazier, 330
Wallis, George, 52
Wal-Mart, 239
Wanamaker, John, 161, *163*, 164, 174, 177, 182
Ward, Montgomery, 174
Warner, Thomas, 48
War of 1812, 37, 44
Washington, George, 39, 43
Waters, Asa, 34–35, 57, 59
Watertown Arsenal, 313n
Watson, Peter, 77–79, 83, 84, 90–91
Webster, Daniel, 7, 8, 40
Weed Sewing Machine Co., 181–82
Welch, Jack, 158
Wellington, Duke of, 31
Western Union, 92, 141–42, 146–48, *148*, 240
Westinghouse, George, 95, 213, 255n
Westinghouse company, 278, 298
West Point, 39
West Shore Railroad, 231
wheat farming, 110–11, 117, 217
Whigs, 7, 8, 10, 99, 136–37
Whiskey Trust, 194
White, Maunsel, 303, 304
White Star line, 268
Whiting, Indiana, refinery, 221–24
Whitman, Walt, 120, 164, 167
Whitney, Eli, 41, 44, 48
Whittier, John Greenleaf, 119
Whitworth, Joseph, 52, 53, 55–56
Willard, Edward, 73
Willcox and Gibbs, 48, 181
Williamson, Harold, 87
Wilmington Railroad, 145
Wilson, William, 310
Winchester rifle, 48
wire and nail makers, 253, 257, 265
women
  department stores and, 161–62, 166–67
  family life and, 185–86
  middle-class, 170–71
  work and, 166–68, 172, *192*
  textile industry and, 57
Woolworth, Frank, 177
Worldcom, 239

XIT ranch, 113

Zunz, Olivier, 167

Illustration Credits

1. *Prelude*

Page 3. Lincoln funeral train route: From Stefan Lorant, *Lincoln: A Picture Story of His Life.*
Page 25. Andrew Carnegie (*upper left*): The Carnegie Library of Pittsburgh; John D. Rockefeller (*upper right*): Courtesy of the Rockefeller Archive Center; Jay Gould (*lower left*): Lynd-
hurst, an historic site of the National Trust for Historic Preservation in the United States;
J. P. Morgan (*lower right*): Archives of The Pierpont Morgan Library, New York.

2. "... *glorious Yankee Doodle*"

Page 32. The Yacht *America*: Courtesy of the Hagley Museum and Library.
Page 36. Blanchard gun-stock machine: Courtesy of the American Precision Museum, photo-
graph by John Alexander. Labels by the author.
Page 46. Rifle gauging set: National Museum of American History, Smithsonian Institution.
Page 58. Evans's grist mill: Rare Books Division, New York Public Library, Astor, Lenox and
Tilden Foundations.

3. *Bandit Capitalism*

Page 65. Jim Fisk: Collection of the New-York Historical Society.
Page 78. Erie ouster: Provided courtesy of HarpWeek, LLC.
Page 95. St. Louis Eads Bridge: *Scientific American*, November 15, 1873.

4. *Wrenchings*

Page 98. Pittsburgh strike: Corbis.
Page 111. Bonanza farm: Fred Hultstrand History In Pictures Collection, NDIRS-NDSU,
Fargo.

5. *Mega-Machine*

Page 121. Corliss engine: Courtesy of the Hagley Museum and Library.
Page 126. Bessemer converter: Courtesy of the Hagley Museum and Library.
Page 148. Gould cartoon: Culver Pictures.
Page 155. John D. Rockefeller: Courtesy of the Rockefeller Archive Center.

6. *The First Mass Consumer Society*

Page 163. Wanamaker's: From Herbert Adams Gibbons, *John Wanamaker*.

Page 175. "Miss Blossom" ad: Ivory Soap Advertising Collection, Archives Center, National Museum of American History, Behring Center, Smithsonian Instutution. Columbia Bicycles catalog: Courtesy of the Connecticut Historical Society Museum.

Page 180. Ferris wheel: Courtesy of the Hagley Museum and Library.

7. *Paper Tigers*

Page 192. Office work: Courtesy, Company Archives, MetLife, Inc.

Page 204. Steel mill town: Photograph from the Records of the Kingsley Association, Archives Service Center, University of Pittsburgh.

Page 212. Andrew Carnegie: The Carnegie Library of Pittsburgh.

Page 223. Standard Oil cartoon: Culver Pictures.

8. *The Age of Morgan*

Page 232. Carnegie at tunnel cut: Pennsylvania State Archives, RG-12 Records of the Dept. of Highways, South Pennsylvania Railroad, Ray's Hill Tunnel, #11903.

Page 234. J. P. Morgan. Archives of The Pierpoint Morgan Library, reprinted with permission of Joanna T. Steichen.

Page 242. Jay Gould: Corbis.

Page 249. Morgan stork cartoon: Archives of The Pierpont Morgan Library.

Page 263. Morgan banking cartoon: Archives of The Pierpont Morgan Library.

9. *America Rules*

Page 282. "The Original Coxey's Army": Courtesy of the Hagley Museum and Library.

10. *The Wrong Lessons*

Page 296. Locomotive lab: Courtesy of the Hagley Museum and Library.

Page 309. "Scientific Shoveling": Frederick Winslow Taylor Collection, Stevens Institute of Technology, Hoboken, N.J., U.S.A.

Page 316. Abandoned steel mill: Photograph by Beth Conant.

About the Author

CHARLES R. MORRIS is the author of nine books, including *American Catholic* and *Money, Greed, and Risk*. His articles have appeared in the *Los Angeles Times*, the *Wall Street Journal*, *The New York Times*, the *Harvard Business Review*, and *The Atlantic Monthly*. He is a lawyer and former banker, and was most recently president of a financial services software company. He lives in New York City.